The Play's the Thing

The Play's the Thing:

An Introduction to Drama

Nedra Pezold Roberts

The Westminster Schools
Atlanta, Georgia

Independent School Press

Wellesley Hills   Massachusetts

PRINTED IN THE UNITED STATES OF AMERICA

0-88334-141-7

8182838485
1234567890

In memory of

David Thomas Lauderdale, Jr.

CONTENTS

The Play's the Thing

WHAT IS DRAMA?

Compared with essays or novels, plays *look* different on the printed page. That simple and remarkable difference may be enough in itself to raise the question, *what is drama?* Of course, this fundamental question can assume various shapes. In the classroom, the question may concern an insistence · that the students all speak of "the play" instead of "the book" or "the story." Sometimes the question concerns an emphasis on reading every stage direction. Sometimes the question concerns the sanity of the teacher in making students draw the stage and set for whatever play is being studied. Such questions are basic, elementary, primary, because in their own way they ask why the study of drama should be any different from the study of short stories. The simplest questions are often the most difficult, and this particular question is actually far too complex to be answered in a brief introduction. We can, however, make a start.

Drama is a literary form. The playwright uses words written down on paper as the mode of expression. However, the printed page is not meant to be the final form of most plays; the page is merely an outline intended to guide actors in performing the play. (By way of analogy, when we turn on a television set we usually expect to see actors putting on a show; we hardly expect to see a picture of the show's script as it came from the typewriter.) The Greek word from which we derive "drama" is *dran,* meaning "to do" or "to act." Unlike most other literary forms, then, drama is action meant to be seen and heard; the play must indeed be *played*, it must be acted out in front of an audience for the process to reach fulfillment and completion.

Like many distinctions, this one is more gray than it is black-and-white. If we think for a moment about our experiences with another literary form, poetry, we will recall times when a poem came alive for us only after hearing it read. This is the way poetry began, with the bard performing his composition or that of someone else before an audience, an audience that was illiterate, that would not have been able to read the poem even if it could have been written down. Moreover, there are many poems that require the reader to "stage" them mentally — especially such poems as Marvell's "To His Coy Mistress" or Browning's "My Last Duchess," well-known examples of a kind of poem called the dramatic monologue. As for plays themselves, there is one kind — called "closet drama" — which is intended from the beginning for the study instead of the stage. We might also think of George Bernard Shaw, who used to write plays meant for *both* the stage and the study, plays with long stage directions and complete little essays which only a reader would discover. And then there was Charles Lamb, who actually preferred reading a Shakespeare play to seeing it performed, because he was convinced he could mount a better production in his mind than a theatrical company could manage on a real stage.

Still, most playwrights intend their dramas to move off the printed page and into the theatre. The audience in the theatre is able to *see* the play performed, while the audience at home or in the classroom must use its "image-ination" much, much more. When Henry Drummond angrily turns on Hornbeck at the end of *Inherit the Wind,* the audience in a threatre can hardly miss the point; however, the reading audience must imagine the facial expressions and physical gestures and sudden tension as the electrical charge sweeps across the stage and out into the theatre audience. In this scene, drama demands more active involvement from readers than most other literary forms require.

The reader, then, must assume many roles personally — audience, director, actors, even lighting technicians — if the play being studied' is to be "seen." The stage directions and descriptions become very important aids, instead of irritating filler to be skipped over. Likewise, drawing a sketch of the set can help fix in our minds the place where the action is performed. A careful sketch of *The Glass Menagerie* better enables us to "see" Laura moving about in the Wingfield apartment, from the sofa to the old Victrola to the table displaying her glass animals; once we can "see" this tiny apartment and its drab decor, we understand the dull futility in the lives of the people who live there.

The reader in performing the play mentally must interpret dialogue and action and is therefore constantly wrestling with questions — what is happening in this scene? what reaction do I have? why? Such questions have to do with critical *analysis.* When we analyze something, we dissect it, we determine what its components are, and we examine those elements minutely; then we can put it all together again, with much more appreciation. This is true of any human activity, whether we are analyzing a touchdown pass through instant replay on television, or analyzing a bordelaise sauce in a French restaurant, or analyzing the caste relationships among the characters in *The Admirable Crichton* in an English class.

Analyzing drama into several parts can be done in many ways. No sooner did Western drama reach its first golden age, in ancient Greece, than Aristotle set out to identify its elements; his six parts of tragedy (plot, character, diction, thought, scenery, song) have influenced students of the drama for over two thousand years, but we are free to revise the list. We may find, for instance, that it is useful to divide the components of drama into two general domains, the literary and the theatrical. Elements that drama has in common with other literary forms include such things as plot, character, and dialogue. Elements peculiar to the theatre might include set design, staging, and props. What can an examination of these elements reveal about the play itself, and what might we then learn about the theme? Theme, after all, is the play's central concern or subject.

To suggest an answer, we might look at some of the language or word choices (Aristotle's *diction)* in *The Hairy Ape* and *Pygmalion.*

In O'Neill's play, Yank's language is not merely appropriate to his character; it actually defines character. When Yank speaks, we learn what kind of person he is, what he thinks and feels, and what ideas he represents. His speech near the end of Scene I is a remarkable mixture of crudity and poetry. Yank wants to see himself as the force within the machine, the personification of progress, "de new dat's moiderin' de old." He is energy itself, he believes — not the life force of nature, but rather the spirit of modern technology. His imagery is explosive, an effect reinforced by his accent; O'Neill's phonetic spellings toughen and harden sound patterns, as when "th" gives way to "t" or "d": "smash trou," "plough trou," "blows dat up," "knocks dat dead." And yet there is poetry in Yank's staccato rhythms, in his vivid images, in his depth of passion. His angry exultation is matched by moods of painful confusion and wretched misery, emotions unknown to machinery; although Yank wants to see himself as primal strength, we see him as our brother, a vulnerable human being who must grope agonizingly toward self-knowledge.

In a different way, the language of Shaw's Eliza Doolittle emphasizes human individuality despite class distinctions. In Act Three, for instance, Mrs. Higgins' at-home provides an artificial, formal setting for elevated conversation. Eliza, impeccably dressed and the very picture of refinement, delivers her opinions on such elegant matters as the restorative powers of gin, the circumstances surrounding her aunt's death, the cheering influence of liquor, and the probable fate of her aunt's hat. There is high comedy in the incongruity between Eliza's riotous subject matter and the upperclass decorum of her manner, between the artless sincerity of her convictions and the studied precision of her pronunciation. However, this tension between matter and form also defines Eliza for us; we recognize her as an open, direct, honest person, one who cannot truly conform to superficially genteel ways. Indeed, Eliza's vitality, which erupts despite the restraints of polite society, exposes the language and life of the Eynesford Hills as effete and empty. Thus it is that Eliza's language helps convey Shaw's thematic denunciation of caste and pretense.

Theatrical elements such as lighting can likewise assist us in understanding a play. It is instructive to notice how Williams uses lighting in his play. On a simple plane, lighting helps delineate mood or character: red is used for heated argument; blue is Laura's color, yellow is Amanda's. On a higher plane, lighting can reveal the very heart of the play. Thus the attentive reader will observe that while the drama is Tom's memory, we often see Laura in the center of a clear pool of light; during one particular argument between Amanda and Tom, mother and son are shouting and gesticulating — but it is Laura's huddled figure that we see brightly illuminated. If we ask why Laura and not Tom commands our attention in this scene, we will find that what is important for Tom as he remembers such incidents is the effect the arguing had on Laura, not the arguments themselves. The point is that Tom is guilt-ridden about running away from home and deserting his vulnerable sister; but he cannot outrun his memory or his guilt, and so at the end of the play he must finally come to terms with himself. Once we recognize how significant such elements as word choice or narrative device or lighting can be, then we will begin searching out other instances — and analysis will turn into a richly rewarding game, not a dry academic exercise.

No drama is complete without an audience, be it people in a theatre watching actors on a stage or students in a classroom reading words on a page. Good drama is enjoyable, but it is also enlightening or edifying; it is not mere escapism. It whisks us away from our lives, in order to bring us back to our life with new awareness, new comprehension, new appreciation. The plays that follow have been carefully selected with these criteria in mind. They are readable and they are teachable, but they are also significant: they give us new perspectives on ourselves, for they are involved in mankind.

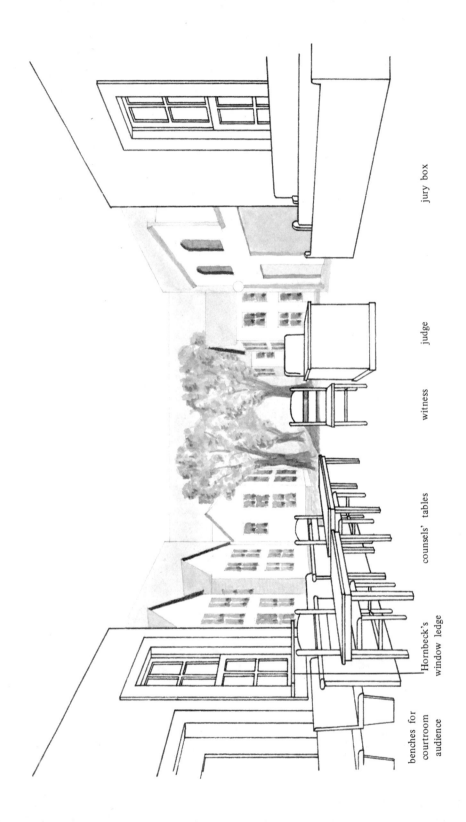

benches for
courtroom
audience

Hornbeck's
window ledge

counsels' tables

witness

judge

jury box

GETTING STARTED: *INHERIT THE WIND*

"The collision of Bryan and Darrow at Dayton was dramatic, but it was not a drama," Jerome Lawrence and Robert E. Lee caution the reader in their headnote to *Inherit the Wind*. The genesis of their famous play is undeniably the infamous Scopes "Monkey Trial" held in the Rhea County Courthouse in Dayton, Tennessee, in the scorching summer of 1925, but what makes *Inherit the Wind* drama is precisely what distinguishes it from journalism or history. Lawrence and Lee freely alter facts in favor of a higher truth, a truth that removes us from the particular to the general, from a literal trial affecting one man's fate to a figurative trial in the sense of an ordeal, a struggle with truth that affects all men. It is this human and humane universality that justifies the authors' concluding note: "It is not 1925. The stage directions set the time as 'Not too long ago.' It might have been yesterday. It could be tomorrow."

Probably few readers of plays take the time or trouble to draw sketches of sets, but the exercise can be exceedingly worthwhile. Unlike many plays, *Inherit the Wind* is performed on different parts of the same set throughout; that is convenient for us, because it means we need only one sketch. On the facing page is one possibility.

At the beginning of Act One, Lawrence and Lee provide fairly complete directions for the set; still, any attempt to implement the directives forces us to consider a number of aspects that the playwrights merely hint at. For example, Hornbeck's window ledge might best be placed behind and above the courtroom spectators, on the opposite side of the stage from the jury box. Such an arrangement would emphasize that formal judgment is being rendered from both quarters: the jurors for the people of Hillsboro, Hornbeck for the readers of the Baltimore *Herald*. If the judge's bench and the witness stand are situated upstage center, facing the audience, then all questions and testimony can be given directly in front of the theatre audience. Brady and Drummond's tables would need to be placed in front of the spectators, but angled so that the audience has a clear view of both men. Actors would then move in a triangle-shaped field bounded by the counsels' tables, the witness stand, and the jury box, making full use of the stage and keeping different groups of actors constantly involved in the action.

7

Readers sometimes grow impatient with stage directions, wanting to get on with the story line; however, to make sense out of dialogue, we must be able to stage the play in our own imagination, and that means the parenthetical information is often as important — or even more important — than the lines of the actors. This is certainly true of the stage description Lawrence and Lee provide. Once we see that Hillsboro is "a sleepy, obscure country town about to be vigorously awakened," and that the converging streets and buildings of the town (in the background) loom over the courtroom (in the foreground) so that "the town is visible always, . . . as much on trial as the individual defendant," then we already know a great deal about the play to follow. We recognize that society itself, represented by Hillsboro, is going to be confronted with a crisis; since we are part of society, we too will be challenged to grow, to leave the comfortable status quo behind. Although we do not yet know what shape the challenge will take, we can guess that the play will present a kind of archetypal movement from ignorance to knowledge, innocence to experience, infancy to maturity. Lawrence and Lee indicate that the setting is significant; they also write, "The crowd is equally important throughout, so that the court becomes a cock-pit, an arena, with the active spectators on all sides of it." From what we know of human nature, we can assume that some of the spectators will be more eager than others to accept the challenge posed, to change, to grow.

Act One

The first act is divided into two scenes, in and around the courthouse. Scene i opens with a mini-drama, in which we meet two of the children Bertram Cates is charged with "corrupting." It is early in the morning, and Howard, dressed in his father's cut-down overalls and equipped with a tin can and improvised fishing pole, is absorbed in digging for fishbait. Melinda skips on stage; Howard dangles a worm in her face and as she backs away he teasingly informs her that she evolved from such a creature. The children hardly realize the importance of their game, but we do. This is the "can of worms" that Cates has opened up, and Howard's demand — "What're yuh skeered of?" — is a question that will recur in different ways throughout the play.

Characters and background information must be introduced efficiently, so the play moves to its next vignette. We meet Cates himself, and the girl he is in love with, Rachel Brown. From their nervous, intimate, honest conversation, we learn what Cates has done and what reaction he has met. Daring to think for himself, Cates has questioned what the law says he must not question; he has realized that life is not as simple as "good or bad, black or white, night or day." But Rachel has been taught to accept others' ideas uncritically, not to discover beliefs for herself; the rules have been laid down, and one has simply to follow them to order to be right. She cannot comprehend why Cates would do otherwise, and so she is the perfect foil in this scene, for in trying to explain his thinking to her, Cates reveals himself to us.

The lights fade in the courthouse area and come up on the town, and we meet representative inhabitants of Hillsboro – who turn out to be representative inhabitants of just about any town. Here are people who think, others who cannot think, those who will not think, those who fear thinking, those who just never thought much about thinking. The town is in a holiday mood, because the great Matthew Harrison Brady is coming to put Hillsboro on the map and bring a boom for local business and local beliefs. Just like Mr. Bannister, everyone wants a front-row seat for the wonderful show.

Into this expectant mood, this carnival atmosphere, wanders E.K. Hornbeck. He is dressed in city clothes, and he sneers contemptuously as he looks around. We soon spot the difference between the two young men, Cates and Hornbeck. Cates is a true sceptic – *skepsis,* meaning doubt or examination; *skeptikos,* meaning thoughtful consideration – who holds ideas in open-minded doubt as he examines them. Cates the humble sceptic puts ideas on trial, but gives them a fair trial; Hornbeck the arrogant cynic finds ideas guilty of falsehood without ever permitting them a hearing. To Hornbeck, all belief is gullibility; doubt and rejection mean the same thing.

Hornbeck is the cynic, then, but he is much more; he is a complex figure demanding our full alertness. For one thing, he is a successful ringmaster at the start of the play: he depicts Hillsboro as a hilarious circus and we share his amusement. Initially, we find Hornbeck's role as outside observer attractive, because that is our own role. Like Hornbeck, we wish to see ourselves as sophisticated and superior to the ignorant, small-minded, backward townsfolk. Moreover, Hornbeck possesses a kind of dignity that goes beyond his own high opinion of himself; Lawrence and Lee endow him with a scintillating control of words that is genuinely impressive, not just slickly clever. In fact,

Hornbeck often speaks not in prose but in blocked, capitalized lines of free verse — as though he were filling the part of some ancient Greek chorus, interpreting and commenting on the action of the play. Even Hornbeck's customary place in the courtroom, a window ledge, places him physically apart from the action and somewhat "above" it all.

Matthew Harrison Brady's arrival has been so adroitly prepared that we share the crowd's anticipation; the excitement of placards and bands, singing and parading, affects us, too. It is inevitably a little disappointing, therefore, when the patriarchal "benign giant" turns out to be an ageing, overweight, disheveled, pompous blowhard. Then, when Hornbeck announces the name of the defense attorney, the crowd is stunned and Brady himself momentarily pales. Now everybody discusses Henry Drummond, as earlier they had buzzed about Brady; again our anticipation is spurred. It is time for Drummond to enter the arena, and then the business of scene i will be finished.

The stage directions at this point are elaborate; there is no mistaking Lawrence and Lee's intentions. The lights dim to signal the approach of twilight, the red lighting creating the double effect of glowing sunset and infernal heat. As Drummond's huge shadow is cast on the backdrop, Melinda — now alone on center stage — screams, "It's the Devil!" (echoing what Jeremiah Brown had said moments earlier) and flees. Hornbeck and Drummond are the only actors left. It registers on us that Drummond, like Brady, is not as large or as frightening as his shadow would have us believe, so that the sardonic humor of Hornbeck's greeting — "Hello, Devil. Welcome to Hell" — comes as comic relief. The lights fade, and in the darkness we have a few seconds to reflect that if Drummond is not truly the Devil, then perhaps Hillsboro is not Hell, either.

Scene ii introduces us to the courtroom where the battle will be waged, because Lawrence and Lee need to give the audience some idea of what the coming trial will be like and what kind of justice Bert Cates can expect. Most of scene ii is given over to the selection of the final two jurymen. Our original impressions of the townspeople are revised and refined; several more individuals emerge from the mass, and we realize that not all these inhabitants are as biased or as silly as Hornbeck would have us presume. However, we do see prejudice, we see ineptness, we see favored treatment for Brady, and we see that Drummond will have to fight for any judicial impartiality or plain fairness here.

And that is precisely what he does. Whether snapping his gaudy suspenders or badgering the judge about "all this damned 'Colonel' talk" or denouncing the "commercial announcement... for Reverend Brown's product," Drummond is constantly jockeying for position against Brady. The polished verbal sparring and calculated histrionic tantrums are all entertaining, to be sure, but at bottom the two legal titans are utterly serious. "It was immoral what you did to that jury," Brady insults Drummond, referring to a celebrated obscenity case, and Drummond retorts, "All I want is to prevent the clock-stoppers from dumping a load of medieval nonsense into the United States Constitution."

The fundamental earnestness of things is reiterated towards the end of the scene. The judge declares a recess, and Brady is ushered away by a mob of adoring fans; nobody approaches the pariah, Drummond, as he packs his brief. The earlier melodramatic wrangling gives way to low-key intimacy, as the defense lawyer soon finds himself caught up in a tense but quiet lovers' quarrel between Rachel and Cates. From these last lines of dialogue we gain new insight into Drummond's character and principles, we develop great sympathy for Rachel, and we conceive profound respect for Cates. Appropriately, Hornbeck is nowhere in sight: like him, we came to Hillsboro as uninvolved outsiders, but by the close of Act One we are very deeply involved in the lives of Drummond, Rachel, and Cates.

Act Two

There are two scenes in Act Two, the prayer meeting before the trial and the trial itself. In one sense, the religious gathering takes us through an imaginative account of Creation in Genesis, while the trial exposes us to Darwin's account of man's development. Such a bloodless paraphrase, however, does an injustice to the powerful emotional clashes and explosive theatrical fireworks that render Act Two so vivid and vibrant. It is a meticulously constructed work of drama, the elements of conflict coming at us from all sides — from the dialogue, from the gestures of the actors, from the subject matter, from the blocking of stage action, from the lighting, from the set design itself.

Scene 1 is vigorous poetic drama, both beautiful and frightening. Brown is a gifted fanatic, who infects the crowd with his own passionate intensity. He speaks of the Word coming to enlighten mankind, but his own words imprison his hearers in darkness. Brown manipulates people with brilliant rhetoric; he is not interested in rational discourse. Brown's avowal of God's love paradoxically reveals his own hatred for sinful humanity. Not only does he attempt boldly to mold the verdict against Cates before the trial even begins, but he calls down a curse upon his own daughter when she tries to defend Bert.

At this point Brady, who has been increasingly alarmed, intervenes to remind the minister of God's mercy in addition to His justice; Brady stops Brown's rantings, soothes the crowd, and sends them home. What is important for readers of the play to notice is that Lawrence and Lee have balanced Brown's little show against the *whole* stage: the courtroom abstract symbol of due process of law no matter how poorly individual trials may live up to that ideal, is in full view throughout Brown's tirade. Furthermore, Lawrence and Lee have placed the actors so that Hornbeck and Drummond are also in full view, on the fringes of the crowd, to balance Brown on his platform. The conclusion of the scene makes the structural balance even clearer, when Brady asks Drummond, "Why is it, my old friend, that you have moved so far away from me?" and Drummond replies, "All motion is relative. Perhaps it is *you* who have moved away – by standing still." Fanaticism insists on a single interpretation of things, but reason always uncovers alternatives.

Scene ii is by far the longest scene in the play; we might expect it to be the theatrical highpoint, the trial everyone has been awaiting. Recapitulating the structure of Act One, scene i, Lawrence and Lee begin with the questioning of Howard. In his cross-examination, Drummond warns that what is actually on trial in Hillsboro is the right to think; he follows up by inquiring whether Howard has indeed been corrupted by his teacher, whether he really believes everything Cates said about evolution. Howard's answer is perfect: "I'm not sure. I gotta think it over."

But now the judge begins to lend his considerable weight to Brady's cause; by the time Brady frees a distraught Rachel from the witness stand, hardly a pretense of judicial objectivity remains. Drummond is overruled at every turn, while Brady is allowed liberty upon liberty. Increasingly isolated and frustrated, Drummond is not permitted to introduce any evidence or any witnesses. The swelling tension peaks when Drummond, knowing he will lose the case in this forum and realizing he must establish grounds for appeal to a higher court ("I want those 'Amens' in the record!"), calls as his sole defense witness none other than Matthew Harrison Brady.

Now Drummond must employ the very thing he is defending: he must use *reason* to eviscerate Brady's position, to demonstrate the logical contradictions in construing the Bible literally. As Brady's testimony begins to collapse into flailing emotion, the popular hero manifests his own inability to think. In contrast with Drummond's waxing assurance, Brady wanes into babbling confusion — confusion which radiates out into the courtroom, provoking the judge to adjourn the session. Brady is left behind to whimper pathetically, "They're laughing at me, Mother!" as his wife cradles his head against her breast and croons, "It's all right, baby. It's all right." The scene is, quite simply, devastating.

Act Three

Act Three is a finely orchestrated whole that opens in calm, rises to crescendo after crescendo, and falls back into tranquillity. There are abundant stage directions, which explain facial expression, gesture, and movement to complement dialogue. It might be argued that the fixed reference point in this kaleidoscopic act is Drummond's Golden Dancer speech, a quiet set-piece about the splendid rocking horse Drummond fell in love with when he was seven, a rocking horse that turned out to be "all shine, and no substance." Golden Dancer represents the attractive illusion that is discovered to be false, the thing that is not what it seems; throughout Act Three, illusion after illusion is stripped away, like layers of onion skin, leaving people, situations, and ideas revealed for what they are.

For instance, we might consider Harry Esterbrook and his radio equipment. Brady, who communicates a magical charisma in his Chautauqua-tent speeches, cannot be effective addressing an audience he does not see; his power lies in personal contact. Brady's weakness is even more evident when the radio engineer physically maneuvers him, as if he were just another piece of sound equipment ("almost . . . an inanimate object," the playwrights hint). When the engineer disconnects his broadcast equipment in the middle of Brady's speech, the action serves to further deflate and humiliate a man who was for so long a monumental hero.

The implications reach far beyond Brady. The radio engineer's action underscores the farce of the entire trial, a travesty of justice whose entertainment value has been exploited by both backwoods politicians and news-media managers. This is the cynical reality that Hornbeck sees so clearly, but what Hornbeck cannot perceive is that a good man can work successfully within such a perverse system. Drummond is sent to Hillsboro by the Baltimore *Herald,* and doubtless Hornbeck's newspaper gets plenty of sales in return for its investment — but Drummond scores a victory also for his idealistic values, values which will survive the transition from print to electronic technology because they are permanent. Brady, on the other hand, cannot make that transition; refusing to evolve with the times, he has become a human fossil.

With the verdict and sentence, chaos erupts and one surprise tumbles upon another. Cates is found guilty, of course, but shoddy political expediency combines with Drummond's splendid defense to nullify the effect. The fine (and bail pending appeal) is so ludicrously small that Brady's victory collapses in ashes. "Which side won?" Melinda calls across the courtroom, and Howard shouts back, "I ain't sure." Cates himself echoes Melinda's perplexity ("Did I win or did I lose?") and Drummond has to interpret events for him ("You won . . . you made it a joke"). But Drummond knows that victories are never decisive, for he also tells Cates, "You don't suppose this kind of thing is ever finished, do you? Tomorrow it'll be something else — and another fella will have to stand up."

The anticlimactic verdict and sentence are followed by a series of theatrical coups. First Brady launches into his prepared speech, despite the noisy anarchy reigning in the courtroom; then the radio man abruptly exits, leaving Brady helplessly brandishing his speech, like some outdated Excalibur; next, amid shouts and screams, Brady collapses. No sooner is the fallen champion carried away than Rachel comes to announce that she has broken with her father: "I was always afraid of what I might think — so it seemed safer not to think at all. . . . I think the sickly ideas die mostly, don't you, Bert?" Her question is indirectly answered by the judge, who reports another jolt: "Brady's dead." And then, for still another startling development, Drummond explodes at Hornbeck. The ensuing clash between the "atheist who believes in God" and the journalist who "never pushed a noun against a verb except to blow up something" provides the final volcanic eruption; after Hornbeck's departure, the stage returns to calm.

Now alone, Drummond brings down the curtain with a convincing example of how essential it is to read stage directions closely. Holding Darwin's book in one hand, he "picks up the Bible in his other hand; he looks from one volume to the other, balancing them thoughtfully, as if his hands were scales. He half-smiles, half-shrugs. Then Drummond slaps the two books together and jams them in his briefcase, side by side. Slowly, he climbs to the street level and crosses the empty square." Drummond's final actions constitute a pantomime statement of theme; the audience, watching in silence, would have plenty of time to recover from the pandemonium of events and contemplate what had been witnessed in the theater.

Inherit the Wind

Introduction

The American theatre has benefited greatly from the team of Jerome Lawrence and Robert Edwin Lee. Since 1942 these men have collaborated on well over a dozen plays and musicals, including such hits as *Look, Ma, I'm Dancin'* (1948), *Auntie Mame* (1956), *Mame* (1966), *The Night Thoreau Spent in Jail* (1970), and *Jabberwock* (1972). However, their best-known play is still *Inherit the Wind* (1955), which starred Ed Begley, Paul Muni, and Tony Randall when it opened on Broadway, and featured Frederick March, Spencer Tracy, and Gene Kelly in the subsequent film adaptation.

Lawrence, who was born in 1915, worked in print and broadcast journalism, holding jobs that ranged from the Wilmington, Ohio *News Journal* to CBS and Paramount Studios, before joining partnership with Lee. He was named visiting professor at Ohio State University from 1969 on. Lee, for his part, was born in 1918 and has been associated with a number of universities, including Northwestern, Ohio Wesleyan, Western Reserve, and Drake. He joined the faculty of the theatre arts department at the University of California, Los Angeles, in 1966. The two men have won many Tony Awards, Donaldson Awards, and critics' awards; *Inherit the Wind,* for instance, seemed to sweep everything on the shelf, from the Outer Circle Award and *Variety's* New York Drama Critics poll to the London Critics Poll of best foreign play of the year (1960) and no fewer than seven Antoinette Perry awards.

Two recent statements help illuminate Lawrence and Lee's joint career, throwing light especially on *Inherit the Wind.* "I believe in change," Lee has said, inevitably reminding us of the difference between Matthew Harrison Brady and Henry Drummond. "I believe it is the purpose of the artist – particularly the playwright – to anticipate tomorrow – to project his imagined view of it – so we can prepare for the future with a maximum of sanity and a minimum of despair." And Lawrence has said, "In our plays we have attempted to grapple with universal themes, even in our comedies. We have tried for a blend between the dramatic and the entertaining: our most serious works are always leavened with laughter *(Inherit the Wind* is an example) and our seemingly frivolous comedies . . . have sub-texts which say something important for the contemporary world."

16

INHERIT THE WIND

by Jerome Lawrence
and Robert E. Lee

"He that troubleth his own house
Shall inherit the wind."
Proverbs 11:29

CHARACTERS

MELINDA	MRS. BLAIR
HOWARD	ELIJAH
RACHEL BROWN	E. K. HORNBECK
MEEKER	HURDY GURDY MAN
BERTRAM CATES	TIMMY
MR. GOODFELLOW	MAYOR
MRS. KREBS	MATTHEW HARRISON BRADY
REV. JEREMIAH BROWN	MRS. BRADY
CORKIN	TOM DAVENPORT
BOLLINGER	HENRY DRUMMOND
PLATT	JUDGE
MR. BANNISTER	DUNLAP
MRS. LOOMIS	SILLERS
HOT DOG MAN	REUTERS MAN
MRS. McCLAIN	HARRY Y. ESTERBROOK

Time: Summer. Not too long ago.

Place: A small town.

Inherit the Wind is not history. The events which took place in Dayton, Tennessee, during the scorching July of 1925 are clearly the genesis of this play. It has, however, an exodus entirely its own.

Only a handful of phrases have been taken from the actual transcript of the famous Scopes Trial. Some of the characters of the play are related to the colorful figures in that battle of giants; but they have life and language of their own — and, therefore, names of their own.

The greatest reporters and historians of the century have written millions of words about the "Monkey Trial." We are indebted to them for their brilliant reportage. And we are grateful to the late Arthur Garfield Hays, who recounted to us much of the unwritten vividness of the Dayton adventure from his own memory and experience.

The collision of Bryan and Darrow at Dayton was dramatic, but it was not a drama. Moreover, the issues of their conflict have acquired new dimension and meaning in the thirty years since they clashed at the Rhea County Courthouse. So *Inherit the Wind* does not pretend to be journalism. It is theatre. It is not 1925. The stage directions set the time as "Not too long ago." It might have been yesterday. It could be tomorrow.

Jerome Lawrence
Robert E. Lee

ACT ONE

Scene i

In and around the Hillsboro Courthouse. The foreground is the actual courtroom, with jury box, judge's bench and a scattering of trial-scarred chairs and counsel tables. The back wall of the courtroom is non-existent. On a raked level above it is the courthouse square, the Main Street and the converging streets of the town. This is not so much a literal view of Hillsboro as it is an impression of a sleepy, obscure country town about to be vigorously awakened.

It is important to the concept of the play that the town is visible always, looming there, as much on trial as the individual defendant. The crowd is equally important throughout, so that the court becomes a cock-pit, an arena, with the active spectators on all sides of it.

It is an hour after dawn on a July day that promises to be a scorcher. HOWARD, a boy of thirteen, wanders onto the courthouse lawn. He is barefoot, wearing a pair of his pa's cutdown overalls. He carries an improvised fishing pole and a tin can. He studies the ground carefully, searching for something. A young girl's voice calls from off-stage.

MELINDA [*calling sweetly*]. How-ard! [HOWARD, *annoyed, turns and looks toward the voice.* MELINDA, *a healthy, pigtailed girl of twelve, skips on.*] Hello, Howard.

[HOWARD *is disinterested, continues to search the ground.*]

HOWARD. 'Lo, Lindy.

MELINDA [*making conversation*]. I think it's gonna be hotter'n yesterday. That rain last night didn't do much good.

HOWARD [*professionally*]. It brought up the worms. [*Suddenly he spots one in the lawn. Swiftly he grabs for it, and holds it up proudly.*] Lookit this fat one!

MELINDA [*shivering*]. How can you touch 'em? It makes me all goose-bumpy! [HOWARD *dangles it in front of her face. She backs away, shuddering.*]

HOWARD. What're yuh skeered of? *You* was a worm once!

MELINDA [*shocked*]. I wasn't neither!

HOWARD. You was so! When the whole world was covered with

19

water, there was nuthin' but worms and blobs of jelly. And you and your whole family was worms!

MELINDA. We was not!

HOWARD. Blobs of jelly, then.

MELINDA. Howard Blair, that's sinful talk! I'm gonna tell my pa and he'll make you wash your mouth out with soap!

HOWARD. Ahhh, your old man's a monkey! [MELINDA *gasps. She turns indignantly and runs off.* HOWARD *shrugs in the manner of a man-of-the-world.*] 'Bye, Lindy. [*He deposits the worm in his tin can, and continues looking for more.* RACHEL *enters. She is twenty-two, pretty, but not beautiful. She wears a cotton summer dress. She carries a small composition-paper suitcase. There is a tense, distraught air about her. She may have been crying. She looks about nervously, as if she doesn't want to be seen. When she sees* HOWARD, *she hesitates; then she crosses quickly downstage into the courthouse area in the hope that the boy will not notice her. But he does see* RACHEL, *and watches her with puzzled curiosity. Then he spots another worm, tugs it out of the ground, and holds it up, wriggling.* HOWARD *addresses the worm.*] What do you wanta be when you grow up?

[RACHEL *stands uncertainly in the courthouse area. This is strange ground to her. Unsure, she looks about.*]

RACHEL [*tentatively, calling*]. Mr. Meeker . . .?

[*After a pause, a door at stage right opens.* MR. MEEKER, *the bailiff, enters. There is no collar on his shirt; his hair is tousled, and there is shaving soap on his face, which he is wiping off with a towel as he enters.*]

MEEKER [*a little irritably*]. Who is it? [*Surprised.*] Why, hello, Rachel. 'Scuse the way I look. [*He wipes the soap out of his ear. Then he notices her suitcase.*] Not goin' away, are you? Excitement's just startin'.

RACHEL [*earnestly*]. Mr. Meeker, don't let my father know I came here.

MEEKER [*shrugs*]. The Reverend don't tell me his business. Don't know why I should tell him mine.

RACHEL. I want to see Bert Cates. Is he all right?

MEEKER. Don't know why he shouldn't be. I always figured the safest place in the world is a jail.

RACHEL. Can I go down and see him?

MEEKER. Ain't a very proper place for a minister's daughter.

RACHEL. I only want to see him for a minute.

MEEKER. Sit down, Rachel. I'll bring him up. You can talk to him right here in the courtroom. [RACHEL *sits in one of the stiff wooden chairs.* MEEKER *starts out, then pauses.*] Long as I've been bailiff here, we've never had nothin' but drunks, vagrants, couple of chicken thieves. [*A little dreamily.*] Our best catch was that fella from Minnesota that chopped up his wife; we had to extradite him. [*Shakes his head.*] Seems kinda queer havin' a school-teacher in our jail. [*Shrugs.*] Might improve the writin' on the walls.

[MEEKER *goes out. Nervously,* RACHEL *looks around at the cold, official furnishings of the courtroom.* MEEKER *returns to the courtroom, followed by* BERT CATES. CATES *is a pale, thin young man of twenty-four. He is quiet, shy, well-mannered, not particularly good-looking.* RACHEL *and* CATES *face each other expressionlessly, without speaking.* MEEKER *pauses in the doorway.*]

MEEKER. I'll leave you two alone to talk. Don't run off, Bert.

[MEEKER *goes out.* RACHEL *and* CATES *look at each other.*]

RACHEL. Hello, Bert.

CATES. Rache, I told you not to come here.

RACHEL. I couldn't help it. Nobody saw me. Mr. Meeker won't tell. [*Troubled.*] I keep thinking of you, locked up here —

CATES [*trying to cheer her up*]. You know something funny? The food's better than the boarding house. And you'd better not tell anybody how cool it is down there, or we'll have a crime wave every summer.

RACHEL. I stopped by your place and picked up some of your things. A clean shirt, your best tie, some handkerchiefs.

CATES. Thanks.

RACHEL [*rushing to him*]. Bert, why don't you tell 'em it was all a joke? Tell 'em you didn't mean to break a law, and you won't do it again!

CATES. I suppose everybody's all steamed up about Brady coming.

RACHEL. He's coming in on a special train out of Chattanooga. Pa's going to the station to meet him. Everybody is!

CATES. Strike up the band.

RACHEL. Bert, it's still not too late. Why can't you admit you're wrong? If the biggest man in the country — next to the President, maybe — if Matthew Harrison Brady comes here to tell the whole world how wrong you are —

CATES. You still think I did wrong?

RACHEL. Why did you do it?

CATES. You know why I did it. I had the book in my hand, Hunter's *Civic Biology.* I opened it up, and read my sophomore science class Chapter 17, Darwin's *Origin of Species.* [RACHEL *starts to protest.*] All it says is that man wasn't just stuck here like a geranium in a flower pot; that living comes from a *long* miracle, it didn't just happen in seven days.

RACHEL. There's a law against it.

CATES. I know that.

RACHEL. Everybody says what you did is bad.

CATES. It isn't as simple as that. Good or bad, black or white, night or day. Do you know, at the top of the world the twilight is six months long?

RACHEL. But we don't live at the top of the world. We live in Hillsboro, and when the sun goes down, it's dark. And why do you try to make it different? [RACHEL *gets the shirt, tie, and handkerchiefs from the suitcase.*] Here.

CATES. Thanks, Rache.

RACHEL. Why can't you be on the right side of things?

CATES. Your father's side. [RACHEL *starts to leave.* CATES *runs after her.*] Rache — love me!

[*They embrace.* MEEKER *enters with a long-handled broom.*]

MEEKER [*clears his throat*]. I gotta sweep.

[RACHEL *breaks away and hurries off.*]

CATES [*calling*]. Thanks for the shirt!

[MEEKER, *who has been sweeping impassively now stops and leans on the broom.*]

MEEKER. Imagine. Matthew Harrison Brady, comin' here. I voted for him for President. Twice. In nineteen hundred, and again in oh-eight. Wasn't old enough to vote for him the first time he ran. But my pa did. [*Turns proudly to* CATES.] I *seen* him once. At a Chautauqua meeting in Chattanooga. [*Impressed, remembering.*] The tent-poles shook! [CATES *moves nervously.*] Who's gonna be your lawyer, son?

CATES. I don't know yet. I wrote to that newspaper in Baltimore. They're sending somebody.

MEEKER [*resumes sweeping*]. He better be loud.

CATES [*picking up the shirt*]. You want me to go back down?

MEEKER. No need. You can stay up here if you want.

CATES [*going toward the jail*]. I'm supposed to be in jail; I'd better be in jail!

[MEEKER *shrugs and follows* CATES *off. The lights fade in the courtroom area, and come up on the town: morning of a hot July day. The STOREKEEPER enters, unlocking his store. MRS. KREBS saunters across the square.*]

STOREKEEPER. Warm enough for you, Mrs. Krebs?

MRS. KREBS. The Good Lord guv us the heat, and the Good Lord guv us the glands to sweat with.

STOREKEEPER. I bet the Devil ain't so obliging.

MRS. KREBS. Don't intend to find out.

[*The* REVEREND JEREMIAH BROWN, *a gaunt, thin-lipped man, strides on. He looks around, scowling.*]

STOREKEEPER. Good morning, Reverend.

BROWN. 'Morning.

MRS. KREBS. 'Morning, Reverend.

BROWN. Mrs. Krebs. [*Shouting off.*] Where's the banner? Why haven't you raised the banner?

CORKIN [*entering, followed by another workman*]. Paint didn't dry 'til jist now.

[*They are carrying a rolled-up canvas banner.*]

BROWN. See that you have it up before Mr. Brady arrives.

[COOPER *enters, gestures "hello" to the others.*]

CORKIN. Fast as we can do it, Reverend.

BROWN. We must show him at once what kind of a community this is.

CORKIN. Yes, Reverend. Come on, Phil. Hep.

[*They rig the banner to halyards between the buildings.*]

MRS. KREBS. Big day, Reverend.

CORKIN. Indeed it is. Picnic lunch ready, Mrs. Krebs?

MRS. KREBS. Fitt'n fer a king.

[BANNISTER, PLATT *and other townspeople gather excitedly. They are colorful small-town citizens, but not caricatured rubes.*]

BOLLINGER [*running on, carrying his cornet*]. Station master says old 94's on time out of Chattanooga. And Brady's on board all right!

COOPER. The minute Brady gets here, people gonna pour in. Town's gonna fill up like a rain barrel in a flood.

STOREKEEPER. That means business!

[MELINDA *and her mother come on and set up a lemonade stand.*]

BANNISTER. Where they gonna stay? Where we gonna sleep all them people?

MRS. KREBS. They got money, we'll sleep 'em.

PLATT. Looks like the biggest day for this town since we put up Coxey's army!

HOWARD [*bolting on*]. Hey! Ted Finney's got out his big bass drum. And y'oughta see what they done to the depot! Ribbons all over the rainspouts!

MELINDA. Lemonade! Lemonade!

[*The workmen hoist the banner above the heads of the crowd, where it hangs for the remainder of the action. The banner blares:* "READ YOUR BIBLE."]

CORKIN. It's all ready, Reverend.

[*The townspeople applaud.* BOLLINGER *toots a ragged fan-fare. A* HAWKER *in a white apron wheels on a hot-dog stand. The crowd mills about, in holiday spirit.*]

HAWKER. Hot dogs! Get your red-hots! Hot dogs!

[MRS. McCLAIN *enters with a shopping bag full of frond fans.*]

MRS. McCLAIN. Get your fans. Compliments of Maley's Funeral Home. Thirty-five cents.

[*The stage is now full of eager and expectant people.* MRS. BLAIR *shoves her way through the crowd, looking for her son.*]

MRS. BLAIR [*calling*]. Howard. Howard!

HOWARD [*racing to her*]. Hey, Ma. This is just like the county fair.

MRS. BLAIR. Now you settle down and stop runnin' around and pay some attention when Mr. Brady gets here. Spit down your hair.

[HOWARD *spits in her hand, and she pastes down a cowlick.*] Hold still! [HOWARD *flashes off through the crowd.* ELIJAH, *a "holy man" from the hills, comes on with a wooden vegetable crate full of books. He is bearded, wild-haired, dressed in a tattered burlap smock. His feet are bare. He sets up shop between the hot dogs and the lemonade, with a placard reading:* "WHERE WILL YOU SPEND ETERNITY?"]

ELIJAH [*in a shrill, screeching voice*]. Buy a Bible! Your guide-book to eternal life!

[E. K. HORNBECK *wanders on, carrying a suitcase. He is a newspaperman in his middle thirties, who sneers politely at everything, including himself. His clothes — those of a sophis-ticated city-dweller — contrast sharply with the attire of the townspeople.* HORNBECK *looks around, with wonderful contempt.*]

MRS. McCLAIN [*to* HORNBECK]. Want a fan? Compliments of Maley's Funeral Home — thirty-five cents!

HORNBECK. I'd die first.

MRS. KREBS [*unctuously, to* HORNBECK]. You're a stranger, aren't you, mister? Want a nice clean place to stay?

HORNBECK. I had a nice clean place to stay, madame,
And I left it to come here.

MRS. KREBS [*undaunted*]. You're gonna need a room.

HORNBECK. I have a reservation at the Mansion House.

MRS. KREBS. Oh? [*She sniffs.*] That's all right, I suppose, for them as *likes* havin' a privy practically in the bedroom!

HORNBECK. The unplumbed and plumbing-less depths!
Ahhhh, Hillsboro — Heavenly Hillsboro.
The buckle on the Bible Belt.

[*The* HAWKER *and* ELIJAH *converge on* HORNBECK *from opposite sides.*]

HAWKER. Hot dog?

ELIJAH. Bible?

[HORNBECK *up-ends his suit case and sits on it.*]

HORNBECK. Now that poses a pretty problem!
Which is hungrier — my stomach or my soul?

[HORNBECK *buys a hot dog.*]

ELIJAH [*miffed*]. Are you an Evolutionist? An infidel? A sinner?

HORNBECK [*munching the hot dog*].
The worst kind. I write for a newspaper.
    [HORNBECK *offers his hand.*]
I'm E. K. Hornbeck, Baltimore *Herald*.
I don't believe I caught your name . . .?

ELIJAH [*impressively*]. They call me . . . Elijah.

HORNBECK [*pleased*].
Elijah! Yes! Why, I had no idea you were still around.
I've read some of your stuff.

ELIJAH [*haughtily*]. I neither read nor write.

HORNBECK. Oh. Excuse me.
I must be thinking of another Elijah.

[*An* ORGAN-GRINDER *enters, with a live monkey on a string.* HORNBECK *spies the monkey gleefully; he greets the monk with arms outstretched.*]

Grandpa!

[*Crosses to the monkey, bends down and shakes the monkey's hand.*]

Welcome to Hillsboro, Sir!
Have you come to testify for the defense
Or for the prosecution?
[*The monkey, oddly enough, doesn't answer.*] No comment?
That's fairly safe. But I warn you, sir,
You can't compete with all these monkeyshines.

[MELINDA *hands the monkey a penny.*]

MELINDA. Look. He took my penny.

HORNBECK. How could you ask for better proof than that?
   There's the father of the human race!

TIMMY [*running on, breathlessly*]. Train's coming! I seen the
   smoke 'way up the track!

[*The train whistle sounds, off.*]

BROWN [*taking command*]. All the members of the Bible League,
   get ready! Let us show Mr. Brady the spirit in which we
   welcome him to Hillsboro.

[MRS. BLAIR *blows her pitch pipe and the townspeople parade off singing "Marching to Zion." Even the* ORGAN-GRINDER *leaves his monkey tied to the hurdy-gurdy and joins the departing crowd. But* HORNBECK *stays behind.*]

HORNBECK. Amen.

   [*To the monkey.*]
Shield your eyes, monk!
You're about to meet the mightiest of your descendents.
A man who wears a cathedral for a cloak,
A church spire for a hat,
Whose tread has the thunder of the legions of the Lion-
Hearted!

   [*The* STOREKEEPER *emerges from his establishment and looks in his own store window.* HORNBECK *turns to him.*]

You're missing the show.

STOREKEEPER. Somebody's got to mind the store.

HORNBECK. May I ask your opinion, sir, on Evolution?

STOREKEEPER. Don't have any opinions. They're bad for business.

[*Off-stage, a cheer. Then the thumping drum into "Gimme That Old-Time Religion" sung by the unseen townspeople.*]

HORNBECK [*to the monkey*].
Sound the trumpet, beat the drum.
Everybody's come to town
To see your competition, monk.
Alive and breathing in the county cooler:
A high-school teacher — wild, untamed!

[*The crowd surges back, augmented, in a jubilant parade. Many are carrying banners, reading:*
ARE YOU A MAN OR A MONKEY?
AMEND THE CONSTITUTION — PROHIBIT DARWIN
SAVE OUR SCHOOLS FROM SIN
MY ANCESTORS AIN'T APES!
WELCOME MATTHEW HARRISON BRADY
DOWN WITH DARWIN
BE A SWEET ANGEL
DON'T MONKEY WITH OUR SCHOOLS!
DARWIN IS WRONG!
DOWN WITH EVOLUTION
SWEETHEART, COME UNTO THE LORD]

[HORNBECK *goes to the background to watch the show.* MATTHEW HARRISON BRADY *comes on, a benign giant of a man, wearing a pith helmet. He basks in the cheers and the excitement, like a patriarch surrounded by his children. He is gray, balding, paunchy, an indeterminate sixty-five. He is followed by* MRS. BRADY; *the* MAYOR; REVEREND BROWN; TOM DAVENPORT, *the circuit district attorney; some newspapermen, and an army of the curious.*]

ALL [*singing*].
Gimme that old-time religion,

Gimme that old-time religion,
Gimme that old-time religion,
It's good enough for me!

It was good enough for father,
It was good enough for father,
It was good enough for father,
And it's good enough for me!

It was good for the Hebrew children,
It was good for the Hebrew children,
It was good for the Hebrew children,
And it's good enough for me!

Gimme that old-time religion,
Gimme that old-time religion,
Gimme that old-time religion,
It's good enough for me!

MAYOR [*speaks*]. Mr. Brady, if you please.

REVEREND [*singing*]. It is good enough for Brady.

CROWD.
It is good enough for Brady,
It is good enough for Brady,
And it's good enough for me!

[*Cheers and applause.* BRADY *seems to carry with him a built-in spotlight. So* MRS. BRADY — *pretty, fashionably dressed, a proper "Second Lady" to the nation's "Second Man" — seems always to be in his shadow. This does not annoy her.* SARAH BRADY *is content that all her thoughts and emotions should gain the name of action through her husband.* BRADY *removes his hat and raises his hand. Obediently, the crowd falls to a hushed anticipatory silence.*]

BRADY. Friends — and I can see most of you are my friends, from the way you have decked out your beautiful city of Hillsboro — [*There is a pleased reaction, and a spattering of applause. When* BRADY *speaks, there can be no doubt of his personal magnetism. Even* HORNBECK, *who slouches contemptuously at far left, is impressed with the speaker's power; for here is a man to be reckoned with.*] Mrs. Brady and I are delighted to be among you! [BRADY *takes his wife's hand and draws her to his side.*] I could only wish one thing: that you had not given us quite so warm a welcome! [BRADY *removes his alpaca coat. The crowd laughs.* BRADY *beams.* MRS. McCLAIN *hands him a frond fan.* BRADY *takes it.*] Bless you. [*He fans himself vigorously.*] My friends of Hillsboro, you know why I have come here. I have not come merely to prosecute a lawbreaker, an arrogant youth who has spoken out against the Revealed Word. I have come because what has happened in a schoolroom of your town has unloosed a wicked attack from the big cities of the North! — an attack upon the law which you have so wisely placed among the statutes of this state. I am here to defend that which is most precious in the hearts of all of us: the Living Truth of the Scriptures!

[*Applause and emotional cheering.*]

PHOTOGRAPHER. Mr. Brady. Mr. Brady, a picture?

BRADY. I shall be happy to oblige! [*The townspeople, chanting "Go Tell It on the Mountain," move upstage.* BRADY *begins to organize a group photograph. To his wife.*] Sarah . . .

MRS. BRADY [*moving out of the camera range*]. No, Matt. Just you and the dignitaries.

BRADY. You are the Mayor, are you not?

MAYOR [*stepping forward, awkwardly*]. I am, sir.

BRADY [*extending his hand*]. My name is Matthew Harrison Brady.

MAYOR. Oh, I know. Everybody knows that. I had a speech of welcome ready, but somehow it didn't seem necessary.

BRADY. I shall be honored to hear your greeting, sir.

[*The* MAYOR *clears his throat and takes some notes from his pocket.*]

MAYOR [*sincerely*]. Mr. Matthew Harrison Brady, this municipality is proud to have within its city limits the warrior who has always fought for us ordinary people. The lady folks of this town wouldn't have the vote if it wasn't for you, fightin' to give 'em all that suffrage. Mr. President Wilson wouldn't never have got to the White House and won the war if it wasn't for you supportin' him. And, in conclusion, the Governor of our state . . .

PHOTOGRAPHER. Hold it! [*The camera clicks.*] Thank you.

[MRS. BRADY *is disturbed by the informality of the pose.*]

MRS. BRADY. Matt — you didn't have your coat on.

BRADY [*to the* PHOTOGRAPHER]. Perhaps we should have a more formal pose. [*As* MRS. BRADY *helps him on with his coat.*] Who is the spiritual leader of the community?

MAYOR. That would be the Reverend Jeremiah Brown.

[REVEREND BROWN *steps forward.*]

BROWN. Your servant, and the Lord's.

[BRADY *and* BROWN *shake hands.*]

BRADY. The Reverend at my left, the Mayor at my right. [*Stiffly, they face the camera.*] We must look grave, gentlemen, but not too serious. Hopeful, I think is the word. We must look hopeful.

[BRADY *assumes the familiar oratorical pose. The camera clicks. Unnoticed, the barefoot* HOWARD *has stuck his head, mouth agape, into the picture. The* MAYOR *refers to the last page of his undelivered speech.*]

MAYOR. In conclusion, the Governor of our state has vested in me the authority to confer upon you a commission as Honorary Colonel in the State Militia.

[*Applause.*]

BRADY [*savoring it*]. "Colonel Brady." I like the sound of that!

BROWN. We thought you might be hungry, Colonel Brady, after your train ride.

MAYOR. So the members of our Ladies' Aid have prepared a buffet lunch.

BRADY. Splendid, splendid — I could do with a little snack.

[*Some of the townspeople, at* BROWN'S *direction, carry on a long picnic table, loaded with foodstuffs, potato salad, fried turkey, pickled fruits, cold meats and all the picnic paraphernalia.* RACHEL *comes on following the table, carrying a pitcher of lemonade which she places on the table.*]

BANNISTER [*an eager beaver*]. You know, Mr. Brady — *Colonel* Brady — all of us here voted for you three times.

BRADY. I trust it was in three separate elections!

[*There is laughter.* TOM DAVENPORT, *a crisp, business-like young man, offers his hand to* BRADY.]

DAVENPORT. Sir, I'm Tom Davenport.

BRADY [*beaming*]. Of course. Circuit district attorney. [*Putting his arm around* DAVENPORT'S *shoulder.*] We'll be a team, won't we, young man! Quite a team! [*The picnic table is in place. The sight of the food being uncovered is a magnetic attraction to Brady. He beams, and moistens his lips.*] Ahhhh, what a handsome repast! [*Some of the women grin sheepishly at the flattery.* BRADY *is a great eater, and he piles mountains of food on his plate.*] What a challenge it is, to fit on the old armor again! To test the steel of our Truth against the blasphemies of Science! To stand —

MRS. BRADY. Matthew, it's a warm day. Remember, the doctor told you not to overeat.

BRADY. Don't worry, Mother. Just a bite or two. [*He hoists a huge drumstick on his plate, then assails a mountain of potato salad.*] Who among you knows the defendant? — Cates, is that his name?

DAVENPORT. Well, we *all* know him, sir.

MAYOR. Just about everybody in Hillsboro knows everybody else.

BRADY. Can someone tell me — is this fellow Cates a criminal by nature?

RACHEL [*almost involuntarily*]. Bert isn't a criminal. He's good, really. He's just —

[RACHEL *seems to shrink from the attention that centers on her. She takes an empty bowl and starts off with it.*]

BRADY. Wait, my child. Is Mr. Cates your friend?

RACHEL [*looking down, trying to get away*]. I can't tell you anything about him —

BROWN [*fiercely*]. Rachel! [*To Brady.*] My daughter will be pleased to answer any questions about Bertram Cates.

BRADY. Your daughter, Reverend? You must be proud, indeed. [BROWN *nods.* BRADY *takes a mouthful of potato salad, turns to* RACHEL.] Now. How did you come to be acquainted with Mr. Cates?

RACHEL [*suffering*]. At school. I'm a schoolteacher, too.

BRADY. I'm sure you teach according to the precepts of the Lord.

RACHEL. I try. My pupils are only second-graders.

BRADY. Has Mr. Cates ever tried to pollute your mind with his heathen dogma?

RACHEL. Bert isn't a heathen!

BRADY [*sympathetically*]. I understand your loyalty, my child. This man, the man in your jailhouse, is a fellow schoolteacher. Likable, no doubt. And you are loath to speak out against him before all these people. [BRADY *takes her arm,¯still carrying his plate. He moves her easily away from the others. As they move.*] Think of me as a friend, Rachel. And tell me what troubles you.

[BRADY *moves her upstage and their conversation continues, inaudible to us.* BRADY *continues to eat,* RACHEL *speaks to him earnestly. The townspeople stand around the picnic table, munching the buffet lunch.*]

BANNISTER. Who's gonna be the defense attorney?

DAVENPORT. We don't know yet. It hasn't been announced.

MAYOR [*he hands a modest picnic plate to* MRS. BRADY]. Whoever it is, he won't have much of a chance against your husband, will he, Mrs. Brady?

[*There are chortles of self-confident amusement. But* HORN-BECK *saunters toward the picnic table.*]

HORNBECK. I disagree.

MAYOR. Who are you?

HORNBECK. Hornbeck. E.K. Hornbeck, of the Baltimore *Herald*.

BROWN [*can't quite place the name, but it has unpleasant connotations*]. Hornbeck . . . Hornbeck . . .

HORNBECK. I am a newspaperman, bearing news.
When this sovereign state determined to indict
The sovereign mind of a less-than-sovereign schoolteacher,
My editors decided there was more than a headline here.
The Baltimore *Herald,* therefore, is happy to announce
That it is sending two representatives to "Heavenly Hillsboro":

The most brilliant reporter in America today,
Myself.
And the most agile legal mind of the Twentieth Century,
Henry Drummond.

[*This name is like a whip-crack.*]

MRS. BRADY [*stunned*]. Drummond!

BROWN. Henry Drummond, the agnostic?

BANNISTER. I heard about him. He got those two Chicago child murderers off just the other day.

BROWN. A vicious, godless man!

[*Blithely,* HORNBECK *reaches across the picnic table and chooses a drumstick. He waves it jauntily toward the astonished party.*]

HORNBECK. A Merry Christmas and a Jolly Fourth of July!

[*Munching the drumstick,* HORNBECK *goes off. Unnoticed,* BRADY *and* RACHEL *have left the scene, missing this significant disclosure. There is a stunned pause.*]

DAVENPORT [*genuinely impressed*]. Henry Drummond for the defense. Well!

BROWN. Henry Drummond is an agent of darkness. [*With resolution.*] We won't let him in the town!

DAVENPORT. I don't know by what law you could keep him out.

MAYOR [*rubbing his chin*]. I'll look it up in the town ordinances.

BROWN. I saw Drummond once. In a courtroom in Ohio. A man was on trial for a most brutal crime. Although he knew — and admitted — the man was guilty, Drummond was perverting the evidence to cast the guilt away from the accused and onto you and me and all of society.

MRS. BRADY. Henry Drummond. Oh, dear me.

BROWN. I can still see him. A slouching hulk of a man, whose head juts out like an animal's. [*He imitates* DRUMMOND'S *slouch.* MELINDA *watches, frightened.*] You look into his face, and you wonder why God made such a man. And then you know that God didn't make him, that he is a creature of the Devil, perhaps even the Devil himself!

[*Little* MELINDA *utters a frightened cry, and buries her head in the folds of her mother's skirt.* BRADY *re-enters with* RACHEL, *who has a confused and guilty look.* BRADY'S *plate has been scraped clean; only the fossil of the turkey leg remains. He looks at the ring of faces, which have been disturbed by* BROWN'S *description of the heretic* DRUMMOND. MRS. BRADY *comes toward him.*]

MRS. BRADY. Matt — they're bringing Henry Drummond for the defense.

BRADY [*pale*]. Drummond? [*The townspeople are impressed by the impact of this name on* BRADY.] Henry Drummond!

BROWN. We won't allow him in the town!

MAYOR [*lamely*]. I think — maybe the Board of Health — [*He trails off.*]

BRADY [*crossing thoughtfully*]. No. [*He turns.*] I believe we should *welcome* Henry Drummond.

MAYOR [*astonished*]. Welcome him!

BRADY. If the enemy sends its Goliath into battle, it magnifies our cause. Henry Drummond has stalked the courtrooms of this land for forty years. When he fights, headlines follow. [*With growing fervor.*] The whole world will be watching our victory over Drummond. [*Dramatically.*] If St. George had slain a dragonfly, who would remember him.

[*Cheers and pleased reactions from the crowd.*]

MRS. BLAIR. Would you care to finish off the pickled apricots, Mr. Brady?

[BRADY *takes them.*]

BRADY. It would be a pity to see them go to waste.

MRS. BRADY. Matt, do you think —

BRADY. Have to build up my strength, Mother, for the battle ahead. [*Munching thoughtfully.*] Now what will Drummond do? He'll try to make us forget the lawbreaker and put the law on trial. [*He turns to* RACHEL.] But we'll have the *answer* for Mr. Drummond. Right here, in some of the things this sweet young lady has told me.

RACHEL. But Mr. Brady —

[BRADY *turns to* BROWN.]

BRADY. A fine girl, Reverend. Fine girl!

[RACHEL *seems tormented, but helpless.*]

BROWN. Rachel has always been taught to do the righteous thing.

[RACHEL *moves off.*]

BRADY. I'm sure she has.

[MELINDA *hands him a glass of lemonade.*]

BRADY. Thank you. A toast, then! A toast to tomorrow! To the beginning of the trial and the success of our cause. A toast, in good American lemonade!

[*He stands lifting his glass. Others rise and join the toast.* BRADY *downs his drink.*]

MRS. BRADY. Mr. Mayor, it's time now for Mr. Brady's nap. He always likes to nap after a meal.

MAYOR. We have a suite ready for you at the Mansion House. I think you'll find your bags already there.

BRADY. Very thoughtful, considerate of you.

MAYOR. If you'll come with me — it's only across the square.

BRADY. I want to thank all the members of the Ladies' Aid for preparing this nice little picnic repast.

MRS. KREBS [*beaming*]. Our pleasure, sir.

BRADY. And if I seemed to pick at my food, I don't want you to think I didn't enjoy it. [*Apologetically.*] But you see, we had a box lunch on the train.

[*There is a good-humored reaction to this, and the* BRADYS *move off accompanied by the throng of admirers, singing "It is good enough for Brady." Simultaneously the lights fade down on the courthouse lawn and fade up on the courtroom area.* HORNBECK *saunters on, chewing at an apple. He glances about the courtroom as if he were searching for something. When* RACHEL *hurries on,* HORNBECK *drops back into a shadow and she does not see him.*]

RACHEL [*distressed*]. Mr. Meeker. Mr. Meeker? [*She calls down toward the jail.*] Bert, can you hear me? Bert, you've got to tell me what to do. I don't know what to do —

[HORNBECK *takes a bite out of his apple.* RACHEL *turns sharply at the sound, surprised to find someone else in the courtroom.*]

HORNBECK [*quietly*].
I give advice, at remarkably low hourly rates.
Ten percent off to unmarried young ladies,
And special discounts to the clergy and their daughters.

RACHEL. What are you doing here?

HORNBECK. I'm inspecting the battlefield
The night before the battle. Before it's cluttered
With the debris of journalistic camp-followers.
   [*Hiking himself up on a window ledge.*]
I'm scouting myself an observation post
To watch the fray.
   [RACHEL *starts to go off.*]
Wait. Why do you want to see Bert Cates?
What's he to you, or you to him?
Can it be that both beauty and biology
Are on our side?
   [*Again she starts to leave. But* HORNBECK *jumps down from his ledge and crosses toward her.*]
There's a newspaper here I'd like to have you see.
It just arrived
From that wicked modern Sodom and Gomorrah,
Baltimore!
   [RACHEL *looks at him quizzically as he fishes a tear sheet out of his pocket.*]
Not the entire edition, of course.
No Happy Hooligan, Barney Google, Abe Kabibble.
Merely the part worth reading: E.K. Hornbeck's
Brilliant little symphony of words.
   [*He offers her the sheet, but she doesn't take it.*]

You should read it.

   [*Almost reluctantly, she starts to read.*]

                    My typewriter's been singing
A sweet, sad song about the Hillsboro heretic,
B. Cates: boy-Socrates, latter-day Dreyfus,
Romeo with a biology book.
   [*He looks over her shoulder, admiring his own writing. He takes another bite out of the apple.*]

I may be rancid butter,
But I'm on your side of the bread.

RACHEL [*looking up, surprised*]. This sounds as if you're a friend of Bert's.

HORNBECK. As much as a critic can be a friend to anyone.

[*He sits backward on a chair, watching her head. He takes another bite out of his apple, then offers it to her.*]

Have a bite?

[RACHEL, *busily reading, shakes her head.*]

Don't worry. I'm not the serpent, Little Eva.
This isn't from the Tree of Knowledge.
You won't find one in the orchards of Heavenly Hillsboro.
Birches, beeches, butternuts. A few ignorance bushes.
No Tree of Knowledge.

[RACHEL *has finished reading the copy; and she looks up at* HORNBECK *with a new respect.*]

RACHEL. Will this be published here, in the local paper?

HORNBECK. In the "Weekly Bugle"? Or whatever it is they call
The leaden stuff they blow through the local linotypes?
I doubt it.

RACHEL. It would help Bert if the people here could read this. It would help them understand . . . ! [*She appraises* HORN-BECK, *puzzled.*] I never would have expected you to write an article like this. You seem so —

HORNBECK. Cynical? That's my fascination.
I do hateful things, for which people love me,
And lovable things for which they hate me.
I am a friend of enemies, the enemy of friends;
I am admired for my detestability.
I am both Poles and the Equator,
With no Temperate Zones between.

RACHEL. You make it sound as if Bert is a hero. I'd like to think that, but I can't. A schoolteacher is a public servant: I think he should do what the law and the school-board want him to. If the superintendent says, "Miss Brown, you're to teach from Whitley's *Second Reader,*" I don't feel I have to give him an argument.

HORNBECK. Ever give your pupils a snap-quiz on existence?

RACHEL. What?

HORNBECK. Where we came from, where we are, where we're going?

RACHEL. All the answers to those questions are in the Bible.

HORNBECK [*with a genuine incredulity*].
All?! You feed the youth of Hillsboro
From the little truck-garden of your mind?

RACHEL [*offended, angry*]. I think there must be something wrong in what Bert believes, if a great man like Mr. Brady comes here to speak out against him.

HORNBECK. Matthew Harrison Brady came here
To find himself a stump to shout from.
That's all.

RACHEL. You couldn't understand. Mr. Brady is the champion of ordinary people, like us.

HORNBECK. Wake up, Sleeping Beauty. The ordinary people
Played a dirty trick on Colonel Brady.
They ceased to exist.

    [RACHEL *looks puzzled*.]

                                     Time was
When Brady was the hero of the hinterland,
Water-boy for the great unwashed.
But they've got inside plumbing in their heads these days!
There's a highway through the backwoods now,
And the trees of the forest have reluctantly made room
For their leafless cousins, the telephone poles.
Henry's Lizzie rattles into town
And leaves behind
The Yesterday-Messiah,
Standing in the road alone
In a cloud of flivver dust.

    [*Emphatically, he brandishes the apple.*]

The boob has been de-boobed.
Colonel Brady's virginal small-towner
Has been *had* —
By Marconi and Montgomery Ward.

[HORNBECK *strolls out of the courtroom and onto the town square; the lights dissolve as before from one area to the other.*

[RACHEL *goes off in the darkness. The store fronts glow with sunset light. The* SHOPKEEPER *pulls the shade in his store window and locks the door.* MRS. McCLAIN *crosses, fanning herself wearily.*]

STOREKEEPER. Gonna be a hot night, Mrs. McClain.

MRS. McCLAIN. I thought we'd get some relief when the sun went down.

[HORNBECK *tosses away his apple core, then leans back and watches as the* SHOPKEEPER *and* MRS. McCLAIN *go off. The* ORGAN-GRINDER *comes on, idly with his monkey.* MELINDA *enters attracted by the melody which tinkles in the twilight. She gives the monkey a penny. The* ORGAN-GRINDER *thanks her, and moves off.* MELINDA *is alone, back to the audience, in center stage.* HORNBECK, *silent and motionless, watches from the side. The faces of the buildings are now red with the dying moment of sunset.*

A long, ominous shadow appears across the buildings, cast from a figure approaching off stage. MELINDA *awed, watches the shadow grow.* HENRY DRUMMOND *enters, carrying a valise. He is hunched over, head jutting forward, exactly as* BROWN *described him. The red of the sun behind him hits his slouching back, and his face is in shadow.* MELINDA *turns and looks at* DRUMMOND, *full in the face.*]

MELINDA [*terrified*]. It's the Devil!

[*Screaming with fear* MELINDA *runs off.* HORNBECK *crosses slowly toward* DRUMMOND, *and offers his hand.*]

HORNBECK. Hello, Devil. Welcome to Hell.

(The lights fade.)

Scene ii

The courtroom. A few days later.

The townspeople are packed into the sweltering courtroom. The shapes of the buildings are dimly visible in the background, as if Hillsboro itself were on trial. Court is in session, fans are pumping. The humorless JUDGE *sits at his bench; he has a nervous habit of flashing an automatic smile after every ruling.* CATES *sits beside* DRUMMOND *at a counsel table.* BRADY *sits grandly at another table, fanning himself with benign self-assurance.* HORN-BECK *is seated on his window ledge.* RACHEL, *tense, is among the spectators. In the jury box, ten of the twelve jurors are already seated.* BANNISTER *is on the witness stand.* DAVENPORT *is examining him.*

DAVENPORT. Do you attend church regularly, Mr. Bannister?

BANNISTER. Only on Sundays.

DAVENPORT. That's good enough for the prosecution. Your Honor, we will accept this man as a member of the jury.

[BANNISTER *starts toward the jury box.*]

JUDGE. One moment, Mr. Bannister. You're not excused.

BANNISTER [*a little petulant*]. I wanted that there front seat in the jury box.

DRUMMOND [*rising*]. Well, hold your horses, Bannister. You may get it yet!

[BANNISTER *returns to the witness chair.*]

JUDGE. Mr. Drummond, you may examine the venireman.

DRUMMOND. Thank you, Your Honor. Mr. Bannister, how come you're so anxious to get that front seat over there?

BANNISTER. Everybody says this is going to be quite a show.

DRUMMOND. I hear the same thing. Ever read anything in a book about Evolution?

BANNISTER. Nope.

DRUMMOND. Or about a fella named Darwin?

41

BANNISTER. Can't say I have.

DRUMMOND. I'll bet you read your Bible.

BANNISTER. Nope.

DRUMMOND. How come?

BANNISTER. Can't read.

DRUMMOND. Well, you are fortunate. [*There are a few titters through the courtroom.*] He'll do.

[BANNISTER *turns toward the* JUDGE, *poised.*]

JUDGE. Take your seat, Mr. Bannister. [BANNISTER *races to the jury box as if shot from a gun, and sits in the remaining front seat, beaming.*] Mr. Meeker, will you call a venireman to fill the twelfth and last seat on the jury?

BRADY [*rising*]. Your Honor, before we continue, will the court entertain a motion on a matter of procedure?

MEEKER [*calling toward the spectators*]. Jesse H. Dunlap. You're next, Jesse.

JUDGE. Will the learned prosecutor state the motion?

BRADY. It has been called to my attention that the temperature in this courtroom is now 97 degrees Fahrenheit. [*He mops his forehead with a large handkerchief.*] And it may get hotter! [*There is laughter.* BRADY *basks in the warmth of his popularity.*] I do not feel that the dignity of the court will suffer if we remove a few superfluous outer garments.

[BRADY *indicates his alpaca coat.*]

JUDGE. Does the defense have any objection to Colonel Brady's motion?

DRUMMOND [*askance*]. I don't know if the dignity of the court can be upheld with these galluses I've got on.

JUDGE. We'll take that chance, Mr. Drummond. Those who wish to remove their coats may do so.

[*With relief, many of the spectators take off their coats and loosen their collar buttons.* DRUMMOND *wears wide, bright purple suspenders. The spectators react.*]

BRADY [*with affable sarcasm*]. Is the counsel for the defense showing us the latest fashion in the great metropolitan city of Chicago?

DRUMMOND [*pleased*]. Glad you asked me that. I brought these along special. [*He cocks his thumbs in the suspenders.*] Just so happens I bought these galluses at Peabody's General Store in *your* home town, Mr. Brady. Weeping Water, Nebraska.

[DRUMMOND *snaps the suspenders jauntily. There is amused reaction at this.* BRADY *is nettled: this is his show, and he wants all the laughs. The* JUDGE *pounds for order.*]

JUDGE. Let us proceed with the selection of the final juror.

[MEEKER *brings* JESSE DUNLAP *to the stand. He is a rugged, righteous-looking man.*]

MEEKER. State your name and occupation.

DUNLAP. Jesse H. Dunlap. Farmer and cabinetmaker.

DAVENPORT. Do you believe in the Bible, Mr. Dunlap?

DUNLAP [*vigorously*]. I believe in the Holy Word of God. And I believe in Matthew Harrison Brady!

[*There is some applause, and a few scattered "Amens."* BRADY *waves acceptance.*]

DAVENPORT. This man is acceptable to the prosecution.

JUDGE. Very well, Mr. Drummond?

DRUMMOND [*quietly, without rising*]. No questions. Not acceptable.

BRADY [*annoyed*]. Does Mr. Drummond refuse this man a place on the jury simply because he believes in the Bible?

DRUMMOND. If you find an Evolutionist in this town, you can refuse him.

BRADY [*angrily*]. I object to the defense attorney rejecting a worthy citizen without so much as asking him a question!

DRUMMOND [*agreeably*]. All right. I'll ask him a question. [*Saunters over to* DUNLAP.] How are you?

DUNLAP [*a little surprised*]. Kinda hot.

DRUMMOND. So am I. Excused.

[DUNLAP *looks at the* JUDGE, *confused.*]

JUDGE. You are excused from jury duty, Mr. Dunlap. You may step down.

[DUNLAP *goes back and joins the spectators, a little miffed.*]

BRADY [*piously*]. I object to the note of levity which the counsel for the defense is introducing into these procedures.

JUDGE. The bench agrees with you in spirit, Colonel Brady.

DRUMMOND [*rising angrily*]. And *I* object to all this damned "Colonel" talk. I am not familiar with Mr. Brady's military record.

JUDGE. Well — he was made an Honorary Colonel in our State Militia. The day he arrived in Hillsboro.

DRUMMOND. The use of this title prejudices the case of my client: it calls up a picture of the prosecution, astride a white horse, ablaze in the uniform of a militia colonel, with all the forces of right and righteousness marshaled behind him.

JUDGE. What can we do?

DRUMMOND. Break him. Make him a private. I have no serious objection to the honorary title of "Private Brady."

[*There is a buzz of reaction. The* JUDGE *gestures for the* MAYOR *to come over for a hurried, whispered conference.*]

MAYOR [*after some whispering*]. Well, we can't take it back —! [*There is another whispered exchange. Then the* MAYOR *steps gingerly toward* DRUMMOND.] By — by authority of — well, I'm sure the Governor won't have any objection — I hereby appoint you, Mr. Drummond, a temporary Honorary Colonel in the State Militia.

DRUMMOND [*shaking his head, amused*]. Gentlemen, what can I say? It is not often in a man's life that he attains the exalted rank of "temporary Honorary Colonel."

MAYOR. It will be made permanent, of course, pending the arrival of the proper papers over the Governor's signature.

DRUMMOND [*looking at the floor*]. I thank you.

JUDGE. Colonel Brady. Colonel Drummond. You will examine the next venireman.

[MEEKER *brings* GEORGE SILLERS *to the stand.*]

MEEKER. State your name and occupation.

SILLERS. George Sillers. I work at the feed store.

DAVENPORT. Tell me, sir. Would you call yourself a religious man?

SILLERS. I guess I'm as religious as the next man.

[BRADY *rises.* DAVENPORT *immediately steps back, deferring to his superior.*]

BRADY. In Hillsboro, sir, that means a great deal. Do you have any children, Mr. Sillers?

SILLERS. Not as I know of.

BRADY. If you had a son, Mr. Sillers, or a daughter, what would you think if that sweet child came home from school and told you that a Godless teacher —

DRUMMOND. Objection! We're supposed to be choosing jury members! The prosecution's denouncing the defendant before the trial has even begun!

JUDGE. Objection sustained.

[*The* JUDGE *and* BRADY *exchange meaningless smiles.*]

BRADY. Mr. Sillers. Do you have any personal opinions with regard to the defendant that might prejudice you on his behalf?

SILLERS. Cates? I don't hardly know him. He bought some peat moss from me once, and paid his bill.

BRADY. Mr. Sillers impresses me as an honest, God-fearing man. I accept him.

JUDGE. Thank you, Colonel Brady. *Colonel* Drummond?

DRUMMOND [*strolling toward the witness chair*]. Mr. Sillers, you just said you were a religious man. Tell me something. Do you work at it very hard?

SILLERS. Well, I'm pretty busy down at the feed store. My wife tends to the religion for both of us.

DRUMMOND. In other words, you take care of this life, and your wife takes care of the next one?

DAVENPORT. Objection.

JUDGE. Objection sustained.

DRUMMOND. While your wife was tending to the religion, Mr. Sillers, did you ever happen to bump into a fella named Charles Darwin?

SILLERS. Not till recent.

DRUMMOND. From what you've heard about this Darwin, do you think your wife would want to have him over for Sunday dinner?

[BRADY *rises magnificently.*]

BRADY. Your Honor, my worthy opponent from Chicago is cluttering the issue with hypothetical questions —

DRUMMOND [*wheeling*]. I'm doing *your* job, Colonel.

DAVENPORT [*leaping up*]. The prosecution is perfectly able to handle its own arguments.

DRUMMOND. Look, I've established that Mr. Sillers isn't working very hard at religion. Now, for your sake, I want to make sure he isn't working at Evolution.

SILLERS [*simply*]. I'm just working at the feed store.

DRUMMOND [*to the* JUDGE]. This man's all right. [*Turning.*] Take a box seat, Mr. Sillers.

BRADY. I am not altogether satisfied that Mr. Sillers will render impartial —

DRUMMOND. Out of order. The prosecution has already accepted this man.

[*The following becomes a simultaneous wrangle among the attorneys.*]

BRADY. I want a fair trial.

DRUMMOND. So do I!

BRADY. Unless the state of mind of the members of the jury conforms to the laws and patterns of society —

DRUMMOND. Conform! Conform! What do you want to do — run the jury through a meat-grinder, so they all come out the same?

DAVENPORT. Your Honor!

BRADY. I've seen what you can do to a jury. Twist and tangle them. Nobody's forgotten the Endicott Publishing case — where you made the jury believe the obscenity was in their own minds, not on the printed page. It was immoral what you did to that jury. Tricking them. Judgment by confusion. Think you can get away with it here?

DRUMMOND. All I want is to prevent the clock-stoppers from dumping a load of medieval nonsense into the United States Constitution.

JUDGE. This is not a Federal court.

DRUMMOND [*slapping his hand on the table*]. Well, dammit, you've got to stop 'em somewhere.

[*The* JUDGE *beats with his gavel.*]

JUDGE. Gentlemen, you are *both* out of order. The bench holds that the jury has been selected. [BRADY *lets his arms fall, with a gesture of sweet charity.*] Because of the lateness of the hour and the unusual heat, the court is recessed until ten o'clock tomorrow morning. [JUDGE *raps gavel, and the court begins to break up. Then the* JUDGE *notices a slip of paper, and raps for order again.*] Oh. The Reverend Brown has asked me to make this announcement. There will be a prayer meeting tonight on the courthouse lawn, to pray for justice and guidance. All are invited.

DRUMMOND. Your Honor. I object to this commercial announcement.

JUDGE. Commercial announcement?

DRUMMOND. For Reverend Brown's product. Why don't you announce that there will be an Evolutionist meeting?

JUDGE. I have no knowledge of such a meeting.

DRUMMOND. That's understandable. It's bad enough that everybody coming into this courtroom has to walk underneath a banner that says: "Read Your Bible!" Your Honor, I want that sign taken down! Or else I want another one put up — just as big, just as big letters — saying "Read Your Darwin!"

JUDGE. That's preposterous!

DRUMMOND. It certainly is!

JUDGE. You are out of order, Colonel Drummond. The court stands recessed.

[*As the formality of the courtroom is relaxed, there is a general feeling of relief. Spectators and jury members adjust their sticky clothes, and start moving off. Many of the townspeople gather around* BRADY, *to shake his hand, get his autograph, and to stand for a moment in the great man's presence. They cluster about him, and follow* BRADY *as he goes off, the shepherd leading his flock. In marked contrast,* DRUMMOND *packs away his brief in a tattered leather case; but no one comes near him.* RACHEL *moves toward* BERT. *They stand face-to-face, wordlessly. Both seem to wish the whole painful turmoil were over. Suddenly,* RACHEL *darts to* DRUMMOND'S *side.* CATES *opens his mouth to stop her, but she speaks rapidly, with pent-up tension.*]

RACHEL. Mr. Drummond. You've got to call the whole thing off. It's not too late. Bert knows he did wrong. He didn't mean to. And he's sorry. Now why can't he just stand up and say to everybody: "I did wrong. I broke a law. I admit it. I won't do it again." Then they'd stop all this fuss, and — everything would be like it was.

[DRUMMOND *looks at* RACHEL, *not unkindly.*]

DRUMMOND. Who are you?

RACHEL. I'm — a friend of Bert's.

[DRUMMOND *turns to* CATES.]

DRUMMOND. How about it, boy? Getting cold feet?

CATES. I never thought it would be like this. Like Barnum and Bailey coming to town.

DRUMMOND [*easily*]. We can call it off. You want to quit?

RACHEL [*coming to* BERT'S *side*]. Yes!

CATES. People look at me as if I was a murderer. Worse than a murderer! That fella from Minnesota who killed his wife — remember, Rachel — half the town turned out to see 'em put him on the train. They just looked at him as if he was a curiosity — not like they *hated* him! Not like he'd done anything really wrong! Just different!

DRUMMOND [*laughs a little to himself*]. There's nothing very original about murdering your wife.

CATES. People I thought were my friends look at me now as if I had horns growing out of my head.

DRUMMOND. You murder a wife, it isn't nearly as bad as murdering an old wives' tale. Kill one of their fairy-tale notions, and they call down the wrath of God, Brady, and the state legislature.

RACHEL. You make a joke out of everything. You seem to think it's so funny!

DRUMMOND. Lady, when you lose your power to laugh, you lose your power to think straight.

CATES. Mr. Drummond, I can't laugh. I'm scared.

DRUMMOND. Good. You'd be a damned fool if you weren't.

RACHEL [*bitterly*]. You're supposed to help Bert; but every time you swear you make it worse for him.

DRUMMOND [*honestly*]. I'm sorry if I offend you. [*He smiles.*] But I don't swear just for the hell of it. [*He fingers his galluses.*] You see, I figure language is a poor enough means of communication as it is. So we ought to use all the words we've got. Besides, there are damned few words that everybody understands.

RACHEL. You don't care anything about Bert! You just want a chance to make speeches against the Bible!

DRUMMOND. I care a great deal about Bert. I care a great deal about what Bert thinks.

RACHEL. Well, I care about what the people in this town think of *him*.

DRUMMOND [*quietly*]. Can you buy back his respectability by making him a coward? [*He spades his hands in his hip pockets.*] I understand what Bert's going through. It's the loneliest feeling in the world — to find yourself standing up when everybody else is sitting down. To have everybody look at you and say, "What's the matter with him?" I know. I know what it feels like. Walking down an empty street, listening to the sound of your own footsteps. Shutters closed, blinds drawn, doors locked against you. And you aren't sure whether you're walking toward something, or if you're just walking away. [*He takes a deep breath, then turns abruptly.*] Cates, I'll change your plea and we'll call off the whole business — on one condition. If you honestly believe you committed a criminal act against the citizens of this state and the minds of their children. If you honestly believe that you're wrong and the law's right. Then the hell with it. I'll pack my grip and go back to Chicago, where it's a cool hundred in the shade.

RACHEL [*eagerly*]. Bert knows he's wrong. Don't you, Bert?

DRUMMOND. Don't prompt the witness.

CATES [*indecisive*]. What do you think, Mr. Drummond?

DRUMMOND. I'm here. That tells you what I think. [*He looks squarely at* CATES.] Well, what's the verdict, Bert? You want to find yourself guilty before the jury does?

CATES [*quietly, with determination*]. No, sir, I'm not gonna quit.

RACHEL [*protesting*]. Bert!

CATES. It wouldn't do any good now, anyhow. [*He turns to* RA-CHEL.] If you'll stick by me, Rache — well, we can fight it out.

[*He smiles at her wanly. All the others have gone now, except* MEEKER *and* DRUMMOND. RACHEL *shakes her head, bewildered, tears forming in her eyes.*]

RACHEL. I don't know what to do; I don't know what to do.

CATES [*frowning*]. What's the matter, Rache?

RACHEL. I don't want to do it, Bert; but Mr. Brady says —

DRUMMOND. What does Brady say?

RACHEL [*looking down*]. They want me to testify against Bert.

CATES [*stunned*]. You can't!

MEEKER. I don't mean to rush you, Bert; but we gotta close up the shop.

[CATES *is genuinely panicked.*]

CATES. Rache, some of the things I've talked to you about are things you just say to your own heart. [*He starts to go with* MEEKER, *then turns back.*] If you get up on the stand and say those things out loud — [*He shakes his head.*] Don't you understand? The words I've said to you — softly, in the dark — just trying to figure out what the stars are for, or what might be on the back side of the moon —

MEEKER. Bert —

CATES. They were questions, Rache. I was just asking questions. If you repeat those things on the witness stand, Brady'll make 'em sound like answers. And they'll crucify me!

[CATES *and* MEEKER *go off. The lights are slowly dimming.* DRUMMOND *puts on his coat, sizing up* RACHEL *as he does so.* RACHEL, *torn, is almost unconscious of his presence or of her surroundings.*]

DRUMMOND [*kindly, quietly*]. What's your name? Rachel what?

RACHEL. Rachel Brown. Can they make me testify?

DRUMMOND. I'm afraid so. It would be nice if nobody ever had to *make* anybody do anything. But — [*He takes his brief case.*] Don't let Brady scare you. He only *seems* to be bigger than the law.

RACHEL. It's not Mr. Brady. It's my father.

DRUMMOND. Who's your father?

RACHEL. The Reverend Jeremiah Brown. [DRUMMOND *whistles softly through his teeth.*] I remember feeling this way when I was a little girl. I would wake up at night, terrified of the dark. I'd think sometimes that my bed was on the ceiling, and the whole house was upside down; and if I didn't hang onto the mattress, I might fall outward into the stars. [*She shivers a little, remembering.*] I wanted to run to my father, and have him tell me I was safe, that everything was all right. But I was always more frightened of him than I was of falling. It's the same way now.

DRUMMOND [*softly*]. Is your mother dead?

RACHEL. I never knew my mother. [*Distraught.*] Is it true? *Is* Bert wicked?

DRUMMOND [*with simple conviction*]. Bert Cates is a good man. Maybe even a great one. And it takes strength for a woman to love such a man. Especially when he's a pariah in the community.

RACHEL. I'm only confusing Bert. And he's confused enough as it is.

DRUMMOND. The man who has everything figured out is probably a fool. College examinations notwithstanding, it takes a very smart fella to say "I don't know the answer!"

[DRUMMOND *puts on his hat, touches the brim of it as a gesture of good-bye and goes slowly off.*]

(Curtain.)

ACT TWO

Scene i

The courthouse lawn. The same night. The oppressive heat of the day has softened into a pleasant summer evening. Two lamp-posts spread a glow over the town square, and TWO WORKMEN *are assembling the platform for the prayer meeting. One of the* WORKMEN *glances up at the* READ YOUR BIBLE *banner.*

FIRST WORKMAN. What're we gonna do about this sign?

SECOND WORKMAN. The Devil don't run this town. Leave it up.

[BRADY *enters, followed by a knot of reporters.* HORN-BECK *brings up the rear; he alone is not bothering to take notes. Apparently this informal press conference has been in progress for some time, and* BRADY *is now bringing it to a climax.*]

BRADY. — and I hope that you will tell the readers of your newspapers that here in Hillsboro we are fighting the fight of the Faithful throughout the world!

[*All write.* BRADY *eyes* HORNBECK, *leaning lazily, not writing.*]

REPORTER [*British accent*]. A question, Mr. Brady.

BRADY. Certainly. Where are you from, young man?

REPORTER. London, sir. Reuters News Agency.

BRADY. Excellent. I have many friends in the United Kingdom.

REPORTER. What is your personal opinion of Henry Drummond?

BRADY. I'm glad you asked me that. I want people everywhere to know I bear no personal animosity toward Henry Drummond. There was a time when we were on the same side of the fence. He gave me active support in my campaign of 1908 — and I welcomed it. [*Almost impassioned, speaking at writing tempo, so all the reporters can get it down.*] But I say that if my own *brother* challenged the faith of millions, as Mr. Drummond is doing, I would oppose him still! [*The* WORKMEN *pound; the townspeople begin to gather.*] I think that's all for this evening, gentlemen. [*The reporters scatter.* BRADY *turns to*

52

HORNBECK.] Mr. Hornbeck, my clipping service has sent me some of your dispatches.

HORNBECK. How flattering to know I'm being clipped.

BRADY. It grieves me to read reporting that is so — biased.

HORNBECK. I'm no reporter, Colonel. I'm a critic.

BRADY. I hope you will stay for Reverend Brown's prayer meeting. It may bring you some enlightenment.

HORNBECK. It may. I'm here on a press pass, and I don't intend To miss any part of the show.

[REVEREND BROWN *enters with* MRS. BRADY *on his arm.* HORNBECK *passes them jauntily, and crosses downstage.*]

BRADY. Good evening, Reverend. How are you, Mother?

MRS. BRADY. The Reverend Brown was good enough to escort me.

BRADY. Reverend, I'm looking forward to your prayer meeting.

BROWN. You will find our people are fervent in their belief.

[MRS. BRADY *crosses to her husband.*]

MRS. BRADY. I know it's warm, Matt; but these night breezes can be treacherous. And you know how you perspire.

[*She takes a small kerchief out of her handbag and tucks it around his neck. He laughs a little.*]

BRADY. Mother is always so worried about my throat.

BROWN [*consulting his watch*]. I always like to begin my meetings at the time announced.

BRADY. Most commendable. Proceed, Reverend. After you.

[BROWN *mounts the few steps to the platform.* BRADY *follows him, loving the feel of the board beneath his feet. This is the squared circle where he had fought so many bouts with the English language, and won. The prayer meeting is motion picture, radio, and tent-show to these people. To them, the* REVEREND BROWN *is a combination Milton Sills and Douglas Fairbanks. He grasps the podium and stares down at them sternly.* BRADY *is benign. He sits with his legs crossed, an arm crooked over one corner of his chair.* BROWN *is milking the expectant pause. Just as he is ready to speak,* DRUMMOND *comes in and stands at the fringe of the crowd.* BROWN *glowers at* DRUMMOND. *The crowd chants.*]

BROWN. Brothers and sisters, I come to you on the Wings of the Word. The Wings of the 'Word are beating loud in the tree-tops! The Lord's Word is howling in the Wind, and flashing in the belly of the Cloud!

WOMAN. I hear it!

MAN. I see it, Reverend!

BROWN. And we *believe* the Word!

ALL. We believe!

BROWN. We believe the Glory of the Word!

ALL. Glory, Glory! Amen, amen!

[RACHEL *comes on, but remains at the fringes of the crowd.*]

BROWN. Hearken to the Word! [*He lowers his voice.*] The Word tells us that the World was created in Seven Days. In the beginning, the earth was without form, and void. And the Lord said, "Let there be light!"

VOICES. Ahhhh . . . !

BROWN. And there *was* light! And the Lord saw the Light and the Light saw the Lord, and the Light said, "Am I good, Lord?" And the Lord said, "Thou art good!"

MAN [*deep-voiced, singing*]. And the evening and the morning were the first day!

VOICES. Amen, amen!

BROWN [*calling out*]. The Lord said, "Let there be Firmament!" And even as He spoke, it was so! And the Firmament bowed down before Him and said, "Am I good, Lord?" And the Lord said, "Thou art good!"

MAN [*singing*]. And the evening and the morning were the second day!

VOICES. Amen, amen!

BROWN. On the Third Day brought He forth the Dry Land, and the Grass, and the Fruit Tree! And on the Fourth Day made

He the Sun, the Moon, and the Stars — and He pronounced them Good!

VOICES. Amen.

BROWN. On the Fifth Day He peopled the sea with fish. And the air with fowl. And made He great whales. And He blessed them all. But on the morning of the Sixth Day, the Lord rose, and His eye was dark, and a scowl lay across His face. [*Shouts.*] Why? Why was the Lord troubled?

ALL. Why? Tell us why? Tell the troubles of the Lord!

BROWN [*dropping his voice almost to a whisper*]. He looked about Him, did the Lord; at all His handiwork, bowed down before Him. And He said, "It is not good, it is not enough, it is not finished. I . . . shall . . . make . . . Me . . . a . . . *Man!*"

[*The crowd burst out into an orgy of hosannahs and waving arms.*]

ALL. Glory! Hosannah! Bless the Lord who created us!

WOMAN [*shouting out*]. Bow down! Bow down before the Lord!

MAN. Are we good, Lord? Tell us! Are we good?

BROWN [*answering*]. The Lord said, "Yea, thou art good! For I have created ye in My Image, after My Likeness! Be fruitful, and multiply, and replenish the Earth, and subdue it!"

MAN [*deep-voiced, singing*]. The Lord made Man master of the Earth . . . !

ALL. Glory, glory! Bless the Lord!

BROWN [*whipping 'em up*]. Do we believe?

ALL [*in chorus*]. Yes!

BROWN. Do we believe the Word?

ALL [*coming back like a whip-crack*]. Yes!

BROWN. Do we believe the Truth of the Word?

ALL. Yes!

BROWN [*pointing a finger toward the jail*]. Do we curse the man who denies the Word?

ALL [*crescendo, each answer mightier than the one before*]. Yes!

BROWN. Do we cast out this sinner in our midst?

ALL. Yes!

[*Each crash of sound from the crowd seems to strike* RACHEL *physically, and shake her.*]

BROWN. Do we call down hellfire on the man who has sinned against the Word?

ALL [*roaring*]. Yes!

BROWN [*deliberately shattering the rhythm, to go into a frenzied prayer, hands clasped together and lifted heavenward*]. O Lord of the Tempest and the Thunder! O Lord of Righteousness and Wrath! We pray that Thou wilt make a sign unto us! Strike down this sinner, as Thou didst Thine enemies of old, in the days of the Pharaohs! [*All lean forward, almost expecting the heavens to open with a thunderbolt.* RACHEL *is white.* BRADY *shifts uncomfortably in his chair; this is pretty strong stuff, even for him.*] Let him feel the terror of Thy sword! For all eternity, let his soul writhe in anguish and damnation —

RACHEL. *No!* [*She rushes to the platform.*] No, Father. Don't pray to destroy Bert!

BROWN. Lord, we call down the same curse on those who ask grace for this sinner — though they be blood of my blood, and flesh of my flesh!

BRADY [*rising, grasping* BROWN'S *arm*]. Reverend Brown, I know it is the great zeal of your faith which makes you utter this prayer! But it is possible to be overzealous, to destroy that which you hope to save — so that nothing is left but emptiness. [BROWN *turns.*] Remember the wisdom of Solomon in the Book of Proverbs — [*Softly.*] "He that troubleth his own house . . . shall inherit the wind." [BRADY *leads* BROWN *to a chair, then turns to the townspeople.*] The Bible also tells us that God forgives His children. And we, the Children of God, should forgive each other. [RACHEL *slips off.*] My good friends, return to your homes. The blessings of the Lord be with you all. [*Slowly the townspeople move off, singing and humming "Go, Tell It On the Mountain."* BRADY *is left alone on stage with* DRUMMOND, *who still watches him impassively.* BRADY *crosses to* DRUMMOND.] We were good friends once. I was always glad of your support. What happened between us? There used to be a mutuality of understanding and admiration. Why is it, my old friend, that you have moved so far away from me?

[*A pause. They study each other.*]

DRUMMOND [*slowly*]. All motion is relative. Perhaps it is *you* who have moved away — by standing still.

[*The words have a sharp impact on BRADY. For a moment, he stands still, his mouth open, staring at DRUMMOND. Then he takes two faltering steps backward, looks at DRUM-MOND again, then moves off the stage. DRUMMOND stands alone. Slowly the lights fade on the silent man. The curtain falls momentarily.*]

Scene ii

The courtroom, two days later. It is bright midday, and the trial is in full swing. The JUDGE is on the bench; the jury, lawyers, officials and spectators crowd the courtroom. HOWARD, the thirteen-year-old boy, is on the witness stand. He is wretched in a starched collar and Sunday suit. The weather is as relentlessly hot as before. BRADY is examining the boy, who is a witness for the prosecution.

BRADY. Go on, Howard. Tell them what else Mr. Cates told you in the classroom.

HOWARD. Well, he said at first the earth was too hot for any life. Then it cooled off a mite, and cells and things begun to live.

BRADY. Cells?

HOWARD. Little bugs like, in the water. After that, the little bugs got to be bigger bugs, and sprouted legs and crawled up on the land.

BRADY. How long did this take, according to Mr. Cates?

HOWARD. Couple million years. Maybe longer. Then comes the fishes and the reptiles and the mammals. Man's a mammal.

BRADY. Along with the dogs and the cattle in the field: did he say that?

HOWARD. Yes, sir.

[DRUMMOND *is about to protest against prompting the witness; then he decides it isn't worth the trouble.*]

BRADY. Now, Howard, how did *man* come out of this slimy mess of bugs and serpents, according to your — "Professor"?

HOWARD. Man was sort of evoluted. From the "Old World Monkeys."

[BRADY *slaps his thigh.*]

BRADY. Did you hear that, my friends? "Old World Monkeys"! According to Mr. Cates, you and I aren't even descended from good American monkeys! [*There is laughter.*] Howard, listen carefully. In all this talk of bugs and *"Evil-ution,"* of slime and ooze, did Mr. Cates ever make any reference to God?

HOWARD. Not as I remember.

BRADY. Or the miracle He achieved in seven days as described in the beautiful Book of Genesis?

HOWARD. No, sir.

[BRADY *stretches out his arms in an all-embracing gesture.*]

BRADY. Ladies and gentlemen —

DRUMMOND. Objection! I ask that the court remind the learned counsel that this is not a Chautauqua tent. He is supposed to be submitting evidence to a jury. There are no ladies on the jury.

BRADY. Your Honor, I have no intention of making a speech. There is no need. I am sure that everyone on the jury, everyone within the sound of this boy's voice, is moved by his tragic confusion. He has been taught that he wriggled up like an animal from the filth and the muck below! [*Continuing fervently, the spirit is upon him.*] I say that these Bible-haters, these *"Evil-utionists,"* are brewers of poison. And the legislature of this sovereign state has had the wisdom to demand that the peddlers of poison — in bottles or in books — clearly label the products they attempt to sell! [*There is applause.* HOWARD *gulps.* BRADY *points at the boy.*] I tell you, if this law is not upheld, this boy will become one of a generation, shorn of its faith by the teachings of Godless science! But if the full penalty of the law is meted out to Bertram Cates, the faithful the whole world over, who are watching us here, and listening to our every word, will call this courtroom blessed!

[*Applause. Dramatically,* BRADY *moves to his chair. Condescendingly, he waves to* DRUMMOND.]

BRADY. Your witness, sir.

[BRADY *sits.* DRUMMOND *rises, slouches toward the witness stand.*]

DRUMMOND. Well, I sure am glad Colonel Brady didn't make a speech! [*Nobody laughs. The courtroom seems to resent* DRUMMOND'S *gentle ridicule of the orator. To many, there is an effrontery in* DRUMMOND'S *very voice — folksy and relaxed. It's rather like a harmonica following a symphony concert.*] Howard, I heard you say that the world used to be pretty hot.

HOWARD. That's what Mr. Cates said.

DRUMMOND. You figure it was any hotter then than it is right now?

HOWARD. Guess it musta been. Mr. Cates read it to us from a book.

DRUMMOND. Do you know what book?

HOWARD. I guess that Mr. Darwin thought it up.

DRUMMOND [*leaning on the arm of the boy's chair*]. You figure anything's wrong about that, Howard?

HOWARD. Well, I dunno —

DAVENPORT [*leaping up, crisply*]. Objection, Your Honor. The defense is asking that a thirteen-year-old boy hand down an opinion on a question of morality!

DRUMMOND [*to the* JUDGE]. I am trying to establish, Your Honor, that Howard — or Colonel Brady — or Charles Darwin — or anyone in this courtroom — or *you,* sir — has the right to *think!*

JUDGE. Colonel Drummond, the right to think is not on trial here.

DRUMMOND [*energetically*]. With all respect to the bench, I hold that the right to think is very much on trial! It is fearfully in danger in the proceedings of this court!

BRADY [*rises*]. A *man* is on trial!

DRUMMOND. A thinking man! And he is threatened with fine and imprisonment because he chooses to speak what he thinks.

JUDGE. Colonel Drummond, would you please rephrase your question.

DRUMMOND [*to* HOWARD]. Let's put it this way, Howard. All this fuss and feathers about Evolution, do you think it hurt you any?

HOWARD. Sir?

DRUMMOND. Did it do you any harm? You still feel reasonably fit? What Mr. Cates told you, did it hurt your baseball game any? Affect your pitching arm?

[*He punches* HOWARD'S *right arm playfully.*]

HOWARD. No, sir. I'm a leftie.

DRUMMOND. A southpaw, eh? Still honor your father and mother?

HOWARD. Sure.

DRUMMOND. Haven't murdered anybody since breakfast?

DAVENPORT. Objection.

JUDGE. Objection sustained.

[DRUMMOND *shrugs.*]

BRADY. Ask him if his Holy Faith in the scriptures has been shattered —

DRUMMOND. When I need your *valuable* help, Colonel, you may rest assured I shall humbly ask for it. [*Turning.*] Howard, do you believe everything Mr. Cates told you?

HOWARD [*frowning*]. I'm not sure. I gotta think it over.

DRUMMOND. Good for you. Your pa's a farmer, isn't he?

HOWARD. Yes, sir.

DRUMMOND. Got a tractor?

HOWARD. Brand new one.

DRUMMOND. You figure a tractor's sinful, because it isn't mentioned in the Bible?

HOWARD [*thinking*]. Don't know.

DRUMMOND. Moses never made a phone call. Suppose that makes the telephone an instrument of the Devil?

HOWARD. I never thought of it that way.

BRADY [rising, booming]. Neither did anybody else! Your Honor, the defense makes the same old error of all Godless men! They confuse material things with the great spiritual realities of the Revealed Word! [*Turning to* DRUMMOND.] Why do you bewilder this child? Does Right have no meaning to you, sir?

[BRADY'S *hands are outstretched, palms upward, pleading.* DRUMMOND *stares at* BRADY *long and thoughtfully.*]

DRUMMOND [*in a low voice*]. Realizing that I may prejudice the case of my client, I must say that "Right" has no meaning to me whatsoever! [*There is a buzz of reaction in the courtroom.*] *Truth* has meaning — as a direction. But one of the peculiar imbecilities of our time is the grid of morality we have placed on human behavior: so that every act of man must be measured against an arbitrary latitude of right and longitude of wrong — in exact minutes, seconds, and degrees! [*He turns to* HOWARD.] Do you have any idea what I'm talking about, Howard?

HOWARD. No, sir.

DRUMMOND. Well, maybe you will. Someday. Thank you, son. That's all.

JUDGE. The witness is excused. [*He raps his gavel, but* HOWARD *remains in the chair, staring goop-eyed at his newly found idol.*] We won't need you any more, Howard: you can go back to your pa now. [HOWARD *gets up, and joins the spectators.*] Next witness.

DAVENPORT. Will Miss Rachel Brown come forward, please?

[RACHEL *emerges from among the spectators. She comes forward quickly, as if wanting to get the whole thing over with. She looks at no one.* CATES *watches her with a hopeless expression:* Et tu, Brute. MEEKER *swears her in perfunctorily.*]

BRADY. Miss Brown. You are a teacher at the Hillsboro Consolidated School?

RACHEL [*flat*]. Yes.

BRADY. So you have had ample opportunity to know the defendant, Mr. Cates, professionally?

RACHEL. Yes.

BRADY [*with exaggerated gentleness*]. Is Mr. Cates a member of the spiritual community to which you belong?

DRUMMOND [*rises*]. Objection! I don't understand this chatter about "spiritual communities." If the prosecution wants to know if they go to the same church, why doesn't he ask that?

JUDGE. Uh — objection overruled. [DRUMMOND *slouches, disgruntled.* CATES *stares at* RACHEL *disbelievingly, while her eyes remain on the floor. The exchange between* DRUMMOND *and the* JUDGE *seems to have unnerved her, however.*] You will answer the question, please.

RACHEL. I did answer it, didn't I? What was the question?

BRADY. Do you and Mr. Cates attend the same church?

RACHEL. Not any more. Bert dropped out two summers ago.

BRADY. Why?

RACHEL. It was what happened with the little Stebbins boy.

BRADY. Would you tell us about that, please?

RACHEL. The boy was eleven years old, and he went swimming in the river, and got a cramp, and drowned. Bert felt awful about it. He lived right next door, and Tommy Stebbins used to come over to the boarding house and look through Bert's microscope. Bert said the boy had a quick mind, and he might even be a scientist when he grew up. At the funeral, Pa preached that Tommy didn't die in a state of grace, because his folks had never had him baptized —

[CATES, *who has been smoldering through this recitation, suddenly leaps angrily to his feet.*]

CATES. Tell 'em what your father really said! That Tommy's soul was damned, writhing in hellfire!

DUNLAP [*shaking a fist at* CATES]. Cates, you sinner!

[*The* JUDGE *raps for order. There is confusion in the courtroom.*]

CATES. Religion's supposed to comfort people, isn't it? Not frighten them to death!

JUDGE. We will have order, please!

[DRUMMOND *tugs* CATES *back to his seat.*]

DRUMMOND. Your Honor, I request that the defendant's remarks be stricken from the record.

[*The* JUDGE *nods.*]

BRADY. But how can we strike this young man's bigoted opinions from the memory of this community? [BRADY *turns, about to play his trump card.*] Now, my dear. Will you tell the jury some more of Mr. Cates' opinions on the subject of religion?

DRUMMOND. Objection! Objection! Objection! Hearsay testimony is not admissible.

JUDGE. The court sees no objection to this line of questioning. Proceed, Colonel Brady.

BRADY. Will you merely repeat in your own words some of the conversations you had with the defendant?

[RACHEL'S *eyes meet* BERT'S. *She hesitates.*]

RACHEL. I don't remember exactly —

BRADY [*helpfully*]. What you told me the other day. That presumably "humorous" remark Mr. Cates made about the Heavenly Father.

RACHEL. Bert said —

[*She stops.*]

BRADY. Go ahead, my dear.

RACHEL [*pathetically*]. I can't —

JUDGE. May I remind you, Miss Brown, that you are testifying under oath, and it is unlawful to withhold pertinent information.

RACHEL. Bert was just talking about some of the things he'd read. He — He —

BRADY. Were you shocked when he told you these things? [RACHEL *looks down.*] Describe to the court your innermost feelings when Bertram Cates said to you: "God did not create Man! Man created God!"

[*There is a flurry of reaction.*]

DRUMMOND [*leaping to his feet*]. Objection!

RACHEL [*blurting*]. Bert didn't say that! He was just joking. What he said was: "God created Man in His own image — and Man, being a gentleman, returned the compliment."

[HORNBECK *guffaws and pointedly scribbles this down.* BRADY *is pleased.* RACHEL *seems hopelessly torn.*]

BRADY. Go on, my dear. Tell us some more. What did he say about the holy state of matrimony? Did he compare it with the breeding of animals?

RACHEL. No, he didn't say that — He didn't *mean* that. That's not what I told you. All' he said was —

[*She opens her mouth to speak, but nothing comes out. An emotional block makes her unable to utter a sound. Her lips move wordlessly.*]

JUDGE. Are you ill, Miss Brown? Would you care for a glass of water?

[*The fatuity of this suggestion makes* RACHEL *crumble into a near breakdown.*]

BRADY. Under the circumstances, I believe the witness should be dismissed.

DRUMMOND. And will the defense have no chance to challenge some of these statements the prosecutor has put in the mouth of the witness?

[CATES *is moved by* RACHEL'S *obvious distress.*]

CATES [*to* DRUMMOND]. Don't plague her. Let her go.

DRUMMOND [*pauses, then sighs*]. No questions.

JUDGE. For the time being, the witness is excused. [REVEREND BROWN *comes forward to help his daughter from the stand. His demeanor is unsympathetic as he escorts her from the courtroom. There is a hushed babble of excitement.*] Does the prosecution wish to call any further witnesses?

DAVENPORT. Not at the present time, Your Honor.

JUDGE. We shall proceed with the case for the defense. Colonel Drummond.

DRUMMOND [*rising*]. Your Honor, I wish to call Dr. Amos D. Keller, head of the Department of Zoology at the University of Chicago.

BRADY. Objection.

[DRUMMOND *turns, startled.*]

DRUMMOND. On what grounds?

BRADY. I wish to inquire what possible relevance the testimony of a *Zoo*-ology professor can have in this trial.

DRUMMOND [*reasonably*]. It has every relevance! My client is on trial for teaching Evolution. Any testimony relating to his alleged infringement of the law must be admitted!

BRADY. Irrelevant, immaterial, inadmissible.

DRUMMOND [*sharply*]. Why? If Bertram Cates were accused of murder, would it be irrelevant to call expert witnesses to examine the weapon? Would you rule out testimony that the so-called murder weapon was incapable of firing a bullet?

JUDGE. I fail to grasp the learned counsel's meaning.

DRUMMOND. Oh. [*With exaggerated gestures, as if explaining things to a small child.*] Your Honor, the defense wishes to place Dr. Keller on the stand to explain to the gentlemen of the jury exactly what the evolutionary theory is. How can they pass judgment on it if they don't know what it's all about?

BRADY. I hold that the very law we are here to enforce excludes such testimony! The people of this state have made it very clear that they do not want this *zoo*-ological hogwash slobbered around the schoolrooms! And I refuse to allow these agnostic scientists to employ this courtroom as a sounding board, as a platform from which they can shout their heresies into the headlines!

JUDGE [*after some thoughtful hesitation*]. Colonel Drummond, the court rules that zoology is irrelevant to the case.

[*The* JUDGE *flashes his customary mechanical and humorless grin.*]

DRUMMOND. Agnostic scientists! Then I call Dr. Allen Page — [*Staring straight at* BRADY.] Deacon of the Congregational Church — and professor of geology and archeology at Oberlin College.

BRADY [*drily*]. Objection!

JUDGE. Objection sustained.

[*Again, the meaningless grin.*]

DRUMMOND [*astonished*]. In one breath, does the court deny the existence of zoology, geology and archeology?

JUDGE. We do not deny the existence of these sciences: but they do not relate to this point of law.

DRUMMOND [*fiery*]. I call Walter Aaronson, philosopher, anthropologist, author! One of the most brilliant minds in the world today! Objection, Colonel Brady?

BRADY [*nodding, smugly*]. Objection.

DRUMMOND. Your Honor! The Defense has brought to Hillsboro — at great expense and inconvenience — fifteen noted scientists! The great thinkers of our time! Their testimony is basic to the defense of my client. For it is my intent to show this court that what Bertram Cates spoke quietly one spring afternoon in the Hillsboro High School is no crime! It is incontrovertible as geometry in every enlightened community of minds!

JUDGE. In *this* community, Colonel Drummond — and in this sovereign state — exactly the opposite is the case. The language of the law is clear; we do not need experts to question the validity of a law that is already on the books.

[DRUMMOND *for once in his life has hit a legal roadblock.*]

DRUMMOND [*scowling*]. In other words, the court rules out any expert testimony on Charles Darwin's *Origin of Species* or *Descent of Man?*

JUDGE. The court so rules.

[DRUMMOND *is flabbergasted. His case is cooked and he knows it. He looks around helplessly.*]

DRUMMOND [*there's the glint of an idea in his eye*]. Would the court admit expert testimony regarding a book known as the Holy Bible?

JUDGE [*hesitates, turns to* BRADY]. Any objection, Colonel Brady?

BRADY. If the counsel can advance the case of the defendant through the use of the Holy Scriptures, the prosecution will take no exception!

DRUMMOND. Good! [*With relish.*] I call to the stand one of the world's foremost experts on the Bible and its teachings — Matthew Harrison Brady!

[*There is an uproar in the courtroom. The* JUDGE *raps for order.*]

DAVENPORT. Your Honor, this is preposterous!

JUDGE [*confused*]. I — well, it's highly unorthodox. I've never known an instance where the defense called the prosecuting attorney as a witness.

[BRADY *rises. Waits for the crowd's reaction to subside.*]

BRADY. Your Honor, this entire trial is unorthodox. If the interests of Right and Justice will be served, I will take the stand.

DAVENPORT [*helplessly*]. But Colonel Brady —

[*Buzz of awed reaction. The giants are about to meet head-on. The* JUDGE *raps the gavel again, nervously.*]

JUDGE [*to* BRADY]. The court will support you if you wish to decline to testify — as a witness against your own case . . .

BRADY [*with conviction*]. Your Honor, I shall not testify *against* anything. I shall speak out, as I have all my life — on behalf of the Living Truth of the Holy Scriptures!

[DAVENPORT *sits, resigned but nervous.*]

JUDGE [*to* MEEKER, *in a nervous whisper*]. Uh — Mr. Meeker, you'd better swear in the witness, please . . .

[DRUMMOND *moistens his lips in anticipation.* BRADY *moves to the witness stand in grandiose style.* MEEKER *holds out a Bible,* BRADY *puts his left hand on the book, and raises his right hand.*]

MEEKER. Do you solemnly swear to tell the truth, the whole truth, and nothing but the truth, so help you God?

BRADY [*booming*]. I do.

MRS. KREBS. And he will!

[BRADY *sits, confident and assured. His air is that of a benign and learned mathematician about to be quizzed by a schoolboy on matters of short division.*]

DRUMMOND. Am I correct, sir, in calling on you as an authority on the Bible?

BRADY. I believe it is not boastful to say that I have studied the Bible as much as any layman. And I have tried to live according to its precepts.

DRUMMOND. Bully for you. Now, I suppose you can quote me chapter and verse right straight through the King James Version, can't you?

BRADY. There are many portions of the Holy Bible that I have committed to memory.

[DRUMMOND *crosses to counsel table and picks up a copy of Darwin.*]

DRUMMOND. I don't suppose you've memorized many passages from the *Origin of Species?*

BRADY. I am not in the least interested in the pagan hypotheses of that book.

DRUMMOND. Never read it?

BRADY. And I never will.

DRUMMOND. Then how in perdition do you have the gall to whoop up this holy war against something you don't know anything about? How can you be so cocksure that the body of scientific knowledge systematized in the writings of Charles Darwin is, in any way, irreconcilable with the spirit of the Book of Genesis?

BRADY. Would you state that question again, please?

DRUMMOND. Let me put it this way. [*He flips several pages in the book.*] On page nineteen of *Origin of Species,* Darwin states — [DAVENPORT *leaps up.*]

DAVENPORT. I object to this, Your Honor. Colonel Brady has been called as an authority on the Bible. Now the "gentleman from Chicago" is using this opportunity to read into the record scientific testimony which you, Your Honor, have previously ruled is irrelevant. If he's going to examine Colonel Brady on the Bible, let him stick to the Bible, the Holy Bible, and only the Bible!

[DRUMMOND *cocks an eye at the bench.*]

JUDGE [*clears his throat*]. You will confine your questions to the Bible.

[DRUMMOND *slaps shut the volume of Darwin.*]

DRUMMOND [*not angrily*]. All right. I get the scent in the wind. [*He tosses the volume of Darwin on the counsel table.*] We'll play in *your* ball park, Colonel. [*He searches for a copy of the Bible, finally gets* MEEKER'S. *Without opening it,* DRUMMOND *scrutinizes the binding from several angles.*] Now let's get this straight. Let's get it clear. This *is* the book that you're an expert on?

[BRADY *is annoyed at* DRUMMOND'S *elementary attitude and condescension.*]

BRADY. That is correct.

DRUMMOND. Now tell me. Do you feel that every word that's written in this book should be taken literally?

BRADY. Everything in the Bible should be accepted, exactly as it is given there.

DRUMMOND [*leafing through the Bible*]. Now take this place where the whale swallows Jonah. Do you figure that actually happened?

BRADY. The Bible does not say "a whale," it says "a big fish."

DRUMMOND. Matter of fact, it says "a great fish" — but it's pretty much the same thing. What's your feeling about that?

BRADY. I believe in a God who can make a whale and who can make a man and make both do what He pleases!

VOICES. Amen, amen!

DRUMMOND [*turning sharply to the clerk*]. I want those "Amens" in the record! [*He wheels back to* BRADY.] I recollect a story about Joshua, making the sun stand still. Now as an expert, you tell me that's as true as the Jonah business. Right? [BRADY *nods, blandly.*] That's a pretty neat trick. You suppose Houdini could do it?

BRADY. I do not question or scoff at the miracles of the Lord — as do ye of little faith.

DRUMMOND. Have you ever pondered just what would naturally happen to the earth if the sun stood still?

BRADY. You can testify to that if I get you on the stand.

[*There is laughter.*]

DRUMMOND. If they say that the sun stood still, they must've had a notion that the sun moves around the earth. Think that's the way of things? Or don't you believe the earth moves around the sun?

BRADY. I have faith in the Bible!

DRUMMOND. You don't have much faith in the solar system.

BRADY [*doggedly*]. The sun stopped.

DRUMMOND. Good. [*Level and direct.*] Now if what you say factually happened — if Joshua halted the sun in the sky — that means the earth stopped spinning on its axis; continents toppled over each other, mountains flew out into space. And the earth, arrested in its orbit, shriveled to a cinder and crashed into the sun. [*Turning.*] How come they missed *this* tidbit of news.

BRADY. They missed it because it didn't happen.

DRUMMOND. It must've happened! According to natural law. Or don't you believe in natural law, Colonel? Would you like to ban Copernicus from the classroom, along with Charles Darwin? Pass a law to wipe out all the scientific development since Joshua. Revelations — period!

BRADY [*calmly, as if instructing a child*]. Natural law was born in the mind of the Heavenly Father. He can change it, cancel it, use it as He pleases. It constantly amazes me that you apostles of science, for all your supposed wisdom, fail to grasp this simple fact.

[DRUMMOND *flips a few pages in the Bible.*]

DRUMMOND. Listen to this: Genesis 4-16. "And Cain went out from the presence of the Lord, and dwelt in the land of Nod, on the East of Eden. And Cain *knew his wife!*" Where the hell did *she* come from?

BRADY. Who?

DRUMMOND. Mrs. Cain. Cain's wife. If, "In the beginning" there were only Adam and Eve, and Cain and Abel, where'd this extra woman spring from? Ever figure that out?

BRADY [*cool*]. No, sir. I will leave the agnostics to hunt for her.

[*Laughter.*]

DRUMMOND. Never bothered you?

BRADY. Never bothered me.

DRUMMOND. Never tried to find out?

BRADY. No.

DRUMMOND. Figure somebody pulled off another creation, over in the next county?

BRADY. The Bible satisfies me, it is enough.

DRUMMOND. It frightens me to imagine the state of learning in this world if everyone had your driving curiosity.

[DRUMMOND *is still probing for a weakness in Goliath's armor. He thumbs a few pages further in the Bible.*]

DRUMMOND. This book now goes into a lot of "begats." [*He reads.*] "And Aphraxad begat Salah; and Salah begat Eber" and so on and so on. These pretty important folks?

BRADY. They are the generations of the holy men and women of the Bible.

DRUMMOND. How did they go about all this "begatting"?

BRADY. What do you mean?

DRUMMOND. I mean, did people "begat" in those days about the same way they get themselves "begat" today?

BRADY. The process is about the same. I don't think your scientists have improved it any.

[*Laughter.*]

DRUMMOND. In other words, these folks were conceived and brought forth through the normal biological function known as *sex*. [*There is hush-hush reaction through the court. HOWARD'S mother clamps her hands over the boy's ears, but he wriggles free.*] What do you think of sex, Colonel Brady?

BRADY. In what spirit is this question asked?

DRUMMOND. I'm not asking what you think of sex as a father, or as a husband. Or a Presidential candidate. You're up here as an expert on the Bible. What's the Biblical evaluation of sex?

BRADY. It is considered "Original Sin."

DRUMMOND [*with mock amazement*]. And all these holy people got themselves "begat" through "Original Sin"? [BRADY *does not answer. He scowls, and shifts his weight in his chair.*] All this sinning make 'em any less holy?

DAVENPORT. Your Honor, where is this leading us? What does it have to do with the State versus Bertram Cates?

JUDGE. Colonel Drummond, the court must be satisfied that this line of questioning has some bearing on the case.

DRUMMOND [*fiery*]. You've ruled out all my witnesses. I must be allowed to examine the one witness you've left me in my own way!

BRADY [*with dignity*]. Your Honor, I am willing to sit here and endure Mr. Drummond's sneering and his disrespect. For he is pleading the case of the prosecution by his contempt for all that is holy.

DRUMMOND. I object, I object, I object.

BRADY. On what grounds? Is it possible that something *is* holy to the celebrated agnostic?

DRUMMOND. *Yes!* [*His voice drops, intensely.*] The individual human mind. In a child's power to master the multiplication table there is more sanctity than in all your shouted "Amens!", "Holy, Holies!" and "Hosannahs!" An idea is a greater monument than a cathedral. And the advance of man's knowledge is more of a miracle than any sticks turned to snakes, or the parting of waters! But are we now to halt the march of progress because Mr. Brady frightens us with a fable? [*Turning to the jury, reasonably.*] Gentlemen, progress has never been a bargain. You've got to pay for it. Sometimes I think there's a man behind a counter who says, "All right, you can have a telephone; but you'll have to give up privacy, the charm of distance. Madam, you may vote; but at a price; you lose the right to retreat behind a powder-puff or a petticoat. Mister, you may conquer the air; but the birds will lose their wonder, and the clouds will smell of gasoline!" [*Thoughtfully, seeming to look beyond the courtroom.*] Darwin moved us forward to a hilltop, where we could look back and see the way from which we came. But for this view, this insight, this knowledge, we must abandon our faith in the pleasant poetry of Genesis.

BRADY. We must *not* abandon faith! Faith is the important thing!

DRUMMOND. Then why did God plague us with the power to think? Mr. Brady, why do you deny the *one* faculty which lifts man above all other creatures on the earth: the power of his brain to reason. What other merit have we? The elephant is larger, the horse is stronger and swifter, the butterfly more beautiful, the mosquito more prolific, even the simple sponge is more durable! [*Wheeling on* BRADY.] Or does a *sponge* think?

BRADY. I don't know. I'm a man, not a sponge.

[*There are a few snickers at this; the crowd seems to be slipping away from* BRADY *and aligning itself more and more with* DRUMMOND.]

DRUMMOND. Do you think a sponge thinks?

BRADY. If the Lord wishes a sponge to think, it thinks.

DRUMMOND. Does a man have the same privileges that a sponge does?

BRADY. Of course.

DRUMMOND [*roaring, for the first time: stretching his arm toward* CATES]. This man wishes to be accorded the same privilege as a sponge! *He wishes to think!*

[*There is some applause. The sound of it strikes* BRADY *exactly as if he had been slapped in the face.*]

BRADY. But your client is wrong! He is deluded! He has lost his way!

DRUMMOND. It's sad that we aren't all gifted with your positive knowledge of Right and Wrong, Mr. Brady. [DRUMMOND *strides to one of the uncalled witnesses seated behind him, and takes from him a rock about the size of a tennis ball.* DRUMMOND *weighs the rock in his hand as he saunters back toward* BRADY.] How old do you think this rock is?

BRADY [*intoning*]. I am more interested in the Rock of Ages, than I am in the Age of Rocks.

[*A couple of die-hard "Amens."* DRUMMOND *ignores this glib gag.*]

DRUMMOND. Dr. Page of Oberlin College tells me that this rock is at least ten million years old.

BRADY [*sarcastically*]. Well, well, Colonel Drummond! You managed to sneak in some of that scientific testimony after all.

[DRUMMOND *opens up the rock, which splits into two halves. He shows it to* BRADY.]

DRUMMOND. Look, Mr. Brady. These are the fossil remains of a pre-historic marine creature, which was found in this very county — and which lived here millions of years ago, when these very mountain ranges were submerged in water.

BRADY. I know. The Bible gives a fine account of the flood. But your professor is a little mixed up on his dates. That rock is not more than six thousand years old.

DRUMMOND. How do you know?

BRADY. A fine Biblical scholar, Bishop Usher, has determined for us the exact date and hour of the Creation. It occurred in the Year 4,004, B.C.

DRUMMOND. That's Bishop Usher's opinion.

BRADY. It is not an opinion. It is literal fact, which the good Bishop arrived at through careful computation of the ages of the prophets as set down in the Old Testament. In fact, he determined that the Lord began the Creation on the 23rd of October in the Year 4,004 B.C. at — uh, at 9 A.M.!

DRUMMOND. That Eastern Standard Time? [*Laughter.*] Or Rocky Mountain Time? [*More laughter.*] It wasn't daylight-saving time, was it? Because the Lord didn't make the sun until the fourth day!

BRADY [*fidgeting*]. That is correct.

DRUMMOND [*sharply*]. The first day. Was it a twenty-four-hour day?

BRADY. The Bible says it was a day.

DRUMMOND. There wasn't any sun. How do you know how long it was?

BRADY [*determined*]. The Bible says it was a day.

DRUMMOND. A normal day, a literal day, a twenty-four-hour day?

[*Pause. BRADY is unsure.*]

BRADY. I do not know.

DRUMMOND. What do you think?

BRADY [*floundering*]. I do not think about things that . . . I do not think about!

DRUMMOND. Do you ever think about things that you *do* think about? [*There is some laughter. But it is dampened by the knowledge and awareness throughout the courtroom, that the trap is about to be sprung.*] Isn't it possible that first day was twenty-*five* hours long? There was no way to measure it, no way to tell! *Could* it have been twenty-five hours?

[*Pause. The entire courtroom seems to lean forward.*]

BRADY [*hesitates — then*]. It is . . . *possible* . . .

[DRUMMOND'S *got him. And he knows it! This is the turning point. From here on, the tempo mounts.* DRUMMOND *is now fully in the driver's seat. He pounds his questions faster and faster.*]

DRUMMOND. Oh. You interpret that the first day recorded in the Book of Genesis could be of indeterminate length.

BRADY [*wriggling*]. I mean to state that the day referred to is not necessarily a twenty-four-hour day.

DRUMMOND. It could have been thirty hours! Or a month! Or a year! Or a hundred years! [*He brandishes the rock underneath* BRADY'S *nose.*] *Or ten million years!*

[DAVENPORT *is able to restrain himself no longer. He realizes that* DRUMMOND *has* BRADY *in his pocket. Red-faced, he leaps up to protest.*]

DAVENPORT. I protest! This is not only irrelevant, immaterial — it is *illegal!* [*There is excited reaction in the courtroom. The* JUDGE *pounds for order, but the emotional tension will not subside.*] I demand to know the purpose of Mr. Drummond's examination! What is he trying to do?

[*Both* BRADY *and* DRUMMOND *crane forward, hurling their answers not at the court, but at each other.*]

BRADY. I'll tell you what he's trying to do! He wants to destroy everybody's belief in the Bible, and in God!

DRUMMOND. You know that's not true. I'm trying to stop you bigots and ignoramuses from controlling the education of the United States! And you know it!

[*Arms out,* DAVENPORT *pleads to the court, but is unheard. The* JUDGE *hammers for order.*]

JUDGE [*shouting*]. I shall ask the bailiff to clear the court, unless there is order here.

BRADY. How dare you attack the Bible?

DRUMMOND. The Bible is a book. A good book. But it's not the *only* book.

BRADY. It is the revealed word of the Almighty. God spake to the men who wrote the Bible.

DRUMMOND. And how do you know that God didn't "spake" to Charles Darwin?

BRADY. I know, because God tells me to oppose the evil teachings of that man.

DRUMMOND. Oh. God speaks to you.

BRADY. Yes.

DRUMMOND. He tells you exactly what's right and what's wrong?

BRADY [*doggedly*]. Yes.

DRUMMOND. And you act accordingly?

BRADY. Yes.

DRUMMOND. So you, Matthew Harrison Brady, through oratory, legislation, or whatever, pass along God's orders to the rest of the world! [*Laughter begins.*] Gentlemen, meet the "Prophet From Nebraska!"

[BRADY'S *oratory is unassailable; but his vanity — exposed by* DRUMMOND'S *prodding — is only funny. The laughter is painful to* BRADY. *He starts to answer* DRUMMOND, *then turns toward the spectators and tries, almost physically, to suppress the amused reaction. This only makes it worse.*]

BRADY [*almost inarticulate*]. I — Please — !

DRUMMOND [*with increasing tempo, closing in*]. Is that the way of things? God tells Brady what is good! To be against Brady is to be against God!

[*More laughter.*]

BRADY [*confused*]. No, no! Each man is a free agent —

DRUMMOND. Then what is Bertram Cates doing in the Hillsboro jail? [*Some applause.*] Suppose Mr. Cates had enough influence and lung power to railroad through the State Legislature a law that only *Darwin* should be taught in the schools!

BRADY. Ridiculous, ridiculous! There is only one great Truth in the world —

DRUMMOND. The Gospel according to Brady! God speaks to Brady, and Brady tells the world! Brady, Brady, Brady, Almighty!

[DRUMMOND *bows grandly. The crowd laughs.*]

BRADY. The Lord is my strength —

DRUMMOND. What if a lesser human being — a Cates, or a Darwin — has the audacity to think that God might whisper to *him?* That an un-Brady thought might still be holy? Must men go to prison because they are at odds with the self-appointed prophet? [BRADY *is now trembling so that it is impossible for him to speak. He rises, towering above his tormentor — rather like a clumsy, lumbering bear that is baited by an agile dog.*] Extend the Testaments! Let us have a Book of Brady! We shall hex the Pentateuch, and slip you in neatly between Numbers and Deuteronomy!

[*At this, there is another burst of laughter.* BRADY *is almost in a frenzy.*]

BRADY [*reaching for a sympathetic ear, trying to find the loyal audience which has slipped away from him*]. My friends — Your Honor — My Followers — Ladies and Gentlemen —

DRUMMOND. The witness is excused.

BRADY [*unheeding*]. All of you know what I stand for! What I believe! I believe, I believe in the truth of the Book of Genesis! [*Beginning to chant.*] Exodus, Leviticus, Numbers, Deuteronomy, Joshua, Judges, Ruth, First Samuel, Second Samuel, First Kings, Second Kings —

DRUMMOND. Your Honor, this completes the testimony. The witness is excused!

BRADY [*pounding the air with his fists*]. Isaiah, Jeremiah, Lamentations, Ezekiel, Daniel, Hosea, Joel, Amos, Obadiah —

[*There is confusion in the court. The* JUDGE *raps.*]

JUDGE. You are excused, Colonel Brady —

BRADY. Jonah, Micah, Nahum, Habakkuk, Zephaniah —

[BRADY *beats his clenched fists in the air with every name.*

There is a rising counterpoint of reaction from the spectators. Gavel.]

JUDGE [*over the confusion*]. Court is adjourned until ten o'clock tomorrow morning!

[*Gavel. The spectators begin to mill about. A number of them, reporters and curiosity seekers, cluster around DRUMMOND. DAVENPORT follows the JUDGE out.*]

DAVENPORT. Your Honor, I want to speak to you about striking all of this from the record.

[*They go out.*]

BRADY [*still erect on the witness stand*]. Haggai, Zechariah, Malachi . . .

[*His voice trails off. He sinks, limp and exhausted into the witness chair. MRS. BRADY looks at her husband, worried and distraught. She looks at DRUMMOND with helpless anger. DRUMMOND moves out of the courtroom, and most of the crowd goes with him. Reporters cluster tight about DRUM-MOND, pads and pencils hard at work. BRADY sits, ignored, on the witness chair. MEEKER takes CATES back to the jail. MRS. BRADY goes to her husband, who still sits on the raised witness chair.*]

MRS. BRADY [*taking his hand*]. Matt —

[BRADY *looks about to see if everyone has left the courtroom, before he speaks.*]

BRADY. Mother. They're laughing at me, Mother!

MRS. BRADY [*unconvincingly*]. No, Matt. No, they're not!

BRADY. I can't stand it when they laugh at me!

[MRS. BRADY *steps up onto the raised level of the witness chair. She stands beside and behind her husband, putting her arms around the massive shoulders and cradling his head against her breast.*]

MRS. BRADY [*soothing*]. It's all right, baby. It's all right. [MRS. BRADY *sways gently back and forth, as if rocking her husband to sleep.*] Baby . . . Baby . . . !

(The curtain falls.)

ACT THREE

The courtroom, the following day. The lighting is low, somber. A spot burns down on the defense table, where DRUMMOND *and* CATES *sit, waiting for the jury to return.* DRUMMOND *leans back in a meditative mood, feet propped on a chair.* CATES, *the focus of the furor, is resting his head on his arms. The courtroom is almost empty. Two spectators doze in their chairs. In comparative shadow,* BRADY *sits, eating a box lunch. He is drowning his troubles with food, as an alcoholic escapes from reality with a straight shot.* HORNBECK *enters, bows low to* BRADY.

HORNBECK. Afternoon, Colonel. Having high tea, I see.
> [BRADY *ignores him.*]
> Is the jury still out? Swatting flies
> And wrestling with justice — in that order?
> > [HORNBECK *crosses to* DRUMMOND. CATES *lifts his head.*]
> I'll hate to see the jury filing in;
> Won't you, Colonel? I'll miss Hillsboro —
> Especially this courthouse:
> A melange of Moorish and Methodist;
> It must have been designed by a congressman!

[HORNBECK *smirks at his own joke, then sits in the shadows and pores over a newspaper. Neither* CATES *nor* DRUMMOND *have paid the slightest attention to him.*]

CATES [*staring straight ahead*]. Mr. Drummond. What's going to happen?

DRUMMOND. What do you think is going to happen, Bert?

CATES. Do you think they'll send me to prison?

DRUMMOND. They could.

CATES. They don't ever let you see anybody from the outside, do they? I mean — you can just talk to a visitor — through a window — the way they show it in the movies?

DRUMMOND. Oh, it's not as bad as all that. [*Turning toward the town.*] When they started this fire here, they never figured it would light up the whole sky. A lot of people's shoes are getting hot. But you can't be too sure.

[*At the other side of the stage,* BRADY *rises majestically from his debris of paper napkins and banana peels, and goes off.*]

CATES [*watching* BRADY *go off*]. He seems so sure. He seems to know what the verdict's going to be.

DRUMMOND. Nobody knows. [*He tugs on one ear.*] I've got a pretty good idea. When you've been a lawyer as long as I have — a thousand years, more or less — you get so you can smell the way a jury's thinking.

CATES. What are they thinking right now?

DRUMMOND [*sighing*]. Someday I'm going to get me an *easy* case. An open-and-shut case. I've got a friend up in Chicago. Big lawyer. Lord how the money rolls in! You know why? He never takes a case unless it's a sure thing. Like a jockey who won't go in a race unless he can ride the favorite.

CATES. You sure picked the long shot this time, Mr. Drummond.

DRUMMOND. Sometimes I think the law *is* like a horse race. Sometimes it seems to me I ride like fury, just to end up back where I started. Might as well be on a merry-go-round, or a rocking horse . . . or . . . [*He half-closes his eyes. His voice is far away, his lips barely move.*] Golden Dancer. . . .

CATES. What did you say?

DRUMMOND. That was the name of my first long shot. Golden Dancer. She was in the big side window of the general store in Wakeman, Ohio. I used to stand out in the street and say to myself, "If I had Golden Dancer I'd have everything in the world that I wanted." [*He cocks an eyebrow.*] I was seven years old, and a very fine judge of rocking horses. [*He looks off again, into the distance.*] Golden Dancer had a bright red mane, blue eyes, and she was gold all over, with purple spots. When the sun hit her stirrups, she was a dazzling sight to see. But she was a week's wages for my father. So Golden Dancer and I always had a plate glass window between us. [*Reaching back for the memory.*] But — let's see, it wasn't Christmas; must've been my birthday — I woke up in the morning and there was Golden Dancer at the foot of my bed! Ma had skimped on the groceries, and my father'd worked nights for a month. [*Re-living the moment.*] I jumped into the saddle and started to rock — [*Almost a whisper.*] And it *broke!* It split in two! The wood was rotten, the whole thing was put together with spit and sealing wax! All shine, and no substance! [*Turning to* CATES.] Bert, whenever you see something bright, shining, perfect-seeming — all gold, with purple spots — look behind the paint! And if it's a lie — show it up for what it really is!

[*A* RADIO MAN *comes on, lugging an old-fashioned carbon microphone. The* JUDGE, *carrying his robe over his arm, comes on and scowls at the microphone.*]

RADIO MAN [*to* JUDGE]. I think this is the best place to put it — if it's all right with you, Your Honor.

JUDGE. There's no precedent for this sort of thing.

RADIO MAN. You understand, sir, we're making history here to-day. This is the first time a public event has ever been broadcast.

JUDGE. Well, I'll allow it — provided you don't interfere with the business of the court.

[*The* RADIO MAN *starts to string his wires. The* MAYOR *hurries on, worried, brandishing a telegram.*]

MAYOR [*to* JUDGE]. Merle, gotta talk to you. Over here. [*He draws the* JUDGE *aside, not wanting to be heard.*] This wire just came. The boys over at the state capitol are getting worried about how things are going. Newspapers all over are raising such a hullaballoo. After all, November, ain't too far off, and it don't do any of us any good to have any of the voters gettin' all steamed up. Wouldn't do no harm to just let things simmer down. [*The* RADIO MAN *reappears.*] Well, go easy, Merle.

[*Tipping his hat to* DRUMMOND, *the* MAYOR *hurries off.*]

RADIO MAN [*crisply, into the mike*]. Testing. Testing.

[DRUMMOND *crosses to the microphone.*]

DRUMMOND [*to the* RADIO MAN]. What's that?

RADIO MAN. An enunciator.

DRUMMOND. You going to broadcast?

RADIO MAN. We have a direct wire to WGN, Chicago. As soon as the jury comes in, we'll announce the verdict.

[DRUMMOND *takes a good look at the microphone, fingers the base.*]

DRUMMOND. Radio! God, this is going to break down a lot of walls.

RADIO MAN [*hastily*]. You're — you're not supposed to say "God" on the radio!

DRUMMOND. Why the hell not?

[*The* RADIO MAN *looks at the microphone, as if it were a toddler that had just been told the facts of life.*]

RADIO MAN. You're not supposed to say "Hell," either.

DRUMMOND [*sauntering away*]. *This* is going to be a barren source of amusement!

[BRADY *re-enters and crosses ponderously to the* RADIO MAN.]

BRADY. Can one speak into either side of this machine?

[*The* RADIO MAN *starts at this rumbling thunder, so close to the ear of his delicate child.*]

RADIO MAN [*in an exaggerated whisper*]. Yes, sir. Either side.

[BRADY *attempts to lower his voice, but it is like putting a leash on an elephant.*]

BRADY. Kindly signal me while I am speaking, if my voice does not have sufficient projection for your radio apparatus.

[RADIO MAN *nods, a little annoyed.* HORNBECK *smirks, amused. Suddenly the air in the courtroom is charged with excitement.* MEEKER *hurries on — and the spectators begin to scurry expectantly back into the courtroom. Voices mutter: "They're comin' in now. Verdict's been reached. Jury's comin' back in."* MEEKER *crosses to the* JUDGE'S *bench, reaches up for the gavel and raps it several times.*]

MEEKER. Everybody rise. [*The spectators come to attention.*] Hear ye, hear ye. Court will reconvene in the case of the State versus Bertram Cates.

[MEEKER *crosses to lead in the jury. They enter, faces fixed and stern.*]

CATES [*whispers to* DRUMMOND]. What do you think? Can you tell from their faces?

[DRUMMOND *is nervous, too. He squints at the returning*

jurors, drumming his fingers on the table top. CATES *looks around, as if hoping to see* RACHEL — *but she is not there. His disappointment is evident. The* RADIO MAN *has received his signal from off-stage, and he begins to speak into the microphone.*]

RADIO MAN [*low, with dramatic intensity*]. Ladies and gentlemen, this is Harry Esterbrook, speaking to you from the courthouse in Hillsboro, where the jury is just returning to the courtroom to render its verdict in the famous Hillsboro Monkey Trial case. The Judge has just taken the bench. And in the next few minutes we shall know whether Bertram Cates will be found innocent or guilty.

[*The* JUDGE *looks at him with annoyance. Gingerly, the* RADIO MAN *aims his microphone at the* JUDGE *and steps back. There is hushed tension all through the courtroom.*]

JUDGE [*clears his throat*]. Gentlemen of the Jury, have you reached a decision?

SILLERS [*rising*]. Yeah. Yes, sir, we have, Your Honor.

[MEEKER *crosses to* SILLERS *and takes a slip of paper from him. Silently, he crosses to the* JUDGE'S *bench again, all eyes following the slip of paper. The* JUDGE *takes it, opens it, raps his gavel.*]

JUDGE. The jury's decision is unanimous. Bertram Cates is found guilty as charged!

[*There is tremendous reaction in the courtroom. Some cheers, applause, "Amens." Some boos.* BRADY *is pleased. But it is not the beaming, powerful, assured* BRADY *of the Chautauqua tent. It is a spiteful, bitter victory for him, not a conquest with a cavalcade of angels.* CATES *stares at his lap.* DRUMMOND *taps a pencil. The* RADIO MAN *talks rapidly, softly into his microphone. The* JUDGE *does not attempt to control the reaction.*]

HORNBECK [*in the manner of a hawker or pitchman*]. Step right up, and get your tickets for the Middle Ages! You only *thought* you missed the Coronation of Charlemagne!

JUDGE [*rapping his gavel, shouting over the noise*]. Quiet, please! This court is still in session. [*The noise quiets down.*] The prisoner will rise, to hear the sentence of this court. [DRUMMOND *looks up quizzically, alert.*] Bertram Cates, I hereby sentence you to —

DRUMMOND [*sharply*]. Your Honor! A question of procedure!

JUDGE [*nettled*]. Well, sir?

DRUMMOND. Is it not customary in this state to allow the defendant to make a statement before sentence is passed?

[*The* JUDGE *is red-faced.*]

JUDGE. Colonel Drummond, I regret this omission. In the confusion, and the — I neglected — [*Up, to* CATES.] Uh, Mr. Cates, if you wish to make any statement before sentence is passed on you, why, you may proceed.

[*Clears throat again.* CATES *rises. The courtroom quickly grows silent again.*]

CATES [*simply*]. Your Honor, I am not a public speaker. I do not have the eloquence of some of the people you have heard in the last few days. I'm just a schoolteacher.

MRS. BLAIR. Not any more you ain't!

CATES [*pause. Quietly*]. I *was* a schoolteacher. [*With difficulty.*] I feel I am . . . I have been convicted of violating an unjust law. I will continue in the future, as I have in the past, to oppose this law in any way I can. I —

[CATES *isn't sure exactly what to say next. He hesitates, then sits down. There is a crack of applause. Not from everybody, but from many of the spectators.* BRADY *is fretful and disturbed. He's won the case. The prize is his, but he can't reach for the candy. In his hour of triumph,* BRADY *expected to be swept from the courtroom on the shoulders of his exultant followers. But the drama isn't proceeding according to plan. The gavel again. The court quiets down.*]

JUDGE. Bertram Cates, this court has found you guilty of violating Public Act Volume 37, Statute Number 31428, as charged. This violation is punishable by fine and/or imprisonment. [*He coughs.*] But since there has been no previous violation of this statute, there is no precedent to guide the bench in passing sentence. [*He flashes the automatic smile.*] The court deems it proper — [*He glances at the* MAYOR.] — to sentence Bertram Cates to pay a fine of — [*He coughs.*] one hundred dollars.

[*The mighty Evolution Law explodes with the pale puff of a wet firecracker. There is a murmur of surprise through the courtroom.* BRADY *is indignant. He rises, incredulous.*]

BRADY. Did your honor say one hundred dollars?

JUDGE. That is correct. [*Trying to get it over with.*] This seems to conclude the business of the trial —

BRADY [*thundering*]. Your Honor, the prosecution takes exception! Where the issues are so titanic, the court must mete out more drastic punishment —

DRUMMOND [*biting in*]. I object!

BRADY. To make an example of this transgressor! To show the world —

DRUMMOND. Just a minute. Just a minute. The amount of the fine is of no concern to me. Bertram Cates has no intention whatsoever of paying this or any other fine. He would not pay it if it were one single dollar. We will appeal this decision to the Supreme Court of this state. Will the court grant thirty days to prepare our appeal?

JUDGE. Granted. The court fixes bond at . . . five hundred dollars. I believe this concludes the business of this trial. Therefore, I declare this court is adjour—

BRADY [*hastily*]. Your Honor! [*He reaches for a thick manuscript.*] Your Honor, with the court's permission, I should like to read into the record a few short remarks which I have prepared —

DRUMMOND. I object to that. Mr. Brady may make any remarks he likes — long, short or otherwise. In a Chautauqua tent or in a political campaign. Our business in Hillsboro is completed. The defense holds that the court shall be adjourned.

BRADY [*frustrated*]. But I have a few remarks —

JUDGE. And we are all anxious to hear them, sir. But Colonel Drummond's point of procedure is well taken. I am sure that everyone here will wish to remain after the court is adjourned to hear your address. [BRADY *lowers his head slightly, in gracious deference to procedure. The* JUDGE *raps the gavel.*] I hereby declare this court is adjourned, sine die.

[*There is a babble of confusion and reaction.* HORNBECK *promptly crosses to* MEEKER *and confers with him in whispers. Spectators, relieved of the court's formality, take a seventh-inning stretch. Fans pump, sticky clothes are plucked away from the skin.*]

MELINDA [*calling to* HOWARD, *across the courtroom*]. Which side won?

HOWARD [*calling back*]. I ain't sure. But the whole thing's over!

[*A couple of* HAWKERS *slip in the courtroom with Eskimo Pies and buckets of lemonade.*]

HAWKER. Eskimo Pies. Get your Eskimo Pies!

[JUDGE *raps with his gavel.*]

JUDGE [*projecting*]. Quiet! Order in the — I mean, your attention, please. [*The spectators quiet down some, but not completely.*] We are honored to hear a few words from Colonel Brady, who wishes to address you —

[*The* JUDGE *is interrupted in his introduction by* MEEKER *and* HORNBECK. *They confer sotto voce. The babble of voices crescendos.*]

HAWKER. Get your Eskimo Pies! Cool off with an Eskimo Pie!

[*Spectators flock to get ice cream and lemonade.* BRADY *preens himself for the speech, but is annoyed by the confusion.* HORNBECK *hands the* JUDGE *several bills from his wallet, and* MEEKER *pencils a receipt. The* JUDGE *bangs the gavel again.*]

JUDGE. We beg your attention, please, ladies and gentlemen! Colonel Brady has some remarks to make which I am sure will interest us all!

[*A few of the faithful fall dutifully silent. But the milling about and the slopping of lemonade continues. Two kids chase each other in and out among the spectators, annoying the perspiring* RADIO MAN. BRADY *stretches out his arms, in the great attention-getting gesture.*]

BRADY. My dear friends . . . ! Your attention, please! [*The bugle voice reduces the noise somewhat further. But it is not the eager, anticipatory hush of olden days. Attention is given him, not as the inevitable due of a mighty monarch, but grudgingly and resentfully.*] Fellow citizens, and friends of the unseen audience. From the hallowed hills of sacred Sinai, in the days of remote antiquity, came the law which has been our bulwark and our shield. Age upon age, men have looked to the law as they would look to the mountains, whence cometh our strength. And here, here in this —

[*The* RADIO MAN *approaches* BRADY *nervously.*]

RADIO MAN. Excuse me, Mr. — uh, Colonel Brady; would you . . . uh . . . point more in the direction of the enunciator . . . ?

[*The* RADIO MAN *pushes* BRADY *bodily toward the microphone. As the orator is maneuvered into position, he seems almost to be an inanimate object, like a huge ornate vase which must be precisely centered on a mantel. In this momentary lull, the audience has slipped away from him again. There's a backwash of restless shifting and murmuring.* BRADY'S *vanity and cussedness won't let him give up, even though he realizes this is a sputtering anticlimax. By God, he'll make them listen!*]

BRADY [*red-faced, his larynx taut, roaring stridently*]. As they would look to the mountains whence cometh our strength. And here, here in this courtroom, we have seen vindicated — [*A few people leave. He watches them desperately, out of the corner of his eye.*] We have seen vindicated —

RADIO MAN [*after an off-stage signal*]. Ladies and gentlemen, our program director in Chicago advises us that our time here is completed. Harry Y. Esterbrook speaking. We return you now to our studios and "Matinee Musicale."

[*He takes the microphone and goes off. This is the final indignity to* BRADY; *he realizes that a great portion of his audience has left him as he watches it go.* BRADY *brandishes his speech, as if it were Excalibur. His eyes start from his head, the voice is a tight, frantic rasp.*]

BRADY. From the hallowed hills of sacred Sinai . . .

[*He freezes. His lips move, but nothing comes out. Paradoxically, his silence brings silence. The orator can hold his audience only by not speaking.*]

STOREKEEPER. Look at him!

MRS. BRADY [*with terror*]. Matt —

[*There seems to be some violent, volcanic upheaval within him. His lower lip quivers, his eyes stare. Very slowly, he seems to be leaning toward the audience. Then, like a figure in a waxworks, toppling from its pedestal, he falls stiffly, face forward.* MEEKER *and* DAVENPORT *spring forward, catch* BRADY *by the shoulders and break his fall. The sheaf of manuscript,*] *clutched in his raised hand, scatters in mid air. The great words flutter innocuously to the courtroom floor. There is a burst of reaction.* MRS. BRADY *screams.*]

DAVENPORT. Get a doctor!

[*Several men lift the prostrate* BRADY, *and stretch him across three chairs.* MRS. BRADY *rushes to his side.*]

JUDGE. Room! Room! Give him room!

MRS. BRADY. Matt! Dear God in Heaven! Matt!

[DRUMMOND, HORNBECK and CATES *watch, silent and concerned — somewhat apart from the crowd. The silence is tense. It is suddenly broken by a fanatic old* WOMAN, *who shoves her face close to* BRADY'S *and shrieks.*]

WOMAN [*wailing*]. O Lord, work us a miracle and save our Holy Prophet!

[*Rudely,* MEEKER *pushes her back.*]

MEEKER [*contemptuously*]. Get away! [*Crisply.*] Move him out of here. Fast as we can. Hank. Bill. Give us a hand here. Get him across the street to Doc's office.

[*Several men lift* BRADY, *with difficulty, and begin to carry him out. A strange thing happens.* BRADY *begins to speak in a hollow, distant voice — as if something sealed up inside of him were finally broken, and the precious contents spilled out into the open at last.*]

BRADY [*as he is carried out; in a strange, unreal voice*]. Mr. Chief Justice, Citizens of these United States. During my term in the White House, I pledge to carry out my program for the betterment of the common people of this country. As your new President, I say what I have said all of my life . . . .

[*The crowd tags along, curious and awed. Only* DRUMMOND, CATES *and* HORNBECK *remain, their eyes fixed on* BRADY'S *exit.* DRUMMOND *stares after him.*]

DRUMMOND. How quickly they can turn. And how painful it can be when you don't expect it. [*He turns.*] I wonder how it feels to be Almost-President three times — with a skull full of undelivered inauguration speeches.

HORNBECK. Something happens to an Also-Ran.
Something happens to the feet of a man

Who always comes in second in a foot-race.
He becomes a national unloved child,
A balding orphan, an aging adolescent
Who never got the biggest piece of candy.
Unloved children, of all ages, insinuate themselves
Into spotlights and rotogravures.
They stand on their hands and wiggle their feet.
Split pulpits with their pounding! And their tonsils
Turn to organ pipes. Show me a shouter,
And I'll show you an also-ran. A might-have-been,
An almost-was.

CATES [*softly*]. Did you see his face? He looked terrible. . . .

[MEEKER *enters.* CATES *turns to him.* MEEKER *shakes his head: "I don't know."*]

MEEKER. I'm surprised more folks ain't keeled over in this heat.

HORNBECK. He's all right. Give him an hour or so
To sweat away the pickles and the pumpernickel.
To let his tongue forget the acid taste
Of vinegar victory.
Mount Brady will erupt again by nightfall,
Spouting lukewarm fire and irrelevant ashes.

[CATES *shakes his head, bewildered.* DRUMMOND *watches him, concerned.*]

DRUMMOND. What's the matter, boy?

CATES. I'm not sure. Did I win or did I lose?

DRUMMOND. You won.

CATES. But the jury found me —

DRUMMOND. What jury? Twelve men? Millions of people will say you won. They'll read in their papers tonight that you smashed a bad law. You made it a joke!

CATES. Yeah. But what's going to happen now? I haven't got a job. I'll bet they won't even let me back in the boarding house.

DRUMMOND. Sure, it's gonna be tough, it's not gonna be any church social for a while. But you'll live. And while they're making you sweat, remember — you've helped the next fella.

CATES. What do you mean?

DRUMMOND. You don't suppose this kind of thing is ever finished, do you? Tomorrow it'll be something else — and another fella will have to stand up. And you've helped give him the guts to do it!

CATES [*turning to* MEEKER, *with new pride in what he's done*]. Mr. Meeker, don't you have to lock me up?

MEEKER. They fixed bail.

CATES. You don't expect a schoolteacher to have five hundred dollars.

MEEKER [*jerking his head toward* HORNBECK]. This fella here put up the money.

HORNBECK. With a year's subscription to the Baltimore *Herald*, We give away — at no cost or obligation — A year of freedom.

[RACHEL *enters, carrying a suitcase. She is smiling, and there is a new lift to her head.* CATES *turns and sees her.*]

CATES. Rachel!

RACHEL. Hello, Bert.

CATES. Where are you going?

RACHEL. I'm not sure. But I'm leaving my father.

CATES. Rache . . .

RACHEL. Bert, it's my fault the jury found you guilty. [*He starts to protest.*] Partly my fault. I helped. [RACHEL *hands* BERT *a book.*] This is your book, Bert. [*Silently, he takes it.*] I've read it. All the way through. I don't understand it. What I do understand, I don't like. I don't want to think that men come from apes and monkeys. But I think that's beside the point.

[DRUMMOND *looks at the girl admiringly.*]

DRUMMOND. That's right. That's beside the point.

[RACHEL *crosses to* DRUMMOND.]

RACHEL. Mr. Drummond, I hope I haven't said anything to offend you. You see, I haven't really thought very much. I was always afraid of what I might think — so it seemed safer not to think at all. But now I know. A thought is like a child inside our body. It has to be born. If it dies inside you, part of you dies, too! [*Pointing to the book.*] Maybe what Mr. Darwin wrote is bad. I don't know. Bad or good, it doesn't make any difference. The ideas have to come out — like children. Some of 'em healthy as a bean plant, some sickly. I think the sickly ideas die mostly, don't you, Bert?

[BERT *nods yes, but he's too lost in new admiration for her to do anything but stare. He does not move to her side.* DRUM-MOND *smiles, as if to say: "That's quite a girl!" The* JUDGE *walks in slowly.*]

JUDGE. Brady's dead.

[*They all react. The* JUDGE *starts toward his chambers.*]

DRUMMOND. I can't imagine the world without Matthew Harrison Brady.

CATES [*to the* JUDGE]. What caused it? Did they say?

[*Dazed, the* JUDGE *goes off without answering.*]

HORNBECK. Matthew Harrison Brady died of a busted belly.

[DRUMMOND *slams down his brief case.*]

HORNBECK. You know what I thought of him,
And I know what you thought.
Let us leave the lamentations to the illiterate!
Why should we weep for him? He cried enough for himself!
The national tear-duct from Weeping Water, Nebraska,
Who flooded the whole nation like a one-man Mississippi!
You know what he was:
A Barnum-bunkum Bible-beating bastard!

[DRUMMOND *rises, fiercely angry.*]

DRUMMOND. You smart-aleck! You have no more right to spit on his religion than you have a right to spit on *my* religion! Or my lack of it!

HORNBECK [*askance*]. Well, what do you know!
Henry Drummond for the defense
Even of his enemies!

DRUMMOND [*low, moved*]. There was much greatness in this man.

HORNBECK. Shall I put that in the obituary?

[DRUMMOND *starts to pack up his brief case.*]

DRUMMOND. Write anything you damn please.

HORNBECK. How do you write an obituary
For a man who's been dead thirty years?
"In Memoriam — M.H.B." Then what?
Hail the apostle whose letters to the Corinthians
Were lost in the mail?
Two years, ten years — and tourists will ask the guide,
"Who died here? Matthew Harrison Who?"
  [*A sudden thought.*]
What did he say to the minister? It fits!
He delivered his own obituary!
  [*He looks about the witness stand and the* JUDGE'S *bench,
  searching for something.*]
They must have one here some place.
  [HORNBECK *pounces on a Bible.*]
Here it is: *his* book!
  [*Thumbing hastily.*]
Proverbs, wasn't it?

DRUMMOND [*quietly*]. "He that troubleth his own house shall
inherit the wind: and the fool shall be servant to the wise in
heart."

[HORNBECK *looks at* DRUMMOND, *surprised. He snaps
the Bible shut, and lays it on the* JUDGE'S *bench.* HORN-
BECK *folds his arms and crosses slowly toward* DRUM-
MOND, *his eyes narrowing.*]

HORNBECK. We're growing an odd crop of agnostics this year!

[DRUMMOND'S *patience is wearing thin.*]

DRUMMOND [*evenly*]. I'm getting damned tired of you, Hornbeck.

HORNBECK. Why?

DRUMMOND. You never pushed a noun against a verb except to
blow up something.

HORNBECK. That's a typical lawyer's trick: accusing the accuser!

DRUMMOND. What am I accused of?

HORNBECK. I charge you with contempt of conscience!
Self-perjury. Kindness aforethought.
Sentimentality in the first degree.

DRUMMOND. Why? Because I refuse to erase a man's lifetime? I tell you Brady had the same right as Cates: the right to be wrong!

HORNBECK. "Be-Kind-To-Bigots" Week. Since Brady's dead, We must be kind. God, how the world is rotten With kindness!

DRUMMOND. A giant once lived in that body. [*Quietly.*] But Matt Brady got lost. Because he was looking for God too high up and too far away.

HORNBECK. You hypocrite! You fraud!
    [*With a growing sense of discovery.*]
You're more religious than *he* was!
    [DRUMMOND *doesn't answer.* HORNBECK *crosses toward the exit hurriedly.*]
Excuse me, gentlemen. I must get me to a typewriter And hammer out the story of an atheist Who believes in God.

    [*He goes off.*]

CATES. Colonel Drummond.

DRUMMOND. Bert, I am resigning my commission in the State Militia. I hand in my sword!

CATES. Doesn't it cost a lot of money for an appeal? I couldn't pay you . . .

    [DRUMMOND *waves him off.*]

DRUMMOND. I didn't come here to be paid. [*He turns.*] Well, I'd better get myself on a train.

RACHEL. There's one out at five-thirteen. Bert, you and I can be on that train, too!

CATES [*smiling, happy*]. I'll get my stuff!

RACHEL. I'll help you!

    [*They start off.* RACHEL *comes back for her suitcase.* CATES *grabs his suit jacket, clasps* DRUMMOND'S *arm.*]

CATES [*calling over his shoulder*]. See you at the depot!

    [RACHEL *and* CATES *go off.* DRUMMOND *is left alone on stage. Suddenly he notices* RACHEL'S *copy of Darwin on the table.*]

DRUMMOND [*calling*]. Say — you forgot —

[*But* RACHEL *and* CATES *are out of earshot. He weighs the volume in his hand; this one book has been the center of the whirlwind. Then* DRUMMOND *notices the Bible on the* JUDGE'S *bench. He picks up the Bible in his other hand; he looks from one volume to the other, balancing them thoughtfully, as if his hands were scales. He half-smiles, half-shrugs. Then* DRUMMOND *slaps the two books together and jams them in his brief case, side by side. Slowly, he climbs to the street level and crosses the empty square.*]

(The curtain falls.)

PYGMALION

A Romance in Five Acts

by George Bernard Shaw

Pygmalion

Introduction

At the tender age of twenty, George Bernard Shaw (1856-1950) left Dublin to descend upon London, and British society and the English drama were never the same again. For a time he wrote music criticism and stage reviews, as well as socialist propaganda for the young Fabian Society, but within a short time others were doing the reviewing and he was doing the plays. London was amused, outraged, and bewildered by this self-proclaimed "upstart son of a downstart father," this brash Irishman who not only considered himself extremely intelligent and witty but also proclaimed the opinion. In retrospect, it seems only typical of Shaw that one of the campaigns about which he was most passionate should be for a thoroughly logical and utterly impractical reform of English spelling along phonetic lines.

Pygmalion was his single greatest commercial bonanza, and the preface to the published play carries that unmistakable Shaw imprint: "I wish to boast that *Pygmalion* has been an extremely successful play, both on stage and screen, all over Europe and North America as well as at home." It is impossible to examine Shaw's plays and ignore the author's intrusive, scintillating personality. Trenchant and obtuse, amiable and obdurate, compassionate and quarrelsome, Shaw was a bundle of contradictions; in his writings, he was likewise master of many styles, from formidable polemic to dazzling improvisation. The Nobel Prize was presented to him in 1925.

If the man is not easily classified, neither are the plays. The astonishing theatrical variety of his work immediately impresses anyone who peruses such dramas as *Mrs. Warren's Profession, Candida, Arms and the Man, Man and Superman, Major Barbara, Caesar and Cleopatra,* or *Saint Joan.* If his dramas have anything at all in common, perhaps it is their courageous exploration of controversial and fundamental themes in startlingly frank virtuoso terms. No other modern dramatist has given us a body of work so significant.

ACT ONE

[*COVENT GARDEN at 11.15 p.m. Torrents of heavy summer rain. Cab whistles blowing frantically in all directions. Pedestrians running for shelter into the market and under the portico of St. Paul's Church, where there are already several people, among them a lady and her daughter in evening dress. They are all peering out gloomily at the rain, except one man with his back turned to the rest, who seems wholly preoccupied with a notebook in which he is writing busily.*
The church clock strikes the first quarter.]

THE DAUGHTER [*in the space between the central pillars, close to the one on her left*]. I'm getting chilled to the bone. What can Freddy be doing all this time? He's been gone twenty minutes.

THE MOTHER [*on her daughter's right*]. Not so long. But he ought to have got us a cab by this.

A BYSTANDER [*on the lady's right*]. He wont get no cab not until half-past eleven, missus, when they come back after dropping their theatre fares.

THE MOTHER. But we must have a cab. We cant stand here until half-past eleven. It's too bad.

THE BYSTANDER. Well, it aint my fault, missus.

THE DAUGHTER. If Freddy had a bit of gumption, he would have got one at the theatre door.

THE MOTHER. What could he have done, poor boy?

THE DAUGHTER. Other people got cabs. Why couldnt he?

[*Freddy rushes in out of the rain from the Southampton Street side, and comes between them closing a dripping umbrella. He is a young man of twenty, in evening dress, very wet round the ankles.*]

THE DAUGHTER. Well, havnt you got a cab?

FREDDY. Theres not one to be had for love or money.

THE MOTHER. Oh, Freddy, there must be one. You cant have tried.

97

THE DAUGHTER. It's too tiresome. Do you expect us to go and get one ourselves?

FREDDY. I tell you theyre all engaged. The rain was so sudden: nobody was prepared; and everybody had to take a cab. Ive been to Charing Cross one way and nearly to Ludgate Circus the other; and they were all engaged.

THE MOTHER. Did you try Trafalgar Square?

FREDDY. There wasnt one at Trafalgar Square.

THE DAUGHTER. Did you try?

FREDDY. I tried as far as Charing Cross Station. Did you expect me to walk to Hammersmith?

THE DAUGHTER. You havnt tried at all.

THE MOTHER. You really are very helpless, Freddy. Go again; and dont come back until you have found a cab.

FREDDY. I shall simply get soaked for nothing.

THE DAUGHTER. And what about us? Are we to stay here all night in this draught, with next to nothing on? You selfish pig —

FREDDY. Oh, very well: I'll go, I'll go. [*He opens his umbrella and dashes off Strandwards, but comes into collision with a flower girl, who is hurrying in for shelter, knocking her basket out of her hands. A blinding flash of lightning, followed instantly by a rattling peal of thunder, orchestrates the incident.*]

THE FLOWER GIRL. Nah then, Freddy: look wh' y' gowin, deah.

FREDDY. Sorry [*He rushes off.*]

THE FLOWER GIRL [*picking up her scattered flowers and replacing them in the basket*]. Theres menners f' yer! Te-oo banches of voylets trod into the mad. [*She sits down on the plinth of the column, sorting her flowers, on the lady's right. She is not at all an attractive person. She is perhaps eighteen, perhaps twenty, hardly older. She wears a little sailor hat of black straw that has long been exposed to the dust and soot of London and has seldom if ever been brushed. Her hair needs washing rather badly: its mousy color can hardly be natural. She wears a shoddy black coat that reaches nearly to her knees and is shaped to her waist. She has a brown skirt with a coarse apron. Her boots are much the worse for wear. She is no doubt as clean as she can afford to be; but compared to the ladies she*] *is very dirty. Her features are no worse than theirs; but their condition leaves something to be desired; and she needs the services of a dentist.*]

THE MOTHER. How do you know that my son's name is Freddy, pray?

THE FLOWER GIRL. Ow, eez ye-ooa san, is e? Wal, fewd dan y' de-ooty bawmz a mather should, eed now bettern to spawl a pore gel's flahrzn than ran awy athaht pyin. Will ye-oo py me f' them? [*Here, with apologies, this desperate attempt to represent her dialect without a phonetic alphabet must be abandoned as unintelligible outside London.*]

THE DAUGHTER. Do nothing of the sort, mother. The idea!

THE MOTHER. Please allow me, Clara. Have you any pennies?

THE DAUGHTER. No. Ive nothing smaller than sixpence.

THE FLOWER GIRL [*hopefully*]. I can give you change for a tanner, kind lady.

THE MOTHER [*to* CLARA]. Give it to me. [CLARA *parts reluctantly.*] Now [*To the girl.*] this is for your flowers.

THE FLOWER GIRL. Thank you kindly, lady.

THE DAUGHTER. Make her give you the change. These things are only a penny a bunch.

THE MOTHER. Do hold your tongue, Clara. [*To the girl.*] You can keep the change.

THE FLOWER GIRL. Oh, thank you, lady.

THE MOTHER. Now tell me how you know that young gentleman's name.

THE FLOWER GIRL. I didnt.

THE MOTHER. I heard you call him by it. Dont try to deceive me.

THE FLOWER GIRL [*protesting*]. Who's trying to deceive you? I called him Freddy or Charlie same as you might yourself if you was talking to a stranger and wished to be pleasant. [*She sits down beside her basket.*]

THE DAUGHTER. Sixpence thrown away! Really, mamma, you might have spared Freddy that. [*She retreats in disgust behind the pillar.*]

An elderly gentleman of the amiable military type rushes into the shelter, and closes a dripping umbrella. He is in the same plight as Freddy, very wet about the ankles. He is in evening dress, with a light overcoat. He takes the place left vacant by the daughter's retirement.

THE GENTLEMAN. Phew!

THE MOTHER [*to* THE GENTLEMAN]. Oh, sir, is there any sign of its stopping?

THE GENTLEMAN. I'm afraid not. It started worse than ever about two minutes ago. [*He goes to the plinth beside the flower girl; puts up his foot on it; and stoops to turn down his trouser ends.*]

THE MOTHER. Oh dear! [*She retires sadly and joins her daughter.*]

THE FLOWER GIRL [*taking advantage of the military gentleman's proximity to establish friendly relations with him*]. If it's worse, it's a sign it's nearly over. So cheer up, Captain; and buy a flower off a poor girl.

THE GENTLEMAN. I'm sorry. I havnt any change.

THE FLOWER GIRL. I can give you change, Captain.

THE GENTLEMAN. For a sovereign? Ive nothing less.

THE FLOWER GIRL. Garn! Oh do buy a flower off me, Captain. I can change half-a-crown. Take this for tuppence.

THE GENTLEMAN. Now dont be troublesome: theres a good girl. [*Trying his pockets.*] I really havnt any change — Stop: heres three hapence, if thats any use to you. [*He retreats to the other pillar.*]

THE FLOWER GIRL [*disappointed, but thinking three half-pence better than nothing*]. Thank you, sir.

THE BYSTANDER [*to the girl*]. You be careful: give him a flower for it. Theres a bloke here behind taking down every blessed word youre saying. [*All turn to the man who is taking notes.*]

THE FLOWER GIRL [*springing up terrified*]. I aint done nothing wrong by speaking to the gentleman. Ive a right to sell flowers if I keep off the kerb. [*Hysterically.*] I'm a respectable girl: so help me, I never spoke to him except to ask him to buy a flower off me. [*General hubbub, mostly sympathetic to the flower girl, but deprecating her excessive sensibility. Cries of* Dont start hollerin. Who's hurting you? Nobody's going to touch you. Whats the good of fussing? Steady on. Easy easy, etc., *come from the elderly staid spectators, who pat her comfortingly. Less patient ones bid her shut her head, or ask her roughly what is wrong with her. A remoter group, not knowing what the matter is, crowd in and increase the noise with question and answer:* Whats the row? Whatshe do? Where is he? A tec taking her down. What! him? Yes: him over there: Took money off the gentleman, etc. *THE FLOWER GIRL, distraught and mobbed, breaks through them to the gentleman, crying wildly.*] Oh, sir, dont let him charge me. You dunno what it means to me. Theyll take away my character and drive me on the streets for speaking to gentlemen. They—

THE NOTE TAKER [*coming forward on her right, the rest crowding after him*]. There, there, there, there! who's hurting you, you silly girl? What do you take me for?

THE BYSTANDER. It's all right: he's a gentleman: look at his boots. [*Explaining to the note taker.*] She thought you was a copper's nark, sir.

THE NOTE TAKER [*with quick interest*]. Whats a copper's nark?

THE BYSTANDER [*inapt at definition*]. It's a — well, it's a copper's nark, as you might say. What else would you call it? A sort of informer.

THE FLOWER GIRL [*still hysterical*]. I take my Bible oath I never said a word —

THE NOTE TAKER [*overbearing but good-humored*]. Oh, shut up, shut up. Do I look like a policeman?

THE FLOWER GIRL [*far from reassured*]. Then what did you take down my words for? How do I know whether you took me down right? You just shew me what youve wrote about me. [*The note taker opens his book and holds it steadily under her nose, though the pressure of the mob trying to read it over his shoulders would upset a weaker man.*] Whats that? That aint proper writing. I cant read that.

THE NOTE TAKER. I can. [*Reads, reproducing her pronunciation exactly.*] "Cheer ap, Keptin; n' baw ya flahr orf a pore gel."

THE FLOWER GIRL [*much distressed*]. It's because I called him Captain. I meant no harm. [*To the gentleman.*] Oh, sir, dont let him lay a charge agen me for a word like that. You —

THE GENTLEMAN. Charge! I make no charge. [*To* THE NOTE TAKER.] Really, sir, if you are a detective, you need not begin protecting me against molestation by young women until I ask you. Anybody could see that the girl meant no harm.

THE BYSTANDERS GENERALLY [*demonstrating against police espionage*]. Course they could. What business is it of yours? You mind your own affairs. He wants promotion, he does. Taking down people's words! Girl never said a word to him. What harm if she did? Nice thing a girl cant shelter from the rain without being insulted, etc., etc., etc. [*She is conducted by the more sympathetic demonstrators back to her plinth, where she resumes her seat and struggles with her emotion.*]

THE BYSTANDER. He aint a tec. He's a blooming busybody: thats what he is. I tell you, look at his boots.

THE NOTE TAKER [*turning on him genially*]. And how are all your people down at Selsey?

THE BYSTANDER [*suspiciously*]. Who told you that my people come from Selsey?

THE NOTE TAKER. Never you mind. They did. [*To the girl.*] How do you come to be up so far east? You were born in Lisson Grove.

THE FLOWER GIRL [*appalled*]. Oh, what harm is there in my leaving Lisson Grove? It wasnt fit for a pig to live in; and I had to pay four-and-six a week. [*In tears.*] Oh, boo—hoo—oo—

THE NOTE TAKER. Live where you like; but stop that noise.

THE GENTLEMAN [*to the girl*]. Come, come! he cant touch you: you have a right to live where you please.

A SARCASTIC BYSTANDER [*thrusting himself between* THE NOTE TAKER *and* THE GENTLEMAN]. Park Lane, for instance. I'd like to go into the Housing Question with you, I would.

THE FLOWER GIRL [*subsiding into a brooding melancholy over her basket, and talking very low-spiritedly to herself*]. I'm a good girl, I am.

THE SARCASTIC BYSTANDER [*not attending to her*]. Do you know where I come from?

THE NOTE TAKER [*promptly*]. Hoxton.

Titterings. Popular interest in the note taker's performance increases.

THE SARCASTIC ONE [*amazed*]. Well, who said I didnt? Bly me! You know everything, you do.

THE FLOWER GIRL [*still nursing her sense of injury*]. Aint no call to meddle with me, he aint.

THE BYSTANDER [*to her*]. Of course he aint. Dont you stand it from him. [*To* THE NOTE TAKER.] See here: what call have you to know about people what never offered to meddle with you? Wheres your warrant?

SEVERAL BYSTANDERS [*encouraged by this seeming point of law*]. Yes: wheres your warrant?

THE FLOWER GIRL. Let him say what he likes. I dont want to have no truck with him.

THE BYSTANDER. You take us for dirt under your feet, dont you? Catch you taking liberties with a gentleman!

THE SARCASTIC BYSTANDER. Yes: tell him where he come from if you want to go fortune-telling.

THE NOTE TAKER. Cheltenham, Harrow, Cambridge, and India.

THE GENTLEMAN. Quite right. [*Great laughter. Reaction in* THE NOTE TAKER's *favor. Exclamations of* He knows all about it. Told him proper. Hear him tell the toff where he come from? etc.]. May I ask, sir, do you do this for your living at a music hall?

THE NOTE TAKER. Ive thought of that. Perhaps I shall some day.

The rain has stopped; and the persons on the outside of the crowd begin to drop off.

THE FLOWER GIRL [*resenting the reaction*]. He's no gentleman, he aint, to interfere with a poor girl.

THE DAUGHTER [*out of patience, pushing her way rudely to the front and displacing* THE GENTLEMAN, *who politely retires to the other side of the pillar*]. What on earth is Freddy doing? I shall get pneumonia if I stay in this draught any longer.

THE NOTE TAKER [*to himself, hastily making a note of her pronunciation of "monia"*]. Earlscourt.

THE DAUGHTER [*violently*]. Will you please keep your impertinent remarks to yourself.

THE NOTE TAKER. Did I say that out loud? I didnt mean to. I beg your pardon. Your mother's Epsom, unmistakeably.

THE MOTHER [*advancing between her daughter and* THE NOTE TAKER]. How very curious! I was brought up in Largelady Park, near Epsom.

THE NOTE TAKER [*uproariously amused*]. Ha! ha! What a devil of a name! Excuse me. [*To the daughter.*] You want a cab, do you?

THE DAUGHTER. Dont dare speak to me.

THE MOTHER. Oh please, please, Clara. [*Her daughter repudiates her with an angry shrug and retires haughtily.*] We should be so grateful to you, sir, if you found us a cab. [THE NOTE TAKER *produces a whistle.*] Oh, thank you. [*She joins her daughter.*]

THE NOTE TAKER *blows a piercing blast.*

THE SARCASTIC BYSTANDER. There! I knowed he was a plainclothes copper.

THE BYSTANDER. That aint a police whistle: thats a sporting whistle.

THE FLOWER GIRL [*still preoccupied with her wounded feelings*]. He's no right to take away my character. My character is the same to me as any lady's.

THE NOTE TAKER. I dont know whether youve noticed it; but the rain stopped about two minutes ago.

THE BYSTANDER. So it has. Why didnt you say so before? and us losing our time listening to your silliness! [*He walks off towards the Strand.*]

THE SARCASTIC BYSTANDER. I can tell where you come from. You come from Anwell. Go back there.

THE NOTE TAKER [*helpfully*]. Hanwell.

THE SARCASTIC BYSTANDER [*affecting great distinction of speech*]. Thenk you, teacher. Haw haw! So long [*He touches his hat with mock respect and strolls off.*]

THE FLOWER GIRL. Frightening people like that! How would he like it himself?

THE MOTHER. It's quite fine now, Clara. We can walk to a motor bus. Come. [*She gathers her skirts above her ankles and hurries off towards the Strand.*]

THE DAUGHTER. But the cab — [*Her mother is out of hearing*]. Oh, how tiresome! [*She follows angrily.*]

All the rest have gone except THE NOTE TAKER, THE GENTLEMAN, *and* THE FLOWER GIRL, *who sits arranging her basket and still pitying herself in murmurs.*

THE FLOWER GIRL. Poor girl! Hard enough for her to live without being worrited and chivied.

THE GENTLEMAN [*returning to his former place on* THE NOTE TAKER's *left*]. How do you do it, if I may ask?

THE NOTE TAKER. Simply phonetics. The science of speech. Thats my profession: also my hobby. Happy is the man who can make a living by his hobby! You can spot an Irishman or a Yorkshireman by his brogue. I can place any man within six miles. I can place him within two miles in London. Sometimes within two streets.

THE FLOWER GIRL. Ought to be ashamed of himself, unmanly coward!

THE GENTLEMAN. But is there a living in that?

THE NOTE TAKER. Oh yes. Quite a fat one. This is an age of up-starts. Men begin in Kentish Town with £80 a year, and end in Park Lane with a hundred thousand. They want to drop Kent-ish Town; but they give themselves away every time they open their mouths. Now I can teach them —

THE FLOWER GIRL. Let him mind his own business and leave a poor girl —

THE NOTE TAKER [*explosively*]. Woman: cease this detestable boohooing instantly; or else seek the shelter of some other place of worship.

THE FLOWER GIRL [*with feeble defiance*]. Ive a right to be here if I like, same as you.

THE NOTE TAKER. A woman who utters such depressing and disgusting sounds has no right to be anywhere — no right to live. Remember that you are a human being with a soul and the divine gift of articulate speech: that your native language is the language of Shakespear and Milton and The Bible: and dont sit there crooning like a bilious pigeon.

THE FLOWER GIRL [*quite overwhelmed, looking up at him in mingled wonder and deprecation without daring to raise her head*]. Ah-ah-ah-ow-ow-ow-oo!

THE NOTE TAKER [*whipping out his book*]. Heavens! what a sound! [*He writes; then holds out the book and reads, reproducing her vowels exactly.*] Ah-ah-ah-ow-ow-ow-oo!

THE FLOWER GIRL [*tickled by the performance, and laughing in spite of herself*]. Garn!

THE NOTE TAKER. You see this creature with her kerbstone English: the English that will keep her in the gutter to the end of her days. Well, sir, in three months I could pass that girl off as a duchess at an ambassador's garden party. I could even get her a place as lady's maid or shop assistant, which requires better English. Thats the sort of thing I do for commercial millionaires. And on the profits of it I do genuine scientific work in phonetics, and a little as a poet on Miltonic lines.

THE GENTLEMAN. I am myself a student of Indian dialects; and —

THE NOTE TAKER [*eagerly*]. Are you? Do you know Colonel Pickering, the author of Spoken Sanscrit?

THE GENTLEMAN. I am Colonel Pickering. Who are you?

THE NOTE TAKER. Henry Higgins, author of Higgins's Universal Alphabet.

PICKERING [*with enthusiasm*]. I came from India to meet you.

HIGGINS. I was going to India to meet you.

PICKERING. Where do you live?

HIGGINS. 27A Wimpole Street. Come and see me to-morrow.

PICKERING. I'm at the Carlton. Come with me now and lets have a jaw over some supper.

HIGGINS. Right you are.

THE FLOWER GIRL [*to Pickering, as he passes her*]. Buy a flower, kind gentleman. I'm short for my lodging.

PICKERING. I really havnt any change. I'm sorry. [*He goes away.*]

HIGGINS [*shocked at the girl's mendacity*]. Liar. You said you could change half-a-crown.

THE FLOWER GIRL [*rising in desperation*]. You ought to be stuffed with nails, you ought. [*Flinging the basket at his feet.*] Take the whole blooming basket for sixpence.

The church clock strikes the second quarter.

HIGGINS [*hearing in it the voice of God, rebuking him for his Pharisaic want of charity to the poor girl*]. A reminder. [*He raises his hat solemnly; then throws a handful of money into the basket and follows* PICKERING.]

THE FLOWER GIRL [*picking up a half-crown*]. Ah-ow-ooh! [*Picking up a couple of florins.*] Aaah-ow-ooh! [*Picking up several coins.*] Aaaaaah-ow-ooh! [*Picking up a half-sovereign.*] Aaaaaaaaaaaah-ow-ooh!!!

FREDDY [*springing out of a taxicab*]. Got one at last. Hallo! [*To the girl*] Where are the two ladies that were here?

THE FLOWER GIRL. They walked to the bus when the rain stopped.

FREDDY. And left me with a cab on my hands! Damnation!

THE FLOWER GIRL [*with grandeur*]. Never mind, young man. I'm going home in a taxi. [*She sails off to the cab. The driver puts his hand behind him and holds the door firmly shut against her. Quite understanding his mistrust, she shews him her handful of money.*] Eightpence aint no object to me, Charlie. [*He grins and opens the door.*] Angel Court, Drury Lane, round the corner of Micklejohn's oil shop. Lets see how fast you can make her hop it. [*She gets in and pulls the door to with a slam as the taxicab starts.*]

FREDDY. Well, I'm dashed!

ACT TWO

[*NEXT DAY at 11 a.m. Higgins's laboratory in Wimpole Street. It is a room on the first floor, looking on the street, and was meant for the drawing room. The double doors are in the middle of the back wall; and persons entering find in the corner to their right two tall file cabinets at right angles to one another against the walls. In this corner stands a flat writing-table, on which are a phonograph, a laryngoscope, a row of tiny organ pipes with bellows, a set of lamp chimneys for singing flames with burners attached to a gas plug in the wall by an indiarubber tube, several tuning-forks of different sizes, a life-size image of half a human head, shewing in section the vocal organs, and a box containing a supply of wax cylinders for the phonograph.*

Further down the room, on the same side, is a fireplace, with a comfortable leather-covered easy-chair at the side of the hearth nearest the door, and a coal-scuttle. There is a clock on the mantelpiece. Between the fireplace and the phonograph table is a stand for newspapers.

On the other side of the central door, to the left of the visitor, is a cabinet of shallow drawers. On it is a telephone and the telephone directory. The corner beyond, and most of the side wall, is occupied by a grand piano, with the keyboard at the end furthest from the door, and a bench for the player extending the full length of the keyboard. On the piano is a dessert dish heaped with fruit and sweets, mostly chocolates.

The middle of the room is clear. Besides the easy-chair, the piano bench, and two chairs at the phonograph table, there is one stray chair. It stands near the fireplace. On the walls, engravings: mostly Piranesis and mezzotint portraits. No paintings.

Pickering is seated at the table, putting down some cards and a tuning-fork which he has been using. Higgins is standing up near him, closing two or three file drawers which are hanging out. He appears in the morning light as a robust, vital, appetizing sort of man of forty or thereabouts, dressed in a professional-looking black frock-coat with a white linen collar and black silk tie. He is of the energetic, scientific type, heartily, even violently interested in everything that can be studied as a scientific subject, and careless about himself and other people, including their feelings. He is, in fact, but for his years and size, rather like a very impetuous baby "taking notice" eagerly and loudly, and requiring almost as much watching to keep him out of unintended mischief. His manner varies from genial bullying when he is in a good humor to stormy petulance when anything goes wrong; but he is so entirely frank and void of malice that he remains likeable even in his least reasonable moments.]

HIGGINS [*as he shuts the last drawer*]. Well, I think thats the whole show.

PICKERING. It's really amazing. I havnt taken half of it in, you know.

HIGGINS. Would you like to go over any of it again?

PICKERING [*rising and coming to the fireplace, where he plants himself with his back to the fire*]. No, thank you; not now. I'm quite done up for this morning.

HIGGINS [*following him, and standing beside him on his left*]. Tired of listening to sounds?

PICKERING. Yes. It's a fearful strain. I rather fancied myself because I can pronounce twenty-four distinct vowel sounds; but your hundred and thirty beat me. I cant hear a bit of difference between most of them.

HIGGINS [*chuckling, and going over to the piano to eat sweets*]. Oh, that comes with practice. You hear no difference at first; but you keep on listening, and presently you find theyre all as different as A from B. [MRS. PEARCE *looks in: she is Higgins's housekeeper.*] Whats the matter?

MRS. PEARCE [*hesitating, evidently perplexed*]. A young woman wants to see you sir.

HIGGINS. A young woman! What does she want?

MRS. PEARCE. Well, sir, she says youll be glad to see her when you know what she's come about. She's quite a common girl, sir. Very common indeed. I should have sent her away, only I thought perhaps you wanted her to talk into your machines. I hope Ive not done wrong; but really you see such queer people sometimes — youll excuse me, I'm sure, sir —

HIGGINS. Oh, thats all right, Mrs. Pearce. Has she an interesting accent?

MRS. PEARCE. Oh, something dreadful, sir, really. I dont know how you can take an interest in it.

HIGGINS [*to* PICKERING]. Lets have her up. Shew her up, Mrs. Pearce. [*He rushes across to his working table and picks out a cylinder to use on the phonograph.*]

MRS. PEARCE [*only half resigned to it*]. Very well, sir. It's for you to say. [*She goes downstairs.*]

HIGGINS. This is rather a bit of luck. I'll shew you how I make records. We'll set her talking; and I'll take it down first in Bell's Visible Speech; then in broad Romic; and then we'll get her on the phonograph so that you can turn her on as often as you like with the written transcript before you.

MRS. PEARCE [*returning*]. This is the young woman, sir.

> THE FLOWER GIRL *enters in state. She has a hat with three ostrich feathers, orange, sky-blue, and red. She has a nearly clean apron, and the shoddy coat has been tidied a little. The pathos of this deplorable figure, with its innocent vanity and consequential air, touches* PICKERING, *who has already straightened himself in the presence of* MRS. PEARCE. *But as to* HIGGINS, *the only distinction he makes between men and women is that when he is neither bullying nor exclaiming to the heavens against some feather-weight cross, he coaxes women as a child coaxes its nurse when it wants to get anything out of her.*

HIGGINS [*brusquely, recognizing her with unconcealed disappointment, and at once, babylike, making an intolerable grievance of it*]. Why, this is the girl I jotted down last night. She's no use: Ive got all the records I want of the Lisson Grove lingo; and I'm not going to waste another cylinder on it. [*To the girl.*] Be off with you: I dont want you.

THE FLOWER GIRL. Dont you be so saucy. You aint heard what I come for yet. [*To* MRS. PEARCE, *who is waiting at the door for further instructions.*] Did you tell him I come in a taxi?

MRS. PEARCE. Nonsense, girl! what do you think a gentleman like Mr. Higgins cares what you came in?

THE FLOWER GIRL. Oh, we are proud! He aint above giving lessons, not him: I heard him say so. Well, I aint come here to ask for any compliment; and if my money's not good enough I can go elsewhere.

HIGGINS. Good enough for what?

THE FLOWER GIRL. Good enough for ye-oo. Now you know, dont you? I'm come to have lessons, I am. And to pay for em too: make no mistake.

HIGGINS [*stupent*]. Well!!! [*Recovering his breath with a gasp.*] What do you expect me to say to you?

THE FLOWER GIRL. Well, if you was a gentleman, you might ask me to sit down, I think. Dont I tell you I'm bringing you business?

HIGGINS. Pickering: shall we ask this baggage to sit down, or shall we throw her out of the window?

THE FLOWER GIRL [*running away in terror to the piano, where she turns at bay*]. Ah-ah-oh-ow-ow-ow-oo! [*Wounded and whimpering.*] I wont be called a baggage when Ive offered to pay like any lady.

  Motionless, the two men stare at her from the other side of the room, amazed.

PICKERING [*gently*]. What is it you want, my girl?

THE FLOWER GIRL. I want to be a lady in a flower shop stead of selling at the corner of Tottenham Court Road. But they wont take me unless I can talk more genteel. He said he could teach me. Well, here I am ready to pay him — not asking any favor — and he treats me as if I was dirt.

MRS. PEARCE. How can you be such a foolish ignorant girl as to think you could afford to pay Mr. Higgins?

THE FLOWER GIRL. Why shouldnt I? I know what lessons cost as well as you do; and I'm ready to pay.

HIGGINS. How much?

THE FLOWER GIRL [*coming back to him, triumphant*]. Now youre talking! I thought youd come off it when you saw a chance of getting back a bit of what you chucked at me last night. [*Confidentially.*] Youd had a drop in, hadnt you?

HIGGINS [*peremptorily*]. Sit down.

THE FLOWER GIRL. Oh, if youre going to make a compliment of it —

HIGGINS [*thundering at her*]. Sit down.

MRS. PEARCE [*severely*]. Sit down, girl. Do as youre told. [*She *places the stray chair near the hearthrug between* HIGGINS *and* PICKERING, *and stands behind it waiting for the girl to sit down.*]

THE FLOWER GIRL. Ah-ah-ah-ow-ow-oo! [*She stands, half rebellious, half bewildered.*]

PICKERING [*very courteous*]. Wont you sit down?

THE FLOWER GIRL [*coyly*]. Dont mind if I do. [*She sits down. PICKERING returns to the hearthrug.*]

HIGGINS. Whats your name?

THE FLOWER GIRL. Liza Doolittle.

HIGGINS [*declaiming gravely*]. Eliza, Elizabeth, Betsy and Bess,
    They went to the woods to get a bird's nes':

PICKERING. They found a nest with four eggs in it:

HIGGINS. They took one apiece, and left three in it.

They laugh heartily at their own wit.

LIZA. Oh, dont be silly.

MRS. PEARCE. You mustnt speak to the gentleman like that.

LIZA. Well, why wont he speak sensible to me?

HIGGINS. Come back to business. How much do you propose to pay me for the lessons?

LIZA. Oh, I know whats right. A lady friend of mine gets French lessons for eighteenpence an hour from a real French gentleman. Well, you wouldnt have the face to ask me the same for teaching me my own language as you would for French; so I wont give more than a shilling. Take it or leave it.

HIGGINS [*walking up and down the room, rattling his keys and his cash in his pockets*]. You know, Pickering, if you consider a shilling, not as a simple shilling, but as a percentage of this girl's income, it works out as fully equivalent to sixty or seventy guineas from a millionaire.

PICKERING. How so?

HIGGINS. Figure it out. A millionaire has about £150 a day. She earns about half-a-crown.

LIZA [*haughtily*]. Who told you I only —

HIGGINS [*continuing*]. She offers me two-fifths of her day's income for a lesson. Two-fifths of a millionaire's income for a day would be somewhere about £60. It's handsome. By George, it's enormous! it's the biggest offer I ever had.

LIZA [*rising, terrified*]. Sixty pounds! What are you talking about? I never offered you sixty pounds. Where would I get —

HIGGINS. Hold your tongue.

LIZA [*weeping*]. But I aint got sixty pounds. Oh'—

MRS. PEARCE. Dont cry, you silly girl. Sit down. Nobody is going to touch your money.

HIGGINS. Somebody is going to touch you, with a broomstick, if you dont stop snivelling. Sit down.

LIZA [*obeying slowly*]. Ah-ah-ah-ow-oo-o! One would think you was my father.

HIGGINS. If I decide to teach you, I'll be worse than two fathers to you. Here! [*He offers her his silk handkerchief.*]

LIZA. Whats this for?

HIGGINS. To wipe your eyes. To wipe any part of your face that feels moist. Remember: thats your handkerchief; and thats your sleeve. Dont mistake the one for the other if you wish to become a lady in a shop.

LIZA, *utterly bewildered, stares helplessly at him.*

MRS. PEARCE. It's no use talking to her like that, Mr. Higgins: she doesnt understand you. Besides, youre quite wrong: she doesnt do it that way at all. [*She takes the handkerchief.*]

LIZA [*snatching it*]. Here! You give me that handkerchief. He give it to me, not to you.

PICKERING [*laughing*]. He did. I think it must be regarded as her property, Mrs. Pearce.

MRS. PEARCE [*resigning herself*]. Serve you right, Mr. Higgins.

PICKERING. Higgins: I'm interested. What about the ambassador's garden party? I'll say youre the greatest teacher alive if you make that good. I'll bet you all the expenses of the experiment you cant do it. And I'll pay for the lessons.

LIZA. Oh, you are real good. Thank you, Captain.

HIGGINS [*tempted, looking at her*]. It's almost irresistible. She's so deliciously low — so horribly dirty —

LIZA [*protesting extremely*]. Ah-ah-ah-ah-ow-ow-oo-oo!!! I aint dirty: I washed my face and hands afore I come, I did.

PICKERING. Youre certainly not going to turn her head with flattery, Higgins.

MRS. PEARCE [*uneasy*]. Oh, dont say that, sir: theres more ways than one of turning a girl's head; and nobody can do it better than Mr. Higgins, though he may not always mean it. I do hope, sir, you wont encourage him to do anything foolish.

HIGGINS [*becoming excited as the idea grows on him*]. What is life but a series of inspired follies? The difficulty is to find them to do. Never lose a chance: it doesnt come every day. I shall make a duchess of this draggletailed guttersnipe.

LIZA [*strongly deprecating this view of her*]. Ah-ah-ah-ow-ow-oo!

HIGGINS [*carried away*]. Yes: in six months — in three if she has a good ear and a quick tongue — I'll take her anywhere and pass her off as anything. We'll start today: now! this moment! Take her away and clean her, Mrs. Pearce. Monkey Brand, if it wont come off any other way. Is there a good fire in the kitchen?

MRS. PEARCE [*protesting*]. Yes; but —

HIGGINS [*storming on*]. Take all her clothes off and burn them. Ring up Whiteley or somebody for new ones. Wrap her up in brown paper til they come.

LIZA. Youre no gentleman, youre not, to talk of such things. I'm a good girl, I am; and I know what the like of you are, I do.

HIGGINS. We want none of your Lisson Grove prudery here, young woman. Youve got to learn to behave like a duchess. Take her away, Mrs. Pearce. If she gives you any trouble, wallop her.

LIZA [*springing up and running between* PICKERING *and* MRS. PEARCE *for protection*]. No! I'll call the police, I will.

MRS. PEARCE. But Ive no place to put her.

HIGGINS. Put her in the dustbin.

LIZA. Ah-ah-ah-ow-ow-oo!

PICKERING. Oh come, Higgins! be reasonable.

MRS. PEARCE [*resolutely*]. You must be reasonable, Mr. Higgins: really you must. You cant walk over everybody like this.

HIGGINS, *thus scolded, subsides. The hurricane is succeeded by a zephyr of amiable surprise.*

HIGGINS [*with professional exquisiteness of modulation*]. I walk over everybody! My dear Mrs. Pearce, my dear Pickering, I never had the slightest intention of walking over anyone. All I propose is that we should be kind to this poor girl. We must help her to prepare and fit herself for her new station in life. If I did not express myself clearly it was because I did not wish to hurt her delicacy, or yours.

LIZA, *reassured, steals back to her chair.*

MRS. PEARCE [*to* PICKERING]. Well, did you ever hear anything like that, sir?

PICKERING [*laughing heartily*]. Never, Mrs. Pearce: never.

HIGGINS [*patiently*]. Whats the matter?

MRS. PEARCE. Well, the matter is, sir, that you cant take a girl up like that as if you were picking up a pebble on the beach.

HIGGINS. Why not?

MRS. PEARCE. Why not! But you dont know anything about her. What about her parents? She may be married.

LIZA. Garn!

HIGGINS. There! As the girl very properly says, Garn! Married indeed! Dont you know that a woman of that class looks a worn out drudge of fifty a year after she's married?

LIZA. Whood marry me?

HIGGINS [*suddenly resorting to the most thrillingly beautiful low tones in his best elocutionary style*]. By George, Eliza, the streets will be strewn with the bodies of men shooting themselves for your sake before Ive done with you.

MRS. PEARCE. Nonsense, sir. You mustnt talk like that to her.

LIZA [*rising and squaring herself determinedly*]. I'm going away. He's off his chump, he is. I dont want no balmies teaching me.

HIGGINS [*wounded in his tenderest point by her insensibility to his elocution*]. Oh, indeed! I'm mad, am I? Very well, Mrs. Pearce: you neednt order the new clothes for her. Throw her out.

LIZA [*whimpering*]. Nah-ow. You got no right to touch me.

MRS. PEARCE. You see now what comes of being saucy. [*Indicating the door.*] This way, please.

LIZA [*almost in tears*]. I didnt want no clothes. I wouldnt have taken them. [*She throws away the handkerchief.*] I can buy my own clothes.

HIGGINS [*deftly retrieving the handkerchief and intercepting her on her reluctant way to the door*]. Youre an ungrateful wicked girl. This is my return for offering to take you out of the gutter and dress you beautifully and make a lady of you.

MRS. PEARCE. Stop, Mr. Higgins. I wont allow it. It's you that are wicked. Go home to your parents, girl; and tell them to take better care of you.

LIZA. I aint got no parents. They told me I was big enough to earn my own living and turned me out.

MRS. PEARCE. Wheres your mother?

LIZA. I aint got no mother. Her that turned me out was my sixth stepmother. But I done without them. And I'm a good girl, I am.

HIGGINS. Very well, then, what on earth is all this fuss about? The girl doesnt belong to anybody — is no use to anybody but me. [*He goes to* MRS. PEARCE *and begins coaxing.*] You can adopt her, Mrs. Pearce: I'm sure a daughter would be a great amusement to you. Now dont make any more fuss. Take her downstairs; and —

MRS. PEARCE. But whats to become of her? Is she to be paid anything? Do be sensible, sir.

HIGGINS. Oh, pay her whatever is necessary: put it down in the housekeeping book. [*Impatiently.*] What on earth will she want with money? She'll have her food and her clothes. She'll only drink if you give her money.

LIZA [*turning on him*]. Oh you are a brute. It's a lie: nobody ever saw the sign of liquor on me. [*She goes back to her chair and plants herself there defiantly.*]

PICKERING [*in good-humored remonstrance*]. Does it occur to you, Higgins, that the girl has some feelings?

HIGGINS [*looking critically at her*]. Oh no, I dont think so. Not any feelings that we need bother about. [*Cheerily.*] Have you, Eliza?

LIZA. I got my feelings same as anyone else.

HIGGINS [*to* PICKERING, *reflectively*]. You see the difficulty?

PICKERING. Eh? What difficulty?

HIGGINS. To get her to talk grammar. The mere pronunciation is easy enough.

LIZA. I dont want to talk grammar. I want to talk like a lady.

MRS. PEARCE. Will you please keep to the point, Mr. Higgins? I want to know on what terms the girl is to be here. Is she to have any wages? And what is to become of her when youve finished your teaching? You must look ahead a little.

HIGGINS [*impatiently*]. Whats to become of her if I leave her in the gutter? Tell me that, Mrs. Pearce.

MRS. PEARCE. Thats her own business, not yours, Mr. Higgins.

HIGGINS. Well, when Ive done with her, we can throw her back into the gutter; and then it will be her own business again; so thats all right.

LIZA. Oh, youve no feeling heart in you: you dont care for nothing but yourself. [*She rises and takes the floor resolutely*.] Here! Ive had enough of this. I'm going. [*Making for the door*.] You ought to be ashamed of yourself, you ought.

HIGGINS [*snatching a chocolate cream from the piano, his eyes suddenly beginning to twinkle with mischief*]. Have some chocolates, Eliza.

LIZA [*halting, tempted*]. How do I know what might be in them? Ive heard of girls being drugged by the like of you.

HIGGINS *whips out his penknife; cuts a chocolate in two; puts one half into his mouth and bolts it; and offers her the other half.*

HIGGINS. Pledge of good faith, Eliza. I eat one half: you eat the other. [LIZA *opens her mouth to retort: he pops the half chocolate into it.*] You shall have boxes of them, barrels of them, every day. You shall live on them. Eh?

LIZA [*who has disposed of the chocolate after being nearly choked by it*]. I wouldnt have ate it, only I'm too ladylike to take it out of my mouth.

HIGGINS. Listen, Eliza. I think you said you came in a taxi.

LIZA. Well, what if I did? Ive as good a right to take a taxi as anyone else.

HIGGINS. You have, Eliza; and in future you shall have as many taxis as you want. You shall go up and down and round the town in a taxi every day. Think of that, Eliza.

MRS. PEARCE. Mr. Higgins: youre tempting the girl. It's not right. She should think of the future.

HIGGINS. At her age! Nonsense! Time enough to think of the future when you havnt any future to think of. No, Eliza: do as this lady does; think of other people's futures; but never think of your own. Think of chocolates, and taxis, and gold, and diamonds.

LIZA. No: I dont want no gold and no diamonds. I'm a good girl, I am. [*She sits down again, with an attempt at dignity.*]

HIGGINS. You shall remain so, Eliza, under the care of Mrs. Pearce. And you shall marry an officer in the Guards, with a beautiful moustache: the son of a marquis, who will disinherit him for marrying you, but will relent when he sees your beauty and goodness —

PICKERING. Excuse me, Higgins; but I really must interfere. Mrs. Pearce is quite right. If this girl is to put herself in your hands for six months for an experiment in teaching, she must understand thoroughly what she's doing.

HIGGINS. How can she? She's incapable of understanding anything. Besides, do any of us understand what we are doing? If we did, would we ever do it?

PICKERING. Very clever, Higgins; but not sound sense. [*To ELIZA.*] Miss Doolittle —

LIZA [*overwhelmed*]. Ah-ah-ow-oo!

HIGGINS. There! Thats all youll get out of Eliza. Ah-ah-ow-oo! No use explaining. As a military man you ought to know that.

Give her her orders: thats what she wants. Eliza: you are to live here for the next six months, learning how to speak beautifully, like a lady in a florist's shop. If youre good and do whatever youre told, you shall sleep in a proper bedroom, and have lots to eat, and money to buy chocolates and take rides in taxis. If youre naughty and idle you will sleep in the back kitchen among the black beetles, and be walloped by Mrs. Pearce with a broomstick. At the end of six months you shall go to Buckingham Palace in a carriage, beautifully dressed. If the King finds out youre not a lady, you will be taken by the police to the Tower of London, where your head will be cut off as a warning to other presumptuous flower girls. If you are not found out, you shall have a present of seven-and-sixpence to start life with as a lady in a shop. If you refuse this offer you will be a most ungrateful and wicked girl; and the angels will weep for you. [*To* PICKERING.] Now are you satisfied, Pickering? [*To* MRS. PEARCE.] Can I put it more plainly and fairly, Mrs. Pearce?

MRS. PEARCE [*patiently*]. I think youd better let me speak to the girl properly in private. I dont know that I can take charge of her or consent to the arrangement at all. Of course I know you dont mean her any harm; but when you get what you call interested in people's accents, you never think or care what may happen to them or you. Come with me, Eliza.

HIGGINS. Thats all right. Thank you, Mrs. Pearce. Bundle her off to the bathroom.

LIZA [*rising reluctantly and suspiciously*]. Youre a great bully, you are. I wont stay here if I dont like. I wont let nobody wallop me. I never asked to go to Bucknam Palace, I didnt. I was never in trouble with the police, not me. I'm a good girl —

MRS. PEARCE. Dont answer back, girl. You dont understand the gentleman. Come with me. [*She leads the way to the door, and holds it open for* ELIZA.]

LIZA [*as she goes out*]. Well, what I say is right. I wont go near the King, not if I'm going to have my head cut off. If I'd known what I was letting myself in for, I wouldnt have come here. I always been a good girl; and I never offered to say a word to him; and I dont owe him nothing; and I dont care; and I wont be put upon; and I have my feelings the same as anyone else —

    MRS. PEARCE *shuts the door; and* ELIZA's *plaints are no*

longer audible. PICKERING *comes from the hearth to the chair and sits astride it with his arms on the back.*

PICKERING. Excuse the straight question, Higgins. Are you a man of good character where women are concerned?

HIGGINS [*moodily*]. Have you ever met a man of good character where women are concerned?

PICKERING. Yes: very frequently.

HIGGINS [*dogmatically, lifting himself on his hands to the level of the piano, and sitting on it with a bounce*]. Well, I havnt. I find that the moment I let a woman make friends with me, she becomes jealous, exacting, suspicious, and a damned nuisance. I find that the moment I let myself make friends with a woman, I become selfish and tyrannical. Women upset everything. When you let them into your life, you find that the woman is driving at one thing and youre driving at another.

PICKERING. At what, for example?

HIGGINS [*coming off the piano restlessly*]. Oh, Lord knows! I suppose the woman wants to live her own life; and the man wants to live his; and each tries to drag the other on to the wrong track. One wants to go north and the other south; and the result is that both have to go east, though they both hate the east wind. [*He sits down on the bench at the keyboard.*] So here I am, a confirmed old bachelor, and likely to remain so.

PICKERING [*rising and standing over him gravely*]. Come, Higgins! You know what I mean. If I'm to be in this business I shall feel responsible for that girl. I hope it's understood that no advantage is to be taken of her position.

HIGGINS. What! That thing! Sacred, I assure you. [*Rising to explain.*] You see, she'll be a pupil; and teaching would be impossible unless pupils were sacred. Ive taught scores of American millionairesses how to speak English: the best looking women in the world. I'm seasoned. They might as well be blocks of wood. *I* might as well be a block of wood. It's —

MRS. PEARCE *opens the door. She has* ELIZA's *hat in her hand.* PICKERING *retires to the easy-chair at the hearth and sits down.*

HIGGINS [*eagerly*]. Well, Mrs. Pearce; is it all right?

MRS. PEARCE [*at the door*]. I just wish to trouble you with a word, if I may, Mr. Higgins.

HIGGINS. Yes, certainly. Come in. [*She comes forward.*] Dont burn that, Mrs. Pearce. I'll keep it as a curiosity. [*He takes the hat.*]

MRS. PEARCE. Handle it carefully, sir, please. I had to promise her not to burn it; but I had better put it in the oven for a while.

HIGGINS [*putting it down hastily on the piano*]. Oh! thank you. Well, what have you to say to me?

PICKERING. Am I in the way?

MRS. PEARCE. Not at all, sir. Mr. Higgins: will you please be very particular what you say before the girl?

HIGGINS [*sternly*]. Of course. I'm always particular about what I say. Why do you say this to me?

MRS. PEARCE [*unmoved*]. No, sir: youre not at all particular when youve mislaid anything or when you get a little impatient. Now it doesnt matter before me; I'm used to it. But you really must not swear before the girl.

HIGGINS [*indignantly*]. I swear! [*Most emphatically.*] I never swear. I detest the habit. What the devil do you mean?

MRS. PEARCE [*stolidly*]. Thats what I mean, sir. You swear a great deal too much. I dont mind your damning and blasting, and what the devil and where the devil and who the devil —

HIGGINS. Mrs. Pearce: this language from your lips! Really!

MRS. PEARCE [*not to be put off*]. — but there is a certain word I must ask you not to use. The girl has just used it herself because the bath was too hot. It begins with the same letter as bath. She knows no better: she learnt it at her mother's knee. But she must not hear it from your lips.

HIGGINS [*loftily*]. I cannot charge myself with having ever uttered it, Mrs. Pearce. [*She looks at him steadfastly. He adds, hiding an uneasy conscience with a judicial air.*] Except perhaps in a moment of extreme and justifiable excitement.

MRS. PEARCE. Only this morning, sir, you applied it to your boots, to the butter, and to the brown bread.

HIGGINS. Oh, that! Mere alliteration, Mrs. Pearce, natural to a poet.

MRS. PEARCE. Well, sir, whatever you choose to call it, I beg you not to let the girl hear you repeat it.

HIGGINS. Oh, very well, very well. Is that all?

MRS. PEARCE. No, sir. We shall have to be very particular with this girl as to personal cleanliness.

HIGGINS. Certainly. Quite right. Most important.

MRS. PEARCE. I mean not to be slovenly about her dress or untidy in leaving things about.

HIGGINS [*going to her solemnly*]. Just so. I intended to call your attention to that. [*He passes on to* PICKERING, *who is enjoying the conversation immensely.*] It is these little things that matter, Pickering. Take care of the pence and the pounds will take care of themselves is as true of personal habits as of money. [*He comes to anchor on the hearthrug, with the air of a man in an unassailable position.*]

MRS. PEARCE. Yes, sir. Then might I ask you not to come down to breakfast in your dressing-gown, or at any rate not to use it as a napkin to the extent you do, sir. And if you would be so good as not to eat everything off the same plate, and to remember not to put the porridge saucepan out of your hand on the clean tablecloth, it would be a better example to the girl. You know you nearly choked yourself with a fishbone in the jam only last week.

HIGGINS [*routed from the hearthrug and drifting back to the piano*]. I may do these things sometimes in absence of mind; but surely I dont do them habitually. [*Angrily.*] By the way: my dressing-gown smells most damnably of benzine.

MRS. PEARCE. No doubt it does, Mr. Higgins. But if you will wipe your fingers —

HIGGINS [*yelling*]. Oh very well, very well: I'll wipe them in my hair in future.

MRS. PEARCE. I hope youre not offended, Mr. Higgins.

HIGGINS [*shocked at finding himself thought capable of an unamiable sentiment*]. Not at all, not at all. Youre quite right, Mrs. Pearce: I shall be particularly careful before the girl. Is that all?

MRS. PEARCE. No, sir. Might she use some of those Japanese dresses you brought from abroad? I really cant put her back into her old things.

HIGGINS. Certainly. Anything you like. Is that all?

MRS. PEARCE. Thank you, sir. Thats all. [*She goes out.*]

HIGGINS. You know, Pickering, that woman has the most extraordinary ideas about me. Here I am, a shy, diffident sort of man. Ive never been able to feel really grown-up and tremendous, like other chaps. And yet she's firmly persuaded that I'm an arbitrary overbearing bossing kind of person. I cant account for it.

MRS. PEARCE *returns.*

MRS. PEARCE. If you please, sir, the trouble's beginning already. Theres a dustman downstairs, Alfred Doolittle, wants to see you. He says you have his daughter here.

PICKERING [*rising*]. Phew! I say! [*He retreats to the hearthrug.*]

HIGGINS [*promptly*]. Send the blackguard up.

MRS. PEARCE. Oh, very well, sir. [*She goes out.*]

PICKERING. He may not be a blackguard, Higgins.

HIGGINS. Nonsense. Of course he's a blackguard.

PICKERING. Whether he is or not, I'm afraid we shall have some trouble with him.

HIGGINS [*confidently*]. Oh no: I think not. If theres any trouble he shall have it with me, not I with him. And we are sure to get something interesting out of him.

PICKERING. About the girl?

HIGGINS. No. I mean his dialect.

PICKERING. Oh!

MRS. PEARCE [*at the door*]. Doolittle, sir. [*She admits DOO-LITTLE and retires.*]

ALFRED DOOLITTLE *is an elderly but vigorous dustman, clad in the costume of his profession, including a hat with a black brim covering his neck and shoulders. He has well marked and rather interesting features, and seems equally free from fear and conscience. He has a remarkably expressive voice, the result of a habit of giving vent to his feelings without reserve. His present pose is that of wounded honor and stern resolution.*

DOOLITTLE [*at the door, uncertain which of the two gentlemen is his man*]. Professor Higgins?

HIGGINS. Here. Good morning. Sit down.

DOOLITTLE. Morning, Governor. [*He sits down magisterially.*] I come about a very serious matter, Governor.

HIGGINS [*to* PICKERING]. Brought up in Hounslow. Mother Welsh, I should think. [DOOLITTLE *opens his mouth, amazed.* HIGGINS *continues.*] What do you want, Doolittle?

DOOLITTLE [*menacingly*]. I want my daughter: thats what I want. See?

HIGGINS. Of course you do. Youre her father, arnt you? You dont suppose anyone else wants her, do you? I'm glad to see you have some spark of family feeling left. She's upstairs. Take her away at once.

DOOLITTLE [*rising, fearfully taken aback*]. What!

HIGGINS. Take her away. Do you suppose I'm going to keep your daughter for you?

DOOLITTLE [*remonstrating*]. Now, now, look here, Governor. Is this reasonable? Is it fairity to take advantage of a man like this? The girl belongs to me. You got her. Where do I come in? [*He sits down again.*]

HIGGINS. Your daughter had the audacity to come to my house and ask me to teach her how to speak properly so that she could get a place in a flower-shop. This gentleman and my housekeeper have been here all the time. [*Bullying him.*] How dare you come here and attempt to blackmail me? You sent her here on purpose.

DOOLITTLE [*protesting*]. No, Governor.

HIGGINS. You must have. How else could you possibly know that she is here?

DOOLITTLE. Dont take a man up like that, Governor.

HIGGINS. The police shall take you up. This is a plant — a plot to extort money by threats. I shall telephone for the police. [*He *goes resolutely to the telephone and opens the directory.*]

DOOLITTLE. Have I asked you for a brass farthing? I leave it to the gentleman here: have I said a word about money?

HIGGINS [*throwing the book aside and marching down on* DOO-LITTLE *with a poser*]. What else did you come for?

DOOLITTLE [*sweetly*]. Well, what would a man come for? Be human, Governor.

HIGGINS [*disarmed*]. Alfred: did you put her up to it?

DOOLITTLE. So help me, Governor, I never did. I take my Bible oath I aint seen the girl these two months past.

HIGGINS. Then how did you know she was here?

DOOLITTLE [*"most musical, most melancholy"*]. I'll tell you, Governor, if youll only let me get a word in. I'm willing to tell you. I'm wanting to tell you. I'm waiting to tell you.

HIGGINS. Pickering: this chap has a certain natural gift of rhetoric. Observe the rhythm of his native woodnotes wild. "I'm willing to tell you: I'm wanting to tell you: I'm waiting to tell you." Sentimental rhetoric! thats the Welsh strain in him. It also accounts for his mendacity and dishonesty.

PICKERING. Oh, please, Higgins: I'm west country myself. [*To* DOOLITTLE.] How did you know the girl was here if you didnt send her?

DOOLITTLE. It was like this, Governor. The girl took a boy in the taxi to give him a jaunt. Son of her landlady, he is. He hung about on the chance of her giving him another ride home. Well, she sent him back for her luggage when she heard you was willing for her to stop here. I met the boy at the corner of Long Acre and Endell Street.

HIGGINS. Public house. Yes?

DOOLITTLE. The poor man's club, Governor: why shouldn't I?

PICKERING: Do let him tell his story, Higgins.

DOOLITTLE. He told me what was up. And I ask you, what was my feelings and my duty as a father? I says to the boy, "You bring me the luggage." I says —

PICKERING. Why didn't you go for it yourself?

DOOLITTLE. Landlady wouldnt have trusted me with it, Governor. She's that kind of woman: you know, I had to give the boy a penny afore he trusted me with it, the little swine. I brought it to her just to oblige you like, and make myself agreeable. Thats all.

HIGGINS. How much luggage?

DOOLITTLE. Musical instrument, Governor. A few pictures, a trifle of jewelry, and a bird-cage. She said she didnt want no clothes. What was I to think from that, Governor? I ask you as a parent what was I to think?

HIGGINS. So you came to rescue her from worse than death, eh?

DOOLITTLE [*appreciatively: relieved at being so well understood*]. Just so, Governor. Thats right.

PICKERING. But why did you bring her luggage if you intended to take her away?

DOOLITTLE. Have I said a word about taking her away? Have I now?

HIGGINS [*determinedly*]. Youre going to take her away, double quick. [*He crosses to the hearth and rings the bell.*]

DOOLITTLE [*rising*]. No, Governor. Dont say that. I'm not the man to stand in my girl's light. Heres a career opening for her, as you might say; and —

MRS. PEARCE *opens the door and awaits orders.*

HIGGINS. Mrs. Pearce: this is Eliza's father. He has come to take her away. Give her to him. [*He goes back to the piano, with an air of washing his hands of the whole affair.*]

DOOLITTLE. No. This is a misunderstanding. Listen here —

MRS. PEARCE. He cant take her away, Mr. Higgins: how can he? You told me to burn her clothes.

DOOLITTLE. Thats right. I cant carry the girl through the streets like a blooming monkey, can I? I put it to you.

HIGGINS. You have put it to me that you want your daughter. Take your daughter. If she has no clothes go out and buy her some.

DOOLITTLE [*desperate*]. Wheres the clothes she come in? Did I burn them or did your missus here?

MRS. PEARCE. I am the housekeeper, if you please. I have sent for some clothes for your girl. When they come you can take her away. You can wait in the kitchen. This way, please.

DOOLITTLE, *much troubled, accompanies her to the door; then hesitates; finally turns confidently to* HIGGINS.

DOOLITTLE. Listen here, Governor. You and me is men of the world, aint we?

HIGGINS. Oh! Men of the world, are we? Youd better go, Mrs. Pearce.

MRS. PEARCE. I think so, indeed, sir. [*She goes, with dignity.*]

PICKERING. The floor is yours, Mr. Doolittle.

DOOLITTLE [*to* PICKERING]. I thank you, Governor. [*To* HIGGINS, *who takes refuge on the piano bench, a little overwhelmed by the proximity of his visitor; for* DOOLITTLE *has a professional flavor of dust about him.*] Well, the truth is, Ive taken a sort of fancy to you, Governor; and if you want the girl, I'm not so set on having her back home again but what I might be open to an arrangement. Regarded in the light of a young woman, she's a fine handsome girl. As a daughter she's not worth her keep; and so I tell you straight. All I ask is my rights as a father; and youre the last man alive to expect me to let her go for nothing; for I can see youre one of the straight sort, Governor. Well, whats a five-pound note to you? And whats Eliza to me? [*He returns to his chair and sits down judicially.*]

PICKERING. I think you ought to know, Doolittle, that Mr. Higgins's intentions are entirely honorable.

DOOLITTLE. Course they are, Governor. If I thought they wasnt, I'd ask fifty.

HIGGINS [*revolted*]. Do you mean to say, you callous rascal, that you would sell your daughter for £50?

DOOLITTLE. Not in a general way I wouldnt; but to oblige a gentleman like you I'd do a good deal, I do assure you.

PICKERING. Have you no morals, man?

DOOLITTLE [*unabashed*]. Cant afford them, Governor. Neither could you if you was as poor as me. Not that I mean any harm, you know. But if Liza is going to have a bit out of this, why not me too?

HIGGINS [*troubled*]. I dont know what to do, Pickering. There can be no question that as a matter of morals it's a positive crime to give this chap a farthing. And yet I feel a sort of rough justice in his claim.

DOOLITTLE. Thats it, Governor. Thats all I say. A father's heart, as it were.

PICKERING. Well, I know the feeling; but really it seems hardly right —

DOOLITTLE. Dont say that, Governor. Dont look at it that way. What am I, Governors both? I ask you, what am I? I'm one of the undeserving poor: thats what I am. Think of what that means to a man. It means that he's up agen middle class morality all the time. If theres anything going, and I put in for a bit of it, it's always the same story: "Youre undeserving; so you cant have it." But my needs is as great as the most deserving widow's that ever got money out of six different charities in one week for the death of the same husband. I dont need less than a deserving man: I need more. I dont eat less hearty than him; and I drink a lot more. I want a bit of amusement, cause I'm a thinking man. I want cheerfulness and a song and a band when I feel low. Well, they charge me just the same for everything as they charge the deserving. What is middle class morality? Just an excuse for never giving me anything. Therefore, I ask you, as two gentlemen, not to play that game on me. I'm playing straight with you. I aint pretending to be deserving. I'm undeserving; and I mean to go on being undeserving. I like it; and thats the truth. Will you take advantage of a man's nature to do him out of the price of his own daughter what he's brought up and fed and clothed by the sweat of his brow until she's growed big enough to be interesting to you two gentlemen? Is five pounds unreasonable? I put it to you; and I leave it to you.

HIGGINS [*rising, and going over to* PICKERING]. Pickering: if we were to take this man in hand for three months, he could choose between a seat in the Cabinet and a popular pulpit in Wales.

PICKERING. What do you say to that, Doolittle?

DOOLITTLE. Not me, Governor, thank you kindly. Ive heard all the preachers and all the prime ministers — for I'm a thinking man and game for politics or religion or social reform same as

all the other amusements — and I tell you it's a dog's life any
way you look at it. Undeserving poverty is my line. Taking one
station in society with another, it's — it's — well, it's the only
one that has any ginger in it, to my taste.

HIGGINS. I suppose we must give him a fiver.

PICKERING. He'll make a bad use of it, I'm afraid.

DOOLITTLE. Not me, Governor, so help me I wont. Dont you be
afraid that I'll save it and spare it and live idle on it. There
wont be a penny of it left by Monday: I'll have to go to work
same as if I'd never had it. It wont pauperize me, you bet. Just
one good spree for myself and the missus, giving pleasure to
ourselves and employment to others, and satisfaction to you to
think it's not been throwed away. You couldnt spend it better.

HIGGINS [*taking out his pocket book and coming between* DOO-
LITTLE *and the piano*]. This is irresistible. Lets give him ten.
[*He offers two notes to the dustman.*]

DOOLITTLE. No, Governor. She wouldnt have the heart to spend
ten; and perhaps I shouldnt neither. Ten pounds is a lot of
money: it makes a man feel prudent like; and then goodbye to
happiness. You give me what I ask you, Governor: not a penny
more, and not a penny less.

PICKERING. Why don't you marry that missus of yours? I rather
draw the line at encouraging that sort of immorality.

DOOLITTLE. Tell her so, Governor: tell her so. I'm willing. It's
me that suffers by it. Ive no hold on her. I got to be agreeable
to her. I got to give her presents. I got to buy her clothes something sinful. I'm a slave to that woman, Governor, just
because I'm not her lawful husband. And she knows it too.
Catch her marrying me! Take my advice, Governor: marry
Eliza while she's young and dont know no better. If you dont
youll be sorry for it after. If you do, she'll be sorry for it after;
but better her than you, because youre a man, and she's only a
woman and dont know how to be happy anyhow.

HIGGINS. Pickering: if we listen to this man another minute, we
shall have no convictions left. [*To* DOOLITTLE.] Five
pounds I think you said.

DOOLITTLE. Thank you kindly, Governor.

HIGGINS. Youre sure you wont take ten?

DOOLITTLE. Not now. Another time, Governor.

HIGGINS [*handing him a five-pound note*]. Here you are.

DOOLITTLE. Thank you, Governor. Good morning. [*He hurries to the door, anxious to get away with his booty. When he opens it he is confronted with a dainty and exquisitely clean young Japanese lady in a simple blue cotton kimono printed cunningly with small white jasmine blossoms. MRS. PEARCE is with her. He gets out of her way deferentially and apologizes.*] Beg pardon, miss.

THE JAPANESE LADY. Garn! Dont you know your own daughter?

DOOLITTLE, HIGGINS, PICKERING [*exclaiming simultaneously*]. Bly me! it's Eliza! Whats that! This! By Jove!

LIZA. Dont I look silly?

HIGGINS. Silly?

MRS. PEARCE [*at the door*]. Now, Mr. Higgins, please dont say anything to make the girl conceited about herself.

HIGGINS [*conscientiously*]. Oh! Quite right, Mrs. Pearce. [*To ELIZA.*] Yes: damned silly.

MRS. PEARCE. Please, sir.

HIGGINS [*correcting himself*]. I mean extremely silly.

LIZA. I should look all right with my hat on. [*She takes up her hat; puts it on; and walks across the room to the fireplace with a fashionable air.*]

HIGGINS. A new fashion, by George! And it ought to look horrible!

DOOLITTLE [*with fatherly pride*]. Well, I never thought she'd clean up as good looking as that, Governor. She's a credit to me, aint she?

LIZA. I tell you, it's easy to clean up here. Hot and cold water on tap, just as much as you like, there is. Woolly towels, there is; and a towel horse so hot, it burns your fingers. Soft brushes to scrub yourself, and a wooden bowl of soap smelling like primroses. Now I know why ladies is so clean. Washing's a treat for them. Wish they saw what it is for the like of me.

HIGGINS. I'm glad the bathroom met with your approval.

LIZA. It didnt: not all of it; and I dont care who hears me say it. Mrs. Pearce knows.

HIGGINS. What was wrong, Mrs. Pearce?

MRS. PEARCE [*blandly*]. Oh, nothing, sir. It doesn't matter.

LIZA. I had a good mind to break it. I didnt know which way to look. But I hung a towel over it, I did.

HIGGINS. Over what?

MRS. PEARCE. Over the looking glass, sir.

HIGGINS. Doolittle: you have brought your daughter up too strictly.

DOOLITTLE. Me! I never brought her up at all, except to give her a lick of a strap now and again. Dont put it on me, Governor. She aint accustomed to it, you see: thats all. But she'll soon pick up your free-and-easy ways.

LIZA. I'm a good girl, I am; and I wont pick up no free-and-easy ways.

HIGGINS. Eliza: if you say again that youre a good girl, your father shall take you home.

LIZA. Not him. You dont know my father. All he come here for was to touch you for some money to get drunk on.

DOOLITTLE. Well, what else would I want money for? To put into the plate in church, I suppose. [*She puts out her tongue at him. He is so incensed by this that* PICKERING *presently finds it necessary to step between them.*] Dont you give me none of your lip; and dont let me hear you giving this gentleman any of it neither, or youll hear from me about it. See?

HIGGINS. Have you any further advice to give her before you go, Doolittle? Your blessing, for instance.

DOOLITTLE. No, Governor: I aint such a mug as to put up my children to all I know myself. Hard enough to hold them in without that. If you want Eliza's mind improved, Governor, you do it yourself with a strap. So long, gentlemen. [*He turns to go.*]

HIGGINS [*impressively*]. Stop. Youll come regularly to see your daughter. It's your duty, you know. My brother is a clergyman; and he could help you in your talks with her.

DOOLITTLE [*evasively*]. Certainly. I'll come, Governor. Not just this week, because I have a job at a distance. But later on you may depend on me. Afternoon, gentlemen. Afternoon, maam. [*He takes off his hat to* MRS. PEARCE, *who disdains the salutation and goes out. He winks at* HIGGINS, *thinking him probably a fellow-sufferer from* MRS. PEARCE's *difficult disposition, and follows her.*]

LIZA. Dont you believe the old liar. He'd as soon you set a bull-dog on him as a clergyman. You wont see him again in a hurry.

HIGGINS. I dont want to, Eliza. Do you?

LIZA. Not me. I dont want never to see him again, I dont. He's a disgrace to me, he is, collecting dust, instead of working at his trade.

PICKERING. What is his trade, Eliza?

LIZA. Taking money out of other people's pockets into his own. His proper trade's a navvy; and he works at it sometimes too — for exercise — and earns good money at it. Aint you going to call me Miss Doolittle any more?

PICKERING. I beg your pardon, Miss Doolittle. It was a slip of the tongue.

LIZA. Oh, I dont mind; only it sounded so genteel. I should just like to take a taxi to the corner of Tottenham Court Road and get out there and tell it to wait for me, just to put the girls in their place a bit. I wouldnt speak to them, you know.

PICKERING. Better wait til we get you something really fashion-able.

HIGGINS. Besides, you shouldnt cut your old friends now that you have risen in the world. Thats what we call snobbery.

LIZA. You dont call the like of them my friends now, I should hope. Theyve took it out of me often enough with their ridicule when they had the chance; and now I mean to get a bit of my own back. But if I'm to have fashionable clothes, I'll wait. I should like to have some. Mrs. Pearce says youre going to give me some to wear in bed at night different to what I wear in the daytime; but it do seem a waste of money when you could get something to shew. Besides, I never could fancy changing into cold things on a winter night.

MRS. PEARCE [*coming back*]. Now, Eliza. The new things have come for you to try on.

LIZA. Ah-ow-oo-ooh! [*She rushes out.*]

MRS. PEARCE [*following her*]. Oh, dont rush about like that, girl. [*She shuts the door behind her.*]

HIGGINS. Pickering: we have taken on a stiff job.

PICKERING [*with conviction*]. Higgins: we have.

ACT THREE

[*It is* MRS. HIGGINS'S *at-home day. Nobody has yet arrived. Her drawing room, in a flat on Chelsea Embankment, has three windows looking on the river; and the ceiling is not so lofty as it would be in an older house of the same pretension. The windows are open, giving access to a balcony with flowers in pots. If you stand with your face to the windows, you have the fireplace on your left and the door in the right-hand wall close to the corner nearest the windows.*

MRS. HIGGINS *was brought up on Morris and Burne Jones; and her room, which is very unlike her son's room in Wimpole Street, is not crowded with furniture and little tables and nicknacks. In the middle of the room there is a big otto-man; and this, with the carpet, the Morris wall-papers, and the Morris chintz window curtains and brocade covers of the otto-man and its cushions, supply all the ornament, and are much too handsome to be hidden by odds and ends of useless things. A few good oil-paintings from the exhibitions in the Grosvenor Gallery thirty years ago (the Burne Jones, not the Whistler side of them) are on the walls. The only landscape is a Cecil Lawson on the scale of a Rubens. There is a portrait of* MRS. HIGGINS *as she was when she defied fashion in her youth in one of the beautiful Rosettian costumes which, when carica-tured by people who did not understand, led to the absurdities of popular estheticism in the eighteen-seventies.*

In the corner diagonally opposite the door MRS. HIGGINS, *now over sixty and long past taking the trouble to dress out of the fashion, sits writing at an elegantly simple writing-table with a bell button within reach of her hand. There is a Chip-pendale chair further back in the room between her and the window nearest her side. At the other side of the room, further forward, is an Elizabethan chair roughly carved in the taste of Inigo Jones. On the same side a piano in a decorated case. The corner between the fireplace and the window is occupied by a divan cushioned in Morris chintz.*

It is between four and five in the afternoon.

The door is opened violently; and HIGGINS *enters with his hat on.*]

MRS. HIGGINS [*dismayed*]. Henry! [*scolding him*] What are you doing here to-day? It is my at-home day: you promised not to come. [*As he bends to kiss her, she takes his hat off, and presents it to him.*]

HIGGINS. Oh bother! [*He throws the hat down on the table.*]

MRS. HIGGINS. Go home at once.

HIGGINS [*kissing her*]. I know, mother. I came on purpose.

MRS. HIGGINS. But you mustnt. I'm serious, Henry. You offend all my friends: they stop coming whenever they meet you.

HIGGINS. Nonsense! I know I have no small talk; but people dont mind. [*He sits on the settee.*]

MRS. HIGGINS. Oh! dont they? Small talk indeed! What about your large talk? Really, dear, you mustnt stay.

HIGGINS. I must. Ive a job for you. A phonetic job.

MRS. HIGGINS. No use, dear. I'm sorry; but I cant get round your vowels; and though I like to get pretty postcards in your patent shorthand, I always have to read the copies in ordinary writing you so thoughtfully send me.

HIGGINS. Well, this isnt a phonetic job.

MRS. HIGGINS. You said it was.

HIGGINS. Not your part of it. Ive picked up a girl.

MRS. HIGGINS. Does that mean that some girl has picked you up?

HIGGINS. Not at all. I dont mean a love affair.

MRS. HIGGINS. What a pity!

HIGGINS. Why?

MRS. HIGGINS. Well, you never fall in love with anyone under forty-five. When will you discover that there are some rather nice-looking young women about?

HIGGINS. Oh, I cant be bothered with young women. My idea of a lovable woman is something as like you as possible. I shall never get into the way of seriously liking young women: some habits lie too deep to be changed. [*Rising abruptly and walking about, jingling his money and his keys in his trouser pockets.*] Besides, theyre all idiots.

MRS. HIGGINS. Do you know what you would do if you really loved me, Henry?

HIGGINS. Oh bother! What? Marry, I suppose?

MRS. HIGGINS. No. Stop fidgeting and take your hands out of your pockets. [*With a gesture of despair, he obeys and sits down again.*] Thats a good boy. Now tell me about the girl.

HIGGINS. She's coming to see you.

MRS. HIGGINS. I dont remember asking her.

HIGGINS. You didnt. I asked her. If youd known her you wouldnt have asked her.

MRS. HIGGINS. Indeed! Why?

HIGGINS. Well, it's like this. She's a common flower girl. I picked her off the kerbstone.

MRS. HIGGINS. And invited her to my at-home!

HIGGINS [*rising and coming to her to coax her*]. Oh, thatll be all right. Ive taught her to speak properly; and she has strict orders as to her behavior. She's to keep to two subjects: the weather and everybody's health — Fine day and How do you do, you know — and not to let herself go on things in general. That will be safe.

MRS. HIGGINS. Safe! To talk about our health! about our insides! perhaps about our outsides! How could you be so silly, Henry?

HIGGINS [*impatiently*]. Well, she must talk about something. [*He controls himself and sits down again.*] Oh, she'll be all right: dont you fuss. Pickering is in it with me. Ive a sort of bet on that I'll pass her off as a duchess in six months. I started on her some months ago; and she's getting on like a house on fire. I shall win my bet. She has a quick ear; and she's been easier to teach than my middle class pupils because she's had to learn a complete new language. She talks English almost as you talk French.

MRS. HIGGINS. Thats satisfactory, at all events.

HIGGINS. Well, it is and it isnt.

MRS. HIGGINS. What does that mean?

HIGGINS. You see, Ive got her pronunciation all right; but you have to consider not only how a girl pronounces, but what she pronounces; and thats where —

They are interrupted by the parlor-maid, announcing guests.

THE PARLOR-MAID. Mrs. and Miss Eynsford Hill. [*She withdraws.*]

HIGGINS. Oh Lord! [*He rises; snatches his hat from the table; and makes for the door; but before he reaches it his mother introduces him.*]

    MRS. *and* MISS EYNSFORD HILL *are the mother and daughter who sheltered from the rain in Covent Garden. The mother is well bred, quiet, and has the habitual anxiety of straitened means. The daughter has acquired a gay air of being very much at home in society: the bravado of genteel poverty.*

MRS. EYNSFORD HILL [*to* MRS. HIGGINS]. How do you do? [*They shake hands.*]

MISS EYNSFORD HILL. How d'you do? [*She shakes.*]

MRS. HIGGINS [*introducing*]. My son Henry.

MISS EYNSFORD HILL. Your celebrated son! I have so longed to meet you, Professor Higgins.

HIGGINS [*glumly, making no movement in her direction*]. Delighted. [*He backs against the piano and bows brusquely.*]

MISS EYNSFORD HILL [*going to him with confident familiarity*]. How do you do?

HIGGINS [*staring at her*]. Ive seen you before somewhere. I havnt the ghost of a notion where; but Ive heard your voice. [*Drearily.*] It doesnt matter. Youd better sit down.

MRS. HIGGINS. I'm sorry to say that my celebrated son has no manners. You mustnt mind him.

MISS EYNSFORD HILL [*gaily*]. I dont. [*She sits in the Elizabethan chair.*]

MRS. EYNSFORD HILL [*a little bewildered*]. Not at all. [*She sits on the ottoman between her daughter and* MRS. HIGGINS, *who has turned her chair away from the writing-table.*]

HIGGINS. Oh, have I been rude? I didnt mean to be.

    He goes to the central window, through which, with his back to the company, he contemplates the river and the flowers in Battersea Park on the opposite bank as if they were a frozen desert.

THE PARLOR-MAID *returns, ushering in* PICKERING.

THE PARLOR-MAID. Colonel Pickering. [*She withdraws.*]

PICKERING. How do you do, Mrs. Higgins?

MRS. HIGGINS. So glad youve come. Do you know Mrs. Eynsford Hill — Miss Eynsford Hill? [*Exchange of bows. The Colonel brings the Chippendale chair a little forward between* MRS. HILL *and* MRS. HIGGINS, *and sits down.*]

PICKERING. Has Henry told you what weve come for?

HIGGINS [*over his shoulder*]. We were interrupted: damn it!

MRS. HIGGINS. Oh Henry, Henry, really!

MRS. EYNSFORD HILL [*half rising*]. Are we in the way?

MRS. HIGGINS [*rising and making her sit down again*]. No, no. You couldnt have come more fortunately: we want you to meet a friend of ours.

HIGGINS [*turning hopefully*]. Yes, by George! We want two or three people. Youll do as well as anybody else.

THE PARLOR-MAID *returns, ushering* FREDDY.

THE PARLOR-MAID. Mr. Eynsford Hill.

HIGGINS [*almost audibly, past endurance*]. God of Heaven! another of them.

FREDDY [*shaking hands with* MRS. HIGGINS]. Ahdedo?

MRS. HIGGINS. Very good of you to come. [*Introducing.*] Colonel Pickering.

FREDDY [*bowing*]. Ahdedo?

MRS. HIGGINS. I dont think you know my son, Professor Higgins.

FREDDY [*going to* HIGGINS]. Ahdedo?

HIGGINS [*looking at him much as if he were a pickpocket*]. I'll take my oath Ive met you before somewhere. Where was it?

FREDDY. I dont think so.

HIGGINS [*resignedly*]. It dont matter, anyhow. Sit down.

He shakes FREDDY's *hand, and almost slings him on to the ottoman with his face to the windows; then comes round to the other side of it.*

HIGGINS. Well, here we are, anyhow! [*He sits down on the otto-man next* MRS. EYNSFORD HILL, *on her left.*] And now, what the devil are we going to talk about until Eliza comes?

MRS. HIGGINS. Henry: you are the life and soul of the Royal Society's soirees; but really youre rather trying on more commonplace occasions.

HIGGINS. Am I? Very sorry. [*Beaming suddenly.*] I suppose I am, you know. [*Uproariously.*] Ha, ha!

MISS EYNSFORD HILL [*who considers* HIGGINS *quite eligible matrimonially*]. I sympathize. I havnt any small talk. If people would only be frank and say what they really think!

HIGGINS [*relapsing into gloom*]. Lord forbid!

MRS. EYNSFORD HILL [*taking up her daughter's cue*]. But why?

HIGGINS. What they think they ought to think is bad enough, Lord knows; but what they really think would break up the whole show. Do you suppose it would be really agreeable if I were to come out now with what *I* really think?

MISS EYNSFORD HILL [*gaily*]. Is it so very cynical?

HIGGINS. Cynical! Who the dickens said it was cynical? I mean it wouldnt be decent.

MRS. EYNSFORD HILL [*seriously*]. Oh! I'm sure you dont mean that, Mr. Higgins.

HIGGINS. You see, we're all savages, more or less. We're supposed to be civilized and cultured — to know all about poetry and philosophy and art and science, and so on; but how many of us know even the meanings of these names? [*To* MISS HILL.] What do you know of poetry? [*To* MRS. HILL.] What do you know of science? [*Indicating* FREDDY.] What does he know of art or science or anything else? What the devil do you imagine I know of philosophy?

MRS. HIGGINS [*warningly*]. Or of manners, Henry?

THE PARLOR-MAID [*opening the door*]. Miss Doolittle. [*She withdraws.*]

HIGGINS [*rising hastily and running to* MRS. HIGGINS]. Here she is, mother. [*He stands on tiptoe and makes signs over his mother's head to* ELIZA *to indicate to her which lady is her hostess.*]

ELIZA, *who is exquisitely dressed, produces an impression of such remarkable distinction and beauty as she enters that they all rise, quite fluttered. Guided by* HIGGINS's *signals, she comes to* MRS. HIGGINS *with studied grace.*

LIZA [*speaking with pedantic correctness of pronunciation and great beauty of tone*]. How do you do, Mrs. Higgins? [*She gasps slightly in making sure of the H in Higgins, but is quite successful.*] Mr. Higgins told me I might come.

MRS. HIGGINS [*cordially*]. Quite right: I'm very glad indeed to see you.

PICKERING. How do you do, Miss Doolittle?

LIZA [*shaking hands with him*]. Colonel Pickering, is it not?

MRS. EYNSFORD HILL. I feel sure we have met before, Miss Doolittle. I remember your eyes.

LIZA. How do you do? [*She sits down on the ottoman gracefully in the place just left vacant by* HIGGINS.]

MRS. EYNSFORD HILL [*introducing*]. My daughter Clara.

LIZA. How do you do?

CLARA [*impulsively*]. How do you do? [*She sits down on the ottoman beside* ELIZA, *devouring her with her eyes.*]

FREDDY [*coming to their side of the ottoman*]. Ive certainly had the pleasure.

MRS. EYNSFORD HILL [*introducing*]. My son Freddy.

LIZA. How do you do?

FREDDY *bows and sits down in the Elizabethan chair, infatuated.*

HIGGINS [*suddenly*]. By George, yes: it all comes back to me! [*They stare at him.*] Covent Garden! [*Lamentably.*] What a damned thing!

MRS. HIGGINS. Henry, please! [*He is about to sit on the edge of the table.*] Dont sit on my writing-table: youll break it.

HIGGINS [*sulkily*]. Sorry.

He goes to the divan, stumbling into the fender and over the fire-irons on his way; extricating himself with muttered imprecations; and finishing his disastrous journey by throwing himself so impatiently on the divan that he almost breaks it. MRS. HIGGINS *looks at him, but controls herself and says nothing.*

A long and painful pause ensues.

MRS. HIGGINS [*at last, conversationally*]. Will it rain, do you think?

LIZA. The shallow depression in the west of these islands is likely to move slowly in an easterly direction. There are no indications of any great change in the barometrical situation.

FREDDY. Ha! ha! how awfully funny!

LIZA. What is wrong with that, young man? I bet I got it right.

FREDDY. Killing!

MRS. EYNSFORD HILL. I'm sure I hope it wont turn cold. Theres so much influenza about. It runs right through our whole family regularly every spring.

LIZA [*darkly*]. My aunt died of influenza: so they said.

MRS. EYNSFORD HILL [*clicks her tongue sympathetically*]!!!

LIZA [*in the same tragic tone*]. But it's my belief they done the old woman in.

MRS. HIGGINS [*puzzled*]. Done her in?

LIZA. Y-e-e-e-es, Lord love you! Why should she die of influenza? She come through diphtheria right enough the year before. I saw her with my own eyes. Fairly blue with it, she was. They all thought she was dead; but my father he kept ladling gin down her throat til she came to so sudden that she bit the bowl off the spoon.

MRS. EYNSFORD HILL [*startled*]. Dear me!

LIZA [*piling up the indictment*]. What call would a woman with that strength in her have to die of influenza? What become of her new straw hat that should have come to me? Somebody pinched it; and what I say is, them as pinched it done her in.

MRS. EYNSFORD HILL. What does doing her in mean?

HIGGINS [*hastily*]. Oh, thats the new small talk. To do a person in means to kill them.

MRS. EYNSFORD HILL [*to ELIZA, horrified*]. You surely dont believe that your aunt was killed?

LIZA. Do I not! Them she lived with would have killed her for a hat-pin, let alone a hat.

MRS. EYNSFORD HILL. But it cant have been right for your father to pour spirits down her throat like that. It might have killed her.

LIZA. Not her. Gin was mother's milk to her. Besides, he'd poured so much down his own throat that he knew the good of it.

MRS. EYNSFORD HILL. Do you mean that he drank?

LIZA. Drank! My word! Something chronic.

MRS. EYNSFORD HILL. How dreadful for you!

LIZA. Not a bit. It never did him no harm what I could see. But then he did not keep it up regular. [*Cheerfully.*] On the burst, as you might say, from time to time. And always more agreeable when he had a drop in. When he was out of work, my mother used to give him fourpence and tell him to go out and not come back until he'd drunk himself cheerful and loving-like. Theres lots of women has to make their husbands drunk to make them fit to live with. [*Now quite at her ease.*] You see, it's like this. If a man has a bit of a conscience, it always takes him when he's sober; and then it makes him low-spirited. A drop of booze just takes that off and makes him happy. [*To FREDDY, who is in convulsions of suppressed laughter.*] Here! what are you sniggering at?

FREDDY. The new small talk. You do it so awfully well.

LIZA. If I was doing it proper, what was you laughing at? [*To HIGGINS.*] Have I said anything I oughtnt?

MRS. HIGGINS [*interposing*]. Not at all, Miss Doolittle.

LIZA. Well, thats a mercy, anyhow. [*Expansively.*] What I always say is —

HIGGINS [*rising and looking at his watch*]. Ahem!

LIZA [*looking round at him; taking the hint; and rising*]. Well: I must go. [*They all rise.* FREDDY *goes to the door.*] So pleased to have met you. Goodbye. [*She shakes hands with* MRS. HIGGINS.]

MRS. HIGGINS. Goodbye.

LIZA. Goodbye, Colonel Pickering.

PICKERING. Goodbye, Miss Doolittle. [*They shake hands.*]

LIZA [*nodding to the others*]. Goodbye, all.

FREDDY [*opening the door for her*]. Are you walking across the Park, Miss Doolittle? If so —

LIZA. Walk! Not bloody likely. [*Sensation.*] I am going in a taxi. [*She goes out.*]

PICKERING *gasps and sits down.* FREDDY *goes out on the balcony to catch another glimpse of* ELIZA.

MRS. EYNSFORD HILL [*suffering from shock*]. Well, I really cant get used to the new ways.

CLARA [*throwing herself discontentedly into the Elizabethan chair*]. Oh, it's all right, mamma, quite right. People will think we never go anywhere or see anybody if you are so old-fashioned.

MRS. EYNSFORD HILL. I daresay I am very old-fashioned; but I do hope you wont begin using that expression, Clara. I have got accustomed to hear you talking about men as rotters, and calling everything filthy and beastly; though I do think it horrible and unladylike. But this last is really too much. Dont you think so, Colonel Pickering?

PICKERING. Dont ask me. Ive been away in India for several years; and manners have changed so much that I sometimes dont know whether I'm at a respectable dinner-table or in a ship's forecastle.

CLARA. It's all a matter of habit. Theres no right or wrong in it. Nobody means anything by it. And it's so quaint, and gives such a smart emphasis to things that are not in themselves very witty. I find the new small talk delightful and quite innocent.

MRS. EYNSFORD HILL [*rising*]. Well, after that, I think it's time for us to go.

PICKERING *and* HIGGINS *rise.*

CLARA [*rising*]. Oh yes: we have three at-homes to go to still. Goodbye, Mrs. Higgins. Goodbye, Colonel Pickering. Goodbye, Professor Higgins.

HIGGINS [*coming grimly at her from the divan, and accompanying her to the door*]. Goodbye. Be sure you try on that small talk at the three at-homes. Dont be nervous about it. Pitch it in strong.

CLARA [*all smiles*]. I will. Goodbye. Such nonsense, all this early Victorian prudery!

HIGGINS [*tempting her*]. Such damned nonsense!

CLARA. Such bloody nonsense!

MRS. EYNSFORD HILL [*convulsively*]. Clara!

CLARA. Ha! ha! [*She goes out radiant, conscious of being thoroughly up to date, and is heard descending the stairs in a stream of silvery laughter.*]

FREDDY [*to the heavens at large*]. Well, I ask you — [*He gives it up, and comes to* MRS. HIGGINS.] Goodbye.

MRS. HIGGINS [*shaking hands*]. Goodbye. Would you like to meet Miss Doolittle again?

FREDDY [*eagerly*]. Yes, I should, most awfully.

MRS. HIGGINS. Well, you know my days.

FREDDY. Yes. Thanks awfully. Goodbye. [*He goes out.*]

MRS. EYNSFORD HILL. Goodbye, Mr. Higgins.

HIGGINS. Goodbye. Goodbye.

MRS. EYNSFORD HILL [*to* PICKERING]. It's no use. I shall never be able to bring myself to use that word.

PICKERING. Dont. It's not compulsory, you know. Youll get on quite well without it.

MRS. EYNSFORD HILL. Only, Clara is so down on me if I am not positively reeking with the latest slang. Goodbye.

PICKERING. Goodbye. [*They shake hands.*]

MRS. EYNSFORD HILL [*to* MRS. HIGGINS]. You mustnt mind Clara. [PICKERING, *catching from her lowered tone that this is not meant for him to hear, discreetly joins* HIGGINS *at the window.*] We're so poor! and she gets so few parties, poor child! She doesnt quite know. [MRS. HIGGINS, *seeing that her eyes are moist, takes her hand sympathetically and goes with her to the door.*] But the boy is nice. Dont you think so?

MRS. HIGGINS. Oh, quite nice. I shall always be delighted to see him.

MRS. EYNSFORD HILL. Thank you, dear. Goodbye. [*She goes out.*]

HIGGINS [*eagerly*]. Well? Is Eliza presentable? [*He swoops on his mother and drags her to the ottoman, where she sits down in* ELIZA's *place with her son on her left.*]

PICKERING *returns to his chair on her right.*

MRS. HIGGINS. You silly boy, of course she's not presentable. She's a triumph of your art and of her dressmaker's; but if you suppose for a moment that she doesnt give herself away in every sentence she utters, you must be perfectly cracked about her.

PICKERING. But dont you think something might be done? I mean something to eliminate the sanguinary element from her conversation.

MRS. HIGGINS. Not as long as she is in Henry's hands.

HIGGINS [*aggrieved*]. Do you mean that my language is improper?

MRS. HIGGINS. No, dearest: it would be quite proper — say on a canal barge; but it would not be proper for her at a garden party.

HIGGINS [*deeply injured*]. Well I must say —

PICKERING [*interrupting him*]. Come, Higgins: you must learn to know yourself. I havnt heard such language as yours since we used to review the volunteers in Hyde Park twenty years ago.

HIGGINS [*sulkily*]. Oh, well, if you say so, I suppose I dont always talk like a bishop.

MRS. HIGGINS [*quieting Henry with a touch*]. Colonel Pickering: will you tell me what is the exact state of things in Wimpole Street?

PICKERING [*cheerfully: as if this completely changed the subject*]. Well, I have come to live there with Henry. We work together at my Indian Dialects; and we think it more convenient —

MRS. HIGGINS. Quite so. I know all about that: it's an excellent arrangement. But where does this girl live?

HIGGINS. With us, of course. Where should she live?

MRS. HIGGINS. But on what terms? Is she a servant? If not, what is she?

PICKERING [*slowly*]. I think I know what you mean, Mrs. Higgins.

HIGGINS. Well, dash me if *I* do! Ive had to work at the girl every day for months to get her to her present pitch. Besides, she's useful. She knows where my things are, and remembers my appointments and so forth.

MRS. HIGGINS. How does your housekeeper get on with her?

HIGGINS. Mrs. Pearce? Oh, she's jolly glad to get so much taken off her hands; for before Eliza came, she used to have to find things and remind me of my appointments. But she's got some silly bee in her bonnet about Eliza. She keeps saying "You dont think, sir": doesnt she, Pick?

PICKERING. Yes: thats the formula. "You dont think, sir." Thats the end of every conversation about Eliza.

HIGGINS. As if I ever stop thinking about the girl and her confounded vowels and consonants. I'm worn out, thinking about her, and watching her lips and her teeth and her tongue, not to mention her soul, which is the quaintest of the lot.

MRS. HIGGINS. You certainly are a pretty pair of babies, playing with your live doll.

HIGGINS. Playing! The hardest job I ever tackled: make no mistake about that, mother. But you have no idea how frightfully interesting it is to take a human being and change her into a quite different human being by creating a new speech for her. It's filling up the deepest gulf that separates class from class and soul from soul.

PICKERING [*drawing his chair closer to* MRS. HIGGINS *and bending over to her eagerly*]. Yes: it's enormously interesting. I assure you, Mrs. Higgins, we take Eliza very seriously. Every week — every day almost — there is some new change. [*Closer again.*] We keep records of every stage — dozens of gramophone disks and photographs —

HIGGINS [*assailing her at the other ear*]. Yes, by George: it's the most absorbing experiment I ever tackled. She regularly fills our lives up: doesn't she, Pick?

PICKERING. We're always talking Eliza.

HIGGINS. Teaching Eliza.

PICKERING. Dressing Eliza.

MRS. HIGGINS. What!

HIGGINS. Inventing new Elizas.

HIGGINS.	*(speaking together)*	You know, she has the most extraordinary quickness of ear:
PICKERING.		I assure you, my dear Mrs. Higgins, that girl
HIGGINS.		just like a parrot. I've tried her with every
PICKERING.		is a genius. She can play the piano quite beautifully.
HIGGINS.		possible sort of sound that a human being can make —
PICKERING.		We have taken her to classical concerts and to music
HIGGINS.		Continental dialects, African dialects, Hottentot
PICKERING.		halls; and it's all the same to her: she plays everything
HIGGINS.		clicks, things it took me years to get hold of; and
PICKERING.		she hears right off when she comes home, whether it's
HIGGINS.		she picks them up like a shot, right away, as if she had
PICKERING.		Beethoven and Brahms or Lehar and Lionel Monckton;
HIGGINS.		been at it all her life.
PICKERING.		though six months ago, she'd never as much as touched a piano —

MRS. HIGGINS [*putting her fingers in her ears, as they are by this time shouting one another down with an intolerable noise*]. Sh-sh-sh—sh! [*They stop.*]

PICKERING. I beg your pardon. [*He draws his chair back apologetically.*]

HIGGINS. Sorry. When Pickering starts shouting nobody can get a word in edgeways.

MRS. HIGGINS. Be quiet, Henry. Colonel Pickering: dont you realize that when Eliza walked into Wimpole Street, something walked in with her?

PICKERING. Her father did. But Henry soon got rid of him.

MRS. HIGGINS. It would have been more to the point if her mother had. But as her mother didnt something else did.

PICKERING. But what?

MRS. HIGGINS [*unconsciously dating herself by the word*]. A problem.

PICKERING. Oh, I see. The problem of how to pass her off as a lady.

HIGGINS. I'll solve that problem. Ive half solved it already.

MRS. HIGGINS. No, you two infinitely stupid male creatures; the problem of what is to be done with her afterwards.

HIGGINS. I dont see anything in that. She can go her own way, with all the advantages I have given her.

MRS. HIGGINS. The advantages of that poor woman who was here just now! The manners and habits that disqualify a fine lady from earning her own living without giving her a fine lady's income! Is that what you mean?

PICKERING [*indulgently, being rather bored*]. Oh, that will be all right, Mrs. Higgins. [*He rises to go.*]

HIGGINS [*rising also*]. We'll find her some light employment.

PICKERING. She's happy enough. Dont you worry about her. Goodbye. [*He shakes hands as if he were consoling a frightened child, and makes for the door.*]

HIGGINS. Anyhow, theres no good bothering now. The thing's done. Goodbye, mother. [*He kisses her, and follows* PICKERING.]

PICKERING [*turning for a final consolation*]. There are plenty of openings. We'll do whats right. Goodbye.

HIGGINS [*to* PICKERING *as they go out together*]. Let's take her to the Shakespear exhibition at Earls Court.

PICKERING. Yes: lets. Her remarks will be delicious.

HIGGINS. She'll mimic all the people for us when we get home.

PICKERING. Ripping. [*Both are heard laughing as they go downstairs.*]

MRS. HIGGINS [*rises with an impatient bounce, and returns to her work at the writing-table. She sweeps a litter of disarranged papers out of her way; snatches a sheet of paper from her stationery case; and tries resolutely to write. At the third line she gives it up; flings down her pen; grips the table angrily and exclaims*]. Oh, men! men!! men!!!

ACT FOUR

[*The Wimpole Street laboratory. Midnight. Nobody in the room. The clock on the mantelpiece strikes twelve. The fire is not alight: it is a summer night.*

Presently HIGGINS *and* PICKERING *are heard on the stairs.*]

HIGGINS [*calling down to* PICKERING]. I say, Pick: lock up, will you? I shant be going out again.

PICKERING. Right. Can Mrs. Pearce go to bed? We dont want anything more, do we?

HIGGINS. Lord, no!

ELIZA *opens the door and is seen on the lighted landing in opera cloak, brilliant evening dress, and diamonds, with fan, flowers, and all accessories. She comes to the hearth, and switches on the electric lights there. She is tired: her pallor contrasts strongly with her dark eyes and hair; and her expression is almost tragic. She takes off her cloak; puts her fan and flowers on the piano; and sits down on the bench, brooding and silent. HIGGINS, in evening dress, with overcoat and hat, comes in, carrying a smoking jacket which he has picked up downstairs. He takes off the hat and overcoat; throws them carelessly on the newspaper stand; disposes of his coat in the same way; puts on the smoking jacket; and throws himself wearily into the easy-chair at the hearth. PICKERING, similarly attired, comes in. He also takes off his hat and overcoat, and is about to throw them on HIGGINS's when he hesitates.*

PICKERING. I say: Mrs. Pearce will row if we leave these things lying about in the drawing room.

HIGGINS. Oh, chuck them over the bannisters into the hall. She'll find them there in the morning and put them away all right. She'll think we were drunk.

PICKERING. We are, slightly. Are there any letters?

HIGGINS. I didnt look. [PICKERING *takes the overcoats and hats and goes downstairs.* HIGGINS *begins half singing half yawning an air from La Fanciulla del Golden West. Suddenly he stops and exclaims.*] I wonder where the devil my slippers are!

150

ELIZA *looks at him darkly; then rises suddenly and leaves the room.*

HIGGINS *yawns again, and resumes his song.*

PICKERING *returns, with the contents of the letter-box in his hand.*

PICKERING. Only circulars, and this coroneted billet-doux for you. [*He throws the circulars into the fender, and posts himself on the hearthrug, with his back to the grate.*]

HIGGINS [*glancing at the billet-doux*]. Money-lender. [*He throws the letter after the circulars.*]

ELIZA *returns with a pair of large down-at-heel slippers. She places them on the carpet before* HIGGINS, *and sits as before without a word.*

HIGGINS [*yawning again*]. Oh Lord! What an evening! What a crew! What a silly tomfoolery! [*He raises his shoe to unlace it, and catches sight of the slippers. He stops unlacing and looks at them as if they had appeared there of their own accord.*] Oh! theyre there, are they?

PICKERING [*stretching himself*]. Well, I feel a bit tired. It's been a long day. The garden party, a dinner party, and the opera! Rather too much of a good thing. But youve won your bet, Higgins. Eliza did the trick and something to spare, eh?

HIGGINS [*fervently*]. Thank God it's over!

ELIZA *flinches violently; but they take no notice of her; and she recovers herself and sits stonily as before.*

PICKERING. Were you nervous at the garden party? *I* was. Eliza didnt seem a bit nervous.

HIGGINS. Oh, she wasnt nervous. I knew she'd be all right. No: it's the strain of putting the job through all these months that has told on me. It was interesting enough at first, while we were at the phonetics; but after that I got deadly sick of it. If I hadnt backed myself to do it I should have chucked the whole thing up two months ago. It was a silly notion: the whole thing has been a bore.

PICKERING. Oh come! the garden party was frightfully exciting. My heart began beating like anything.

HIGGINS. Yes, for the first three minutes. But when I saw we were going to win hands down, I felt like a bear in a cage, hanging about doing nothing. The dinner was worse: sitting gorging there for over an hour, with nobody but a damned fool of a fashionable woman to talk to! I tell you, Pickering, never again for me. No more artificial duchesses. The whole thing has been simple purgatory.

PICKERING. Youve never been broken in properly to the social routine. [*Strolling over to the piano*.] I rather enjoy dipping into it occasionally myself: it makes me feel young again. Anyhow, it was a great success: an immense success. I was quite frightened once or twice because Eliza was doing it so well. You see, lots of the real people cant do it at all: theyre such fools that they think style comes by nature to people in their position; and so they never learn. Theres always something professional about doing a thing superlatively well.

HIGGINS. Yes: thats what drives me mad: the silly people dont know their own silly business. [*Rising*.] However, it's over and done with; and now I can go to bed at last without dreading tomorrow.

ELIZA's *beauty becomes murderous.*

PICKERING. I think I shall turn in too. Still, it's been a great occasion: a triumph for you. Goodnight. [*He goes.*]

HIGGINS [*following him*]. Goodnight. [*Over his shoulder, at the door.*] Put out the lights, Eliza; and tell Mrs. Pearce not to make coffee for me in the morning: I'll take tea. [*He goes out.*]

ELIZA *tries to control herself and feel indifferent as she rises and walks across the hearth to switch off the lights. By the time she gets there she is on the point of screaming. She sits down in* HIGGINS's *chair and holds on hard to the arms. Finally she gives way and flings herself furiously on the floor, raging.*

HIGGINS [*in despairing wrath outside*]. What the devil have I done with my slippers? [*He appears at the door.*]

LIZA [*snatching up the slippers, and hurling them at him one after the other with all her force*]. There are your slippers. And there. Take your slippers; and may you never have a day's luck with them!

HIGGINS [*astounded*]. What on earth —! [*He comes to her.*]

Whats the matter? Get up. [*He pulls her up.*] Anything wrong?

LIZA [*breathless*]. Nothing wrong — with you. Ive won your bet for you, havnt I? Thats enough for you. I dont matter, I suppose.

HIGGINS. You won my bet! You! Presumptuous insect! *I* won it. What did you throw those slippers at me for?

LIZA. Because I wanted to smash your face. I'd like to kill you, you selfish brute. Why didnt you leave me where you picked me out of — in the gutter? You thank God it's all over, and that now you can throw me back again there, do you? [*She crisps her fingers frantically.*]

HIGGINS [*looking at her in cool wonder*]. The creature is nervous, after all.

LIZA [*gives a suffocated scream of fury, and instinctively darts her nails at his face.*]!!

HIGGINS [*catching her wrists*]. Ah! would you? Claws in, you cat. How dare you shew your temper to me? Sit down and be quiet. [*He throws her roughly into the easy-chair.*]

LIZA [*crushed by superior strength and weight*]. Whats to become of me? Whats to become of me?

HIGGINS. How the devil do I know whats to become of you? What does it matter what becomes of you?

LIZA. You dont care. I know you dont care. You wouldnt care if I was dead. I'm nothing to you — not so much as them slippers.

HIGGINS [*thundering*]. Those slippers.

LIZA [*with bitter submission*]. Those slippers. I didnt think it made any difference now.

A pause. ELIZA hopeless and crushed. HIGGINS a little uneasy.

HIGGINS [*in his loftiest manner*]. Why have you begun going on like this? May I ask whether you complain of your treatment here?

LIZA. No.

HIGGINS. Has anybody behaved badly to you? Colonel Pickering? Mrs. Pearce? Any of the servants?

LIZA. No.

HIGGINS. I presume you dont pretend that *I* have treated you badly?

LIZA. No.

HIGGINS. I am glad to hear it. [*He moderates his tone.*] Perhaps youre tired after the strain of the day. Will you have a glass of champagne? [*He moves towards the door.*]

LIZA. No. [*Recollecting her manners.*] Thank you.

HIGGINS [*good-humored again*]. This has been coming on you for some days. I suppose it was natural for you to be anxious about the garden party. But thats all over now. [*He pats her kindly on the shoulder. She writhes.*] Theres nothing more to worry about.

LIZA. No. Nothing more for you to worry about. [*She suddenly rises and gets away from him by going to the piano bench, where she sits and hides her face.*] Oh God! I wish I was dead.

HIGGINS [*staring after her in sincere surprise*]. Why? In heaven's, name, why? [*Reasonably, going to her.*] Listen to me, Eliza. All this irritation is purely subjective.

LIZA. I dont understand. I'm too ignorant.

HIGGINS. It's only imagination. Low spirits and nothing else. Nobody's hurting you. Nothing's wrong. You go to bed like a good girl and sleep it off. Have a little cry and say your prayers: that will make you comfortable.

LIZA. I heard your prayers. "Thank God it's all over!"

HIGGINS [*impatiently*]. Well, dont you thank God it's all over? Now you are free and can do what you like.

LIZA [*pulling herself together in desperation*]. What am I fit for? What have you left me fit for? Where am I to go? What am I to do? Whats to become of me?

HIGGINS [*enlightened, but not at all impressed*]. Oh thats whats worrying you, is it? [*He thrusts his hands into his pockets, and walks about in his usual manner, rattling the contents of his pockets, as if condescending to a trivial subject out of pure kindness.*] I shouldnt bother about it if I were you. I should imagine you wont have much difficulty in settling yourself somewhere or other, though I hadnt quite realized that you were going away. [*She looks quickly at him: he does not look at her, but examines the dessert stand on the piano and decides that he will eat an apple.*] You might marry, you know. [*He bites a large piece out of the apple and munches it noisily.*] You see, Eliza, all men are not confirmed old bachelors like me and the Colonel. Most men are the marrying sort (poor devils!); and youre not bad-looking: it's quite a pleasure to look at you sometimes — not now, of course, because youre crying and looking as ugly as the very devil; but when youre all right and quite yourself, youre what I should call attractive. That is, to the people in the marrying line, you understand. You go to bed and have a good nice rest; and then get up and look at yourself in the glass; and you wont feel so cheap.

ELIZA *again looks at him, speechless, and does not stir.*

    The look is quite lost on him: he eats his apple with a dreamy expression of happiness, as it is quite a good one.

HIGGINS [*a genial afterthought occurring to him*]. I daresay my mother could find some chap or other who would do very well.

LIZA. We were above that at the corner of Tottenham Court Road.

HIGGINS [*waking up*]. What do you mean?

LIZA. I sold flowers. I didnt sell myself. Now youve made a lady of me I'm not fit to sell anything else. I wish youd left me where you found me.

HIGGINS [*slinging the core of the apple decisively into the grate*]. Tosh, Eliza. Dont you insult human relations by dragging all this cant about buying and selling into it. You neednt marry the fellow if you dont like him.

LIZA. What else am I to do?

HIGGINS. Oh, lots of things. What about your old idea of a florist's shop? Pickering could set you up in one: he's lots of money. [*Chuckling.*] He'll have to pay for all those togs you have been wearing to-day; and that, with the hire of the jewelry, will make a big hole in two hundred pounds. Why, six months ago you would have thought it the millennium to have a flower shop of your own. Come! youll be all right. I must clear off to bed: I'm devilish sleepy. By the way, I came down for something: I forget what it was.

LIZA. Your slippers.

HIGGINS. Oh yes, of course. You shied them at me. [*He picks them up, and is going out when she rises and speaks to him.*]

LIZA. Before you go, sir —

HIGGINS [*dropping the slippers in his surprise at her calling him Sir*]. Eh?

LIZA. Do my clothes belong to me or to Colonel Pickering?

HIGGINS [*coming back into the room as if her question were the very climax of unreason*]. What the devil use would they be to Pickering?

LIZA. He might want them for the next girl you pick up to experiment on.

HIGGINS [*shocked and hurt*]. Is that the way you feel towards us?

LIZA. I dont want to hear anything more about that. All I want to know is whether anything belongs to me. My own clothes were burnt.

HIGGINS. But what does it matter? Why need you start bothering about that in the middle of the night?

LIZA. I want to know what I may take away with me. I dont want to be accused of stealing.

HIGGINS [*now deeply wounded*]. Stealing! You shouldnt have said that, Eliza. That shews a want of feeling.

LIZA. I'm sorry. I'm only a common ignorant girl; and in my station I have to be careful. There cant be any feelings between the like of you and the like of me. Please will you tell me what belongs to me and what doesnt?

HIGGINS [*very sulky*]. You may take the whole damned houseful if you like. Except the jewels. Theyre hired. Will that satisfy you? [*He turns on his heel and is about to go in extreme dudgeon.*]

LIZA [*drinking in his emotion like nectar, and nagging him to provoke a further supply*]. Stop, please. [*She takes off her jewels.*] Will you take these to your room and keep them safe? I dont want to run the risk of their being missing.

HIGGINS [*furious*]. Hand them over. [*She puts them into his hands.*]If these belonged to me instead of to the jeweller, I'd ram them down your ungrateful throat. [*He perfunctorily thrusts them into his pockets, unconsciously decorating himself with the protruding ends of the chains.*]

LIZA [*taking a ring off*]. This ring isnt the jeweller's: it's the one you bought me in Brighton. I dont want it now. [*Higgins dashes the ring violently into the fireplace, and turns on her so threateningly that she crouches over the piano with her hands over her face, and exclaims.*] Dont you hit me.

HIGGINS. Hit you! You infamous creature, how dare you accuse me of such a thing? It is you who have hit me. You have wounded me to the heart.

LIZA [*thrilling with hidden joy*]. I'm glad. Ive got a little of my own back, anyhow.

HIGGINS [*with dignity, in his finest professional style*]. You have caused me to lose my temper: a thing that has hardly ever happened to me before. I prefer to say nothing more to-night. I am going to bed.

LIZA [*pertly*]. Youd better leave a note for Mrs. Pearce about the coffee; for she wont be told by me.

HIGGINS [*formally*]. Damn Mrs. Pearce; and damn the coffee; and damn you; and damn my own folly in having lavished hard-earned knowledge and the treasure of my regard and intimacy on a heartless guttersnipe. [*He goes out with impressive decorum, and spoils it by slamming the door savagely.*]

ELIZA *smiles for the first time; expresses her feelings by a wild pantomime in which an imitation of* HIGGINS's *exit is confused with her own triumph; and finally goes down on her knees on the hearthrug to look for the ring.*

ACT FIVE

[MRS. HIGGINS's *drawing room. She is at her writing-table as before.* THE PARLOR-MAID *comes in.*]

THE PARLOR-MAID [*at the door*]. Mr. Henry, maam, is downstairs with Colonel Pickering.

MRS. HIGGINS. Well, shew them up.

THE PARLOR-MAID. Theyre using the telephone, maam. Telephoning to the police, I think.

MRS. HIGGINS. What!

THE PARLOR-MAID [*coming further in and lowering her voice*]. Mr. Henry is in a state, maam. I thought I'd better tell you.

MRS. HIGGINS. If you had told me that Mr. Henry was not in a state it would have been more surprising. Tell them to come up when theyve finished with the police. I suppose he's lost something.

THE PARLOR-MAID. Yes, maam. [*Going.*]

MRS. HIGGINS. Go upstairs and tell Miss Doolittle that Mr. Henry and the Colonel are here. Ask her not to come down til I send for her.

THE PARLOR-MAID. Yes, maam.

HIGGINS *bursts in. He is, as* THE PARLOR-MAID *has said, in a state.*

HIGGINS. Look here, mother: heres a confounded thing!

MRS. HIGGINS. Yes, dear. Good morning. [*He checks his impatience and kisses her, whilst* THE PARLOR-MAID *goes out.*] What is it?

HIGGINS. Eliza's bolted.

MRS. HIGGINS [*calmly continuing her writing*]. You must have frightened her.

HIGGINS. Frightened her! nonsense! She was left last night, as usual, to turn out the lights and all that; and instead of going to bed she changed her clothes and went right off: her bed wasnt slept in. She came in a cab for her things before seven this morning; and that fool Mrs. Pearce let her have them without telling me a word about it. What am I to do?

MRS. HIGGINS. Do without, I'm afraid, Henry. The girl has a perfect right to leave if she chooses.

HIGGINS [*wandering distractedly across the room*]. But I cant find anything. I dont know what appointments Ive got. I'm — [PICKERING *comes in. MRS. HIGGINS puts down her pen and turns away from the writing-table.*]

PICKERING [*shaking hands*]. Good morning, Mrs. Higgins. Has Henry told you? [*He sits down on the ottoman.*]

HIGGINS. What does that ass of an inspector say? Have you offered a reward?

MRS. HIGGINS [*rising in indignant amazement*]. You dont mean to say you have set the police after Eliza.

HIGGINS. Of course. What are the police for? What else could we do? [*He sits in the Elizabethan chair.*]

PICKERING. The inspector made a lot of difficulties. I really think he suspected us of some improper purpose.

MRS. HIGGINS. Well, of course he did. What right have you to go to the police and give the girl's name as if she were a thief, or a lost umbrella, or something? Really! [*She sits down again, deeply vexed.*]

HIGGINS. But we want to find her.

PICKERING. We cant let her go like this, you know, Mrs. Higgins. What were we to do?

MRS. HIGGINS. You have no more sense, either of you, than two children. Why —

THE PARLOR-MAID *comes in and breaks off the conversation.*

THE PARLOR-MAID. Mr. Henry: a gentleman wants to see you very particular. He's been sent on from Wimpole Street.

HIGGINS. Oh, bother! I cant see anyone now. Who is it?

THE PARLOR-MAID. A Mr. Doolittle, sir.

PICKERING. Doolittle! Do you mean the dustman?

THE PARLOR-MAID. Dustman! Oh no, sir: a gentleman.

HIGGINS [*springing up excitedly*]. By George, Pick, it's some relative of hers that she's gone to. Somebody we know nothing about. [*To* THE PARLOR-MAID.] Send him up, quick.

THE PARLOR-MAID. Yes, sir. [*She goes.*]

HIGGINS [*eagerly, going to· his mother*]. Genteel relatives! now we shall hear something. [*He sits down in the Chippendale chair.*]

MRS. HIGGINS. Do you know any of her people?

PICKERING. Only her father: the fellow we told you about.

THE PARLOR-MAID [*announcing*]. Mr. Doolittle. [*She withdraws.*]

> DOOLITTLE *enters. He is brilliantly dressed in a new fashionable frock-coat, with white waistcoat and grey trousers. A flower in his buttonhole, a dazzling silk hat, and patent leather shoes complete the effect. He is too concerned with the business he has come on to notice* MRS. HIGGINS. *He walks straight to* HIGGINS, *and accosts him with vehement reproach.*

DOOLITTLE [*indicating his own person*]. See here! Do you see this? You done this.

HIGGINS. Done what, man?

DOOLITTLE. This, I tell you. Look at it. Look at this hat. Look at this coat.

PICKERING. Has Eliza been buying you clothes?

DOOLITTLE. Eliza! not she. Not half. Why would she buy me clothes?

MRS. HIGGINS. Good morning, Mr. Doolittle. Wont you sit down?

DOOLITTLE [*taken aback as he becomes conscious that he has forgotten his hostess*]. Asking your pardon, maam. [*He approaches her and shakes her proffered hand.*] Thank you. [*He sits down on the ottoman, on* PICKERING'S *right.*] I am that full of what has happened to me that I cant think of anything else.

HIGGINS. What the dickens has happened to you?

DOOLITTLE. I shouldnt mind if it had only happened to me: anything might happen to anybody and nobody to blame but Providence, as you might say. But this is something that you done to me: yes, you, Henry Higgins.

HIGGINS. Have you found Eliza? Thats the point.

DOOLITTLE. Have you lost her?

HIGGINS. Yes.

DOOLITTLE. You have all the luck, you have. I aint found her; but she'll find me quick enough now after what you done to me.

MRS. HIGGINS. But what has my son done to you, Mr. Doolittle?

DOOLITTLE. Done to me! Ruined me. Destroyed my happiness. Tied me up and delivered me into the hands of middle class morality.

HIGGINS [*rising intolerantly and standing over* DOOLITTLE]. Youre raving. Youre drunk. Youre mad. I gave you five pounds. After that I had two conversations with you, at half-a-crown an hour. Ive never seen you since.

DOOLITTLE. Oh! Drunk! am I! Mad? am I? Tell me this. Did you or did you not write a letter to an old blighter in America that was giving five millions to found Moral Reform Societies all over the world, and that wanted you to invent a universal language for him?

HIGGINS. What! Ezra D. Wannafeller! He's dead. [*He sits down again carelessly.*]

DOOLITTLE. Yes: he's dead; and I'm done for. Now did you or did you not write a letter to him to say that the most original moralist at present in England, to the best of your knowledge, was Alfred Doolittle, a common dustman.

HIGGINS. Oh, after your last visit I remember making some silly joke of the kind.

DOOLITTLE. Ah! you may well call it a silly joke. It put the lid on me right enough. Just give him the chance he wanted to shew that Americans is not like us: that they recognize and respect merit in every class of life, however humble. Them words is in his blooming will, in which, Henry Higgins, thanks to your silly joking, he leaves me a share in his Pre-digested

Cheese Trust worth three thousand a year on condition that I lecture for his Wannafeller Moral Reform World League as often as they ask me up to six times a year.

HIGGINS. The devil he does! Whew! [*Brightening suddenly.*] What a lark!

PICKERING. A safe thing for you, Doolittle. They wont ask you twice.

DOOLITTLE. It aint the lecturing I mind. I'll lecture them blue in the face, I will, and not turn a hair. It's making a gentleman of me that I object to. Who asked him to make a gentleman of me? I was happy. I was free. I touched pretty nigh everybody for money when I wanted it, same as I touched you, Henry Higgins. Now I am worrited; tied neck and heels; and everybody touches me for money. It's a fine thing for you, says my solicitor. Is it? says I. You mean it's a good thing for you, I says. When I was a poor man and had a solicitor once when they found a pram in the dust cart, he got me off, and got shut of me and got me shut of him as quick as he could. Same with the doctors: used to shove me out of the hospital before I could hardly stand on my legs, and nothing to pay. Now they finds out that I'm not a healthy man and cant live unless they looks after me twice a day. In the house I'm not let do a hand's turn for myself: somebody else must do it and touch me for it. A year ago I hadnt a relative in the world except two or three that wouldnt speak to me. Now Ive fifty, and not a decent week's wages among the lot of them. I have to live for others and not for myself: thats middle class morality. You talk of losing Eliza. Dont you be anxious: I bet she's on my doorstep by this: she that could support herself easy by selling flowers if I wasnt respectable. And the next one to touch me will be you, Henry Higgins. I'll have to learn to speak middle class language from you, instead of speaking proper English. Thats where youll come in; and I daresay thats what you done it for.

MRS. HIGGINS. But, my dear Mr. Doolittle, you need not suffer all this if you are really in earnest. Nobody can force you to accept this bequest. You can repudiate it. Isnt that so, Colonel Pickering?

PICKERING. I believe so.

DOOLITTLE [*softening his manner in deference to her sex*]. Thats the tragedy of it, maam. It's easy to say chuck it; but I havnt the nerve. Which of us has? We're all intimidated. Intimidated, maam: thats what we are. What is there for me if I chuck it but the workhouse in my old age? I have to dye my hair already to keep my job as a dustman. If I was one of the deserving poor, and had put by a bit, I could chuck it; but then why should I, acause the deserving poor might as well be millionaires for all the happiness they ever has. They dont know what happiness is. But I, as one of the undeserving poor, have nothing between me and the pauper's uniform but this here blasted three thousand a year that shoves me into the middle class. (Excuse the expression, maam: youd use it yourself if you had my provocation.) Theyve got you every way you turn: it's a choice between the Skilly of the workhouse and the Char Bydis of the middle class; and I havnt the nerve for the workhouse. Intimidated: thats what I am. Broke. Brought up. Happier men than me will call for my dust, and touch me for their tip; and I'll look on helpless, and envy them. And thats what your son has brought me to. [*He is overcome by emotion.*]

MRS. HIGGINS. Well, I'm very glad youre not going to do anything foolish, Mr. Doolittle. For this solves the problem of Eliza's future. You can provide for her now.

DOOLITTLE [*with melancholy resignation*]. Yes, maam: I'm expected to provide for everyone now, out of three thousand a year.

HIGGINS [*jumping up*]. Nonsense! he cant provide for her. He shant provide for her. She doesnt belong to him. I paid him five pounds for her. Doolittle: either youre an honest man or a rogue.

DOOLITTLE [*tolerantly*]. A little of both, Henry, like the rest of us: a little of both.

HIGGINS. Well, you took that money for the girl; and you have no right to take her as well.

MRS. HIGGINS. Henry: dont be absurd. If you want to know where Eliza is, she is upstairs.

HIGGINS [*amazed*]. Upstairs!!! Then I shall jolly soon fetch her downstairs. [*He makes resolutely for the door.*]

MRS. HIGGINS [*rising and following him*]. Be quiet, Henry. Sit down.

HIGGINS. I —

MRS. HIGGINS. Sit down, dear; and listen to me.

HIGGINS. Oh very well, very well, very well. [*He throws himself ungraciously on the ottoman, with his face towards the windows.*] But I think you might have told us this half an hour ago.

MRS. HIGGINS. Eliza came to me this morning. She passed the night partly walking about in a rage, partly trying to throw herself into the river and being afraid to, and partly in the Carlton Hotel. She told me of the brutal way you two treated her.

HIGGINS [*bounding up again*]. What!

PICKERING [*rising also*]. My dear Mrs. Higgins, she's been telling you stories. We didnt treat her brutally. We hardly said a word to her; and we parted on particularly good terms. [*Turning on HIGGINS.*] Higgins: did you bully her after I went to bed?

HIGGINS. Just the other way about. She threw my slippers in my face. She behaved in the most outrageous way. I never gave her the slightest provocation. The slippers came bang into my face the moment I entered the room — before I had uttered a word. And used perfectly awful language.

PICKERING [*astonished*]. But why? What did we do to her?

MRS. HIGGINS. I think I know pretty well what you did. The girl is naturally rather affectionate, I think. Isnt she, Mr. Doolittle?

DOOLITTLE. Very tender-hearted, maam. Takes after me.

MRS. HIGGINS. Just so. She had become attached to you both. She worked very hard for you, Henry! I dont think you quite realize what anything in the nature of brain work means to a girl like that. Well, it seems that when the great day of trial came, and she did this wonderful thing for you without making a single mistake, you two sat there and never said a word to her, but talked together of how glad you were that it was all over and how you had been bored with the whole thing. And then you were surprised because she threw your slippers at you! *I* should have thrown the fire-irons at you.

HIGGINS. We said nothing except that we were tired and wanted to go to bed. Did we, Pick?

PICKERING [*shrugging his shoulders*]. That was all.

MRS. HIGGINS [*ironically*]. Quite sure?

PICKERING. Absolutely. Really, that was all.

MRS. HIGGINS. You didnt thank her, or pet her, or admire her, or tell her how splendid she'd been.

HIGGINS [*impatiently*]. But she knew all about that. We didnt make speeches to her, if thats what you mean.

PICKERING [*conscience stricken*]. Perhaps we were a little inconsiderate. Is she very angry?

MRS. HIGGINS [*returning to her place at the writing-table*]. Well, I'm afraid she wont go back to Wimpole Street, especially now that Mr. Doolittle is able to keep up the position you have thrust on her; but she says she is quite willing to meet you on friendly terms and to let bygones be bygones.

HIGGINS [*furious*]. Is she, by George? Ho!

MRS. HIGGINS. If you promise to behave yourself, Henry, I'll ask her to come down. If not, go home; for you have taken up quite enough of my time.

HIGGINS. Oh, all right. Very well. Pick: you behave yourself. Let us put on our best Sunday manners for this creature that we picked out of the mud. [*He flings himself sulkily into the Elizabethan chair.*]

DOOLITTLE [*remonstrating*]. Now, now, Henry Higgins! have some consideration for my feelings as a middle class man.

MRS. HIGGINS. Remember your promise, Henry. [*She presses the bell-button on the writing-table.*] Mr. Doolittle: will you be so good as to step out on the balcony for a moment. I dont want Eliza to have the shock of your news until she has made it up with these two gentlemen. Would you mind?

DOOLITTLE. As you wish, lady. Anything to help Henry to keep her off my hands. [*He disappears through the window.*]

THE PARLOR-MAID *answers the bell.* PICKERING *sits down in* DOOLITTLE's *place.*

MRS. HIGGINS. Ask Miss Doolittle to come down, please.

THE PARLOR-MAID. Yes, maam. [*She goes out.*]

MRS. HIGGINS. Now, Henry: be good.

HIGGINS. I am behaving myself perfectly.

PICKERING. He is doing his best, Mrs. Higgins.

>*A pause.* HIGGINS *throws back his head; stretches out his legs; and begins to whistle.*

MRS. HIGGINS. Henry, dearest, you dont look at all nice in that attitude.

HIGGINS [*pulling himself together*]. I was not trying to look nice, mother.

MRS. HIGGINS. It doesnt matter, dear. I only wanted to make you speak.

HIGGINS. Why?

MRS. HIGGINS. Because you cant speak and whistle at the same time.

>HIGGINS *groans. Another very trying pause.*

HIGGINS [*springing up, out of patience*]. Where the devil is that girl? Are we to wait here all day?

>ELIZA *enters, sunny, self-possessed, and giving a staggeringly convincing exhibition of ease of manner. She carries a little work-basket, and is very much at home.* PICKERING *is too much taken aback to rise.*

LIZA. How do you do, Professor Higgins? Are you quite well?

HIGGINS [*choking*]. Am I — [*He can say no more.*]

LIZA. But of course you are: you are never ill. So glad to see you again, Colonel Pickering. [*He rises hastily; and they shake hands.*] Quite chilly this morning, isn't it? [*She sits down on his left. He sits beside her.*]

HIGGINS. Dont you dare try this game on me. I taught it to you; and it doesnt take me in. Get up and come home; and dont be a fool.

>ELIZA *takes a piece of needlework from her basket, and begins to stitch at it, without taking the least notice of this outburst.*

MRS. HIGGINS. Very nicely put, indeed, Henry. No woman could resist such an invitation.

HIGGINS. You let her alone, mother. Let her speak for herself. You will jolly soon see whether she has an idea that I havnt put into her head or a word that I havnt put into her mouth. I tell you I have created this thing out of the squashed cabbage leaves of Covent Garden; and now she pretends to play the fine lady with me.

MRS. HIGGINS [*placidly*]. Yes, dear; but youll sit down, wont you?

HIGGINS *sits down again, savagely.*

LIZA [*to* PICKERING, *taking no apparent notice of* HIGGINS, *and working away deftly*]. Will you drop me altogether now that the experiment is over, Colonel Pickering?

PICKERING. Oh dont. You mustnt think of it as an experiment. It shocks me, somehow.

LIZA. Oh, I'm only a squashed cabbage leaf —

PICKERING [*impulsively*]. No.

LIZA [*continuing quietly*]. — but I owe so much to you that I should be very unhappy if you forgot me.

PICKERING. It's very kind of you to say so, Miss Doolittle.

LIZA. It's not because you paid for my dresses. I know you are generous to everybody with money. But it was from you that I learnt really nice manners; and that is what makes one a lady, isnt it? You see it was so very difficult for me with the example of Professor Higgins always before me. I was brought up to be just like him, unable to control myself, and using bad language on the slightest provocation. And I should never have known that ladies and gentlemen didnt behave like that if you hadnt been there.

HIGGINS. Well!!

PICKERING. Oh, thats only his way, you know. He doesnt mean it.

LIZA. Oh, *I* didnt mean it either, when I was a flower girl. It was only my way. But you see I did it; and thats what makes the difference after all.

PICKERING. No doubt. Still, he taught you to speak; and I couldnt have done that, you know.

LIZA [*trivially*]. Of course: that is his profession.

HIGGINS. Damnation!

LIZA [*continuing*]. It was just like learning to dance in the fashionable way: there was nothing more than that in it. But do you know what began my real education?

PICKERING. What?

LIZA [*stopping her work for a moment*]. Your calling me Miss Doolittle that day when I first came to Wimpole Street. That was the beginning of self-respect for me. [*She resumes her stitching.*] And there were a hundred little things you never noticed, because they came naturally to you. Things about standing up and taking off your hat and opening doors —

PICKERING. Oh, that was nothing.

LIZA. Yes: things that shewed you thought and felt about me as if I were something better than a scullery-maid; though of course I know you would have been just the same to a scullery-maid if she had been let into the drawing room. You never took off your boots in the dining room when I was there.

PICKERING. You mustnt mind that. Higgins takes off his boots all over the place.

LIZA. I know. I am not blaming him. It is his way, isnt it? But it made such a difference to me that you didnt do it. You see, really and truly, apart from the things anyone can pick up (the dressing and the proper way of speaking, and so on), the difference between a lady and a flower girl is not how she behaves, but how she's treated. I shall always be a flower girl to Professor Higgins, because he always treats me as a flower girl, and always will; but I know I can be a lady to you, because you always treat me as a lady, and always will.

MRS. HIGGINS. Please dont grind your teeth, Henry.

PICKERING. Well, this is really very nice of you, Miss Doolittle.

LIZA. I should like you to call me Eliza, now, if you would.

PICKERING. Thank you. Eliza, of course.

LIZA. And I should like Professor Higgins to call me Miss Doolittle.

HIGGINS. I'll see you damned first.

MRS. HIGGINS. Henry! Henry!

PICKERING [*laughing*]. Why dont you slang back at him? Dont stand it. It would do him a lot of good.

LIZA. I cant. I could have done it once; but now I cant go back to it. Last night, when I was wandering about, a girl spoke to me; and I tried to get back into the old way with her; but it was no use. You told me, you know, that when a child is brought to a foreign country, it picks up the language in a few weeks, and forgets its own. Well, I am a child in your country. I have forgotten my own language, and can speak nothing but yours. Thats the real break-off with the corner of Tottenham Court Road. Leaving Wimpole Street finishes it.

PICKERING [*much alarmed*]. Oh! but youre coming back to Wimpole Street, arnt you? Youll forgive Higgins?

HIGGINS [*rising*]. Forgive! Will she, by George! Let her go. Let her find out how she can get on without us. She will relapse into the gutter in three weeks without me at her elbow.

> DOOLITTLE *appears at the centre window. With a look of dignified reproach at* HIGGINS, *he comes slowly and silently to his daughter, who, with her back to the window, is unconscious of his approach.*

PICKERING. He's incorrigible, Eliza. You wont relapse, will you?

LIZA. No: not now. Never again. I have learnt my lesson. I dont believe I could utter one of the old sounds if I tried. [DOOLITTLE *touches her on her left shoulder. She drops her work, losing her self-possession utterly at the spectacle of her father's splendor.*] A-a-a-a-ah-ow-ooh!

HIGGINS [*with a crow of triumph*]. Aha! Just so. A-a-a-a-ahowooh! A-a-a-a-ahowooh! A-a-a-a-ahowooh! Victory! Victory! [*He throws himself on the divan, folding his arms, and spraddling arrogantly.*]

DOOLITTLE. Can you blame the girl? Dont look at me like that, Eliza. It aint my fault. Ive come into some money.

LIZA. You must have touched a millionaire this time, dad.

DOOLITTLE. I have. But I'm dressed something special today. I'm going to St. George's, Hanover Square. Your stepmother is going to marry me.

LIZA [*angrily*]. Youre going to let yourself down to marry that low common woman!

PICKERING [*quietly*]. He ought to, Eliza. [*To* DOOLITTLE.] Why has she changed her mind?

DOOLITTLE [*sadly*]. Intimidated, Governor. Intimidated. Middle class morality claims its victim. Wont you put on your hat, Liza, and come and see me turned off?

LIZA. If the Colonel says I must, I—I'll [*almost sobbing*] I'll demean myself. And get insulted for my pains, like enough.

DOOLITTLE. Dont be afraid: she never comes to words with anyone now, poor woman! respectability has broke all the spirit out of her.

PICKERING [*squeezing* ELIZA's *elbow gently*]. Be kind to them, Eliza. Make the best of it.

LIZA [*forcing a little smile for him through her vexation*]. Oh well, just to shew theres no ill feeling. I'll be back in a moment. [*She goes out.*]

DOOLITTLE [*sitting down beside* PICKERING]. I feel uncommon nervous about the ceremony, Colonel. I wish youd come and see me through it.

PICKERING. But youve been through it before, man. You were married to Eliza's mother.

DOOLITTLE. Who told you that, Colonel?

PICKERING. Well, nobody told me. But I concluded—naturally—

DOOLITTLE. No: that aint the natural way, Colonel: it's only the middle class way. My way was always the undeserving way. But dont say nothing to Eliza. She dont know: I always had a delicacy about telling her.

PICKERING. Quite right. We'll leave it so, if you dont mind.

DOOLITTLE. And youll come to the church, Colonel, and put me through straight?

PICKERING. With pleasure. As far as a bachelor can.

MRS. HIGGINS. May I come, Mr. Doolittle? I should be very sorry to miss your wedding.

DOOLITTLE. I should indeed be honored by your condescension, maam; and my poor old woman would take it as a tremenjous compliment. She's been very low, thinking of the happy days that are no more.

MRS. HIGGINS [*rising*]. I'll order the carriage and get ready. [*The men rise, except* HIGGINS.] I shant be more than fifteen minutes. [*As she goes to the door* ELIZA *comes in, hatted and buttoning her gloves.*] I'm going to the church to see your father married, Eliza. You had better come in the brougham with me. Colonel Pickering can go on with the bridegroom.

MRS. HIGGINS *goes out.* ELIZA *comes to the middle of the room between the centre window and the ottoman.* PICKERING *joins her.*

DOOLITTLE. Bridegroom! What a word! It makes a man realize his position, somehow. [*He takes up his hat and goes towards the door.*]

PICKERING. Before I go, Eliza, do forgive him and come back to us.

LIZA. I dont think papa would allow me. Would you, dad?

DOOLITTLE [*sad but magnanimous*]. They played you off very cunning, Eliza, them two sportsmen. If it had been only one of them, you could have nailed him. But you see, there was two; and one of them chaperoned the other, as you might say. [*To* PICKERING.] It was artful of you, Colonel; but I bear no malice: I should have done the same myself. I been the victim of one woman after another all my life; and I dont grudge you two getting the better of Eliza. I shant interfere. It's time for us to go, Colonel. So long, Henry. See you in St. George's, Eliza. [*He goes out.*]

PICKERING [*coaxing*]. Do stay with us, Eliza. [*He follows* DOO-LITTLE.]

ELIZA *goes out on the balcony to avoid being alone with* HIGGINS. *He rises and joins her there. She immediately comes back into the room and makes for the door; but he goes along the balcony quickly and gets his back to the door before she reaches it.*

HIGGINS. Well, Eliza, youve had a bit of your own back, as you call it. Have you had enough? and are you going to be reasonable? Or do you want any more?

LIZA. You want me back only to pick up your slippers and put up with your tempers and fetch and carry for you.

HIGGINS. I havnt said I wanted you back at all.

LIZA. Oh, indeed. Then what are we talking about?

HIGGINS. About you, not about me. If you come back I shall treat you just as I have always treated you. I cant change my nature; and I dont intend to change my manners. My manners are exactly the same as Colonel Pickering's.

LIZA. Thats not true. He treats a flower girl as if she was a duchess.

HIGGINS. And I treat a duchess as if she was a flower girl.

LIZA. I see. [*She turns away composedly, and sits on the ottoman, facing the window.*] The same to everybody.

HIGGINS. Just so.

LIZA. Like father.

HIGGINS [*grinning, a little taken down*]. Without accepting the comparison at all points, Eliza, it's quite true that your father is not a snob, and that he will be quite at home in any station of life to which his eccentric destiny may call him. [*Seriously.*] The great secret, Eliza, is not having bad manners or good manners or any other particular sort of manners, but having the same manner for all human souls: in short, behaving as if you were in Heaven, where there are no third-class carriages, and one soul is as good as another.

LIZA. Amen. You are a born preacher.

HIGGINS [*irritated*]. The question is not whether I treat you rudely, but whether you ever heard me treat anyone else better.

LIZA [*with sudden sincerity*]. I dont care how you treat me. I dont mind your swearing at me. I dont mind a black eye: Ive had one before this. But [*standing up and facing him*] I wont be passed over.

HIGGINS. Then get out of my way; for I wont stop for you. You talk about me as if I were a motor bus.

LIZA. So you are a motor bus: all bounce and go, and no consideration for anyone. But I can do without you: dont think I cant.

HIGGINS. I know you can. I told you you could.

LIZA [*wounded, getting away from him to the other side of the ottoman with her face to the hearth*]. I know you did, you brute. You wanted to get rid of me.

HIGGINS. Liar.

LIZA. Thank you. [*She sits down with dignity.*]

HIGGINS. You never asked yourself, I suppose, whether *I* could do without you.

LIZA [earnestly]. Dont you try to get round me. Youll have to do without me.

HIGGINS [*arrogant*]. I can do without anybody. I have my own soul: my own spark of divine fire. But [*with sudden humility*] I shall miss you, Eliza. [*He sits down near her on the ottoman.*] I have learnt something from your idiotic notions: I confess that humbly and gratefully. And I have grown accustomed to your voice and appearance. I like them, rather.

LIZA. Well, you have both of them on your gramophone and in your book of photographs. When you feel lonely without me, you can turn the machine on. It's got no feelings to hurt.

HIGGINS. I cant turn your soul on. Leave me those feelings; and you can take away the voice and the face. They are not you.

LIZA. Oh, you are a devil. You can twist the heart in a girl as easy as some could twist her arms to hurt her. Mrs. Pearce warned me. Time and again she has wanted to leave you; and you always got round her at the last minute. And you dont care a bit for her. And you dont care a bit for me.

HIGGINS. I care for life, for humanity; and you are a part of it that has come my way and been built into my house. What more can you or anyone ask?

LIZA. I wont care for anybody that doesnt care for me.

HIGGINS. Commercial principles, Eliza. Like [*reproducing her Covent Garden pronunciation with professional exactness*] s'yollin voylets (selling violets), isn't it?

LIZA. Dont sneer at me. It's mean to sneer at me.

HIGGINS. I have never sneered in my life. Sneering doesnt become either the human face or the human soul. I am expressing my righteous contempt for Commercialism. I dont and wont trade in affection. You call me a brute because you couldnt buy a claim on me by fetching my slippers and finding my spectacles. You were a fool: I think a woman fetching a man's slippers is a disgusting sight: did I ever fetch your slippers? I think a good deal more of you for throwing them in my face. No use slaving for me and then saying you want to be cared for: who cares for a slave? If you come back, come back for the sake of good fellowship; for youll get nothing else. Youve had a thousand times as much out of me as I have out of you; and if you dare to set up your little dog's tricks of fetching and carrying slippers against my creation of a Duchess Eliza, I'll slam the door in your silly face.

LIZA. What did you do it for if you didnt care for me?

HIGGINS [*heartily*]. Why, because it was my job.

LIZA. You never thought of the trouble it would make for me.

HIGGINS. Would the world ever have been made if its maker had been afraid of making trouble? Making life means making trouble. Theres only one way of escaping trouble; and thats killing things. Cowards, you notice, are always shrieking to have troublesome people killed.

LIZA. I'm no preacher: I dont notice things like that. I notice that you dont notice me.

HIGGINS [*jumping up and walking about intolerantly*]. Eliza: youre an idiot. I waste the treasures of my Miltonic mind by spreading them before you. Once for all, understand that I go my way and do my work without caring twopence what happens to either of us. I am not intimidated, like your father and your stepmother. So you can come back or go to the devil: which you please.

LIZA. What am I to come back for?

HIGGINS [*bouncing up on his knees on the ottoman and leaning over it to her*]. For the fun of it. Thats why I took you on.

LIZA [*with averted face*]. And you may throw me out to-morrow if I dont do everything you want me to?

HIGGINS. Yes; and you may walk out to-morrow if I dont do everything you want me to.

LIZA. And live with my stepmother?

HIGGINS. Yes, or sell flowers.

LIZA. Oh! if I could go back to my flower basket! I should be independent of both you and father and all the world! Why did you take my independence from me? Why did I give it up? I'm a slave now, for all my fine clothes.

HIGGINS. Not a bit. I'll adopt you as my daughter and settle money on you if you like. Or would you rather marry Pickering?

LIZA [*looking fiercely round at him*]. I wouldnt marry you if you asked me; and youre nearer my age than what he is.

HIGGINS [*gently*]. Than he is: not "than what he is."

LIZA [*losing her temper and rising*]. I'll talk as I like. Youre not my teacher now.

HIGGINS [*reflectively*]. I dont suppose Pickering would, though. He's as confirmed an old bachelor as I am.

LIZA. Thats not what I want; and dont you think it. Ive always had chaps enough wanting me that way. Freddy Hill writes to me twice and three times a day, sheets and sheets.

HIGGINS [*disagreeably surprised*]. Damn his impudence! [*He recoils and finds himself sitting on his heels.*]

LIZA. He has a right to if he likes, poor lad. And he does love me.

HIGGINS [*getting off the ottoman*]. You have no right to encourage him.

LIZA. Every girl has a right to be loved.

HIGGINS. What! By fools like that?

LIZA. Freddy's not a fool. And if he's weak and poor and wants me, may be he'd make me happier than my betters that bully me and dont want me.

HIGGINS. Can he make anything of you? Thats the point.

LIZA. Perhaps I could make something of him. But I never thought of us making anything of one another; and you never think of anything else. I only want to be natural.

HIGGINS. In short, you want me to be as infatuated about you as Freddy? Is that it?

LIZA. No I dont. Thats not the sort of feeling I want from you. And dont you be too sure of yourself or of me. I could have been a bad girl if I'd liked. Ive seen more of some things than you, for all your learning. Girls like me can drag gentlemen down to make love to them easy enough. And they wish each other dead the next minute.

HIGGINS. Of course they do. Then what in thunder are we quarrelling about?

LIZA [*much troubled*]. I want a little kindness. I know I'm a common ignorant girl, and you a book-learned gentleman; but I'm not dirt under your feet. What I done [*correcting herself*] what I did was not for the dresses and the taxis: I did it because we were pleasant together and I come — came — to care for you; not to want you to make love to me, and not forgetting the difference between us, but more friendly like.

HIGGINS. Well, of course. Thats just how I feel. And how Pickering feels. Eliza: youre a fool.

LIZA. Thats not a proper answer to give me. [*She sinks on the chair at the writing-table in tears.*]

HIGGINS. It's all youll get until you stop being a common idiot. If youre going to be a lady, youll have to give up feeling neglected if the men you know dont spend half their time snivelling over you and the other half giving you black eyes. If you cant stand the coldness of my sort of life, and the strain of it, go back to the gutter. Work til you are more a brute than a human being; and then cuddle and squabble and drink til you fall asleep. Oh, it's a fine life, the life of the gutter. It's real: it's warm: it's violent: you can feel it through the thickest skin: you can taste it and smell it without any training or any work. Not like Science and Literature and Classical Music and Philosophy and Art. You find me cold, unfeeling, selfish, dont you? Very well: be off with you to the sort of people you like. Marry some sentimental hog or other with lots of money, and a thick pair of lips to kiss you with and a thick pair of boots to kick you with. If you cant appreciate what youve got, youd better get what you can appreciate.

LIZA [*desperate*]. Oh, you are a cruel tyrant. I cant talk to you: you turn everything against me: I'm always in the wrong. But you know very well all the time that youre nothing but a bully. You know I cant go back to the gutter, as you call it, and that I have no real friends in the world but you and the Colonel. You know well I couldnt bear to live with a low common man after

you two; and it's wicked and cruel of you to insult me by
pretending I could. You think I must go back to Wimpole
Street because I have nowhere else to go but father's. But dont
you be too sure that you have me under your feet to be trampled on and talked down. I'll marry Freddy, I will, as soon as
he's able to support me.

HIGGINS [*sitting down beside her*]. Rubbish! you shall marry an
ambassador. You shall marry the Governor-General of India
or the Lord-Lieutenant of Ireland, or somebody who wants a
deputy-queen. I'm not going to have my masterpiece thrown
away on Freddy.

LIZA. You think I like you to say that. But I havnt forgot what
you said a minute ago; and I wont be coaxed round as if I was
a baby or a puppy. If I cant have kindness, I'll have independence.

HIGGINS. Independence? Thats middle class blasphemy. We are
all dependent on one another, every soul of us on earth.

LIZA [*rising determinedly*]. I'll let you see whether I'm dependent
on you. If you can preach, I can teach. I'll go and be a teacher.

HIGGINS. Whatll you teach, in heaven's name?

LIZA. What you taught me. I'll teach phonetics.

HIGGINS. Ha! ha! ha!

LIZA. I'll offer myself as an assistant to Professor Nepean.

HIGGINS [*rising in fury*]. What! That imposter! that humbug!
that toadying ignoramus! Teach him my methods! my
discoveries! You take one step in his direction and I'll wring
your neck. [*He lays hands on her.*] Do you hear?

LIZA [*defiantly non-resistant*]. Wring away. What do I care? I
knew youd strike me some day. [*He lets her go, stamping with
rage at having forgotten himself, and recoils so hastily that he
stumbles back into his seat on the ottoman.*] Aha! Now I know
how to deal with you. What a fool I was not to think of it
before! You cant take away the knowledge you gave me. You
said I had a finer ear than you. And I can be civil and kind to
people, which is more than you can. Aha! Thats done you,
Henry Higgins, it has. Now I dont care that [*snapping her
fingers*] for your bullying and your big talk. I'll advertize it in
the papers that your duchess is only a flower girl that you

taught, and that she'll teach anybody to be a duchess just the same in six months for a thousand guineas. Oh, when I think of myself crawling under your feet and being trampled on and called names, when all the time I had only to lift up my finger to be as good as you, I could just kick myself.

HIGGINS [*wondering at her*]. You damned impudent slut, you! But it's better than snivelling; better than fetching slippers and finding spectacles, isnt it? [*Rising.*] By George, Eliza, I said I'd make a woman of you; and I have. I like you like this.

LIZA. Yes: you turn round and make up to me now that I'm not afraid of you, and can do without you.

HIGGINS. Of course I do, you little fool. Five minutes ago you were like a millstone round my neck. Now youre a tower of strength: a consort battleship. You and I and Pickering will be three old bachelors together instead of only two men and a silly girl.

MRS. HIGGINS *returns, dressed for the wedding.* ELIZA *instantly becomes cool and elegant.*

MRS. HIGGINS. The carriage is waiting, Eliza. Are you ready?

LIZA. Quite. Is the Professor coming?

MRS. HIGGINS. Certainly not. He cant behave himself in church. He makes remarks out loud all the time on the clergyman's pronunciation.

LIZA. Then I shall not see you again, Professor. Goodbye. [*She goes to the door.*]

MRS. HIGGINS [*coming to* HIGGINS]. Goodbye, dear.

HIGGINS. Goodbye, mother. [*He is about to kiss her, when he recollects something.*] Oh, by the way, Eliza, order a ham and a Stilton cheese, will you? And buy me a pair of reindeer gloves, number eights, and a tie to match that new suit of mine, at Eale & Binman's. You can choose the color. [*His cheerful, careless, vigorous voice shows that he is incorrigible.*]

LIZA [*disdainfully*]. Buy them yourself. [*She sweeps out.*]

MRS. HIGGINS. I'm afraid youve spoiled that girl, Henry. But never mind, dear: I'll buy you the tie and gloves.

HIGGINS [*sunnily*]. Oh, dont bother. She'll buy em all right enough. Goodbye.

They kiss. MRS. HIGGINS *runs out.* HIGGINS, *left alone, rattles his cash in his pockets; chuckles; and disports himself in a highly self-satisfied manner.*

*   *   *   *

The rest of the story need not be shewn in action, and indeed, would hardly need telling if our imaginations were not so enfeebled by their lazy dependence on the ready-mades and reach-me-downs of the ragshop in which Romance keeps its stock of "happy endings" to misfit all stories. Now, the history of ELIZA DOOLITTLE, though called a romance because the transfiguration it records seems exceedingly improbable, is common enough. Such transfigurations have been achieved by hundreds of resolutely ambitious young women since Nell Gwynne set them the example by playing queens and fascinating kings in the theatre in which she began by selling oranges. Nevertheless, people in all directions have assumed, for no other reason than that she became the heroine of a romance, that she must have married the hero of it. This is unbearable, not only because her little drama, if acted on such a thoughtless assumption, must be spoiled, but because the true sequel is patent to anyone with a sense of human nature in general, and of feminine instinct in particular.

Eliza, in telling Higgins she would not marry him if he asked her, was not coquetting: she was announcing a well-considered decision. When a bachelor interests, and dominates, and teaches, and becomes important to a spinster, as Higgins with Eliza, she always, if she has character enough to be capable of it, considers very seriously indeed whether she will play for becoming that bachelor's wife, especially if he is so little interested in marriage that a determined and devoted woman might capture him if she set herself resolutely to do it. Her decision will depend a good deal on whether she is really free to choose; and that, again, will depend on her age and income. If she is at the end of her youth, and has no security for her livelihood, she will marry him because she must marry anybody who will provide for her. But at Eliza's age a good-looking girl does not feel that pressure: she feels free to pick and choose. She is therefore guided by her instinct in the matter. Eliza's instinct tells her not to marry Higgins. It does not tell her to give him up. It is not in the slightest doubt as to his remaining one of the strongest personal interests in her life. It would be very sorely strained if there was another woman likely to supplant her with him. But as she feels sure of him on that last point, she has no doubt at all as to her course, and would not have any, even if the difference of twenty years in age, which seems so great to youth, did not exist between them.

As our own instincts are not appealed to by her conclusion, let us see whether we cannot discover some reason in it. When Higgins excused his indifference to young women on the ground that they had an irresistible rival in his mother, he gave the clue to his inveterate old-bachelordom. The case is uncommon only to the extent that remarkable mothers are uncommon. If an imaginative boy has a sufficiently rich mother who has intelligence, personal grace, dignity of character without harshness, and a cultivated sense of the best art of her time to enable her to make her house beautiful, she sets a standard for him against which very few women can struggle, besides effecting for him a disengagement of his affections, his sense of beauty, and his idealism from his specifically sexual impulses. This makes him a standing puzzle to the huge number of uncultivated people who have been brought up in tasteless homes by commonplace or disagreeable parents, and to whom, consequently, literature, painting, sculpture, music, and affectionate personal relations come as modes of sex if they come at all. The word passion means nothing else to them; and that Higgins could have a passion for phonetics and idealize his mother instead of Eliza, would seem to them absurd and unnatural. Nevertheless, when we look round and see that hardly anyone is too ugly or disagreeable to find a wife or a husband if he or she wants one, whilst many old maids and bachelors are above the average in quality and culture, we cannot help suspecting that the disentanglement of sex from the associations with which it is so commonly confused, a disentanglement which persons of genius achieve by sheer intellectual analysis, is sometimes produced or aided by parental fascination.

Now, though Eliza was incapable of thus explaining to herself Higgins's formidable powers of resistance to the charm that prostrated Freddy at the first glance, she was instinctively aware that she could never obtain a complete grip of him, or come between him and his mother (the first necessity of the married woman). To put it shortly, she knew that for some mysterious reason he had not the makings of a married man in him, according to her conception of a husband as one to whom she would be his nearest and fondest and warmest interest. Even had there been no mother-rival, she would still have refused to accept an interest in herself that was secondary to philosophic interests. Had Mrs. Higgins died, there would still have been Milton and the Universal Alphabet. Landor's remark that to those who have the greatest power of loving, love is a secondary affair, would not have recommended Landor to Eliza. Put that along with her resentment of Higgins's domineering superiority, and her mistrust of his coaxing cleverness in getting round her and evading her wrath when he had gone too far with his impetuous bullying, and you will see that Eliza's instinct had good grounds for warning her not to marry her Pygmalion.

And now, whom did Eliza marry? For if Higgins was a predestinate old bachelor, she was most certainly not a predestinate old maid. Well, that can be told very shortly to those who have not guessed it from the indications she has herself given them.

Almost immediately after Eliza is stung into proclaiming her considered determination not to marry Higgins, she mentions the fact that young Mr. Frederick Eynsford Hill is pouring out his love for her daily through the post. Now Freddy is young, practically twenty years younger than Higgins: he is a gentleman (or, as Eliza would qualify him, a toff), and speaks like one; he is nicely dressed, is treated by the Colonel as an equal, loves her unaffectedly, and is not her master, nor ever likely to dominate her in spite of his advantage of social standing. Eliza has no use for the foolish romantic tradition that all women love to be mastered, if not actually bullied and beaten. "When you go to women," says Nietzsche, "take your whip with you." Sensible despots have never confined that precaution to women: they have taken their whips with them when they have dealt with men, and been slavishly idealized by the men over whom they have flourished the whip much more than by women. No doubt there are slavish women as well as slavish men: and women, like men, admire those that are stronger than themselves. But to admire a strong person and to live under that strong person's thumb are two different things. The weak may not be admired and hero-worshipped; but they are by no means disliked or shunned; and they never seem to have the least difficulty in marrying people who are too good for them. They may fail in emergencies; but life is not one long emergency: it is mostly a string of situations for which no exceptional strength is needed, and with which even rather weak people can cope if they have a stronger partner to help them out. Accordingly, it is a truth everywhere in evidence that strong people, masculine or feminine, not only do not marry stronger people, but do not shew any preference for them in selecting their friends. When a lion meets another with a louder roar "the first lion thinks the last a bore." The man or woman who feels strong enough for two, seeks for every other quality in a partner than strength.

The converse is also true. Weak people want to marry strong people who do not frighten them too much; and this often leads them to make the mistake we describe metaphorically as "biting off more than they can chew." They want too much for too little; and when the bargain is unreasonable beyond all bearing, the union becomes impossible: it ends in the weaker party being either discarded or borne as a cross, which is worse. People who are not only weak, but silly or obtuse as well, are often in these difficulties.

This being the state of human affairs, what is Eliza fairly sure to do when she is placed between Freddy and Higgins? Will she look forward to a lifetime of fetching Higgins's slippers or to a lifetime of Freddy fetching hers? There can be no doubt about the answer. Unless Freddy is biologically repulsive to her, and Higgins biologically attractive to a degree that overwhelms all her other instincts, she will, if she marries either of them, marry Freddy.

And that is just what Eliza did.

Complications ensued; but they were economic, not romantic. Freddy had no money and no occupation. His mother's jointure, a last relic of the opulence of Largelady Park, had enabled her to struggle along in Earlscourt with an air of gentility, but not to procure any serious secondary education for her children, much less give the boy a profession. A clerkship at thirty shillings a week was beneath Freddy's dignity, and extremely distasteful to him besides. His prospects consisted of a hope that if he kept up appearances somebody would do something for him. The something appeared vaguely to his imagination as a private secretaryship or a sinecure of some sort. To his mother it perhaps appeared as a marriage to some lady of means who could not resist her boy's niceness. Fancy her feelings when he married a flower girl who had become déclassée under extraordinary circumstances which were now notorious!

It is true that Eliza's situation did not seem wholly ineligible. Her father, though formerly a dustman, and now fantastically disclassed, had become extremely popular in the smartest society by a social talent which triumphed over every prejudice and every disadvantage. Rejected by the middle class, which he loathed, he had shot up at once into the highest circles by his wit, his dustmanship (which he carried like a banner), and his Nietzschean transcendence of good and evil. At intimate ducal dinners he sat on the right hand of the Duchess; and in country houses he smoked in the pantry and was made much of by the butler when he was not feeding in the dining room and being consulted by cabinet ministers. But he found it almost as hard to do all this on four thousand a year as Mrs. Eynsford Hill to live in Earlscourt on an income so pitiably smaller that I have not the heart to disclose its exact figure. He absolutely refused to add the last straw to his burden by contributing to Eliza's support.

Thus Freddy and Eliza, now Mr. and Mrs. Eynsford Hill, would have spent a penniless honeymoon but for a wedding present of £500 from the Colonel to Eliza. It lasted a long time because Freddy did not know how to spend money, never having had any to spend, and Eliza, socially trained by a pair of old bachelors, wore her clothes as long as they held together and looked pretty, without the least regard to their being many months out of fashion. Still, £500 will not last two young people for ever; and they both knew, and Eliza felt as well, that they must shift for themselves in the end. She could quarter herself on Wimpole Street because it had come to be her home; but she was quite aware that she ought not to quarter Freddy there, and that it would not be good for his character if she did.

Not that the Wimpole Street bachelors objected. When she consulted them, Higgins declined to be bothered about her housing problem when that solution was so simple. Eliza's desire to have Freddy in the house with her seemed of no more importance than if she had wanted an extra piece of bedroom furniture. Pleas as to Freddy's character, and the moral obligation on him to earn his own living, were lost on Higgins. He denied that Freddy had any character, and declared that if he tried to do any useful work some competent person would have the trouble of undoing it: a procedure involving a net loss to the community, and great unhappiness to Freddy himself, who was obviously intended by Nature for such light work as amusing Eliza, which, Higgins declared, was a much more useful and honorable occupation than working in the city. When Eliza referred again to her project of teaching phonetics, Higgins abated not a jot of his violent opposition to it. He said she was not within ten years of being qualified to meddle with his pet subject; and as it was evident that the Colonel agreed with him, she felt she could not go against them in this grave matter, and that she had no right, without Higgins's consent, to exploit the knowledge he had given her; for his knowledge seemed to her as much his private property as his watch: Eliza was no communist. Besides, she was superstitiously devoted to them both, more entirely and frankly after her marriage than before it.

It was the Colonel who finally solved the problem, which had cost him much perplexed cogitation. He one day asked Eliza, rather shyly, whether she had quite given up her notion of keeping a flower shop. She replied that she had thought of it, but had put it out of her head, because the Colonel had said, that day at Mrs. Higgins's, that it would never do. The Colonel confessed that when he said that, he had not quite recovered from the dazzling impression of the day before. They broke the matter to Higgins that evening. The sole comment vouchsafed by him very nearly led to a serious quarrel with Eliza. It was to the effect that she would have in Freddy an ideal errand boy.

Freddy himself was next sounded on the subject. He said he had been thinking of a shop himself; though it had presented itself to his pennilessness as a small place in which Eliza should sell tobacco at one counter whilst he sold newspapers at the opposite one. But he agreed that it would be extraordinarily jolly to go early every morning with Eliza to Covent Garden and buy flowers on the scene of their first meeting: a sentiment which earned him many kisses from his wife. He added that he had always been afraid to propose anything of the sort, because Clara would make an awful row about a step that must damage her matrimonial chances, and his mother could not be expected to like it after clinging for so many years to that step of the social ladder on which retail trade is impossible.

This difficulty was removed by an event highly unexpected by Freddy's mother. Clara, in the course of her incursions into those artistic circles which were the highest within her reach, discovered that her conversational qualifications were expected to include a grounding in the novels of Mr. H.G. Wells. She borrowed them in various directions so energetically that she swallowed them all within two months. The result was a conversion of a kind quite common today. A modern Acts of the Apostles would fill fifty whole Bibles if anyone were capable of writing it.

Poor Clara, who appeared to Higgins and his mother as a disagreeable and ridiculous person, and to her own mother as in some inexplicable way a social failure, had never seen herself in either light; for, though to some extent ridiculed and mimicked in West Kensington like everybody else there, she was accepted as a rational and normal — or shall we say inevitable? — sort of human being. At worst they called her The Pusher; but to them no more than to herself had it ever occurred that she was pushing the air, and pushing it in a wrong direction. Still, she was not happy. She was growing desperate. Her one asset, the fact that her mother was what the Epsom greengrocer called a carriage lady, had no exchange value, apparently. It had prevented her from getting educated, because the only education she could have afforded was education with the Earlscourt greengrocer's daughter. It had led her to seek the society of her mother's class; and that class simply would not have her, because she was much poorer then the greengrocer, and, far from being able to afford a maid, could not afford even a housemaid, and had to scrape along at home with an illiberally treated general servant. Under such circumstances nothing could give her an air of being a genuine product of Largelady Park. And yet its tradition made her regard a marriage with anyone within her reach as an unbearable humiliation. Commercial people and professional people in a small way were odious to her. She ran after painters and novelists; but she did not charm them; and her bold attempts to pick up and practice artistic and literary talk irritated them. She was, in short, an utter failure, an ignorant, incompetent, pretentious, unwelcome, penniless, useless little snob; and though she did not admit these disqualifications (for nobody ever faces unpleasant truths of this kind until the possibility of a way out dawns on them) she felt their effects too keenly to be satisfied with her position.

Clara had a startling eyeopener when, on being suddenly wakened to enthusiasm by a girl of her own age who dazzled her and produced in her a gushing desire to take her for a model, and gain her friendship, she discovered that this exquisite apparition had graduated from the gutter in a few months time. It shook her so violently, that when Mr. H.G. Wells lifted her on the point of his puissant pen, and placed her at the angle of view from which the life she was leading and the society to which she clung appeared in its true relation to real human needs and worthy social structure, he effected a conversion and a conviction of sin comparable to the most sensational feats of General Booth or Gypsy Smith. Clara's snobbery went bang. Life suddenly began to move with her. Without knowing how or why, she began to make friends and enemies. Some of the acquaintances to whom she had been a tedious or indifferent or ridiculous affliction, dropped her: others became cordial. To her amazement she found that some "quite nice" people were saturated with Wells, and that this accessibility to ideas was the secret of their niceness. People she had thought deeply religious, and had tried to conciliate on that tack with disastrous results, suddenly took an interest in her, and revealed a hostility to conventional religion which she had never conceived possible except among the most desperate characters. They made her read Galsworthy; and Galsworthy exposed the vanity of Largelady Park and finished her. It exasperated her to think that the dungeon in which she had languished for so many unhappy years had been unlocked all the time, and that the impulses she had so carefully struggled with and stifled for the sake of keeping well with society, were precisely those by which alone she could have come into any sort of sincere human contact. In the radiance of these discoveries, and the tumult of their reaction, she made a fool of herself as freely and conspicuously as when she so rashly adopted Eliza's expletive in Mrs. Higgins's drawing room; for the newborn Wellsian had to find her bearings almost as ridiculously as a baby; but nobody hates a baby for its ineptitudes, or thinks the worse of it for trying to eat the matches; and Clara lost no friends by her follies. They laughed at her to her face this time; and she had to defend herself and fight it out as best she could.

When Freddy paid a visit to Earlscourt (which he never did when he could possibly help it) to make the desolating announcement that he and his Eliza were thinking of blackening the Largelady scutcheon by opening a shop, he found the little household already convulsed by a prior announcement from Clara that she also was going to work in an old furniture shop in Dover Street, which had been started by a fellow Wellsian. This appointment Clara owed, after all, to her old social accomplishment of Push. She had made up her mind that, cost what it might, she would see Mr. Wells in the flesh; and she had achieved her end at a garden' party. She had better luck than so rash an enterprise deserved. Mr. Wells came up to her expectations. Age had not withered him, nor could custom stale his infinite variety in half an hour. His pleasant neatness and compactness, his small hands and feet, his teeming ready brain, his unaffected accessibility, and a certain fine apprehensiveness which stamped him as susceptible from his topmost hair to his tipmost toe, proved irresistible. Clara talked of nothing else for weeks and weeks afterwards. And as she happened to talk to the lady of the furniture shop, and that lady also desired above all things to know Mr. Wells and sell pretty things to him, she offered Clara a job on the chance of achieving that end through her.

And so it came about that Eliza's luck held, and the expected opposition to the flower shop melted away. The shop is in the arcade of a railway station not very far from the Victoria and Albert Museum; and if you live in that neighborhood you may go there any day and buy a buttonhole from Eliza.

Now here is a last opportunity for romance. Would you not like to be assured that the shop was an immense success, thanks to Eliza's charms and her early business experience in Covent Garden? Alas! the truth is the truth: the shop did not pay for a long time, simply because Eliza and her Freddy did not know how to keep it. True, Eliza had not to begin at the very beginning: she knew the names and prices of the cheaper flowers; and her elation was unbounded when she found that Freddy, like all youths educated at cheap, pretentious, and thoroughly inefficient schools, knew a little Latin. It was very little, but enough to make him appear to her a Porson or Bentley, and to put him at his ease with botanical nomenclature. Unfortunately he knew nothing else; and Eliza, though she could count money up to eighteen shillings or so, and had acquired a certain familiarity with the language of Milton from her struggles to qualify herself for winning Higgins's bet, could not write out a bill without utterly disgracing the establishment. Freddy's power of stating in Latin that Balbus built a wall and that Gaul was divided into three parts did not carry with it the slightest knowledge of accounts or business: Colonel Pickering had to explain to him what a cheque book and a bank account meant. And the pair were by no means easily teachable. Freddy backed up Eliza in her obstinate refusal to believe that they could save money by engaging a bookkeeper with some knowledge of the business. How, they argued, could you possibly save money by going to extra expense when you already could not make both ends meet? But the Colonel, after making the ends meet over and over again, at last gently insisted; and Eliza, humbled to the dust by having to beg from him so often, and stung by the uproarious derision of Higgins, to whom the notion of Freddy succeeding at anything was a joke that never palled, grasped the fact that business, like phonetics, has to be learned.

On the piteous spectacle of the pair spending their evenings in shorthand schools and polytechnic classes, learning bookkeeping and typewriting with incipient junior clerks, male and female, from the elementary schools, let me not dwell. There were even classes at the London School of Economics, and a humble personal appeal to the director of that institution to recommend a course bearing on the flower business. He, being a humorist, explained to them the method of the celebrated Dickensian essay on Chinese Metaphysics by the gentleman who read an article on China and an article on Metaphysics and combined the information. He suggested that they should combine the London School with Kew Gardens. Eliza, to whom the procedure of the Dickensian gentleman seemed perfectly correct (as in fact it was) and not in the least funny (which was only her ignorance), took his advice with entire gravity. But the effort that cost her the deepest humiliation was a request to Higgins, whose pet artistic fancy, next to Milton's verse, was calligraphy, and who himself wrote a most beautiful Italian hand, that he would teach her to write. He declared that she was congenitally incapable of forming a single letter worthy of the least of Milton's words; but she persisted; and again he suddenly threw himself into the task of teaching her with a combination of stormy intensity, concentrated patience, and occasional bursts of interesting disquisition on the beauty and nobility, the august mission and destiny, of human handwriting. Eliza ended by acquiring an extremely uncommercial script which was a positive extension of her personal beauty, and spending three times as much on stationery as anyone else because certain qualities and shapes of paper became indispensable to her. She could not even address an envelope in the usual way because it made the margins all wrong.

Their commercial schooldays were a period of disgrace and despair for the young couple. They seemed to be learning nothing about flower shops. At last they gave it up as hopeless, and shook the dust of the shorthand schools, and the polytechnics, and the London School of Economics from their feet for ever. Besides, the business was in some mysterious way beginning to take care of itself. They had somehow forgotten their objections to employing other people. They came to the conclusion that their own way was the best, and that they had really a remarkable talent for business. The Colonel, who had been compelled for some years to keep a sufficient sum on current account at his bankers to make up their deficits, found that the provision was unnecessary: the young people were prospering. It is true that there was not quite fair play between them and their competitors in trade. Their week-ends in the country cost them nothing, and saved them the price of their Sunday dinners; for the motor car was the Colonel's; and he and Higgins paid the hotel bills. Mr. F. Hill, florist and greengrocer (they soon discovered that there was money in asparagus; and asparagus led to other vegetables), had an air which stamped the business as classy; and in private life he was still Frederick Eynsford Hill, Esquire. Not that there was any swank about him: nobody but Eliza knew that he had been christened Frederick Challoner. Eliza herself swanked like anything.

That is all. That is how it has turned out. It is astonishing how much Eliza still manages to meddle in the housekeeping at Wimpole Street in spite of the shop and her own family. And it is notable that though she never nags her husband, and frankly loves the Colonel as if she were his favorite daughter, she has never got out of the habit of nagging Higgins that was established on the fatal night when she won his bet for him. She snaps his head off on the faintest provocation, or on none. He no longer dares to tease her by assuming an abysmal inferiority of Freddy's mind to his own. He storms and bullies and derides: but she stands up to him so ruthlessly that the Colonel has to ask her from time to time to be kinder to Higgins; and it is the only request of his that brings a mulish expression into her face. Nothing but some emergency or calamity great enough to break down all likes and dislikes, and throw them both back on their common humanity -— and may they be spared any such trial! — will ever alter this. She knows that Higgins does not need her, just as her father did not need her. The very scrupulousness with which he told her that day that he had become used to having her there, and dependent on her for all sorts of little services, and that he should miss her if she went away (it would never have occurred to Freddy or the Colonel to say anything of the sort) deepens her inner certainty that she is "no more to him than them slippers''; yet she has a sense, too, that his indifference is deeper than the infatuation of commoner souls. She is immensely interested in him. She has even secret mischievous moments in which she wishes she could get him alone, on a desert island, away from all ties and with nobody else in the world to consider, and just drag him off his pedestal and see him making love like any common man. We all have private imaginations of that sort. But when it comes to business, to the life that she really leads as distinguished from the life of dreams and fancies, she likes Freddy and she likes the Colonel; and she does not like Higgins and Mr Doolittle. Galatea never does quite like Pygmalion: his relation to her is too godlike to be altogether agreeable.

Pygmalion

Springboard

1. George Bernard Shaw was a fascinating human being who held interesting and unconventional ideas about everything from English spelling to political and economic systems. Find out what you can about Shaw, and examine how your new knowledge changes your reading of *Pygmalion.*

2. Shaw's title refers to a Greek myth about an artist who fell in love with a statue he had sculpted. Higgins claims that he has been able to "take a human being and change her into quite a different human being by creating a new speech for her." In what ways does Shaw's play follow the myth? In what ways does the play break with the myth? (You might also be interested in comparing the myth and the play with the subsequent musical version, *My Fair Lady.*)

3. Shaw's original version of *Pygmalion* (reprinted in this text) was strictly a stage play. In 1930, he "corrected" the play, making small changes in the dialogue, adding scenes suitable for film or for stages with elaborate mechanical apparatus, and altering the wording but not the sense of the ending. Find a copy of the later version of the play and compare it with the original version. How has Shaw's addition of scenes changed the structure of the play? Have any of the changes been thematic ones? Has Shaw changed any of the characters? Have his alterations made *Pygmalion* a better play? Why or why not?

(Act One)

4. Speech — the selection of words and their pronunciation — is the culprit Higgins identifies to Pickering as responsible for keeping lower-class "upstarts" trapped. In a class-conscious society such as Higgins describes, what specific changes allow a person mobility, and how far-reaching must these changes be?

5. Eliza resents slurs on her character. She constantly asserts that her rights, her morals, her sense of propriety are the same as those of any "lady." She says she is a "good girl" and knows how a gentleman should behave towards a lady. What does she mean? What can be gathered about her values from

what we see of her here? How acute is her business sense? How good a saleswoman is she? Is she weak or helpless?

(Act Two)

6.   Take a close look at Higgins' laboratory, as described in the stage directions. What can you learn about the man from observing this workroom?

7.   We learn from Mrs. Pearce's scolding of Higgins that he is as capable of bad language and slovenly habits as Eliza, that upper-class breeding does not automatically insure good social behavior and sensitivity to others' feelings. (Examine carefully the adjectives "good" and "bad" in the preceding sentence!) What do you suppose Shaw sees as the important differences between social classes?

8.   Mrs. Pearce argues that Higgins should look to the future when making decisions that will affect the lives of others. In other words, he should consider the broad consequences of his actions. He replies, "Do any of us understand what we are doing? If we did, would we ever do it?" How valid is his answer?

9.   This act presents a series of value systems, some peculiar to a class (Doolittle's description of himself as one of the "undeserving poor" beset upon by middle-class morality), some that cut across classes (the essential worth of any human being). What kinds of value systems do you think ennoble the human spirit? What kinds demean it?

10.   How does Shaw get us to approve of a situation in which an unmarried young girl lives with two bachelors? Would we want Eliza returned to the curb in Covent Garden or to her father's care? What convinces us that the alternative − staying in Higgins' house − is far better for Eliza? Why do we believe that she will not be compromised or taken advantage of?

(Act Three)

11.   What does Henry's relationship with his mother show us of his character? How does he behave in her presence? If you were a psychiatrist or a family therapist, what might you conclude?

12. Is Higgins' manner of address to the Eynsford Hills any different from his manner of address to Eliza or his mother? Why or why not?

13. Mrs. Higgins' "at home" presents us with a clash between form and substance, appearance and reality. Eliza's bearing, voice modulation, and pronunciation are clearly inappropriate to the subject of her conversation. What other examples of disharmony do we see at this gathering? Should we find this scene funny, painful, or what?

14. Is there a significant difference, during the "at home," between the genuineness of Eliza's subject matter and that of Higgins? Whose *outward* bearing and comportment is more suitable for Mrs. Higgins' polite company, Eliza's or Henry's?

15. Clara Eynsford Hill wishes people would "be frank and say what they really think." Higgins responds that such honesty would be disastrous. Do you agree with him? What evidence does the play offer us in supporting or refuting Higgins' position?

(Act Four)

16. Eliza asks, "What's to become of me?" In order to answer, we need also ask what has become of her so far. How different is she from the Eliza in Act One who wanted to talk like a fine lady so she could work in a flower shop? Pickering has already offered to set Eliza up in her own shop, so what does she really mean when she asks what is to become of her?

17. A word often used in connection with Henry Higgins is *careless*. He is careless of manners, dress, swearing, eating, etc. What is there that he does *care* deeply about? How does he "care" for people?

18. Eliza says to Higgins, "There can't be any feelings between the like of you and the like of me." What does she mean? Higgins tells her, "You have wounded me to the heart." How is such a thing possible, if Higgins disregards the importance of feelings? Precisely what is the nature of the feelings these two people have for each other?

(Act Five)

19. Why are Higgins and Pickering upset over Eliza's disappearance? They do not share the same feelings toward her; what is the difference?

20. What has happened to change Doolittle's life and his place in society? Why has Doolittle allowed himself to be intimidated by "middle-class morality"? What does being intimidated mean to Doolittle? How does he define middle-class morality? Does society really have differing moralities for separate classes? How might the class structure and morality of Pygmalion's England differ from those of our own time and place?

21. As in Act One, the three men — Higgins, Pickering, and Doolittle — once again discuss values: economic, social, moral. How do changes come about in one's system of values? Use Eliza, Doolittle, and the Eynsford Hills as examples in presenting your reply; be sure to distinguish between the external and the internal nature of values.

22. When Eliza appears, she is "sunny, self-possessed, and giving a staggeringly convincing exhibition of ease of manner." Higgins immediately reproaches her for trying a "game" on him. What is the game he has in mind? What specifically is the nature of games, and why does Higgins use that word to describe Eliza's manner? What sort of manner would Higgins approve of from Eliza?

23. Eliza says that Pickering taught her really nice manners and that "that is what makes one a lady, isn't it?" Is she right? When she explains that she began to have respect for herself because Pickering treated her with respect, does she mean that the Eliza we saw in Act One had no self-respect. What does Eliza mean here by *respect?* Why does she feel that Higgins shows her little respect?

24. Eliza argues that she wants only a little show of kindness from Higgins, some recognition of the tenderness of feelings. In truth, she craves some display of regard that would signify she is special to him. How does Higgins justify the impossibility for him of treating anyone in a "special" way? Think your way through his position carefully; do you accept it yourself?

25. Keeping in mind the serious discussion between Eliza and Higgins, explain the ending of the play. What — if anything — has been resolved?

The Hairy Ape

Introduction

Eugene O'Neill (1888-1953) is America's pre-eminent dramatist, in part because he virtually invented serious American theatre all by himself. That is a phenomenal achievement, but when we also consider the tremendous creative energy, the technical artistry, and the incessant experimentation that marked his career, then we can understand why O'Neill is the one American playwright to date who possesses a world-wide reputation. Often marred by faults − awkwardly lumbering, intellectually inchoate, heavy-handed, excessive − his plays nonetheless carry a passionate intensity, a relentless turbulence, a sweeping power that can quite simply leave the theatregoer awed and drained.

O'Neill's achievement looms even larger when we contemplate the wreckage of his own life. Born in a Broadway hotel room, he grew up on the move; his parents, itinerant actors and unstable individuals, were hardly able to provide the home he needed. Aside from his sole comedy, *Ah, Wilderness!* (1933), O'Neill drew on his own dismal experience to fashion art out of life. Nowhere is this more obvious than in the autobiographical (and interminable!) *Long Day's Journey into Night* (1956), which he banned from performance until after his death.

O'Neill was plagued by three bad marriages, the suicide of his eldest son, severe alcoholism, and a series of physical ailments which culminated in Parkinson's disease. Perhaps this last blow was the most devastating, for O'Neill fell silent once the tremor in his hands became too violent for him to hold a pencil. Strangely enough, all attempts to type or dictate his work failed; it seems that O'Neill absolutely had to have the physical contact of pencil on paper. He was unable to put a play on Broadway during the dozen years between *Days without End* (1934) and *The Iceman Cometh* (1946), and in 1949 he finally conceded that no more work could be expected of him.

Among O'Neill's notable excursions into symbolism, expressionism, and psychologically subjective drama are *The Emperor Jones* (1920), *Anna Christie* (1921), *Desire under the Elms* (1924), *The Great God Brown* (1926), *Strange Interlude* (1928), and *Mourning Becomes Electra* (1931). Some of the finest expressionism and symbolism in America drama is to be found in *The Hairy Ape* (1922). O'Neill won Pulitzer Prizes in 1920, 1922, and 1928; he was awarded the Nobel Prize in 1936.

THE HAIRY APE

*A Comedy of Ancient and Modern
Life in Eight Scenes*

by Eugene O'Neill

CHARACTERS

ROBERT SMITH, "YANK"
PADDY
LONG
MILDRED DOUGLAS
HER AUNT
SECOND ENGINEER
A GUARD
A SECRETARY OF AN ORGANIZATION
STOKERS, LADIES, GENTLEMEN, ETC.

SCENES

Scene I

[*The firemen's forecastle of a transatlantic liner an hour after sailing from New York for the voyage across. Tiers of narrow, steel bunks, three deep, on all sides. An entrance in rear. Benches on the floor before the bunks. The room is crowded with men, shouting, cursing, laughing, singing — a confused, inchoate uproar swelling into a sort of unity, a meaning — the bewildered, furious, baffled defiance of a beast in a cage. Nearly all the men are drunk. Many bottles are passed from hand to hand. All are dressed in dungaree pants, heavy ugly shoes. Some wear singlets, but the majority are stripped to the waist.*

The treatment of this scene, or of any other scene in the play, should by no means be naturalistic. The effect sought after is a cramped space in the bowels of a ship, imprisoned by white steel. The lines of bunks, the uprights supporting them, cross each other like the steel framework of a cage. The ceiling crushes down upon the men's heads. They cannot stand upright. This accentuates the natural stooping posture which shoveling coal and the resultant overdevelopment of back and shoulder muscles have given them. The men themselves should resemble those pictures in which the appearance of Neanderthal Man is guessed at. All are hairy-chested, with long arms of tremendous power, and low, receding brows above their small, fierce, resentful eyes. All the civilized white races are represented, but except for the slight differentiation in color of hair, skin, eyes, all these men are alike.

The curtain rises on a tumult of sound. YANK *is seated in the foreground. He seems broader, fiercer, more truculent, more powerful, more sure of himself than the rest. They respect his superior strength — the grudging respect of fear. Then, too, he represents to them a self-expression, the very last word in what they are, their most highly developed individual.*]

VOICES. Gif me trink dere, you!
  'Ave a wet!
  Salute!
  Gesundheit!
  Skoal!
  Drunk as a lord, God stiffen you!
  Here's how!

Luck!
Pass back that bottle, damn you!
Pourin' it down his neck!
Ho, Froggy! Where the devil have
    you been?
La Touraine.
I hit him smash in yaw, py Gott!
Jenkins — the First — he's a rotten
    swine —
And the coppers nabbed him — and I
    run —
I like peer better. It don't pig head
    gif you.
A slut, I'm sayin'. She robbed me
    aslape —
To hell with 'em all!
You're a bloody liar!
Say dot again! [*Commotion. Two
men about to fight are pulled apart.*]
No scrappin' now!
Tonight —
See who's the best man!
Bloody Dutchman!
Tonight on the for'ard square.
I'll bet on Dutchy.
He packa da wallop, I tell you!
Shut up, Wop!
No fightin', maties. We're all chums,
    ain't we?
[*A voice starts bawling a song.*]
"Beer, beer, glorious beer!
Fill yourselves right up to here."

YANK [*For the first time seeming to take notice of the uproar
    about him, turns around threateningly — in a tone of con-
    temptuous authority*]. Choke off dat noise! Where d'yuh get
    dat beer stuff? Beer, hell! Beer's for goils — and Dutchmen.
    Me for somep'n wit a kick to it! Gimme a drink, one of youse
    guys. [*Several bottles are eagerly offered. He takes a tremen-
    dous gulp at one of them; then, keeping the bottle in his hand,
    glares belligerently at the owner, who hastens to acquiesce in
    this robbery by saying*] All righto, Yank. Keep it and have
    another. [YANK *contemptuously turns his back on the crowd*

again. For a second there is an embarrassed silence. Then —]

VOICES. We must be passing the Hook.
    She's beginning to roll to it.
    Six days in hell — and then Southampton.
    Py Yesus, I vish somepody take my
        first vatch for me!
    Gittin' seasick, Square-head?
    Drink up and forget it!
    What's in your bottle?
    Gin.
    Dot's a nigger trink.
    Absinthe? It's doped. You'll go off
        your chump, Froggy!
    Cochon!
    Whisky, that's the ticket!
    Where's Paddy?
    Going asleep.
    Sing us that whisky song, Paddy.

[They all turn to an old, wizened Irishman who is dozing, very drunk, on the benches forward. His face is extremely monkey-like with all the sad, patient pathos of that animal in his small eyes.]

        Singa da song, Caruso Pat!
        He's gettin' old. The drink is too
            much for him.
        He's too drunk.

PADDY [*Blinking about him, starts to his feet resentfully, swaying, holding on to the edge of a bunk*]. I'm never too drunk to sing. 'Tis only when I'm dead to the world I'd be wishful to sing at all. [*With a sort of sad contempt.*] "Whisky Johnny," ye want? A chanty, ye want? Now that's a queer wish from the ugly like of you. God help you. But no mather, [*He starts to sing in a thin, nasal, doleful tone.*]

    "Oh, whisky is the life of man!
      Whisky! O Johnny! [*They all join in on this.*]
    Oh, whisky is the life of man!
      Whisky for my Johnny! [*Again chorus.*]
    Oh, whisky drove my old man mad!
      Whisky! O Johnny!
    Oh, whisky drove my old man mad!
      Whisky for my Johnny!"

YANK [*Again turning around scornfully*]. Aw hell! Nix on dat old
sailing ship stuff! All dat bull's dead, see? And you're dead,
too, yuh damned old Harp, on'y yuh don't know it. Take it
easy, see. Give us a rest. Nix on de loud noise. [*With a cynical
grin.*] Can't youse see I'm tryin' to t'ink?

ALL [*Repeating the word after him as one with the same cynical
amused mockery*]. Think! [*The chorused word has a brazen
metallic quality as if their throats were phonograph horns. It is
followed by a general uproar of hard, barking laughter.*]

VOICES. Don't be cracking your head wit ut,
Yank.
You gat headache, py yingo!
One thing about it — it rhymes with
drink!
Ha, ha, ha!
Drink, don't think!
Drink, don't think!
Drink, don't think! [*A whole chorus of
voices has taken up this refrain,
stamping on the floor, pounding on
the benches with fists.*]

YANK [*Taking a gulp from his bottle — good-naturedly*]. Aw
right. Can de noise. I got yuh de foist time. [*The uproar subsides. A very drunken sentimental tenor begins to sing.*]

"Far away in Canada,
Far across the sea,
There's a lass who fondly waits
Making a home for me —"

YANK [*Fiercely contemptuous*]. Shut up, yuh lousy boob! Where
d'yuh get dat tripe? Home? Home, hell! I'll make a home for
yuh! I'll knock yuh dead. Home! T'hell wit home! Where
d'yuh get dat tripe? Dis is home, see? What d'yuh want wit
home? [*Proudly.*] I runned away from mine when I was a kid.
On'y too glad to beat it, dat was me. Home was lickings for
me, dat's all. But yuh can bet your shoit no one ain't never
licked me since! Wanter try it, any of youse? Huh! I guess not.
[*In a more placated but still contemptuous tone.*] Goils waitin'
for yuh, huh? Aw, hell! Dat's all tripe. Dey don't wait for no
one. Dey'd double-cross yuh for a nickel. Dey're all tarts, get
me? Treat 'em rough, dat's me. To hell wit 'em. Tarts, dat's
what, de whole bunch of 'em.

LONG [*Very drunk, jumps on a bench excitedly, gesticulating with a bottle in his hand*]. Listen 'ere, Comrades. Yank 'ere is right. 'E says this 'ere stinkin' ship is our 'ome. And 'e says as 'ome is 'ell. And 'e's right! This is 'ell. We lives in 'ell, Comrades — and right enough we'll die in it. [*Raging.*] And who's ter blame, I arsks yer? We ain't. We wasn't born this rotten way. All men is born free and ekal. That's in the bleedin' Bible, maties. But what d'they care for the Bible — them lazy, bloated swine what travels first cabin? Them's the ones. They dragged us down 'til we're on'y wage slaves in the bowels of a bloody ship, sweatin', burnin' up, eatin' coal dust! Hit's them's ter blame — the damned Capitalist clarss! [*There had been a gradual murmur of contemptuous resentment rising among the men until now he is interrupted by a storm of cat-calls, hisses, boos, hard laughter.*]

VOICES. Turn it off!
  Shut up!
  Sit down!
  Closa da face!
  Tamn fool! [*Etc.*]

YANK [*Standing up and glaring at* LONG]. Sit down before I knock yuh down! [LONG *makes haste to efface himself.* YANK *goes on contemptuously.*] De Bible, huh? De Cap'tlist class, huh? Aw nix on dat Salvation Army-Socialist bull. Git a soapbox! Hire a hall! Come and be saved, huh? Jerk us to Jesus, huh? Aw g'wan! I've listened to lots of guys like you, see. Yuh're all wrong. Wanter know what I t'ink? Yuh ain't no good for no one. Yuh're de bunk. Yuh ain't got no noive, get me? Yuh're yellow, dat's what. Yellow, dat's you. Say! What's dem slobs in de foist cabin got to do wit us? We're better men dan dey are, ain't we? Sure! One of us guys could clean up de whole mob wit one mit. Put one of 'em down here for one watch in de stokehole, what'd happen? Dey'd carry him off on a stretcher. Dem boids don't amount to nothin'. Dey're just baggage. Who makes dis old tub run? Ain't it us guys? Well den, we belong, don't we? We belong and dey don't. Dat's all. [*A loud chorus of approval.* YANK *goes on.*] As for dis bein' hell — aw, nuts! Yuh lost your noive, dat's what. Dis is a man's job, get me? It belongs. It runs dis tub. No stiffs need apply. But yuh're a stiff, see? Yuh're yellow, dat's you.

VOICES. [*With a great hard pride in them*].
    Righto!
    A man's job!
    Talk is cheap, Long.
    He never could hold up his end.
    Divil take him!
    Yank's right. We make it go.
    Py Gott, Yank say right ting!
    We don't need no one cryin' over us.
    Makin' speeches.
    Throw him out!
    Yellow!
    Chuck him overboard!
    I'll break his jaw for him!
    [*They crowd around* LONG *threateningly.*]

YANK [*Half good-natured again — contemptuously*]. Aw, take it
    easy. Leave him alone. He ain't woith a punch. Drink up.
    Here's how, whoever owns dis. [*He takes a long swallow from
    his bottle. All drink with him. In a flash all is hilarious
    amiability again, back-slapping, loud talk, etc.*]

PADDY [*Who has been sitting in a blinking, melancholy daze —
    suddenly cries out in a voice full of old sorrow*]. We belong to
    this, you're saying? We make the ship to go, you're saying?
    Yerra then, that Almighty God have pity on us! [*His voice runs
    into the wail of a keen, he rocks back and forth on his bench.
    The men stare at him, startled and impressed in spite of them-
    selves.*] Oh, to be back in the fine days of my youth, ochone!
    Oh, there was fine beautiful ships them days — clippers wid tall
    masts touching the sky — fine strong men in them — men that
    was sons of the sea as if 'twas the mother that bore them. Oh,
    the clean skins of them, and the clear eyes, the straight backs
    and full chests of them! Brave men they was, and bold men
    surely! We'd be sailing out, bound down round the Horn
    maybe. We'd be making sail in the dawn, with a fair breeze,
    singing a chanty song wid no care to it. And astern the land
    would be sinking low and dying out, but we'd give it no heed
    but a laugh, and never a look behind. For the day that was, was
    enough, for we was free men — and I'm thinking 'tis only slaves
    do be giving heed to the day that's gone or the day to come —
    until they're old like me. [*With a sort of religious exaltation.*]
    Oh, to be scudding south again wid the power of the Trade
    Wind driving her on steady through the nights and the days!

Full sail on her! Nights and days! Nights when the foam of the wake would be flaming wid fire, when the sky'd be blazing and winking wid stars. Or the full of the moon maybe. Then you'd see her driving through the gray night, her sails stretching aloft all silver and white, not a sound on the deck, the lot of us dreaming dreams, till you'd believe 'twas no real ship at all you was on but a ghost ship like the *Flying Dutchman* they say does be roaming the seas forevermore widout touching a port. And there was the days, too. A warm sun on the clean decks. Sun warming the blood of you, and wind over the miles of shiny green ocean like strong drink to your lungs. Work — aye, hard work — but who'd mind that at all? Sure, you worked under the sky and 'twas work wid skill and daring to it. And wid the day done, in the dog watch, smoking me pipe at ease, the look-out would be raising land maybe, and we'd see the mountains of South Americy wid the red fire of the setting sun painting their white tops and the clouds floating by them! [*His tone of exaltation ceases. He goes on mournfully.*] Yerra, what's the use of talking? 'Tis a dead man's whisper. [*To* YANK *resentfully.*] 'Twas them days men belonged to ships, not now. 'Twas them days a ship was part of the sea, and a man was part of a ship, and the sea joined all together and made it one. [*Scornfully.*] Is it one wid this you'd be, Yank — black smoke from the funnels smudging the sea, smudging the decks — the bloody engines pounding and throbbing and shaking — wid divil a sight of sun or a breath of clean air — choking our lungs wid coal dust — breaking our backs and hearts in the hell of the stokehole — feeding the bloody furnace — feeding our lives along wid the coal, I'm thinking — caged in by steel from a sight of the sky like bloody apes in the Zoo! [*With a harsh laugh.*] Ho-ho, divil mend you! Is it to belong to that you're wishing? Is it a flesh and blood wheel of the engines you'd be?

YANK [*Who has been listening with a contemptuous sneer, barks out the answer*]. Sure ting! Dat's me. What about it?

PADDY [*As if to himself — with great sorrow*]. Me time is past due. That a great wave wid sun in the heart of it may sweep me over the side sometime I'd be dreaming of the days that's gone!

YANK. Aw, yuh crazy Mick! [*He springs to his feet and advances on Paddy threateningly — then stops, fighting some queer struggle within himself — lets his hands fall to his sides — contemptuously.*] Aw, take it easy. Yuh're aw right, at dat. Yuh're bugs, dat's all — nutty as a cuckoo. All dat tripe yuh been pullin' — Aw, dat's all right. On'y it's dead, get me? Yuh don't belong no more, see. Yuh don't get de stuff. Yuh're too old. [*Disgustedly.*] But aw say, come up for air onct in a while, can't yuh? See what's happened since yuh croaked. [*He suddenly bursts forth vehemently, growing more and more excited.*] Say! Sure! Sure I meant it! What de hell — Say, lemme talk! Hey! Hey, you old Harp! Hey, youse guys! Say, listen to me — wait a moment — I gotta talk, see. I belong and he don't. He's dead but I'm livin'. Listen to me! Sure I'm part of de engines! Why de hell not? Dey move, don't dey? Dey're speed, ain't dey? Dey smash trou, don't dey? Twenty-five knots a hour! Dat's goin' some! Dat's new stuff! Dat belongs! But him, he's too old. He gets dizzy. Say, listen. All dat crazy tripe about nights and days; all dat crazy tripe about stars and moons; all dat crazy tripe about suns and winds, fresh air and de rest of it — Aw hell, dat's all a dope dream! Hittin' de pipe of de past, dat's what he's doin'. He's old and don't belong no more. But me, I'm young! I'm in de pink! I move wit it! It, get me! I mean de ting dat's de guts of all dis. It ploughs trou all de tripe he's been sayin'. It blows dat up! It knocks dat dead! It slams dat offen de face of de oith! It, get me! De engines and de coal and de smoke and all de rest of it! He can't breathe and swallow coal dust, but I kin, see? Dat's fresh air for me! Dat's food for me! I'm new, get me? Hell in de stokehole? Sure! It takes a man to work in hell. Hell, sure, dat's my fav'rite climate. I eat it up! I git fat on it! It's me makes it hot! It's me makes it roar! It's me makes it move! Sure, on'y for me everyting stops. It all goes dead, get me? De noise and smoke and all de engines movin' de woild, dey stop. Dere ain't nothin' no more! Dat's what I'm sayin'. Everyting else dat makes de woild move, somep'n makes it move. It can't move witout somep'n else, see? Den yuh get down to me. I'm at de bottom, get me! Dere ain't nothin' foither. I'm de end! I'm de start! I start somep'n and de woild moves! It — dat's me! — de new dat's moiderin' de old! I'm de ting in coal dat makes it boin; I'm steam and oil for de engines; I'm de ting in noise dat makes yuh hear it; I'm smoke and express trains and steamers and factory whistles; I'm de ting in gold dat makes money! And I'm what makes iron into steel! Steel, dat stands for de whole ting! And I'm steel — steel — steel! I'm de muscles in steel, de punch behind it. [*As he says this he pounds with his fist against the steel bunks. All the men, roused to a pitch of frenzied self-glorification by his speech, do likewise. There is a deafening metallic roar, through which* YANK'S *voice can be heard bellowing.*] Slaves, hell! We run de whole woiks. All de rich guys dat tink dey're somep'n, dey ain't nothin'! Dey don't belong. But us guys, we're in de move, we're at de bottom, de whole ting is us! [PADDY *from the start of* YANK'S *speech has been taking one gulp after another from his bottle, at first frightenedly, as if he were afraid to listen, then desperately, as if to drown his senses, but finally has achieved complete indifferent, even amused, drunkenness.* YANK *sees his lips moving. He quells the uproar with a shout.*] Hey, youse guys, take it easy! Wait a moment! De nutty Harp is sayin' somep'n.

PADDY [*Is heard now — throws his head back with a mocking burst of laughter*]. Ho-ho-ho-ho-ho —

YANK [*Drawing back his fist, with a snarl*]. Aw! Look out who yuh're givin' the bark!

PADDY [*Begins to sing "The Miller of Dee" with enormous good nature*].

> "I care for nobody, no, not I,
>   And nobody cares for me."

YANK [*Good-natured himself in a flash, interrupts* PADDY *with a slap on the bare back like a report*]. Dat's de stuff! Now yuh're gettin' wise to somep'n. Care for nobody, dat's de dope! To hell wit 'em all! And nix on nobody else carin'. I kin care for myself, get me! [*Eight bells sound, muffled, vibrating through the steel walls as if some enormous brazen gong were imbedded in the heart of the ship. All the men jump up mechanically, file through the door silently close upon each other's heels in what is very like a prisoners' lockstep.* YANK *slaps* PADDY *on the back.*] Our watch, yuh old Harp! [*Mockingly.*] Come on down in hell. Eat up de coal dust. Drink in de heat. It's it, see! Act like yuh like it, yuh better — or croak yuhself.

PADDY [*With jovial defiance*]. To the divil wid it! I'll not report this watch. Let thim log me and be damned. I'm no slave the like of you. I'll be sittin' here at me ease, and drinking, and thinking, and dreaming dreams.

YANK [*Contemptuously*]. Tinkin' and dreamin', what'll that get yuh? What's tinkin' got to do wit it? We move, don't we? Speed, ain't it? Fog, dat's all you stand for. But we drive trou dat, don't we? We split dat up and smash trou — twenty-five knots a hour! [*Turns his back on* PADDY *scornfully.*] Aw, yuh make me sick! Yuh don't belong! [*He strides out the door in rear. Paddy hums to himself, blinking drowsily.*]

[*The curtain falls.*]

Scene II

[*Two days out. A section of the promenade deck.* MILDRED DOUGLAS' *and her aunt are discovered reclining in deck chairs. The former is a girl of twenty, slender, delicate, with a pale, pretty face marred by a self-conscious expression of disdainful superiority. She looks fretful, nervous and discontented, bored by her own anemia. Her aunt is a pompous and proud — and fat — old lady. She is a type even to the point of a double chin and lorgnettes. She is dressed pretentiously as if afraid her face alone would never indicate her position in life.* MILDRED *is dressed all in white.*

The impression to be conveyed by this scene is one of the beautiful, vivid life of the sea all about — sunshine on the deck in a great flood, the fresh sea wind blowing across it. In the midst of all this, these two incongruous, artificial figures, inert and disharmonious, the elder like a gray lump of dough touched up with rouge, the younger looking as if the vitality of her stock had been sapped before she was conceived, so that she is the expression not of its life energy but merely of the artificialities that energy had won for itself in the spending.]

Nouveau-Riche

MILDRED [*Looking up with affected dreaminess*]. How the black smoke swirls back against the sky! Is it not beautiful?

AUNT [*Without looking up*]. I dislike smoke of any kind.

MILDRED. My great-grandmother smoked a pipe — a clay pipe.

AUNT [*Ruffling*]. Vulgar!

MILDRED. She was too distant a relative to be vulgar. Time mellows pipes.

AUNT [*Pretending boredom but irritated*]. Did the sociology you took up at college teach you that — to play the ghoul on every possible occasion, excavating old bones? Why not let your great-grandmother rest in her grave?

MILDRED [*Dreamily*]. With her pipe beside her — puffing in Paradise.

AUNT [*With spite*]. Yes, you are a natural born ghoul. You are even getting to look like one, my dear.

MILDRED [*In a passionless tone*]. I detest you, Aunt. [*Looking at her critically.*] Do you know what you remind me of? Of a cold pork pudding against a background of linoleum tablecloth in the kitchen of a — but the possibilities are wearisome. [*She closes her eyes.*]

AUNT [*With a bitter laugh*]. Merci for your candor. But since I am and must be your chaperon — in appearance — at least — let us patch up some sort of armed truce. For my part you are quite free to indulge any pose of eccentricity that beguiles you — as long as you observe the amenities — *social rules*

MILDRED [*Drawling*]. The inanities? *shallow rules*

AUNT [*Going on as if she hadn't heard*]. After exhausting the morbid thrills of social service work on New York's East Side — how they must have hated you, by the way, the poor that you made so much poorer in their own eyes! — you are now bent on making your slumming international. Well, I hope Whitechapel will provide the needed nerve tonic. Do not ask me to chaperon you there, however. I told your father I would not. I loathe deformity. We will hire an army of detectives and you may investigate everything — they allow you to see.

Honest
(cynical)
pessimism
w/
sarcasm

contrast
to
Yank

Yank :
pure
energy
mil :
waste

MILDRED [*Protesting with a trace of genuine earnestness*]. Please do not mock at my attempts to discover how the other half lives. Give me credit for some sort of groping sincerity in that at least. I would like to help them. I would like to be of some use in the world. Is it my fault I don't know how? I would like to be sincere, to touch life somewhere. [*With weary bitterness.*] But I'm afraid I have neither the vitality nor integrity. All that was burnt out in our stock before I was born. Grandfather's blast furnaces, flaming to the sky, melting steel, making millions — then father keeping those home fires burning, making more millions — and little me at the tail-end of it all. I'm a waste product in the Bessemer process — like the millions. Or rather, I inherit the acquired trait of the by-product, wealth, but none of the energy, none of the strength of the steel that made it. I am sired by gold and damned by it, as they say at the race track — damned in more ways than one. [*She laughs mirthlessly.*]

AUNT [*Unimpressed — superciliously*]. You seem to be going in for sincerity today. It isn't becoming to you, really — except as an obvious pose. Be as artificial as you are, I advise. There's a sort of sincerity in that, you know. And, after all, you must confess you like that better.

MILDRED [*Again affected and bored*]. Yes, I suppose I do. Pardon me for my outburst. When a leopard complains of its spots, it must sound rather grotesque. [*In a mocking tone.*] Purr, little leopard. Purr, scratch, tear, kill, gorge yourself and be happy — only stay in the jungle, where your spots are camouflage. In a cage they make you conspicuous.

AUNT. I don't know what you are talking about.

MILDRED. It would be rude to talk about anything to you. Let's just talk. [*She looks at her wrist watch.*] Well, thank goodness, it's about time for them to come for me. That ought to give me a new thrill, Aunt.

AUNT [*Affectedly troubled*]. You don't mean to say you're going? The dirt — the heat must be frightful —

MILDRED. Grandfather started as a puddler. I should have inherited an immunity to heat that would make a salamander shiver. It will be fun to put it to the test.

AUNT. But don't you have to have the captain's — or someone's — permission to visit the stokehole?

MILDRED [*With a triumphant smile*]. I have it — both his and the chief engineer's. Oh, they didn't want to at first, in spite of my social service credentials. They didn't seem a bit anxious that I should investigate how the other half lives and works on a ship. So I had to tell them that my father, the president of Nazareth Steel, chairman of the board of directors of this line, had told me it would be all right.

AUNT. He didn't.

MILDRED. How naive age makes one! But I said he did, Aunt. I even said he had given me a letter to them — which I had lost. And they were afraid to take the chance that I might be lying. [*Excitedly.*] So it's ho! for the stokehole. The second engineer is to escort me. [*Looking at her watch again.*] It's time. And here he comes, I think. [*The SECOND ENGINEER enters. He is a husky, fine-looking man of thirty-five or so. He stops before the two and tips his cap, visibly embarrassed and ill-at-ease.*]

SECOND ENGINEER. Miss Douglas?

MILDRED. Yes. [*Throwing off her rugs and getting to her feet.*] Are we all ready to start?

SECOND ENGINEER. In just a second, ma'am. I'm waiting for the Fourth. He's coming along.

MILDRED [*With a scornful smile*]. You don't care to shoulder this responsibility alone, is that it?

SECOND ENGINEER [*Forcing a smile*]. Two are better than one. [*Disturbed by her eyes, glances out to sea — blurts out.*] A fine day we're having.

MILDRED. Is it?

SECOND ENGINEER. A nice warm breeze —

MILDRED. It feels cold to me.

SECOND ENGINEER. But it's hot enough in the sun —

MILDRED. Not hot enough for me. I don't like Nature. I was never athletic.

SECOND ENGINEER [*Forcing a smile*]. Well, you'll find it hot enough where you're going.

MILDRED. Do you mean hell?

SECOND ENGINEER [*Flabbergasted, decides to laugh*]. Ho-ho! No, I mean the stokehole.

MILDRED. My grandfather was a puddler. He played with boiling steel.

SECOND ENGINEER [*All at sea — uneasily*]. Is that so? Hum, you'll excuse me, ma'am, but are you intending to wear that dress?

MILDRED. Why not?

SECOND ENGINEER. You'll likely rub against oil and dirt. It can't be helped.

MILDRED. It doesn't matter. I have lots of white dresses.

SECOND ENGINEER. I have an old coat you might throw over —

MILDRED. I have fifty dresses like this. I will throw this one into the sea when I come back. That ought to wash it clean, don't you think?

SECOND ENGINEER [*Doggedly*]. There's ladders to climb down that are none too clean — and dark alleyways —

MILDRED. I will wear this very dress and none other.

SECOND ENGINEER. No offense meant. It's none of my business. I was only warning you —

MILDRED. Warning? That sounds thrilling.

SECOND ENGINEER [*Looking down at the deck — with a sigh of relief*]. There's the Fourth now. He's waiting for us. If you'll come —

MILDRED. Go on. I'll follow you. [*He goes.* MILDRED *turns a mocking smile on her aunt.*] An oaf — but a handsome, virile oaf.

AUNT [*Scornfully*]. Poser!

MILDRED. Take care. He said there were dark alleyways —

AUNT [*In the same tone*]. Poser!

MILDRED [*Biting her lips angrily*]. You are right. But would that my millions were not so anemically chaste!

AUNT. Yes, for a fresh pose I have no doubt you would drag the name of Douglas in the gutter!

MILDRED. From which it sprang. Good-by, Aunt. Don't pray too hard that I may fall into the fiery furnace.

AUNT. Poser!

MILDRED [*Viciously*]. Old hag! [*She slaps her aunt insultingly across the face and walks off, laughing gaily.*]

AUNT [*Screams after her*]. I said poser!

[*The curtain falls.*]

Scene III

[*The stokehole. In the rear, the dimly-outlined bulks of the furnaces and boilers. High overhead one hanging electric bulb sheds just enough light through the murky air laden with coal dust to pile up masses of shadows everywhere. A line of men, stripped to the waist, is before the furnace doors. They bend over, looking neither to right nor left, handling their shovels as*

*if they were part of their bodies, with a strange, awkward,
swinging rhythm. They use the shovels to throw open the furnace doors. Then, from these fiery round holes in the black a
flood of terrific light and heat pours full upon the men who are
outlined in silhouette in the crouching, inhuman attitudes of
chained gorillas. The men shovel with a rhythmic motion,
swinging as on a pivot from the coal which lies in heaps on the
floor behind to hurl it into the flaming mouths before them.
There is a tumult of noise — the brazen clang of the furnace
doors as they are flung open or slammed shut, the grating,
teeth-gritting grind of steel against steel, of crunching coal. This
clash of sounds stuns one's ears with its rending dissonance. But
there is order in it, rhythm, a mechanical regulated recurrence, a
tempo. And rising above all, making the air hum with the quiver
of liberated energy, the roar of leaping flames in the furnaces,
the monotonous throbbing beat of the engines.*

*As the curtain rises, the furnace doors are shut. The men are
taking a breathing spell. One or two are arranging the coal
behind them, pulling it into more accessible heaps. The others
can be dimly made out leaning on their shovels in relaxed attitudes of exhaustion.*]

PADDY [*From somewhere in the line — plaintively*]. Yerra, will
this divil's own watch nivir end? Me back is broke. I'm
destroyed entirely.

YANK [*From the center of the line — with exuberant scorn*]. Aw,
yuh make me sick! Lie down and croak, why don't yuh?
Always beefin', dat's you! Say, dis is a cinch! Dis was made
for me! It's my meat, get me! [*A whistle is blown — a thin,
shrill note from somewhere overhead in the darkness. YANK
curses without resentment.*] Dere's de damn engineer crackin'
de whip. He tinks we're loafin'.

PADDY [*Vindictively*]. God stiffen him!

YANK [*In an exultant tone of command*]. Come on, youse guys!
Git into de game! She's gettin' hungry! Pile some grub in her.
Trow it into her belly! Come on now, all of youse! Open her up!
[*At this last all the men, who have followed his movements of
getting into position, throw open their furnace doors with a
deafening clang. The fiery light floods over their shoulders as
they bend round for the coal. Rivulets of sooty sweat have
traced maps on their backs. The enlarged muscles form bunches
of high light and shadow.*]

YANK [*Chanting a count as he shovels without seeming effort*].
One — two — tree — [*His voice rising exultantly in the joy of battle.*] Dat's de stuff! Let her have it! All togedder now! Sling it into her! Let her ride! Shoot de piece now! Call de toin on her! Drive her into it! Feel her move. Watch her smoke! Speed, dat's her middle name! Give her coal, youse guys! Coal, dat's her booze! Drink it up, baby! Let's see yuh sprint! Dig in and gain a lap! Dere she go-o-es. [*This last in the chanting formula of the galley gods at the six-day bike race. He slams his furnace door shut. The others do likewise with as much unison as their wearied bodies will permit. The effect is one fiery eye after another being blotted out with a series of accompanying bangs.*]

PADDY [*Groaning*]. Me back is broke. I'm bate out — bate — [*There is a pause. Then the inexorable whistle sounds again from the dim regions above the electric light. There is a growl of cursing rage from all sides.*]

YANK [*Shaking his fist upward — contemptuously*]. Take it easy dere, you! Who d'yuh tinks runnin' dis game, me or you? When I git ready, we move. Not before! When I git ready, get me!

VOICES [*Approvingly*].
That's the stuff!
Yank tal him, py golly!
Yank ain't afeerd.
Goot poy, Yank!
Give him hell!
Tell 'im 'e's a bloody swine!
Bloody slave-driver!

YANK [*Contemptuously*]. He ain't got no noive. He's yellow, get me? All de engineers is ·yellow. Dey got streaks a mile wide. Aw, to hell with him! Let's move, youse guys. We had a rest. Come on, she needs it! Give her pep! It ain't for him. Him and his whistle, dey don't belong. But we belong, see! We gotter feed de baby! Come on! [*He turns and flings his furnace door open. They all follow his lead. At this instant the* SECOND *and* FOURTH ENGINEERS *enter from the darkness on the left with* MILDRED *between them. She starts, turns paler, her pose is crumbling, she shivers with fright in spite of the blazing heat, but forces herself to leave the* ENGINEERS *and take a few steps near the men. She is right behind* YANK. *All this ·happens quickly while the men have their backs turned.*]

YANK. Come on, youse guys! [*He is turning to get coal when the whistle sounds again in a peremptory, irritating note. This drives* YANK *into a sudden fury. While the other men have turned full around and stopped dumbfounded by the spectacle of* MILDRED *standing there in her white dress,* YANK *does not turn far enough to see her. Besides, his head is thrown back, he blinks upward through the murk trying to find the owner of the whistle, he brandishes his shovel murderously over his head in one hand, pounding on his chest, gorilla-like, with the other, shouting.*] Toin off dat whistle! Come down outa dere, yuh yellow, brass-buttoned, Belfast bum, yuh! Come down and I'll knock yer brains out! Yuh lousy, stinkin, yellow mut of a Catholic-moiderin' bastard! Come down and I'll moider yuh! Pullin' dat whistle on me, huh? I'll show yuh! I'll crash yer skull in! I'll drive yer teet' down yer troat! I'll slam yer nose trou de back of yer head! I'll cut yer guts out for a nickel, yuh lousy boob, yuh dirty, crummy, muck-eatin' son of a — [*Suddenly he becomes conscious of all the other men staring at something directly behind his back. He whirls defensively with a snarling, murderous growl, crouching to spring, his lips drawn back over his teeth, his small eyes gleaming ferociously. He sees* MILDRED, *like a white apparition in the full light from the open furnace doors. He glares into her eyes, turned to stone. As for her, during his speech she has listened, paralyzed with horror, terror, her whole personality crushed, beaten in, collapsed, by the terrific impact of this unknown, abysmal brutality, naked and shameless. As she looks at his gorilla face, as his eyes bore into hers, she utters a low, choking cry and shrinks away from him, putting both hands up before her eyes to shut out the sight of his face, to protect her own. This startles* YANK *to a reaction. His mouth falls open, his eyes grow bewildered.*]

MILDRED [*About to faint — to the* ENGINEERS, *who now have her one by each arm — whimperingly*]. Take me away! Oh, the filthy beast! [*She faints. They carry her quickly back, disappearing in the darkness at the left, rear. An iron door clangs shut. Rage and bewildered fury rush back on* YANK. *He feels himself insulted in some unknown fashion in the very heart of his pride. He roars.*] God damn yuh! [*And hurls his shovel after them at the door which has just closed. It hits the steel bulkhead with a clang and falls clattering on the steel floor. From overhead the whistle sounds again in a long, angry, insistent command.*]

[*The curtain falls.*]

Scene IV

[*The firemen's forecastle.* YANK'S *watch has just come off duty and had dinner. Their faces and bodies shine from a soap and water scrubbing but around their eyes, where a hasty dousing does not touch, the coal dust sticks like black make-up, giving them a queer, sinister expression.* YANK *has not washed either face or body. He stands out in contrast to them, a blackened, brooding figure. He is seated forward on a bench in the exact attitude of Rodin's "The Thinker." The others, most of them smoking pipes, are staring at* YANK *half-apprehensively, as if fearing an outburst; half-amusedly, as if they saw a joke somewhere that tickled them.*]

VOICES. He ain't ate nothin'.
　　Py golly, a fallar gat to gat grub in him.
　　Divil a lie.
　　Yank feeda da fire, no feeda da face.
　　Ha-ha.
　　He ain't even washed hisself.
　　He's forgot.
　　Hey, Yank, you forgot to wash.

YANK [*Sullenly*]. Forgot nothin'! To hell wit washin'.

VOICES. It'll stick to you.
　　It'll get under your skin.
　　Give yer the bleedin' itch, that's wot.
　　It makes spots on you — like a leopard.
　　Like a piebald nigger, you mean.
　　Better wash up, Yank.
　　You sleep better.
　　Wash up, Yank.
　　Wash up! Wash up!

YANK [*Resentfully*]. Aw say, youse guys. Lemme alone. Can't youse see I'm tryin' to tink?

ALL [*Repeating the word after him as one with cynical mockery*]. Think! [*The word has a brazen, metallic quality as if their throats were phonograph horns. It is followed by a chorus of hard, barking laughter.*]

YANK [*Springing to his feet and glaring at them belligerently*]. Yes, tink! Tink, dat's what I said! What about it? [*They are silent, puzzled by his sudden resentment at what used to be one of his jokes.* YANK *sits down again in the same attitude of "The Thinker."*]

VOICES. Leave him alone.
He's got a grouch on.
Why wouldn't he?

PADDY [*With a wink at the others*]. Sure I know what's the matther. 'Tis aisy to see. He's fallen in love, I'm telling you.

ALL [*Repeating the word after him as one with cynical mockery*]. Love! [*The word has a brazen, metallic quality as if their throats were phonograph horns. It is followed by a chorus of hard, barking laughter.*]

YANK [*With a contemptuous snort*]. Love, hell! Hate, dat's what. I've fallen in hate, get me?

PADDY [*Philosophically*]. 'Twould take a wise man to tell one from the other. [*With a bitter, ironical scorn, increasing as he goes on.*] But I'm telling you it's love that's in it. Sure what else but love for us poor bastes in the stokehole would be bringing a fine lady, dressed like a white quane, down a mile of ladders and steps to be havin' a look at us? [*A growl of anger goes up from all sides.*]

LONG [*Jumping on a bench — hecticly*]. Hinsultin' us! Hinsultin' us, the bloody cow! And them bloody engineers! What right 'as they got to be exhibitin' us 's if we was bleedin' monkeys in a menagerie? Did we sign for hinsults to our dignity as 'onest workers? Is that in the ship's articles? You kin bloody well bet it ain't! But I knows why they done it. I arsked a deck steward 'o she was and 'e told me. 'Er old man's a bleedin' millionaire, a bloody Capitalist! 'E's got enuf bloody gold to sink this bleedin' ship! 'E makes arf the bloody steel in the world! 'E owns this bloody boat! And you and me, Comrades, we're 'is slaves! And the skipper and mates and engineers, they're 'is slaves! And she's 'is bloody daughter and we're all 'er slaves, too! And she gives 'er orders as 'ow she wants to see the bloody animals below decks and down they take 'er! [*There is a roar of rage from all sides.*]

YANK [*Blinking at him bewilderedly*]. Say! Wait a moment! Is all dat straight goods?

LONG. Straight as string! The bleedin' steward as waits on 'em, 'e told me about 'er. And what're we goin' ter do, I arsks yer? 'Ave we got ter swaller 'er hinsults like dogs? It ain't in the ship's articles. I tell yer we got a case. We kin go to law —

YANK [*With abysmal contempt*]. Hell! Law!

ALL [*Repeating the word after him as one with cynical mockery*]. Law! [*The word has a brazen metallic quality as if their throats were phonograph horns. It is followed by a chorus of hard, barking laughter.*]

LONG [*Feeling the ground slipping from under his feet — desperately*]. As voters and citizens we kin force the bloody governments —

YANK [*With abysmal contempt*]. Hell! Governments!

ALL [*Repeating the word after him as one with cynical mockery*]. Governments! [*The word has a brazen metallic quality as if their throats were phonograph horns. It is followed by a chorus of hard, barking laughter.*]

LONG [*Hysterically*]. We're free and equal in the sight of God —

YANK [*With abysmal contempt*]. Hell! God!

ALL [*Repeating the word after him as one with cynical mockery*]. God! [*The word has a brazen metallic quality as if their throats were phonograph horns. It is followed by a chorus of hard, barking laughter.*]

YANK [*Witheringly*]. Aw, join de Salvation Army!

ALL. Sit down! Shut up! Damn fool! Sea-lawyer! [LONG *slinks back out of sight.*]

PADDY [*Continuing the trend of his thoughts as if he had never been interrupted — bitterly*]. And there she was standing behind us, and the Second pointing at us like a man you'd hear in a circus would be saying: In this cage is a queerer kind of baboon than ever you'd find in darkest Africy. We roast them in their own sweat — and be damned if you won't hear some of thim saying they like it! [*He glances scornfully at* YANK.]

YANK [*With a bewildered uncertain growl*]. Aw!

PADDY. And there was Yank roarin' curses and turning round wid his shovel to brain her — and she looked at him, and him at her —

YANK [*Slowly*]. She was all white. I thought she was a ghost. Sure.

PADDY [*With heavy, biting sarcasm*]. 'Twas love at first sight, divil a doubt of it! If you'd seen the endearin' look on her pale mug when she shriveled away with her hands over her eyes to shut out the sight of him! Sure, 'twas as if she'd seen a great hairy ape escaped from the Zoo!

YANK [*Stung — with a growl of rage*]. Aw!

PADDY. And the loving way Yank heaved his shovel at the skull of her, only she was out the door! [*A grin breaking over his face.*] 'Twas touching, I'm telling you! It put the touch of home, swate home in the stokehole. [*There is a roar of laughter from all.*]

YANK [*Glaring at* PADDY *menacingly*]. Aw, choke dat off, see!

PADDY [*Not heeding him — to the others*]. And her grabbin' at the Second's arm for protection. [*With a grotesque imitation of a woman's voice.*] Kiss me, Engineer dear, for it's dark down here and me old man's in Wall Street making money! Hug me tight, darlin', for I'm afeerd in the dark and me mother's on deck makin' eyes at the skipper! [*Another roar of laughter.*]

YANK [*Threateningly*]. Say! What yuh tryin' to do, kid me, yuh old Harp?

PADDY. Divil a bit! Ain't I wishin' myself you'd brained her?

YANK [*Fiercely*]. I'll brain her! I'll brain her yet, wait 'n see! [*Coming over to* PADDY *slowly.*] Say, is dat what she called me — a hairy ape?

PADDY. She looked it at you if she didn't say the word itself.

YANK [*Grinning horribly*]. Hairy ape, huh? Sure! Dat's de way she looked at me, aw right! Hairy ape! So dat's me, huh? [*Bursting into rage — as if she were still in front of him.*] Yuh skinny tart! Yuh white-faced bum, yuh! I'll show yuh who's a ape! [*Turning to the others, bewilderment seizing him again.*] Say, youse guys. I was bawlin' him out for pullin' de whistle on us. You heard me. And den I seen youse lookin' at somep'n and I tought he'd sneaked down to come up in back of me, and I hopped round to knock him dead wit de shovel. And dere she was wit de light on her! Christ, yuh coulda pushed me over with a finger! I was scared, get me? Sure! I tought she was a ghost,

see? She was all in white like dey wrap around stiffs. You seen
her. Kin yuh blame me? She didn't belong, dat's what. And den
when I come to and seen it was a real skoit and seen de way she
was lookin' at me — like Paddy said — Christ, I was sore, get
me? I don't stand for dat stuff from nobody. And I flung de
shovel — on'y she'd beat it. [*Furiously.*] I wished it'd banged
her! I wished it'd knocked her block off!

LONG. And be 'anged for murder or 'lectrocuted? She ain't
bleedin' well worth it.

YANK. I don't give a damn what! I'd be square wit her, wouldn't
I? Tink I wanter let her put somep'n over on me? Tink I'm
goin' to let her git away wit dat stuff? Yuh don't know me! No
one ain't never put nothin' over on me and got away wit it,
see! — not dat kind of stuff — no guy and no skoit neither! I'll
fix her! Maybe she'll come down again —

VOICE. No chance, Yank. You scared her out of a year's growth.

YANK. I scared her? Why de hell should I scare her? Who de hell
is she? Ain't she de same as me? Hairy ape, huh? [*With his old
confident bravado.*] I'll show her I'm better'n her, if she on'y
knew it. I belong and she don't, see! I move and she's dead!
Twenty-five knots a hour, dat's me! Dat carries her but I make
dat. She's on'y baggage. Sure! [*Again bewilderedly.*] But,
Christ, she was funny lookin'! Did yuh pipe her hands? White
and skinny. Yuh could see de bones through 'em. And her
mush, dat was dead white, too. And her eyes, dey was like
dey'd seen a ghost. Me, dat was! Sure! Hairy ape! Ghost, huh?
Look at dat arm! [*He extends his right arm, swelling out the
great muscles.*] I coulda took her wit dat, wit' just my little
finger even, and broke her in two. [*Again bewilderedly.*] Say,
who is dat skoit, huh? What is she? What's she come from?
Who made her? Who give her de noive to look at me like dat?
Dis ting's got my goat right. I don't get her. She's new to me.
What does a skoit like her mean, huh? She don't belong, get
me! I can't see her. [*With growing anger.*] But one ting I'm
wise to, aw right, aw right! Youse all kin bet your shoits I'll git
even wit her. I'll show her if she tinks she — She grinds de
organ and I'm on de string, huh? I'll fix her! Let her come
down again and I'll fling her in de furnace! She'll move den!
She won't shiver at nothin' den! Speed, dat'll be her! She'll
belong den! [*He grins horribly.*]

PADDY. She'll never come. She's had her bellyfull, I'm telling

you. She'll be in bed now, I'm thinking, wid ten doctors and
nurses feedin' her salts to clean the fear out of her.

YANK [*Enraged*]. Yuh tink I made her sick, too, do yuh? Just
lookin' at me, huh? Hairy ape, huh? [*In a frenzy of rage.*] I'll
fix her! I'll tell her where to git off! She'll git down on her knees
and take it back or I'll bust de face offen her! [*Shaking one fist
upward and beating on his chest with the other.*] I'll find yuh!
I'm comin', d'yuh hear? I'll fix yuh, God damn yuh! [*He makes
a rush for the door.*]

VOICES. Stop him!
    He'll get shot!
    He'll murder her!
    Trip him up!
    Hold him!
    He's gone crazy!
    Gott, he's strong!
    Hold him down!
    Look out for a kick!
    Pin his arms!

[*They have all piled on him and, after a fierce struggle, by
sheer weight of numbers have borne him to the floor just inside
the door.*]

PADDY [*Who has remained detached*]. Kape him down till he's
cooled off. [*Scornfully.*] Yerra, Yank, you're a great fool. Is it
payin' attention at all you are to the like of that skinny sow
widout one drop of rale blood in her?

YANK [*Frenziedly, from the bottom of the heap*]. She's done me
doit! She done me doit, didn't she? I'll git square wit her! I'll
get her some way! Git offen me, youse guys! Lemme up! I'll
show her who's a ape!

[*The curtain falls.*]

Scene V

[*Three weeks later. A corner of Fifth Avenue in the Fifties on a
fine Sunday morning. A general atmosphere of clean, well-
tidied, wide street; a flood of mellow, tempered sunshine; gentle, genteel breezes. In the rear, the show windows of two shops,
a jewelry establishment on the corner, a furrier's next to it. Here*]

the adornments of extreme wealth are tantalizingly displayed. The jeweler's window is gaudy with glittering diamonds, emeralds, rubies, pearls, etc., fashioned in ornate tiaras, crowns, necklaces, collars, etc. From each piece hangs an enormous tag from which a dollar sign and numerals in intermittent electric lights wink out the incredible prices. The same in the furrier's. Rich furs of all varieties hang there bathed in a downpour of artificial light. The general effect is of a background of magnificence cheapened and made grotesque by commercialism, a background in tawdry disharmony with the clear light and sunshine on the street itself. Up the side street YANK and LONG come swaggering. LONG is dressed in shore clothes, wears a black Windsor tie, cloth cap. YANK is in his dirty dungarees. A fireman's cap with black peak is cocked defiantly on the side of his head. He has not shaved for days and around his fierce, resentful eyes — as around those of LONG to a lesser degree — the black smudge of coal dust still sticks like make-up. They hesitate and stand together at the corner, swaggering, looking about them with a forced, defiant contempt.]

LONG [*Indicating it all with an oratorical gesture*]. Well, 'ere we are. Fif' Avenoo. This 'ere's their bleedin' private lane, as yer might say. [*Bitterly.*] We're trespassers 'ere. Proletarians keep orf the grass!

YANK [*Dully*]. I don't see no grass, yuh boob. [*Staring at the sidewalk.*] Clean, ain't it? Yuh could eat a fried egg offen it. The white wings got some job sweepin' dis up. [*Looking up and down the avenue — surlily.*] Where's all de white-collar stiffs yuh said was here — and de skoits — *her* kind?

LONG. In church, blarst 'em! Arskin' Jesus to give 'em more money.

YANK. Choich, huh? I useter go to choich onct — sure — when I was a kid. Me old man and woman, dey made me. Dey never went demselves, dough. Always got too big a head on Sunday mornin', dat was dem. [*With a grin.*] Dey was scrappers for fair, bot' of dem. On Satiday nights when dey bot' got a skinful dey could put up a bout oughter been staged at de Garden. When dey got trough dere wasn't a chair or table with a leg under it. Or else dey bot' jumped on me for somep'n. Dat was where I loined to take punishment. [*With a grin and a swagger.*] I'm a chip offen de old block, get me?

LONG. Did yer old man follow the sea?

YANK. Naw. Worked along shore. I runned away when me old lady croaked with de tremens. I helped at truckin' and in de market. Den I shipped in de stokehole. Sure. Dat belongs. De rest was nothin'. [*Looking around him.*]I ain't never seen dis before. De Brooklyn waterfront, dat was where I was dragged up. [*Taking a deep breath.*] Dis ain't so bad at dat, huh?

LONG. Not bad? Well, we pays for it wiv our bloody sweat, if yer wants to know!

YANK [*With sudden angry disgust*]. Aw, hell! I don't see no one, see — like her. All dis gives me a pain. It don't belong. Say, ain't dere a back room around dis dump? Let's go shoot a ball. All dis is too clean and quiet and dolled-up, get me? It gives me a pain.

LONG. Wait and yer'll bloody well see —

YANK. I don't wait for no one. I keep on de move. Say, what yuh drag me up here for, anyway? Tryin' to kid me, yuh simp, yuh?

LONG. Yer wants to get back at 'er, don't yer? That's what yer been sayin' every bloomin' hour since she hinsulted yer.

YANK [*Vehemently*]. Sure ting I do! Didn't I try to get even wit her in Southampton? Didn't I sneak on de dock and wait for her by de gangplank? I was goin' to spit in her pale mug, see! Sure, right in her pop-eyes! Dat woulda made me even, see? But no chanct. Dere was a whole army of plainclothes bulls around. Dey spotted me and gimme de bum's rush. I never seen her. But I'll git square wit her yet, you watch! [*Furiously.*] De lousy tart! She tink she kin get away with moider — but not wit me! I'll fix her! I'll tink of a way!

LONG [*As disgusted as he dares to be*]. Ain't that why I brought yer up 'ere — to show yer? Yer been lookin' at this 'ere 'ole affair wrong. Yer been actin' an' talkin' 's if it was all a bleedin' personal matter between yer and that bloody cow. I wants to convince yer she was on'y a representative of 'er clarss. I wants to awaken yer bloody clarss consciousness. Then yer'll see it's 'er clarss yer've got to fight, not 'er alone. There's a 'ole mob of 'em like 'er, Gawd blind 'em!

YANK [*Spitting on his hands — belligerently*]. De more de merrier when I gits started. Bring on de gang!

LONG. Yer'll see 'em in arf a mo', when that church lets out. [*He *turns and sees the window display in the two stores for the first time.*] Blimey! Look at that, will yer? [*They both walk back and stand looking in the jeweler's. LONG flies into a fury.*] Just look at this 'ere bloomin' mess! Just look at it! Look at the bleedin' prices on 'em — more'n our 'ole bloody stokehole makes in ten voyages sweatin' in 'ell! And they — 'er and 'er bloody clarss — buys 'em for toys to dangle on 'em! One of these 'ere, would buy scoff for a starvin' family for a year!

YANK. Aw, cut de sob stuff! T' hell wit de starvin' family! Yuh'll be passin' de hat to me next. [*With naive admiration.*] Say, dem tings is pretty, huh? Bet yuh dey'd hock for a piece of change aw right. [*Then turning away, bored.*] But aw hell, what good are dey? Let 'er have 'em. Dey don't belong no more'n she does. [*With a gesture of sweeping the jewelers into oblivion.*] All dat don't count, get me?

LONG [*Who has moved to the furrier's — indignantly*]. And I s'pose this 'ere don't count neither — skins of poor, 'armless animals slaughtered so as 'er and 'ers can keep their bleedin' noses warm!

YANK [*Who has been staring at something inside — with queer excitement*]. Take a slant at dat! Give it de once-over! Monkey fur — two t'ousand bucks! [*Bewilderedly.*] Is dat straight goods — monkey fur? What de hell —?

LONG [*Bitterly*]. It's straight enuf. [*With grim humor.*] They wouldn't bloody well pay that for 'airy ape's skin — no, nor for the 'ole livin' ape with all 'is 'ead, and body, and soul thrown in!

YANK [*Clenching his fists, his face growing pale with rage as if the skin in the window were a personal insult*]. Trowin' it up in my face! Christ! I'll fix her!

LONG [*Excitedly*]. Church is out. 'Ere they come, the bleedin' swine. [*After a glance at YANK'S lowering face — uneasily.*] Easy goes, Comrade. Keep yer bloomin' temper. Remember force defeats itself. It ain't our weapon. We must impress our demands through peaceful means — the votes of the on-marching proletarians of the bloody world!

YANK [*With abysmal contempt*]. Votes, hell! Votes is a joke, see. Votes for women! Let dem do it!

LONG [*Still more uneasily*]. Calm, now. Treat 'em wiv the proper contempt. Observe the bleedin' parasites but 'old yer 'orses.

YANK [*Angrily*]. Git away from me! Yuh're yellow, dat's what. Force, dat's me! De punch, dat's me every time, see! [*The crowd from church enter from the right, sauntering slowly and affectedly, their heads held stiffly up, looking neither to right nor left, talking in toneless, simpering voices. The women are rouged, calcimined, dyed, overdressed to the nth degree. The men are in Prince Alberts, high hats, spats, canes, etc. A procession of gaudy marionettes, yet wih something of the relentless horror of Frankenstein monsters in their detached, mechanical unawareness.*]

VOICES. Dear Doctor Caiaphas! He is so sincere!
What was the sermon? I dozed off.
About the radicals, my dear — and the false
    doctrines that are being preached.
We must organize a hundred per`cent
    American bazaar.
And let everyone contribute one one-
    hundredth per cent of their income tax.
What an original idea!
We can devote the proceeds to rehabilitating
    the veil of the temple.
But that has been done so many times.

YANK [*Glaring from one to the other of them — with an insulting snort of scorn*]. Huh! Huh! [*Without seeming to see him, they make wide detours to avoid the spot where he stands in the middle of the sidewalk.*]

LONG [*Frightenedly*]. Keep yer bloomin' mouth shut, I tells yer.

YANK [*Viciously*]. G'wan! Tell it to Sweeney! [*He swaggers away and deliberately lurches into a top-hatted gentleman, then glares at him pugnaciously.*] Say, who d'yuh tink yuh're bumpin'? Tink yuh own de oith?

GENTLEMAN [*Coldly and affectedly*]. I beg your pardon. [*He has not looked at* YANK *and passes on without a glance, leaving him bewildered.*]

LONG [*Rushing up and grabbing* YANK'S *arm*]. 'Ere! Come away! This wasn't what I meant. Yer'll 'ave the bloody coppers down on us.

YANK [*Savagely — giving him a push that sends him sprawling*]. G'wan!

LONG [*Picks himself up — hysterically*]. I'll pop orf then. This ain't what I meant. And whatever 'appens yer can't blame me. [*He slinks off left.*]

YANK. *T' hell wit youse!* [*He approaches a lady — with a vicious grin and a smirking wink.*] Hello, Kiddo. How's every little ting? Got anyting on for tonight? I know an old boiler down to de docks we kin crawl into. [*The lady stalks by without a look, without a change of pace.* YANK *turns to others — insultingly.*] Holy smokes, what a mug! Go hide yuhself before de horses shy at yuh. Gee, pipe de heine on dat one! Say, youse, yuh look like de stoin of a ferryboat. Paint and powder! All dolled up to kill! Yuh look like stiffs laid out for de boneyard! Aw, g'wan, de lot of youse! Yuh give me de eyeache. Yuh don't belong, get me! Look at me, why don't youse dare? I belong, dat's me! [*Pointing to skyscraper across the street which is in process of construction — with bravado.*] See dat building goin' up dere? See de steel work? Steel, dat's me! Youse guys live on it and tink yuh're somep'n. But I'm *in* it, see I'm de hoistin' engine dat makes it go up! I'm it — de inside and bottom of it! Sure! I'm steel and steam and smoke and de rest of it! It moves — speed — twenty-five stories up — and me at de top and bottom — movin'! Youse simps don't move. Yuh're on'y dolls I winds up to see 'm spin. Yuh're de garbage, get me — de leavins — der ashes we dump over de side! Now, what's 'a' yuh gotta say? [*But as they seem neither to see nor hear him, he flies into a fury.*] Bums! Pigs! Tarts! Bitches! [*He turns in rage on the men, bumping viciously into them but not jarring them the least bit. Rather it is he who recoils after each collision. He keeps growling.*] Git off de oith! G'wan, yuh bum! Look where yuh're goin', can't yuh? Git outa here! Fight, why don't yuh? Put up yer mits! Don't be a dog! Fight or I'll knock yuh dead! [*But, without seeming to see him, they all answer with mechanical affected politeness.*] I beg your pardon. [*Then at a cry from one of the women they all scurry to the furrier's window.*]

THE WOMAN [*Ecstatically, with a gasp of delight*]. Monkey fur! [*The whole crowd of men and women chorus after her in the same tone of affected delight.*] Monkey fur!

YANK [*With a jerk of his head back on his shoulders, as if he had received a punch full in the face — raging*]. I see yuh, all in white! I see yuh, yuh white-faced tart, yuh! Hairy ape, huh?

I'll hairy ape yuh! [*He bends down and grips at the street curbing as if to pluck it out and hurl it. Foiled in this, snarling with passion, he leaps to the lamppost on the corner and tries to pull it up for a club. Just at that moment a bus is heard rumbling up. A fat, high-hatted, spatted gentleman runs out from the side street. He calls out plaintively.*] Bus! Bus! Stop there! [*And runs full tilt into the bending straining* YANK, *who is bowled off his balance.*]

YANK [*Seeing a fight — with a roar of joy as he springs to his feet*]. At last! Bus, huh! I'll bust yuh! [*He lets drive a terrific swing, his fist landing full on the fat gentleman's face. But the gentleman stands unmoved as if nothing had happened.*]

GENTLEMAN. I beg your pardon. [*Then irritably.*] You have made me lose my bus. [*He claps his hands and begins to scream.*] Officer! Officer! [*Many police whistles shrill out on the instant and a whole platoon of policemen rush in on* YANK *from all sides. He tries to fight but is clubbed to the pavement and fallen upon. The crowd at the window have not moved or noticed this disturbance. The clanging gong of the patrol wagon approaches with a clamoring din.*]

[*The curtain falls.*]

Scene VI

[*Night of the following day. A row of cells in the prison on Blackwell's Island. The cells extend back diagonally from right front to left rear. They do not stop, but disappear in the dark background as if they ran on, numberless, into infinity. One electric bulb from the low ceiling of the narrow corridor sheds its light through the heavy steel bars of the cell at the extreme front and reveals part of the interior.* YANK *can be seen within, crouched on the edge of his cot in the attitude of Rodin's "The Thinker." His face is spotted with black and blue bruises. A bloodstained bandage is wrapped around his head.*]

YANK [*Suddenly starting as if awakening from a dream, reaches out and shakes the bars — aloud to himself, wonderingly*]. Steel. Dis is de Zoo, huh? [*A burst of hard barking laughter comes from the unseen occupants of the cells, runs back down the tier, and abruptly ceases.*]

VOICES [*Mockingly*].

The Zoo? That's a new name for this coop — a damn good name!

Steel, eh? You said a mouthful. This is the old iron house.

Who is that boob talkin'?

He's the bloke they brung in out of his head. The bulls had beat him up fierce.

YANK [*Dully*]. I musta been dreamin'. I tought I was in a cage at de Zoo — but de apes don't talk, do dey?

VOICES [*With mocking laughter*].

You're in a cage aw right.

A coop!

A pen!

A sty!

A kennel! [*Hard laughter — a pause.*]

Say, guy! Who are you? No, never mind lying. What are you?

Yes, tell us your sad story. What's your game?

What did they jug yuh for?

YANK [*Dully*]. I was a fireman — stokin' on de liners. [*Then with sudden rage, rattling his cell bars.*] I'm a hairy ape, get me? And I'll bust youse all in de jaw if yuh don't lay off kiddin' me.

VOICES. Huh! You're a hard-boiled duck, ain't you!

When you spit, it bounces! [*Laughter.*]

Aw, can it. He's a regular guy. Ain't you?

What did he say he was — a ape?

YANK [*Defiantly*]. Sure ting! Ain't dat what youse all are — apes? [*A silence. Then a furious rattling of bars from down the corridor.*]

A VOICE [*Thick with rage*]. I'll show yuh who's a ape, yuh bum!

VOICES. Ssshh! Nix!

Can de noise!

Piano!

You'll have the guard down on us!

YANK [*Scornfully*]. De guard? Yuh mean de keeper, don't yuh? [*Angry exclamations from all the cells.*]

VOICE [*Placatingly*]. Aw, don't pay no attention to him. He's off his nut from the beatin'-up he got. Say, you guy! We're waitin' to hear what they landed you for — or ain't yuh tellin'?

YANK. Sure, I'll tell youse. Sure! Why de hell not? On'y — youse won't get me. Nobody gets me but me, see? I started to tell de Judge and all he says was: "Toity days to tink it over." Tink it over! Christ, dat's all I been doin' for weeks! [*After a pause.*] I was tryin' to git even with someone, see? — someone dat done me doit.

VOICES [*Cynically*]. De old stuff, I bet. Your goil, huh?
Give yuh the double-cross, huh?
That's them every time!
Did yuh beat up de odder guy?

YANK [*Disgustedly*]. Aw, yuh're all wrong! Sure dere was a skoit in it — but not what youse mean, not dat old tripe. Dis was a new kind of skoit. She was dolled up all in white — in de stokehole. I tought she was a ghost. Sure. [*A pause.*]

VOICES [*Whispering*]. Gee, he's still nutty.
Let him rave. It's fun listenin'.

YANK [*Unheeding — groping in his thoughts*]. Her hands — dey was skinny and white like dey wasn't real but painted on somep'n. Dere was a million miles from me to her — twenty-five knots an hour. She was like some dead ting de cat brung in. Sure, dat's what. She didn't belong. She belonged in de window of a toy store, or on de top of a garbage can, see! Sure! [*He breaks out angrily.*] But would yuh believe it, she had de noive to do me doit. She lamped me like she was seein' somep'n broke loose from de menagerie. Christ, yuh'd oughter seen her eyes! [*He rattles the bars of his cell furiously.*] But I'll get back at her yet, you watch! And if I can't find her I'll take it out on de gang she runs wit. I'm wise to where dey hangs out now. I'll show her who belongs! I'll show her who's in de move and who ain't. You watch my smoke!

VOICES [*Serious and joking*]. Dat's de talkin'!
Take her for all she's got!
What was this dame, anyway? Who was she, eh?

YANK. I dunno. First cabin stiff. Her old man's a millionaire, dey says — name of Douglas.

VOICES. Douglas? That's the president of the Steel Trust, I bet.
Sure. I seen his mug in de papers.
He's filthy with dough.

VOICE. Hey, feller, take a tip from me. If you want to get back at that dame, you better join the Wobblies. You'll get some action, then.

YANK. Wobblies? What de hell's dat?

VOICE. Ain't you ever heard of the I.W.W.?

YANK. Naw. What is it?

VOICE. A gang of blokes — a tough gang. I been readin' about 'em today in the paper. The guard give me the *Sunday Times.* There's a long spiel about 'em. It's from a speech made in the Senate by a guy named Senator Queen. [*He is in the cell next to* YANK'S. *There is a rustling of paper.*] Wait'll I see if I got light enough and I'll read you. Listen. [*He reads.*] "There is a menace existing in this country today which threatens the vitals of our fair Republic — as foul a menace against the very life-blood of the American Eagle as was the foul conspiracy of Cataline against the eagles of ancient Rome!"

VOICE [*Disgustedly*]. Aw, hell! Tell him to salt de tail of dat eagle!

VOICE [*Reading*]. "I refer to that devil's brew of rascals, jailbirds, murderers and cutthroats who libel all honest working men by calling themselves the Industrial Workers of the World; but in the light of their nefarious plots, I call them the Industrious Wreckers of the World!" ‹ *evil*

YANK [*With vengeful satisfaction*]. Wreckers, dat's de right dope! Dat belongs! Me for dem!

VOICE. Ssshh! [*Reading.*] "This fiendish organization is a foul ulcer on the fair body of our Democracy —"

VOICE. Democracy, hell! Give him the boid, fellers — the raspberry! [*They do.*]

VOICE. Ssshh! [*Reading.*] "Like Cato I say to this Senate, the I.W.W. must be destroyed! For they represent an ever-present dagger pointed at the heart of the greatest nation the world has ever known, where all men are born free and equal, with equal opportunities to all, where the Founding Fathers have guaranteed to each one happiness, where Truth, Honor, Liberty, Justice, and the Brotherhood of Man are a religion absorbed with one's mother's milk, taught at our father's knee, sealed, signed, and stamped upon in the glorious Constitution of these United States!" [*A perfect storm of hisses, catcalls, boos, and hard laughter.*]

VOICES [*Scornfully*]. Hurrah for de Fort' of July!
Pass de hat!
Liberty!
Justice!
Honor!
Opportunity!
Brotherhood!

ALL [*With abysmal scorn*]. Aw, hell!

VOICE. Give that Queen Senator guy the bark! All togedder now — one — two — tree — [*A terrific chorus of barking and yapping.*]

GUARD [*From a distance*]. Quiet, there, youse — or I'll get the hose. [*The noise subsides.*]

YANK [*With growling rage*]. I'd like to catch dat senator guy alone for a second. I'd loin him some trute!

VOICE. Ssshh! Here's where he gits down to cases on the Wobblies. [*Reads.*] "They plot with fire in one hand and dynamite in the other. They stop not before murder to gain their ends, nor at the outraging of defenseless womanhood. They would tear down society, put the lowest scum in the seats of the mighty, turn Almighty God's revealed plan for the world topsy-turvy, and make of our sweet and lovely civilization a shambles, a desolation where man, God's masterpiece, would soon degenerate back to the ape!"

VOICE [*To* YANK]. Hey, you guy. There's your ape stuff again.

YANK [*With a growl of fury*]. I got him. So dey blow up tings, do dey? Dey turn tings round, do dey? Hey, lend me dat paper, will yuh?

VOICE. Sure. Give it to him. On'y keep it to yourself, see. We don't wanter listen to no more of that slop.

VOICE. Here you are. Hide it under your mattress.

YANK [*Reaching out*]. Tanks. I can't read much but I kin manage. [*He sits, the paper in the hand at his side, in the attitude of Rodin's "The Thinker." A pause. Several snores from down the corridor. Suddenly* YANK *jumps to his feet with a furious groan as if some appalling thought had crashed on him — bewilderedly.*] Sure — her old man — president of de Steel Trust — makes half de steel in de world — steel — where I tought I belonged — drivin' trou — movin' — in dat — to make her — and cage me in for her to spit on! Christ [*He shakes the bars of his cell door till the whole tier trembles. Irritated, protesting exclamations from those awakened or trying to get to sleep.*] He made dis — dis cage! Steel! *It* don't belong, dat's what! Cages, cells, locks, bolts, bars — dat's what it means! — holdin' me down wit him at de top! But I'll manage trou! Fire, dat melts it! I'll be fire — under de heap — fire dat never goes out — hot as hell — breakin' out in de night — [*While he has been saying this last he has shaken his cell door to a clanging accompaniment. As he comes to the "breakin' out" he seizes one bar with both hands and, putting his two feet up against the others so that his position is parallel to the floor like a monkey's, he gives a great wrench backwards. The bar bends like a licorice stick under his tremendous strength. Just at this moment the* PRISON GUARD *rushes in, dragging a hose behind him.*]

GUARD [*Angrily*]. I'll loin youse bums to wake me up! [*Sees* YANK.] Hello, it's you, huh? Got the D.Ts., hey? Well, I'll cure 'em. I'll drown your snakes for yuh! [*Noticing the bar.*] Hell, look at dat bar bended! On'y a bug is strong enough for dat!

YANK [*Glaring at him*]. Or a hairy ape, yuh big yellow bum! Look out! Here I come! [*He grabs another bar.*]

GUARD [*Scared now — yelling off left*]. Toin de hose on, Ben! — full pressure! And call de others — and a straitjacket! [*The curtain is falling. As it hides* YANK *from view, there is a splattering smash as the stream of water hits the steel of* YANK'S *cell.*]

[*The curtain falls.*]

Scene VII

[*Nearly a month later. An I.W.W. local near the waterfront, showing the interior of a front room on the ground floor, and the street outside. Moonlight on the narrow street, buildings massed in black shadow. The interior of the room, which is general assembly room, office, and reading room, resembles some dingy settlement boys' club. A desk and high stool are in one corner. A table with papers, stacks of pamphlets, chairs about it, is at center. The whole is decidedly cheap, banal,*

*commonplace and unmysterious as a room could well be. The
Secretary is perched on the stool making entries in a large
ledger. An eye shade casts his face into shadows. Eight or ten
men, longshoremen, iron workers, and the like are grouped
about the table. Two are playing checkers. One is writing a letter. Most of them are smoking pipes. A big signboard is on the
wall at the rear, "Industrial Workers of the World — Local
No. 57."*]

YANK [*Comes down the street outside. He is dressed as in Scene
Five. He moves cautiously, mysteriously. He comes to a point
opposite the door; tiptoes softly up to it, listens, is impressed
by the silence within, knocks carefully, as if he were guessing
at the password to some secret rite. Listens. No answer.
Knocks again a bit louder. No answer. Knocks impatiently,
much louder*].

SECRETARY [*Turning around on his stool*]. What the hell is that
— someone knocking? [*Shouts.*] Come in, why don't you?
[*All the men in the room look up.* YANK *opens the door slowly, gingerly, as if afraid of an ambush. He looks around for
secret doors, mystery, is taken aback by the commonplaceness
of the room and the men in it, thinks he may have gotten in the
wrong place, then sees the signboard on the wall and is
reassured.*]

YANK [*Blurts out*]. Hello.

MEN [*Reservedly*]. Hello.

YANK [*More easily*]. I tought I'd bumped into de wrong dump.

SECRETARY [*Scrutinizing him carefully*]. Maybe you have. Are
you a member?

YANK. Naw, not yet. Dat's what I come for — to join.

SECRETARY. That's easy. What's your job — longshore?

YANK. Naw. Fireman — stoker on de liners.

SECRETARY [*With satisfaction*]. Welcome to our city. Glad to
know you people are waking up at last. We haven't got many
members in your line.

YANK. Naw. Dey're all dead to de woild.

SECRETARY. Well, you can help to wake 'em. What's your
name? I'll make out your card.

YANK [*Confused*]. Name? Lemme tink.

SECRETARY [*Sharply*]. Don't you know your own name?

YANK. Sure; but I been just Yank for so long — Bob, dat's it — Bob Smith.

SECRETARY [*Writing*]. Robert Smith. [*Fills out the rest of the card.*] Here you are. Cost you half a dollar.

YANK. Is dat all — four bits? Dat's easy. [*Gives the* SECRETARY *the money.*]

SECRETARY [*Throwing it in drawer*]. Thanks. Well, make yourself at home. No introductions needed. There's literature on the table. Take some of those pamphlets with you to distribute aboard ship. They may bring results. Sow the seed, only go about it right. Don't get caught and fired. We got plenty out of work. What we need is men who can hold their jobs — and work for us at the same time.

YANK. Sure. [*But he still stands, embarrassed and uneasy.*]

SECRETARY [*Looking at him — curiously*]. What did you knock for? Think we had a coon in uniform to open doors?

YANK. Naw. I tought it was locked — and dat yuh'd wanter give me the once-over trou a peephole or somep'n to see if I was right.

SECRETARY [*Alert and suspicious but with an easy laugh*]. Think we were running a crap game? That door is never locked. What put that in your nut?

YANK [*With a knowing grin, convinced that this is all camouflage, a part of the secrecy*]. Dis burg is full of bills, ain't it?

SECRETARY [*Sharply*]. What have the cops got to do with us? We're breaking no laws.

YANK [*With a knowing wink*]. Sure. Youse wouldn't for woilds. Sure. I'm wise to dat.

SECRETARY. You seem to be wise to a lot of stuff none of us knows about.

YANK [*With another wink*]. Aw, dat's aw right, see. [*Then made a bit resentful by the suspicious glances from all sides.*] Aw, can it! Youse needn't put me trou de toid degree. Can't youse see I belong? Sure! I'm reg'lar. I'll stick, get me? I'll shoot de woiks for youse. Dat's why I wanted to join in.

SECRETARY [*Breezily, feeling him out*]. That's the right spirit. Only are you sure you understand what you've joined? It's all plain and aboveboard; still, some guys get a wrong slant on us. [*Sharply.*] What's your notion of the purpose of the I.W.W.?

YANK. Aw, I know all about it.

SECRETARY [*Sarcastically*]. Well, give us some of your valuable information.

YANK [*Cunningly*]. I know enough not to speak outa my toin. [*Then resentfully again.*] Aw, say! I'm reg'lar. I'm wise to de game. I know yuh got to watch your step wit a stranger. For all youse know, I might be a plain-clothes dick, or somep'n, dat's what yuh're tinkin', huh? Aw, forget it! I belong, see? Ask any guy down to de docks if I don't.

SECRETARY. Who said you didn't?

YANK. After I'm 'nitiated, I'll show yuh.

SECRETARY [*Astounded*]. Initiated? There's no initiation.

YANK [*Disappointed*]. Ain't there no password — no grip nor nothin'?

SECRETARY. What'd you think this is — the Elks — or the Black Hand?

YANK. De Elks, hell! De Black Hand, dey're a lot of yellow back-stickin' Ginees. Naw. Dis is a man's gang, ain't it?

SECRETARY. You said it! That's why we stand on our two feet in the open. We got no secrets.

YANK [*Surprised but admiringly*]. Yuh mean to say yuh always run wide open — like dis?

SECRETARY. Exactly.

YANK. Den yuh sure got your noive wit youse!

SECRETARY [*Sharply*]. Just what was it made you want to join us? Come out with that straight.

YANK. Yuh call me? Well, I got noive, too! Here's my hand. Yuh wanter blow tings up, don't yuh? Well, dat's me! I belong!

SECRETARY [*With pretended carelessness*]. You mean change the unequal conditions of society by legitimate direct action — or with dynamite?

YANK. Dynamite! Blow it offen de oith — steel — all de cages — all de factories, steamers, buildings, jails — de Steel Trust and all dat makes it go.

SECRETARY. So — that's your idea, eh? And did you have any special job in that line you wanted to propose to us? [*He makes a sign to the men, who get up cautiously one by one and group behind* YANK.]

YANK [*Boldly*]. Sure, I'll come out wit it. I'll show youse I'm one of de gang. Dere's dat millionaire guy, Douglas —

SECRETARY. President of the Steel Trust, you mean? Do you want to assassinate him?

YANK. Naw, dat don't get yuh nothin'. I mean blow up de factory, de woiks, where he makes de steel. Dat's what I'm after — to blow up de steel, knock all de steel in de woild up to de moon. Dat'll fix tings! [*Exactly, with a touch of bravado.*] I'll do it by me lonesome! I'll show yuh! Tell me where his woiks is, how to git there, all de dope. Gimme de stuff, de old butter — and watch me do de rest! Watch de smoke and see it move! I don't give a damn if dey nab me — long as it's done! I'll soive life for it — and give 'em de laugh! [*Half to himself.*] And I'll write her a letter and tell her de hairy ape done it. Dat'll square tings.

SECRETARY [*Stepping away from* YANK]. Very interesting. [*He gives a signal. The men, huskies all, throw themselves on* YANK *and before he knows it they have his legs and arms pinioned. But he is too flabbergasted to make a struggle, anyway. They feel him over for weapons.*]

MAN. No gat, no knife. Shall we give him what's what and put the boots to him?

SECRETARY. No. He isn't worth the trouble we'd get into. He's too stupid. [*He comes closer and laughs mockingly in* YANK'S *face.*] Ho-ho! By God, this is the biggest joke they've put up on us yet. Hey, you Joke! Who sent you — Burns or Pinkerton? No, by God, you're such a bonehead I'll bet you're in the Secret Service! Well, you dirty spy, you rotten agent provocator, you can go back and tell whatever skunk is paying you blood-money for betraying your brothers that he's wasting his coin. You couldn't catch a cold. And tell him that all he'll ever get on us, or ever has got, is just his own sneaking plots that he's framed up to put us in jail. We are what our manifesto says we are, neither more nor less — and we'll give him a copy of that any time he calls. And as for you — [*He glares scornfully at* YANK, *who is sunk in an oblivious stupor.*] Oh, hell, what's the use of talking? You're a brainless ape.

YANK [*Aroused by the word to fierce but futile struggles*]. What's dat, yuh Sheeny bum, yuh! ´

SECRETARY. Throw him out, boys. [*In spite of his struggles, this is done with gusto and éclat. Propelled by several parting kicks,* YANK *lands sprawling in the middle of the narrow cobbled street. With a growl he starts to get up and storm the closed door, but stops bewildered by the confusion in his brain, pathetically impotent. He sits there, brooding, in as near to the attitude of Rodin's "Thinker" as he can get in his position.*]

YANK [*Bitterly*]. So dem boids don't tink I belong, neider. Aw, to hell wit 'em! Dey're in de wrong pew — de same old bull — soapboxes and Salvation Army — no guts! Cut out an hour offen de job a day and make me happy! Gimme a dollar more a day and make me happy! Tree square a day, and cauliflowers in de front yard — ekal rights — a woman and kids — a lousy vote — and I'm all fixed for Jesus, huh? Aw, hell! What does dat get yuh? Dis ting's in your inside, but it ain't your belly. Feedin' your face — sinkers and coffee — dat don't touch it. It's way down — at de bottom. Yuh can't grab it, and yuh can't stop it. It moves, and everything moves. It stops and de whole woild stops. Dat's me now — I don't tick, see? — I'm a busted Ingersoll, dat's what. Steel was me, and I owned de woild. Now I ain't steel, and de woild owns me. Aw, hell! I can't see — it's all dark, get me? It's all wrong! [*He turns a bitter mocking face up like an ape gibbering at the moon.*] Say, youse up dere, Man in de Moon, yuh look so wise, gimme de answer, huh? Slip me de inside dope, de information right from de stable — where do I get off at, huh?

A POLICEMAN [*Who has come up the street in time to hear this last — with grim humor*]. You'll get off at the station, you boob, if you don't get up out of that and keep movin'.

YANK [*Looking up at him — with a hard, bitter laugh*]. Sure! Lock me up! Put me in a cage! Dat's de on'y answer yuh know. G'wan, lock me up!

POLICEMAN. What you been doin'?

YANK. Enuf to gimme life for! I was born, see? Sure, dat's de charge. Write it in de blotter. I was born, get me!

POLICEMAN [*Jocosely*]. God pity your old woman! [*Then matter-of-fact.*] But I've no time for kidding. You're soused. I'd run you in but it's too long a walk to the station. Come on now, get up, or I'll fan your ears with this club. Beat it now! [*He hauls* YANK *to his feet.*]

YANK [*In a vague mocking tone*]. Say, where do I go from here?

POLICEMAN [*Giving him a push — with a grin, indifferently*]. Go to hell.

[*The curtain falls.*]

Scene VIII

[*Twilight of the next day. The monkey house at the Zoo. One spot of clear gray light falls on the front of one cage so that the interior can be seen. The other cages are vague, shrouded in shadow from which chatterings pitched in a conversational tone can be heard. On the one cage a sign from which the word "gorilla" stands out. The gigantic animal himself is seen squatting on his haunches on a bench in much the same attitude as Rodin's "Thinker." YANK enters from the left. Immediately a chorus of angry chattering and screeching breaks out. The gorilla turns his eyes but makes no sound or move.*]

YANK [*With a hard, bitter laugh*]. Welcome to your city, huh? Hail, hail, de gang's all here! [*At the sound of his voice the chattering dies away into an attentive silence. YANK walks up to the gorilla's cage and, leaning over the railing, stares in at its occupant, who stares back at him, silent and motionless. There is a pause of dead stillness. Then YANK begins to talk in a friendly confidential tone, half-mockingly, but with a deep undercurrent of sympathy.*] Say, yuh're some hard-lookin' guy, ain't yuh? I seen lots of tough nuts dat de gang called gorillas, but yuh're de foist real one I ever seen. Some chest yuh got, and shoulders, and dem arms and mits! I bet yuh got a punch in eider fist dat'd knock 'em all silly. [*This with genuine admiration. The gorilla, as if he understood, stands upright, swelling out his chest and pounding on it with his fist. YANK grins sympathetically.*] Sure, I get yuh. Yuh challenge de whole woild, huh? Yuh got what I was sayin' even if yuh muffed de woids. [*Then bitterness creeping in.*] And why wouldn't yuh get me? Ain't we both members of de same club — de Hairy Apes? [*They stare at each other — a pause — then*

YANK *goes on slowly and bitterly*.] So yuh're what she seen when she looked at me, de white-faced tart! I was you to her, get me? On'y outa de cage — broke out — free to moider her, see? Sure! Dat's what she tought. She wasn't wise dat I was in a cage, too — worser'n yours — sure — a damn sight — 'cause you got some chanct to bust loose — but me — [*He grows confused.*] Aw, hell! It's all wrong, ain't it? [*A pause.*] I s'pose yuh wanter know what I'm doin' here, huh? I been warmin' a bench down to de Battery — ever since last night. Sure. I seen de sun come up. Dat was pretty, too — all red and pink and green. I was lookin' at de skyscrapers — steel — and all de ships comin' in, sailin' out, all over de oith — and dey was steel, too. De sun was warm, dey wasn't no clouds, and dere was a breeze blowin'. Sure, it was great stuff. I got it aw right — what Paddy said about dat bein' de right dope — on'y I couldn't get *in* it, see? I couldn't belong in dat. It was over my head. And I kept tinkin' — and den I beat it up here to see what youse was like. And I waited till dey was all gone to git yuh alone. Say, how d'yuh feel sittin' in dat pen all de time, havin' to stand for 'em comin' and starin' at yuh — de white-faced, skinny tarts and de boobs what marry 'em — makin' fun of yuh, laughin' at yuh, gittin' scared of yuh — damn 'em! [*He pounds on the rail with his fist. The gorilla rattles the bars of his cage and snarls. All the other monkeys set up an angry chattering in the darkness. YANK goes on excitedly.*] Sure! Dat's de way it hits me, too. On'y yuh're lucky, see? Yuh don't belong wit 'em and you know it. But me, I belong wit 'em — but I don't, see? Dey don't belong wit me, dat's what. Get me? Tinkin' is hard — [*He passes one hand across his forehead with a painful gesture. The gorilla growls impatiently. YANK goes on gropingly.*] It's dis way, what I'm drivin' at. Youse can sit and dope dream in de past, green woods, de jungle and de rest of it. Den yuh belong and dey don't. Den yuh kin laugh at 'em, see? Yuh're de champ of de woild. But me — I ain't got no past to tink in, nor nothin' dat's comin', on'y what's now — and dat don't belong. Sure, you're de best off! Yuh can't tink, can yuh? Yuh can't talk neider. But I kin make a bluff at talkin' and tinkin' — a'most git away wit it — a'most! — and dat's where de joker comes in. [*He laughs.*] I ain't on oith and I ain't in heaven, get me? I'm in de middle tryin' to separate 'em, takin' all de woist punches from bot' of 'em. Maybe dat's what dey call hell, huh? But you, yuh're at de bottom. You belong! Sure! Yuh're de on'y one in de woild dat does, yuh lucky stiff! [*The gorilla growls proudly.*] And dat's why dey gotter put yuh in a cage, see? [*The gorilla roars angrily.*] Sure! Yuh get me. It beats it when you try to tink it or talk it — it's way down — deep — behind — you 'n' me we feel it. Sure! Bot' members of dis club! [*He laughs — then in a savage tone.*] What de hell! T' hell wit it! A little action, dat's our meat! Dat belongs! Knock 'em down and keep bustin' 'em till dey croaks yuh wit a gat — wit steel! Sure! Are yuh game? Dey've looked at youse, ain't dey — in a cage? Wanter get even? Wanter wind up like a sport 'stead of croakin' slow in dere? [*The gorilla roars an emphatic affirmative.* YANK *goes on with a sort of furious exaltation.*] Sure! Yuh're reg'lar! Yuh'll stick to de finish! Me 'n' you, huh? — bot' members of this club! Wè'll put up one last star bout dat'll knock 'em offen deir seats! Dey'll have to make de cages stronger after we're trou! [*The gorilla is straining at his bars, growling, hopping from one foot to the other.* YANK *takes a jimmy from under his coat and forces the lock on the cage door. He throws this open.*] Pardon from de governor! Step out and shake hands! I'll take yuh for a walk down Fif' Avenoo. We'll knock 'em offen de oith and croak wit de band playin'. Come on, Brother. [*The gorilla scrambles gingerly out of his cage. Goes to* YANK *and stands looking at him.* YANK *keeps his mocking tone — holds out his hand.*] Shake — de secret grip of our order. [*Something, the tone of mockery, perhaps, suddenly enrages the animal. With a spring he wraps his huge arms around* YANK *in a murderous hug. There is a crackling snap of crushed ribs — a gasping cry, still mocking, from* YANK.] Hey, I didn't say kiss me! [*The gorilla lets the crushed body slip to the floor; stands over it uncertainly, considering; then picks it up, throws it in the cage, shuts the door, and shuffles off menacingly into the darkness at left. A great uproar of frightened chattering and whimpering comes from the other cages. Then* YANK *moves, groaning, opening his eyes, and there is silence. He mutters painfully.*] Say — dey oughter match him — wit Zybszko. He got me, aw right. I'm trou. Even him didn't tink I belonged. [*Then, with sudden passionate despair.*] Christ, where do I get off at? Where do I fit in? [*Checking himself as suddenly.*] Aw, what de hell! No squawkin', see! No quittin', get me! Croak wit your boots on! [*He grabs hold of the bars of the cage and hauls himself painfully to his feet — looks around him bewilderedly — forces a mocking laugh.*] In de cage, huh? [*In the strident tones of a circus barker*.] Ladies and gents, step forward and take a slant at de one and only — [*His voice weakened*.] — one and original — Hairy Ape from de wilds of — [*He slips in a heap on the floor and dies. The monkeys set up a chattering, whimpering wail. And, perhaps, the Hairy Ape at last belongs.*]

[*The curtain falls.*]

12 I.D.'s:

    QUOTES: SPEAKER ; SITUATION ; SIGNIFICANCE

    STAGE DIRECTIONS ; SIGNIFICANCE

2 ESSAY TYPE QUESTIONS:

    1 PARA

    2 PARA   } ALL INCLUSIVE

BELONGING
CAGE
STEEL
THINKING
APE
IMPOTENCE (INABILITY TO DO ANYTHING)
NATURE VS. MACHINE
SOCIAL CLASSES (GROUPS)
LANGUAGE
PAYS. — APPEARANCE

The Hairy Ape

Springboard

1.   What is the significance of O'Neill's title?

2.   Why does O'Neill's headnote to the play define it as "A Comedy of Ancient and Modern Life . . ."? What are the ramifications of the word "comedy"? Why include the adjective "ancient"?

3.   *The Hairy Ape* is an example of *expressionism* in the theatre. O'Neill intends that all the elements of drama and theatre (not solely dialogue) express the mood, the visual impression, and the theme he is communicating. In the opening of Scene I, he cautions that "the treatment of this scene, or of any other scene in the play, should by no means be naturalistic." In light of this caveat, examine O'Neill's use of lighting, exaggerated gesture and posture, set design, costuming, and slang and poetry (often mixed) in the dialogue.

4.   As the action of the play moves from water (Scenes I-IV) to land (Scenes V-VIII), how does Yank's idea of "belonging" change?

(Scene I)

5.   The stage set and the demeanor of the men evoke the sense of beasts defiant in their cramped cage: these hairy-chested men cannot comfortably stand upright, yet they convey immense power. How is this whole impression successfully accomplished?

6.   Yank cannot understand and becomes impatient with Paddy's longing for the old days of sailing when the wind moved the ships, and sailors worked up on deck in the open air and sky: "Oh, the clean skins of them, and the clear eyes, the straight backs and full chests of them!" What is it that Paddy knows but Yank has not yet learned?

7.   Yank's long speech toward the end of this scene is his answer to Paddy's memories. Yank sees his own dignity and importance deriving from the fact that he "belongs," he is "it." Explain Yank's definition of the apparently simple declaration, "it belongs." What does it mean for something *not* to belong? And what is "it"?

8.   What is Yank's opinion of *thought* as opposed to *action?*

(Scene II)

9.   Details in the stage directions for this scene explain the function, impressions, and attitudes of characters as they reveal a contrast between what might be called a vitality of power and an anemia of existence. Characters are deliberately designed as *types.* What "type" does Mildred's aunt represent? What "type" does Mildred herself portray?

10.   Mildred is dressed all in white. What are the implications of this color, when we consider Mildred's assessment of her own existence? What are the implications and ironies when we consider the traditional associations with young women dressed in that color?

11.   What does Mildred mean by the description of herself as "a waste product in the Bessemer process – like the millions"?

12.   What is the difference between Yank's and Mildred's views of steel and hell?

13.   What does Mildred's aunt mean when she calls Mildred a "poser"? Name other characters in the play who are posers. Explain why you consider each one a poser.

(Scene III)

14.   What images are suggested by the opening stage directions? Explain what this group of men would look like, what their physical actions would be, and what the set and lighting would do to enhance the picture presented.

15.   In anger at the whistle from the bridge, Yank bellows, "Who d'yuh tinks runnin' dis game, me or you? When I git ready, we move. Not before!" Is Yank's assessment of the situation valid? Who really does run the ship? (Hint: this may not be as easy a question as it seems!)

16.   What does Mildred recognize in Yank's fierce rage? What does Yank realize for the first time when he sees Mildred's reaction to him? What does the audience recognize, as Mildred's anemia is presented next to Yank's unleashed energy?

17. Consider the pantomime that ends this scene. What does it achieve through gesture and action that words might over-explain?

(Scene IV)

18. Considering the opinion of "thinking" that Yank expresses in Scene I, what irony is achieved by Yank's physical pose in the attitude of Rodin's "The Thinker" when this scene opens?

19. How has seeing Mildred's reaction changed the way Yank views himself and his work? What connection is there between the literal, physical dirt on Yank's body and the emotional insult he feels from Mildred's reaction to him?

20. What does Yank mean when he vows to get even with Mildred? Why is such a thing really impossible? Is Mildred at all aware of what she has taken away from Yank?

21. What is the difference between Long's and Paddy's reactions to Mildred's invasion of their "hell"? What does each of these men feel about Yank's anger? What prompts Paddy's cynical tone?

(Scene V)

22. Long resents the world of Fifth Avenue for political reasons, Yank for personal ones. With this distinction in mind, explain the reactions the two men have to the monkey-fur coat and the crowd of church-goers.

23. O'Neill stages a pantomime parade of the rich who do not look at Yank or Long and indeed seem unable even to see them. Why do these people bewilder Yank so?

24. Long cautions Yank to remember that "force defeats itself. It ain't our weapon." How does Yank himself view force and power? Why doesn't Yank's force work against the fashionable people?

25. Yank declares loudly that he belongs and these "painted" people do not belong. Yet his presence has little effect on them. When he bumps into them, he doesn't jar them at all. What is O'Neill saying to the audience here through the pantomime and Yank's impotence?

26. What explicitly does the closing pantomime demonstrate?

(Scene VI)

27. What is O'Neill's purpose in having the unseen prisoner read Senator Queen's statement in the newspaper?

28. Yank has always considered himself to be steel: steel belongs. In this scene, he is inside a literal steel cage. When Yank learns that Mildred's father makes steel and that her ancestors have built their fortune on steel, what metaphorical cage does Yank also find himself in? How does this new realization affect him? What does he mean when he says he will be fire instead of steel?

29. Yank calls himself "a hairy ape" at the end of Scene VI, but now there is a bravado, a pride of defiance, in the name. What is the source of Yank's new-found pride and defiance?

(Scene VII)

30. The stage directions establish the tone for this scene. We are told that the setting is "decidedly cheap, banal, commonplace and unmysterious," and yet Yank thinks he can find help here in effecting his revenge. Explain the irony.

31. Yank has difficulty remembering his real name, Bob Smith. He has always been called "Yank." What meaning does the nickname usually have? Does the name suitably fit Yank? Why do you suppose O'Neill allows Yank almost to forget his original name?

32. In Scene I, Yank tells the other firemen that he is not a joiner; in Scene VII, he joins the "Industrial Workers of the World — Local No. 57." What has turned him into a joiner? What is O'Neill's purpose in allowing Yank to join a group? (Incidentally, who were the "wobblies" of the real I.W.W.?)

33. What does Yank mean when he says, "Steel was me, and I owned the woild. Now I ain't steel, and the woild owns me"?

(Scene VIII)

34. To preserve our sense of Yank's tragedy, it is essential

that the actor who plays the gorilla do so convincingly. Yet O'Neill has cautioned us at the opening of the play that no scene should receive naturalistic treatment. Considering the content of Scene VIII, explain and discuss some of the special problems — and insights — the audience might encounter seeing an actor on stage in a gorilla suit.

35.   How does Yank now define *cage?* What makes a cage? What is trapped inside a cage? What kinds of cages can be escaped? What kinds cannot?

36.   What does Yank see as the difference between the gorilla and himself as prisoners? Why does Yank consider the gorilla lucky and himself unlucky?

THE ADMIRABLE CRICHTON

by James M. Barrie

The Admirable Crichton

Introduction

The ninth child of a Scottish weaver, James Matthew Barrie (1860-1937) was a very successful journalist, novelist *(The Little Minister* is a perennial favorite), and playwright. He was honored beyond the dreams of most men, being made a baronet, appointed to the Order of Merit, and named rector of St. Andrews University and chancellor of Edinburgh University. Despite all this, Sir James never overcame his innate timidity and habitual melancholy.

His temperamental shyness in the face of life may explain why so many of his works take refuge in sentimentality and fantasy. Although the reading and theatregoing public loved his magical spells, the critics generally found Barrie guilty in the first degree of coyness, whimsy, escapism, and dewy-eyed emotionalism.

Of recent years, however, we have become more appreciative of the considerable technical cunning in even the most syrupy Barrie plays, while with the perspective of time such dramas as *Dear Brutus* (1917) and *What Every Woman Knows* (1908) reveal the bracing influence of turn-of-the-century "drama of ideas" and the new realism of Ibsen and Strindberg. Even such children's plays as *Peter Pan* (1907) and *Mary Rose* (1920) have turned out — like all good literature for children, of course — to have their serious, adult side.

But Barrie's most consequential statement on the human condition appears in *The Admirable Crichton* (1902), written just shortly after he had determined to devote himself to the stage. This play presents a sharp and even bitter commentary on snobbery, social caste, and advantage based on heredity rather than merit. What makes the play so remarkable is the brilliance with which Barrie veils his astringent observations in humor and fantasy. Edwardian audiences enjoyed the broad jokes and witty humor and thrilled to the fantastic island adventure, while today we notice above all the cutting social satire on those human weaknesses that prevent men from being better than they have been. The Edwardians saw one aspect of *Crichton* and we see another; they and we are both right, but the play itself is a more exacting and more balanced blend of fantasy, humor, and satire.

CHARACTERS

THE HON. ERNEST WOOLLEY
CRICHTON
LADY CATHERINE
LADY AGATHA
LADY MARY
TREHERNE
LORD BROCKLEHURST
THE EARL OF LOAM
FISHER
TWEENY
OTHER SERVANTS AT LOAM HOUSE
NAVAL OFFICER
LADY BROCKLEHURST

SETTING

ACT ONE.	LOAM HOUSE, MAYFAIR, LONDON.
ACT TWO.	A DESERT ISLE IN THE PACIFIC.
	TWO MONTHS LATER.
ACT THREE.	SAME AS ACT II.
	TWO YEARS LATER.
ACT FOUR.	LOAM HOUSE, LONDON.
	SEVERAL MONTHS LATER.

TIME — ABOUT 1900.

ACT ONE

AT LOAM HOUSE, MAYFAIR

A moment before the curtain rises, the HON. ERNEST WOOLLEY *drives up to the door of Loam House in Mayfair. There is a happy smile on his pleasant, insignificant face, and this presumably means that he is thinking of himself. He is too busy over nothing, this man about town, to be always thinking of himself, but, on the other hand, he almost never thinks of any other person. Probably* ERNEST'S *great moment is when he wakes of a morning and realizes that he really is* ERNEST, *for we must all wish to be that which is our ideal. We can conceive him springing out of bed light-heartedly and waiting for his man to do the rest. He is dressed in excellent taste, with just the little bit more which shows that he is not without a sense of humour: the dandiacal are often saved by carrying a smile at the whole thing in their spats, let us say.* ERNEST *left Cambridge the other day, a member of the Athenoeum (which he would be sorry to have you confound with a club in London of the same name). He is a bachelor, but not of arts, no mean epigrammatist (as you shall see), and a favourite of the ladies. He is almost a celebrity in restaurants, where he dines frequently, returning to sup; and during this last year he has probably paid as much in them for the privilege of handing his hat to an attendant as the rent of a working-man's flat. He complains brightly that he is hard up, and that if somebody or other at Westminster does not look out the country will go to the dogs. He is no fool. He has the shrewdness to float with the current because it is a labour-saving process, but he has sufficient pluck to fight, if fight he must (a brief contest, for he would soon be toppled over). He has a light nature, which would enable him to bob up cheerily in new conditions and return unaltered to the old ones. His selfishness is his most endearing quality. If he has his way he will spend his life like a cat in pushing his betters out of the soft places, and until he is old he will be fondled in the process.*

He gives his hat to one footman and his cane to another, and mounts the great staircase unassisted and undirected. As a nephew of the house he need show no credentials even to CRICHTON, *who is guarding a door above.*

It would not be good taste to describe CRICHTON, *who is only a servant; if to the scandal of all good houses he is to stand out as a*

249

figure in the play, he must do it on his own, as they say in the pantry and the boudoir. We are not going to help him. We have had misgivings ever since we found his name in the title, and we shall keep him out of his rights as long as we can. Even though we softened to him he would not be a hero in these clothes of servitude; and he loves his clothes. How to get him out of them? It would require a cataclysm. To be an indoor servant at all is to CRICHTON *a badge of honour; to be a butler at thirty is the realization of his proudest ambitions. He is devotedly attached to his master, who, in his opinion, has but one fault, he is not sufficiently contemptuous of his inferiors. We are immediately to be introduced to this solitary failing of a great English peer.*

This perfect butler, then, opens a door, and ushers ERNEST *into a certain room. At the same moment the curtain rises on this room, and the play begins.*

It is one of several reception-rooms in Loam House, not the most magnificent but quite the softest; and of a warm afternoon all that those who are anybody crave for is the softest. The larger rooms are magnificent and bare, carpetless, so that it is an accomplishment to keep one's feet on them; they are sometimes lent for charitable purposes; they are also all in use on the night of a dinner-party, when you may find yourself alone in one, having taken a wrong turning; or alone, save for two others who are within hailing distance. This room, however, is comparatively small and very soft. There are so many cushions in it that you wonder why, if you are an outsider and don't know that it needs six cushions to make one fair head comfy. The couches themselves are cushions as large as beds, and there is an art of sinking into them and of waiting to be helped out of them. There are several famous paintings on the walls, of which you may say 'Jolly thing that,' without losing caste as knowing too much; and in cases there are glorious miniatures, but the daughters of the house cannot tell you of whom; 'there is a catalogue somewhere.' There are a thousand or so of roses in basins, several library novels, and a row of weekly illustrated newspapers lying against each other like fallen soldiers. If any one disturbs this row CRICHTON *seems to know of it from afar and appears noiselessly and replaces the wanderer. One thing unexpected in such a room is a great array of tea-things.* ERNEST *spots them with a twinkle, and has his epigram at once unsheathed. He dallies, however, before delivering the thrust.*

ERNEST. I perceive, from the tea-cups, Crichton, that the great
    function is to take place here.

CRICHTON [*with a respectful sigh*]. Yes, sir.

ERNEST [*chuckling heartlessly*]. The servants' hall coming up to have tea in the drawing-room! [*With terrible sarcasm.*] No wonder you look happy, Crichton.

CRICHTON [*under the knife*]. No, sir.

ERNEST. Do you know, Crichton, I think that with an effort you might look even happier. [CRICHTON *smiles wanly.*] You don't approve of his lordship's compelling his servants to be his equals — once a month?

CRICHTON. It is not for me, sir, to disapprove of his lordship's Radical views.

ERNEST. Certainly not. And, after all, it is only once a month that he is affable to you.

CRICHTON. On all other days of the month, sir, his lordship's treatment of us is everything that could be desired.

ERNEST. [*This is the epigram.*] Tea-cups! Life, Crichton, is like a cup of tea; the more heartily we drink, the sooner we reach the dregs.

CRICHTON [*obediently*]. Thank you, sir.

ERNEST [*becoming confidential, as we do when we have need of an ally*]. Crichton, in case I should be asked to say a few words to the servants, I have strung together a little speech. [*His hand strays to his pocket.*] I was wondering where I should stand.

[*He tries various places and postures, and comes to rest leaning over a high chair, whence, in dumb show, he addresses a gathering. CRICHTON, with the best intentions, gives him a footstool to stand on, and departs, happily unconscious that ERNEST in some dudgeon has kicked the footstool across the room.*]

ERNEST [*addressing an imaginary audience, and desirous of startling them at once*]. Suppose you were all little fishes at the bottom of the sea —

[*He is not quite satisfied with his position, though sure that the fault must lie with the chair for being too high, not with him for being too short. CRICHTON'S suggestion was not perhaps a bad one after all. He lifts the stool, but hastily conceals it behind him on the entrance of the LADIES CATHERINE and*]

AGATHA, *two daughters of the house.* CATHERINE *is twenty, and* AGATHA *two years younger. They are very fashionable young women indeed, who might wake up for a dance, but they are very lazy,* CATHERINE *being two years lazier than* AGATHA.]

ERNEST [*uneasily jocular, because he is concealing the footstool*]. And how are my little friends to-day?

AGATHA [*contriving to reach a settee*]. Don't be silly, Ernest. If you want to know how we are, we are dead. Even to think of entertaining the servants is so exhausting.

CATHERINE [*subsiding nearer the door*]. Besides which, we have had to decide what frocks to take with us on the yacht, and that is such a mental strain.

ERNEST. You poor overworked things. [*Evidently* AGATHA *is his favourite, for he helps her to put her feet on the settee, while* CATHERINE *has to dispose of her own feet.*] Rest your weary limbs.

CATHERINE [*perhaps in revenge*]. But why have you a footstool in your hand?

AGATHA. Yes?

ERNEST. Why? [*Brilliantly; but to be sure he has had time to think it out.*] You see, as the servants are to be the guests I must be butler. I was practising. This is a tray, observe.

[*Holding the footstool as a tray, he minces across the room like an accomplished footman. The gods favour him, for just here* LADY MARY *enters, and he holds out the footstool to her.*]

Tea, my lady?

[LADY MARY *is a beautiful creature of twenty-two, and is of a natural hauteur which is at once the fury and the envy of her sisters. If she chooses she can make you seem so insignificant that you feel you might be swept away with the crumb-brush. She seldom chooses, because of the trouble of preening herself as she does it; she is usually content to show that you merely tire her eyes. She often seems to be about to go to sleep in the middle of a remark: there is quite a long and anxious pause, and then she continues, like a clock that hesitates, bored in the middle of its strike.*]

LADY MARY [*arching her brows*]. It is only you, Ernest; I thought there was some one here [*and she also bestows herself on cushions*].

ERNEST [*a little piqued, and deserting the footstool*]. Had a very tiring day also, Mary?

LADY MARY [*yawning*]. Dreadfully. Been trying on engagement-rings all the morning.

ERNEST [*who is fond of gossip as the oldest club member*]. What's that? [*To* AGATHA.] Is it Brocklehurst?

[*The energetic* AGATHA *nods.*]

You have given your warm young heart to Brocky?

[LADY MARY *is impervious to his humour, but he continues bravely.*]

I don't wish to fatigue you, Mary, by insisting on a verbal answer, but if, without straining yourself, you can signify Yes or No, won't you make the effort?

[*She indolently flashes a ring on her most important finger, and he starts back melodramatically.*]

The ring! Then I am too late, too late! [*Fixing* LADY MARY *sternly, like a prosecuting counsel.*] May I ask, Mary, does Brocky know? Of course, it was that terrible mother of his who pulled this through. Mother does everything for Brocky. Still, in the eyes of the law you will be, not her wife, but his, and, therefore, I hold that Brocky ought to be informed. Now —

[*He discovers that their languorous eyes have closed.*]

If you girls are shamming sleep in the expectation that I shall awaken you in the manner beloved of ladies, abandon all such hopes.

[CATHERINE *and* AGATHA *look up without speaking.*]

LADY MARY [*speaking without looking up*]. You impertinent boy.

ERNEST [*eagerly plucking another epigram from his quiver*]. I knew that was it, though I don't know everything. Agatha, I'm not young enough to know everything.

[*He looks hopefully from one to another, but though they try to grasp this, his brilliance baffles them.*]

AGATHA [*his secret admirer*]. *Young* enough?

ERNEST [*encouragingly*]. Don't you see? I'm not young enough to know everything.

AGATHA. I'm sure it's awfully clever, but it's so puzzling.

[*Here* CRICHTON *ushers in an athletic pleasant-faced young clergyman,* MR. TREHERNE, *who greets the company.*]

CATHERINE. Ernest, say it to Mr. Treherne.

ERNEST. Look here, Treherne, I'm not young enough to know everything.

TREHERNE. How do you mean, Ernest?

ERNEST [*a little nettled*]. I mean what I say.

LADY MARY. Say it again; say it more slowly.

ERNEST. I'm—not—young—enough—to—know—everything.

TREHERNE. *I* see. What you really mean, my boy, is that you are not old enough to know everything.

ERNEST. No, I don't.

TREHERNE. I assure you that's it.

LADY MARY. Of course it is.

CATHERINE. Yes, Ernest, that's it.

[ERNEST, *in desperation, appeals to* CRICHTON.]

ERNEST. I am not young enough, Crichton, to know everything.

[*It is an anxious moment, but a smile is at length extorted from* CRICHTON *as with a corkscrew.*]

CRICHTON. Thank you, sir. [*He goes.*]

ERNEST [*relieved*]. Ah, if you had that fellow's head, Treherne, you would find something better to do with it than play cricket. I hear you bowl with your head.

TREHERNE [*with proper humility*]. I'm afraid cricket is all I'm good for, Ernest.

CATHERINE [*who thinks he has a heavenly nose*]. Indeed, it isn't. You are sure to get on, Mr. Treherne.

TREHERNE. Thank you, Lady Catherine.

CATHERINE. But it was the bishop who told me so. He said a clergyman who breaks both ways is sure to get on in England.

TREHERNE. I'm jolly glad.

[*The master of the house comes in, accompanied by* LORD BROCKLEHURST. *The* EARL OF LOAM *is a widower, a philanthropist, and a peer of advanced ideas. As a widower he is at least able to interfere in the domestic concerns of his house — to rummage in the drawers, so to speak, for which he has felt an itching all his blameless life; his philanthropy has opened quite a number of other drawers to him; and his advanced ideas have blown out his figure. He takes in all the weightiest monthly reviews, and prefers those that are uncut, because he perhaps never looks better than when cutting them; but he does not read them, and save for the cutting it would suit him as well merely to take in the covers. He writes letters to the papers, which are printed in a type to scale with himself, and he is very jealous of those other correspondents who get his type. Let laws and learning, art and commerce die, but leave the big type to an intellectual aristocracy. He is really the reformed House of Lords which will come some day.*

Young LORD BROCKLEHURST *is nothing save for his rank. You could pick him up by the handful any day in Piccadilly or Holborn, buying socks — or selling them.*]

LORD LOAM [*expansively*]. You are here, Ernest. Feeling fit for the voyage, Treherne?

TREHERNE. Looking forward to it enormously.

LORD LOAM. That's right. [*He chases his children about as if they were chickens.*] Now then, Mary, up and doing, up and doing. Time we had the servants in. They enjoy it so much.

LADY MARY. They hate it.

LORD LOAM. Mary, to your duties. [*And he points severely to the tea-table.*]

ERNEST [*twinkling*]. Congratulations, Brocky.

LORD BROCKLEHURST [*who detests humour*]. Thanks.

ERNEST. Mother pleased?

LORD BROCKLEHURST [*with dignity*]. Mother is very pleased.

ERNEST. That's good. Do you go on the yacht with us?

LORD BROCKLEHURST. Sorry I can't. And look here, Ernest, I will *not* be called Brocky.

ERNEST. Mother don't like it?

LORD BROCKLEHURST. She does not. [*He leaves* ERNEST, *who forgives him and begins to think about his speech.* CRICHTON *enters.*]

LORD LOAM [*speaking as one man to another*]. We are quite ready, Crichton. [CRICHTON *is distressed.*]

LADY MARY [*sarcastically*]. How Crichton enjoys it!

LORD LOAM [*frowning*]. He is the only one who doesn't; pitiful creature.

CRICHTON [*shuddering under his lord's displeasure*]. I can't help being a Conservative, my lord.

LORD LOAM. Be a man, Crichton. You are the same flesh and blood as myself.

CRICHTON [*in pain*]. Oh, my lord!

LORD LOAM [*sharply*]. Show them in; and, by the way, they were not all here last time.

CRICHTON. All, my lord, except the merest trifles.

LORD LOAM. It must be every one. [*Lowering.*] And remember this, Crichton, for the time being you are my equal. [*Testily.*] I shall soon show you whether you are not my equal. Do as you are told.

[CRICHTON *departs to obey, and his lordship is now a general. He has no pity for his daughters, and uses a terrible threat.*]

And girls, remember, no condescension. The first who condescends recites. [*This sends them skurrying to their labours.*]

By the way, Brocklehurst, can you do anything?

LORD BROCKLEHURST. How do you mean?

LORD LOAM. Can you do anything — with a penny or a handkerchief, make them disappear, for instance?

LORD BROCKLEHURST. Good heavens, no.

LORD LOAM. It's a pity. Every one in our position ought to be able to do something. Ernest, I shall probably ask you to say a few words; something bright and sparkling.

ERNEST. But, my dear uncle, I have prepared nothing.

LORD LOAM. Anything impromptu will do.

ERNEST. Oh — well — if anything strikes me on the spur of the moment.

[*He unostentatiously gets the footstool into position behind the chair.* CRICHTON *reappears to announce the guests, of whom the first is the housekeeper. They should be well-mannered. Nothing farcical, please.*]

CRICHTON [*reluctantly*]. Mrs. Perkins.

LORD LOAM [*shaking hands*]. Very delighted, Mrs. Perkins. Mary, our friend, Mrs. Perkins.

LADY MARY. How do you do, Mrs. Perkins? Won't you sit here?

LORD LOAM [*threateningly*]. Agatha!

AGATHA [*hastily*]. How do you do? Won't you sit down?

LORD LOAM [*introducing*]. Lord Brocklehurst — my valued friend, Mrs. Perkins.

[LORD BROCKLEHURST *bows and escapes. He has to fall back on* ERNEST.]

LORD BROCKLEHURST. For heaven's sake, Ernest, don't leave me for a moment; this sort of thing is utterly opposed to all my principles.

ERNEST [*airily*]. You stick to me, Brocky, and I'll pull you through.

CRICHTON. Monsieur Fleury.

ERNEST. The chef.

LORD LOAM [*shaking hands with the chef*]. Very charmed to see you, Monsieur Fleury.

FLEURY. Thank you very much.

[FLEURY *bows to* AGATHA, *who is not effusive.*]

LORD LOAM [*warningly*]. Agatha — recitation!

[*She tosses her head, but immediately finds a seat and tea for*

M. FLEURY. TREHERNE *and* ERNEST *move about, making themselves amiable.* LADY MARY *is presiding at the tea-tray.*]

CRICHTON. Mr. Rolleston.

LORD LOAM [*shaking hands with his valet*]. How do you do, Rolleston?

[CATHERINE *looks after the wants of* ROLLESTON.]

CRICHTON. Mr. Tompsett.

[TOMPSETT, *the coachman, is received with honours, from which he shrinks, but with quiet dignity.*]

CRICHTON. Miss Fisher.

[*This superb creature is no less than* LADY MARY'S *maid, and even* LORD LOAM *is a little nervous.*]

LORD LOAM. This is a pleasure, Miss Fisher.

ERNEST [*unabashed*]. If I might venture, Miss Fisher — [*and he takes her unto himself*].

CRICHTON. Miss Simmons.

LORD LOAM [*to* CATHERINE'S *maid*]. You are always welcome, Miss Simmons.

ERNEST [*perhaps to kindle jealousy in* MISS FISHER]. At last we meet. Won't you sit down?

CRICHTON. Mademoiselle Jeanne.

LORD LOAM. Charmed to see you, Mademoiselle Jeanne.

[*A place is found for* AGATHA'S *maid, and the scene is now an animated one; but still our host thinks his girls are not sufficiently sociable. He frowns on* LADY MARY.]

LADY MARY [*in alarm*]. Mr. Treherne, this is Fisher, my maid.

LORD LOAM [*sharply*]. Your what, Mary?

LADY MARY. My friend.

CRICHTON. Thomas.

LORD LOAM. How do you do, Thomas?

[*The first footman gives him a reluctant hand.*]

CRICHTON. John.

LORD LOAM. How do you do, John?

[ERNEST *signs to* LORD BROCKLEHURST, *who hastens to him.*]

ERNEST [*introducing*]. Brocklehurst, this is John. I think you have already met on the door-step.

CRICHTON. Jane.

[*She comes, wrapping her hands miserably in her apron.*]

LORD LOAM [*doggedly*]. Give me your hand, Jane.

CRICHTON. Gladys.

ERNEST. How do you do, Gladys? You know my uncle?

LORD LOAM. Your hand, Gladys.

[*He bestows her on* AGATHA.]

CRICHTON. Tweeny.

[*She is a very humble and frightened kitchenmaid, of whom we are to see more.*]

LORD LOAM. So happy to see you.

FISHER. John, I saw you talking to Lord Brocklehurst just now; introduce me.

LORD BROCKLEHURST [*who is really a second-rate* JOHN]. That's an uncommon pretty girl; if I must feed one of them, Ernest, that's the one.

[*But* ERNEST *tries to part him and* FISHER *as they are about to shake hands.*]

ERNEST. No you don't, it won't do, Brocky. [*To* MISS FISHER.] You are too pretty, my dear. Mother wouldn't like it. [*Discovering* TWEENY.] Here is something safer. Charming girl, Brocky, dying to know you; let me introduce you. Tweeny, Lord Brocklehurst — Lord Brocklehurst, Tweeny.

[BROCKLEHURST *accepts his fate; but he still has an eye for* FISHER, *and something may come of this.*]

LORD LOAM [*severely*]. They are not all here, Crichton.

CRICHTON [*with a sigh*]. Odds and ends.

[*A* STABLE-BOY *and a* PAGE *are shown in, and for a moment no daughter of the house advances to them.*]

LORD LOAM [*with a roving eye on his children*]. Which is to recite?

[*The last of the company are, so to say, embraced.*]

LORD LOAM [*to* TOMPSETT, *as they partake of tea together*]. And how are all at home?

TOMPSETT. Fairish, my lord, if 'tis the horses you are inquiring for?

LORD LOAM. No, no, the family. How's the baby?

TOMPSETT. Blooming, your lordship.

LORD LOAM. A very fine boy. I remember saying so when I saw him; nice little fellow.

TOMPSETT [*not quite knowing whether to let it pass*]. Beg pardon, my lord, it's a girl.

LORD LOAM. A girl? Aha! ha! ha! exactly what I said. I distinctly remember saying, If it's spared it will be a girl.

[CRICHTON *now comes down.*]

LORD LOAM. Very delighted to see you, Crichton.

[CRICHTON *has to shake hands.*]

Mary, you know Mr. Crichton?

[*He wanders off in search of other prey.*]

LADY MARY. Milk and sugar, Crichton?

CRICHTON. I'm ashamed to be seen talking to you, my lady.

LADY MARY. To such a perfect servant as you all this must be most distasteful. [CRICHTON *is too respectful to answer.*] Oh, please to speak, or I shall have to recite. You do hate it, don't you?

CRICHTON. It pains me, your ladyship. It disturbs the etiquette of the servants' hall. After last month's meeting the page-boy, in a burst of equality, called me Crichton. He was dismissed.

LADY MARY. I wonder — I really do — how you can remain with us.

CRICHTON. I should have felt compelled to give notice, my lady, if the master had not had a seat in the Upper House. I cling to that.

LADY MARY. Do go on speaking. Tell me, what did Mr. Ernest mean by saying he was not young enough to know everything?

CRICHTON. I have no idea, my lady.

LADY MARY. But you laughed.

CRICHTON. My lady, he is the second son of a peer.

LADY MARY. Very proper sentiments. You are a good soul, Crichton.

LORD BROCKLEHURST [*desperately to* TWEENY]. And now tell me, have you been to the Opera? What sort of weather have you been having in the kitchen? [TWEENY *gurgles.*] For heaven's sake, woman, be articulate.

CRICHTON [*still talking to* LADY MARY]. No, my lady; his lordship may compel us to be equal upstairs, but there will never be equality in the servants' hall.

LORD LOAM [*overhearing this*]. What's that? No equality? Can't you see, Crichton, that our divisions into classes are artificial, that if we were to return to Nature, which is the aspiration of my life, all would be equal?

CRICHTON. If I may make so bold as to contradict your lordship —

LORD LOAM [*with an effort*]. Go on.

CRICHTON. The divisions into classes, my lord, are not artificial. They are the natural outcome of a civilised society. [*To* LADY MARY.] There must always be a master and servants in all civilised communities, my lady, for it is natural, and whatever is natural is right.

LORD LOAM [*wincing*]. It is very unnatural for me to stand here and allow you to talk such nonsense.

CRICHTON [*eagerly*]. Yes, my lord, it is. That is what I have been striving to point out to your lordship.

AGATHA [*to* CATHERINE]. What is the matter with Fisher? She is looking daggers.

CATHERINE. The tedious creature; some question of etiquette, I suppose.

[*She sails across to* FISHER.]

How are you, Fisher?

FISHER [*with a toss of her head*]. I am nothing, my lady, I am nothing at all.

AGATHA. Oh dear, who says so?

FISHER [*affronted*]. His.lordship has asked that kitchen wench to have a second cup of tea.

CATHERINE. But why not?

FISHER. If it pleases his lordship to offer it to *her* before offering it to *me* —

AGATHA. So that is it. Do you want another cup of tea, Fisher?

FISHER. No, my lady — but my position — I should have been asked first.

AGATHA. Oh dear.

[*All this has taken some time, and by now the feeble appetites of the uncomfortable guests have been satiated. But they know there is still another ordeal to face — his lordship's monthly speech. Every one awaits it with misgiving — the servants lest they should applaud, as last time, in the wrong place, and the daughters because he may be personal about them, as the time before.* ERNEST *is annoyed that there should be this speech at all when there is such a much better one coming, and* BROCKLEHURST *foresees the degradation of the peerage. All are thinking of themselves alone save* CRICHTON, *who knows his master's weakness, and fears he may stick in the middle.* LORD LOAM, *however, advances cheerfully to his doom. He sees* ERNEST'S *stool, and artfully stands on it, to his nephew's natural indignation. The three ladies knit their lips, the servants look down their noses, and the address begins.*]

LORD LOAM. My friends, I am glad to see you all looking so happy. It used to be predicted by the scoffer that these meetings would prove distasteful to you. Are they distasteful? I hear you laughing at the question.

[*He has not heard them, but he hears them now, the watchful* CRICHTON *giving them a lead.*]

No harm in saying that among us to-day is one who was formerly hostile to the movement, but who to-day has been won over. I refer to Lord Brocklehurst, who, I am sure, will presently say to me that if the charming lady now by his side has derived as much pleasure from his company as he has derived from hers, he will be more than satisfied.

[*All look at* TWEENY, *who trembles.*]

For the time being the artificial and unnatural — I say un-natural [*glaring at* CRICHTON, *who bows slightly*] — barriers of society are swept away. Would that they could be swept away for ever.

[*The* PAGE-BOY cheers, and has the one moment of prom-inence in his life. He grows up, marries and has children, but is never really heard of again.]

But that is entirely and utterly out of the question. And now for a few months we are to be separated. As you know, my daughters and Mr. Ernest and Mr. Treherne are to accompany me on my yacht, on a voyage to distant parts of the earth. In less than forty-eight hours we shall be under weigh.

[*But for* CRICHTON'S *eye the reckless* PAGE-BOY *would repeat his success.*]

Do not think our life on the yacht is to be one long idle holi-day. My views on the excessive luxury of the day are well known, and what I preach I am resolved to practise. I have therefore decided that my daughters, instead of having one maid each as at present, shall on this voyage have but one maid between them.

[*Three maids rise; also three mistresses.*]

CRICHTON. My lord!

LORD LOAM. My mind is made up.

ERNEST. I cordially agree.

LORD LOAM. And now, my friends, I should like to think that there is some piece of advice I might give you, some thought, some noble saying over which you might ponder in my absence. In this connection I remember a proverb, which has had a great effect on my own life. I first heard it many years ago. I have never forgotten it. It constantly cheers and guides me. That proverb is — that proverb was — the proverb I speak of —

[*He grows pale and taps his forehead.*]

LADY MARY. Oh dear, I believe he has forgotten it.

LORD LOAM [*desperately*]. The proverb — that proverb to which I refer —

[*Alas, it has gone. The distress is general. He has not even the sense to sit down. He gropes for the proverb in the air. They try applause, but it is no help.*]

I have it now — [*not he*].

LADY MARY [*with confidence*]. Crichton.

[*He does not fail her. As quietly as if he were in goloshes, mind as well as feet, he dismisses the domestics; they go according to precedence but without servility, and there must be no attempt at 'comic effect.' Then he signs to* MR. TREHERNE, *and they conduct* LORD LOAM *with dignity from the room. His hands are still catching flies; he still mutters, 'The proverb —'; but he continues, owing to* CRICHTON'S *treatment, to look every inch a peer. The ladies have now an opportunity to air their indignation.*]

LADY MARY. One maid among three grown women!

LORD BROCKLEHURST. Mary, I think I had better go. That dreadful kitchen-maid —

LADY MARY. I can't blame you, George.

[*He salutes her.*]

LORD BROCKLEHURST. Your father's views are shocking to me, and I am glad I am not to be one of the party on the yacht. My respect for myself, Mary, my natural anxiety as to what mother will say. I shall see you, darling, before you sail.

[*He bows to the others and goes.*]

ERNEST. Selfish brute, only thinking of himself. What about my speech?

LADY MARY. One maid among three of us. What's to be done?

ERNEST. Pooh! You must do for yourselves, that's all.

LADY MARY. Do for ourselves. How can we know where our things are kept?

AGATHA. Are you aware that dresses button up the back?

CATHERINE. How are we to get into our shoes and be prepared for the carriage?

LADY MARY. Who is to put us to bed, and who is to get us up, and how shall we ever know it's morning if there is no one to pull up the blinds?

[CRICHTON *crosses on his way out.*]

ERNEST. How is his lordship now?

CRICHTON. A little easier, sir.

LADY MARY. Crichton, send Fisher to me.

[*He goes.*]

ERNEST. I have no pity for you girls, I —

LADY MARY. Ernest, go away, and don't insult the broken-hearted.

ERNEST. And uncommon glad am I to go. Ta-ta, all of you. He asked me to say a few words. I came here to say a few words, and I'm not at all sure that I couldn't bring an action against him.

[*He departs, feeling that he has left a dart behind him. The girls are alone with their tragic thoughts.*]

LADY MARY [*become a mother to the younger ones at last*]. My poor sisters, come here. [*They go to her doubtfully.*] We must make this draw us closer together. I shall do my best to help you in every way. Just now I cannot think of myself at all.

AGATHA. But how unlike you, Mary.

LADY MARY. It is my duty to protect my sisters.

CATHERINE. I never knew her so sweet before, Agatha. [*Cautiously.*] What do you propose to do, Mary?

LADY MARY. I propose when we are on the yacht to lend Fisher to you when I don't need her myself.

AGATHA. Fisher?

LADY MARY [*who has the most character of the three*]. Of course, as the eldest, I have decided that it is *my* maid we shall take with us.

CATHERINE [*speaking also for* AGATHA]. Mary, you toad.

AGATHA. Nothing on earth would induce Fisher to lift her hand for either me or Catherine.

LADY MARY. I was afraid of it, Agatha. That is why I am so sorry for you.

[*The further exchange of pleasantries is interrupted by the arrival of* FISHER.]

LADY MARY. Fisher, you heard what his lordship said?

FISHER. Yes, my lady.

LADY MARY [*coldly, though the others would have tried blandishment*]. You have given me some satisfaction of late, Fisher, and to mark my approval I have decided that you shall be the maid who accompanies us.

FISHER [*acidly*]. I thank you, my lady.

LADY MARY. That is all; you may go.

FISHER [*rapping it out*]. If you please, my lady, I wish to give notice.

[CATHERINE *and* AGATHA *gleam, but* LADY MARY *is of sterner stuff.*]

LADY MARY [*taking up a book*]. Oh, certainly — you may go.

CATHERINE. But why, Fisher?

FISHER. I could not undertake, my lady, to wait upon three. *We* don't do it. [*In an indignant outburst to* LADY MARY.] Oh, my lady, to think that this affront —

LADY MARY [*looking up*]. I thought I told you to go, Fisher.

[FISHER *stands for a moment irresolute; then goes. As soon as she has gone* LADY MARY *puts down her book and weeps. She is a pretty woman, but this is the only pretty thing we have seen her do yet.*]

AGATHA [*succinctly*]. Serves you right.

[CRICHTON *comes.*]

CATHERINE. It will be Simmons after all. Send Simmons to me.

CRICHTON [*after hesitating*]. My lady, might I venture to speak?

CATHERINE. What is it?

CRICHTON. I happen to know, your ladyship, that Simmons desires to give notice for the same reason as Fisher.

CATHERINE. Oh!

AGATHA [*triumphant*]. Then, Catherine, we take Jeanne.

CRICHTON. And Jeanne also, my lady.

[LADY MARY *is reading, indifferent though the heavens fall, but her sisters are not ashamed to show their despair to* CRICHTON.]

AGATHA. We can't blame them. Could any maid who respected herself be got to wait upon three?

LADY MARY [*with languid interest*]. I suppose there are such persons, Crichton?

CRICHTON [*guardedly*]. I have heard, my lady, that there are such.

LADY MARY [*a little desperate*]. Crichton, what's to be done? We sail in two days; could one be discovered in the time?

AGATHA [*frankly a supplicant*]. Surely you can think of some one?

CRICHTON [*after hesitating*]. There is in this establishment, your ladyship, a young woman —

LADY MARY. Yes?

CRICHTON. A young woman, on whom I have for some time cast an eye.

CATHERINE [*eagerly*]. Do you mean as a possible lady's-maid?

CRICHTON. I had thought of her, my lady, in another connection.

LADY MARY. Ah!

CRICHTON. But I believe she is quite the young person you require. Perhaps if you could see her, my lady —

LADY MARY. I shall certainly see her. Bring her to me. [*He goes.*] You two needn't wait.

CATHERINE. Needn't we? We see your little game, Mary.

AGATHA. We shall certainly remain and have our two-thirds of her.

[*They sit there doggedly until* CRICHTON *returns with* TWEENY, *who looks scared.*]

CRICHTON. This, my lady, is the young person.

CATHERINE [*frankly*]. Oh dear!

[*It is evident that all three consider her quite unsuitable.*]

LADY MARY. Come here, girl. Don't be afraid.

[TWEENY *looks imploringly at her idol.*]

CRICHTON. Her appearance, my lady, is homely, and her manners, as you may have observed, deplorable, but she has a heart of gold.

LADY MARY. What is your position downstairs?

TWEENY [*bobbing*]. I'm a tweeny, your ladyship.

CATHERINE. A what?

CRICHTON. A tweeny; that is to say, my lady, she is not at present, strictly speaking, anything; a *between* maid; she helps the vegetable maid. It is she, my lady, who conveys the dishes from the one end of the kitchen table, where they are placed by the cook, to the other end, where they enter into the charge of Thomas and John.

LADY MARY. I see. And you and Crichton are — ah — keeping company?

[CRICHTON *draws himself up.*]

TWEENY [*aghast*]. A butler don't keep company, my lady.

LADY MARY [*indifferently*]. Does he not?

CRICHTON. No, your ladyship, we butlers may — [*he makes a gesture with his arms*] — but we do not keep company.

AGATHA. I know what it is; you are engaged?

[TWEENY *looks longingly at* CRICHTON.]

CRICHTON. Certainly not, my lady. The utmost I can say at present is that I have cast a favourable eye.

[*Even this is much to* TWEENY.]

LADY MARY. As you choose. But I am afraid, Crichton, she will not suit us.

CRICHTON. My lady, beneath this simple exterior are concealed a very sweet nature and rare womanly gifts.

AGATHA. Unfortunately, that is not what we want.

CRICHTON. And it is she, my lady, who dresses the hair of the ladies'-maids for our evening meals.

[*The ladies are interested at last.*]

LADY MARY. She dresses Fisher's hair?

TWEENY. Yes, my lady, and I does them up when they goes to parties.

CRICHTON [*pained, but not scolding*]. Does!

TWEENY. Doos. And it's me what alters your gowns to fit them.

CRICHTON. *What* alters!

TWEENY. Which alters.

AGATHA. Mary?

LADY MARY. I shall certainly have her.

CATHERINE. *We* shall certainly have her. Tweeny, we have decided to make a lady's-maid of you.

TWEENY. Oh lawks!

AGATHA. We are doing this for you so that your position socially may be more nearly akin to that of Crichton.

CRICHTON [*gravely*]. It will undoubtedly increase the young person's chances.

LADY MARY. Then if I get a good character for you from Mrs. Perkins, she will make the necessary arrangements.

[*She resumes reading.*]

TWEENY [*elated*]. My lady!

LADY MARY. By the way, I hope you are a good sailor.

TWEENY [*startled*]. You don't mean, my lady, I'm to go on the ship?

LADY MARY. Certainly.

TWEENY. But — [*to* CRICHTON.] You ain't going, sir?

CRICHTON. No.

TWEENY [*firm at last*]. Then neither ain't I.

AGATHA. You must.

TWEENY. Leave him! Not me.

LADY MARY. Girl, don't be silly. Crichton will be — considered in your wages.

TWEENY. I ain't going.

CRICHTON. I feared this, my lady.

TWEENY. Nothing'll budge me.

LADY MARY. Leave the room.

[CRICHTON *shows* TWEENY *out with marked politeness.*]

AGATHA. Crichton, I think you might have shown more displeasure with her.

CRICHTON [*contrite*]. I was touched, my lady. I see, my lady, that to part from her would be a wrench to me, though I could not well say so in her presence, not having yet decided how far I shall go with her.

[*He is about to go when* LORD LOAM *returns, fuming.*]

LORD LOAM. The ingrate! The smug! The fop!

CATHERINE. What is it now, father?

LORD LOAM. That man of mine, Rolleston, refuses to accompany us because you are to have but one maid.

AGATHA. Hurrah!

LADY MARY [*in better taste*]. Darling father, rather than you should lose Rolleston, we will consent to take all the three of them.

LORD LOAM. Pooh, nonsense! Crichton, find me a valet who can do without three maids.

CRICHTON. Yes, my lord. [*Troubled.*] In the time — the more suitable the party, my lord, the less willing will he be to come without the — the usual perquisites.

LORD LOAM. Any one will do.

CRICHTON [*shocked*]. My lord!

LORD LOAM. The ingrate! The puppy!

[AGATHA *has an idea, and whispers to* LADY MARY.]

LADY MARY. I ask a favour of a servant? — never!

AGATHA. Then I will. Crichton, would it not be very distressing to you to let his lordship go, attended by a valet who might prove unworthy? It is only for three months; don't you think that you — you yourself — you —

[*As* CRICHTON *sees what she wants he pulls himself up with noble, offended dignity, and she is appalled.*]

I beg your pardon.

[*He bows stiffly.*]

CATHERINE [*to* CRICHTON]. But think of the joy to Tweeny.

[CRICHTON *is moved, but he shakes his head.*]

LADY MARY [*so much the cleverest*]. Crichton, do you think it safe to let the master you love go so far away without you while he has these dangerous views about equality?

[CRICHTON *is profoundly stirred. After a struggle he goes to his master, who has been pacing the room.*]

CRICHTON. My lord, I have found a man.

LORD LOAM. Already? Who is he?

[CRICHTON *presents himself with a gesture.*]

Yourself?

CATHERINE. Father, how good of him.

LORD LOAM [*pleased, but thinking it a small thing*]. Uncommon good. Thank you, Crichton. This helps me nicely out of a hole; and how it will annoy Rolleston! Come with me, and we shall tell him. Not that I think you have lowered yourself in any way. Come along.

[*He goes, and* CRICHTON *is to follow him, but is stopped by* AGATHA *impulsively offering him her hand.*]

CRICHTON [*who is much shaken*]. My lady — a valet's hand!

AGATHA. I had no idea you would feel it so deeply; why did you do it?

[CRICHTON *is too respectful to reply.*]

LADY MARY [*regarding him*]. Crichton, I am curious. I insist upon an answer.

CRICHTON. My lady, I am the son of a butler and a lady's-maid — perhaps the happiest of all combinations; and to me the most beautiful thing in the world is a haughty, aristocratic English house, with every one kept in his place. Though I were equal to your ladyship, where would be the pleasure to me? It would be counterbalanced by the pain of feeling that Thomas and John were equal to me.

CATHERINE. But father says if we were to return to Nature —

CRICHTON. If we did, my lady, the first thing we should do would be to elect a head. Circumstances might alter cases; the same person might not be master; the same persons might not be servants. I can't say as to that, nor should we have the deciding of it. Nature would decide for us.

LADY MARY. You seem to have thought it all out carefully, Crichton.

CRICHTON. Yes, my lady.

CATHERINE. And you have done this for us, Crichton, because you thought that — that father needed to be kept in his place?

CRICHTON. I should prefer you to say, my lady, that I have done it for the house.

AGATHA. Thank you, Crichton. Mary, be nicer to him. [*But* LADY MARY *has begun to read again.*] If there was any way in which we could show our gratitude?

CRICHTON. If I might venture, my lady, would you kindly show it by becoming more like Lady Mary? That disdain is what we like from our superiors. Even so do we, the upper servants, disdain the lower servants, while they take it out of the odds and ends.

[*He goes, and they bury themselves in cushions.*]

AGATHA. Oh dear, what a tiring day.

CATHERINE. I feel dead. Tuck in your feet, you selfish thing.

[LADY MARY *is lying reading on another couch.*]

LADY MARY. I wonder what he meant by circumstances might alter cases.

AGATHA [*yawning*]. Don't talk, Mary, I was nearly asleep.

LADY MARY. I wonder what he meant by the same person might not be master, and the same persons might not be servants.

CATHERINE. Do be quiet, Mary, and leave it to Nature; he said Nature would decide.

LADY MARY. I wonder —

[*But she does not wonder very much. She would wonder more if she knew what was coming. Her book slips unregarded to the floor. The ladies are at rest until it is time to dress.*]

ACT TWO

THE ISLAND

Two months have elapsed, and the scene is a desert island in the Pacific, on which our adventurers have been wrecked.

The curtain rises on a sea of bamboo, which shuts out all view save the foliage of palm trees and some gaunt rocks. Occasionally CRICHTON *and* TREHERNE *come momentarily into sight, hacking and hewing the bamboo, through which they are making a clearing between the ladies and the shore; and by and by, owing to their efforts, we shall have an unrestricted outlook on to a sullen sea that is at present hidden. Then we shall also be able to note a mast standing out of the water — all that is left, saving floating wreckage, of the ill-fated yacht the* Bluebell. *The beginnings of a hut will also be seen, with* CRICHTON *driving its walls into the ground or astride its roof of saplings, for at present he is doing more than one thing at a time. In a red shirt, with the ends of his sailor's breeches thrust into wading-boots, he looks a man for the moment; we suddenly remember some one's saying — perhaps it was ourselves — that a cataclysm would be needed to get him out of his servant's clothes, and apparently it has been forthcoming. It is no longer beneath our dignity to cast an inquiring eye on his appearance. His features are not distinguished, but he has a strong jaw and green eyes, in which a yellow light burns that we have not seen before. His dark hair, hitherto so decorously sleek, has been ruffled this way and that by wind and weather, as if they were part of the cataclysm and wanted to help his chance. His muscles must be soft and flabby still, but though they shriek aloud to him to desist, he rains lusty blows with his axe, like one who has come upon the open for the first time in his life, and likes it. He is as yet far from being an expert woodsman — mark the blood on his hands at places where he has hit them instead of the tree; but note also that he does not waste time in bandaging them — he rubs them in the earth and goes on. His face is still of the discreet pallor that befits a butler, and he carries the smaller logs as if they were a salver; not in a day or a month will he shake off the badge of servitude, but without knowing it he has begun.*

But for the hatchets at work, and an occasional something horrible falling from a tree into the ladies' laps, they hear nothing save the mournful surf breaking on a coral shore.

They sit or recline huddled together against a rock, and they are farther from home, in every sense of the word, than ever before. Thirty-six hours ago, they were given three minutes in which to dress, without a maid, and reach the boats, and they have not made the best of that valuable time. None of them has boots, and had they known this prickly island they would have thought first of boots. They have a sufficiency of garments, but some of them were gifts dropped into the boat — LADY MARY'S tarpaulin coat and hat, for instance, and CATHERINE'S blue jersey and red cap, which certify that the two ladies were lately before the mast. AGATHA is too gay in ERNEST'S dressing-gown, and clutches it to her person with both hands as if afraid that it may be claimed by its rightful owner. There are two pairs of bath slippers between the three of them, and their hair cries aloud and in vain for hairpins.

By their side, on an inverted bucket, sits ERNEST, clothed neatly in the garments of day and night, but, alas, bare-footed. He is the only cheerful member of this company of four, but his brightness is due less to a manly desire to succour the helpless than to his having been lately in the throes of composition, and to his modest satisfaction with the result. He reads to the ladies, and they listen, each with one scared eye to the things that fall from trees.

ERNEST [*who has written on the fly-leaf of the only book saved from the wreck*]. This is what I have written. 'Wrecked, wrecked, wrecked! on an island in the Tropics, the following: the Hon. Ernest Woolley, the Rev. John Treherne, the Ladies, Mary, Catherine, and Agatha Lasenby, with two servants. We are the sole survivors of Lord Loam's steam yacht *Bluebell,* which encountered a fearful gale in these seas, and soon became a total wreck. The crew behaved gallantly, putting us all into the first boat. What became of them I cannot tell, but we, after dreadful sufferings, and insufficiently clad, in whatever garments we could lay hold of in the dark' —

LADY MARY. Please don't describe our garments.

ERNEST. — 'succeeded in reaching this island, with the loss of only one of our party, namely, Lord Loam, who flung away his life in a gallant attempt to save a servant who had fallen overboard.'

[*The ladies have wept long and sore for their father, but there is something in this last utterance that makes them look up.*]

AGATHA. But, Ernest, it was Crichton who jumped overboard trying to save father.

ERNEST [*with the candour that is one of his most engaging qualities*]. Well, you know, it was rather silly of uncle to fling away his life by trying to get into the boat first; and as this document may be printed in the English papers, it struck me, an English peer, you know —

LADY MARY [*every inch an English peer's daughter*]. Ernest, that is very thoughtful of you.

ERNEST [*continuing, well pleased*]. — 'By night the cries of wild cats and the hissing of snakes terrify us extremely' — [*this does not satisfy him so well, and he makes a correction*] — 'terrify the ladies extremely. Against these we have no weapons except one cutlass and a hatchet. A bucket washed ashore is at present our only comfortable seat' —

LADY MARY [*with some spirit*]. And Ernest is sitting on it.

ERNEST. H'sh! Oh, do be quiet. — 'To add to our horrors, night falls suddenly in these parts, and it is then that savage animals begin to prowl and roar.'

LADY MARY. Have you said that vampire bats suck the blood from our toes as we sleep?

ERNEST. No, that's all. I end up, 'Rescue us or we perish. Rich reward. Signed Ernest Woolley, in command of our little party.' This is written on a leaf taken out of a book of poems that Crichton found in his pocket. Fancy Crichton being a reader of poetry! Now I shall put it into the bottle and fling it into the sea.

[*He pushes the precious document into a soda-water bottle, and rams the cork home. At the same moment, and without effort, he gives birth to one of his most characteristic epigrams.*]

The tide is going out, we mustn't miss the post.

[*They are so unhappy that they fail to grasp it, and a little petulantly he calls for* CRICHTON, *ever his stand-by in the hour of epigram.* CRICHTON *breaks through the undergrowth quickly, thinking the ladies are in danger.*]

CRICHTON. Anything wrong, sir?

ERNEST [*with fine confidence*]. The tide, Crichton, is a postman who calls at our island twice a day for letters.

CRICHTON [*after a pause*]. Thank you, sir.

[*He returns to his labours, however, without giving the smile which is the epigrammatist's right, and* ERNEST *is a little disappointed in him.*]

ERNEST. Poor Crichton! I sometimes think he is losing his sense of humour. Come along, Agatha.

[*He helps his favourite up the rocks, and they disappear gingerly from view.*]

CATHERINE. How horribly still it is.

LADY MARY [*remembering some recent sounds*]. It is best when it is still.

CATHERINE [*drawing closer to her*]. Mary, I have heard that they are always very still just before they jump.

LADY MARY. Don't. [*A distinct chopping is heard, and they are startled.*]

LADY MARY [*controlling herself*]. It is only Crichton knocking down trees.

CATHERINE [*almost imploringly*]. Mary, let us go and stand beside him.

LADY MARY [*coldly*]. Let a servant see that I am afraid!

CATHERINE. Don't, then; but remember this, dear, they often drop on one from above.

[*She moves away, nearer to the friendly sound of the axe, and* LADY MARY *is left alone. She is the most courageous of them as well as the haughtiest, but when something she had thought to be a stick glides toward her, she forgets her dignity and screams.*]

LADY MARY [*calling*]. Crichton, Crichton!

[*It must have been* TREHERNE *who was tree-felling, for* CRICHTON *comes to her from the hut, drawing his cutlass.*]

CRICHTON [*anxious*]. Did you call, my lady?

LADY MARY [*herself again, now that he is there*]. I! Why should I?

CRICHTON. I made a mistake, your ladyship. [*Hesitating.*] If you are afraid of being alone, my lady —

LADY MARY. Afraid! Certainly not. [*Doggedly.*] You may go.

[*But she does not complain when he remains within eyesight cutting the bamboo. It is heavy work, and she watches him silently.*]

LADY MARY. I wish, Crichton, you could work without getting so hot.

CRICHTON [*mopping his face*]. I wish I could, my lady. [*He continues his labours.*]

LADY MARY [*taking off her oilskins*]. It makes me hot to look at you.

CRICHTON. It almost makes me cool to look at your ladyship.

LADY MARY [*who perhaps thinks he is presuming*]. Anything I can do for you in that way, Crichton, I shall do with pleasure.

CRICHTON [*quite humbly*]. Thank you, my lady.

[*By this time most of the bamboo has been cut, and the shore and sea are visible, except where they are hidden by the half completed hut. The mast rising solitary from the water adds to the desolation of the scene, and at last tears run down* LADY MARY'S *face.*]

CRICHTON. Don't give way, my lady, things might be worse.

LADY MARY. My poor father.

CRICHTON. If I could have given my life for his —

LADY MARY. You did all a man could do. Indeed I thank you, Crichton. [*With some admiration and more wonder.*] You are a man.

CRICHTON. Thank you, my lady.

LADY MARY. But it is all so awful. Crichton, is there any hope of a ship coming?

CRICHTON [*after hesitation*]. Of course there is, my lady.

LADY MARY [*facing him bravely*]. Don't treat me as a child. I have got to know the worst, and to face it. Crichton, the truth.

CRICHTON [*reluctantly*]. We were driven out of our course, my lady; I fear far from the track of commerce.

LADY MARY. Thank you; I understand.

[*For a moment, however, she breaks down. Then she clenches her hands and stands erect.*]

CRICHTON [*watching her, and forgetting perhaps for the moment that they are not just a man and woman*]. You're a good pluckt 'un, my lady.

LADY MARY [*falling into the same error*]. I shall try to be. [*Extricating herself.*] Crichton, you presume!

CRICHTON. I beg your ladyship's pardon; but you are.

[*She smiles, as if it were a comfort to be told this even by* CRICHTON.]

And until a ship comes we are three men who are going to do out best for you ladies.

LADY MARY [*with a curl of the lip*]. Mr. Ernest does no work.

CRICHTON [*cheerily*]. But he will, my lady.

LADY MARY. I doubt it.

CRICHTON [*confidently, but perhaps thoughtlessly*]. No work — no dinner — will make a great change in Mr. Ernest.

LADY MARY. No work — no dinner. When did you invent that rule, Crichton?

CRICHTON [*loaded with bamboo*]. I didn't invent it, my lady. I seem to see it growing all over the island.

LADY MARY [*disquieted*]. Crichton, your manner strikes me as curious.

CRICHTON [*pained*]. I hope not, your ladyship.

LADY MARY [*determined to have it out with him*]. You are not implying anything so unnatural, I hope, as that if I and my sisters don't work there will be no dinner for *us?*

CRICHTON [*brightly*]. If it is unnatural, my lady, that is the end of it.

LADY MARY. If? Now I understand. The perfect servant at home holds that we are all equal now. I see.

CRICHTON [*wounded to the quick*]. My lady, can you think me so inconsistent?

LADY MARY. That is it.

CRICHTON [*earnestly*]. My lady, I disbelieved in equality at home because it was against nature, and for that same reason I as utterly disbelieve in it on an island.

LADY MARY [*relieved by his obvious sincerity*]. I apologise.

CRICHTON [*continuing unfortunately*]. There must always, my lady, be one to command and others to obey.

LADY MARY [*satisfied*]. One to command, others to obey. Yes. [*Then suddenly she realises that there may be a dire meaning in his confident words.*] Crichton!

CRICHTON [*who has intended no dire meaning*]. What is it, my lady?

[*But she only stares into his face and then hurries from him. Left alone he is puzzled, but being a practical man he busies himself gathering firewood, until* TWEENY *appears excitedly carrying cocoa-nuts in her skirt. She has made better use than the ladies of her three minutes' grace for dressing.*]

TWEENY [*who can be happy even on an island if* CRICHTON *is with her*]. Look what I found.

CRICHTON. Cocoa-nuts. Bravo!

TWEENY. They grows on trees with this round them.

CRICHTON. Where did you think they grew?

TWEENY. I thought as how they grew in rows on top of little sticks.

CRICHTON [*wrinkling his brows*]. Oh Tweeny, Tweeny!

TWEENY [*anxiously*]. Have I offended of your feelings again, sir?

CRICHTON. A little.

TWEENY [*in a despairing outburst*]. I'm full o' vulgar words and ways; and though I may keep them in their holes when you are by, as soon as I'm by myself out they comes in a rush like beetles when the house is dark. I says them gloating-like, in my head — 'Blooming' I says, and 'All my eye,' and 'Ginger,' and 'Nothink'; and all the time we was being wrecked I was praying to myself, 'Please the Lord it may be an island as it's natural to be vulgar on.'

[*A shudder passes through* CRICHTON, *and she is abject.*]

That's the kind I am, sir. I'm 'opeless. You'd better give me up.

[*She is a pathetic, forlorn creature, and his manhood is stirred.*]

CRICHTON [*wondering a little at himself for saying it*]. I won't give you up. It is strange that one so common should attract one so fastidious; but so it is. [*Thoughtfully.*] There is something about you, Tweeny, there is a *je ne sais quoi* about you.

TWEENY [*knowing only that he has found something in her to commend*]. Is there, is there? Oh, I am glad.

CRICHTON [*putting his hand on her shoulder like a protector*]. We shall fight your vulgarity together. [*All this time he has been arranging sticks for his fire.*] Now get some dry grass.

[*She brings his grass, and he puts it under the sticks. He produces an odd lens from his pocket, and tries to focus the sun's rays.*]

TWEENY. Why, what's that?

CRICHTON [*the ingenious creature*]. That's the glass from my watch and one from Mr. Treherne's, with a little water between them. I'm hoping to kindle a fire with it.

TWEENY [*properly impressed*]. Oh, sir!

[*After one failure the grass takes fire, and they are blowing on it when excited cries near by bring them shortly to their feet. AGATHA runs to them, white of face, followed by ERNEST.*]

ERNEST. Danger! Crichton, a tiger-cat!

CRICHTON [*getting his cutlass*]. Where?

AGATHA. It is at our heels.

ERNEST. Look out, Crichton.

CRICHTON. H'sh!

[*TREHERNE comes to his assistance, while LADY MARY and CATHERINE join AGATHA in the hut.*]

ERNEST. It will be on us in a moment.

[*He seizes the hatchet and guards the hut. It is pleasing to see that ERNEST is no coward.*]

TREHERNE. Listen!

ERNEST. The grass is moving. It's coming.

[*It comes. But it is no tiger-cat; it is LORD LOAM crawling on*] *his hands and knees, a very exhausted and dishevelled peer, wondrously attired in rags. The girls see him, and with glad cries rush into his arms.*]

LADY MARY. Father!

LORD LOAM. Mary — Catherine — Agatha! Oh dear, my dears, my dears, oh dear!

LADY MARY. Darling.

AGATHA. Sweetest.

CATHERINE. Love.

TREHERNE. Glad to see you, sir.

ERNEST. Uncle, uncle, dear old uncle.

[*For a time such happy cries fill the air, but presently* TRE-HERNE *is thoughtless.*]

TREHERNE. Ernest thought you were a tiger-cat.

LORD LOAM [*stung somehow to the quick*]. Oh, did you? I knew you at once, Ernest; I knew you by the way you ran.

[ERNEST *smiles forgivingly.*]

CRICHTON [*venturing forward at last*]. My lord, I am glad.

ERNEST [*with upraised finger*]. But you are also idling, Crichton. [*Making himself more comfortable on the ground.*] We mustn't waste time. To work, to work.

CRICHTON [*after contemplating him without rancour*]. Yes, sir.

[*He gets a pot from the hut and hangs it on a tripod over the fire, which is now burning brightly.*]

TREHERNE. Ernest, you'be a little more civil. Crichton, let me help.

[*He is soon busy helping* CRICHTON *to add to the strength of the hut.*]

LORD LOAM [*gazing at the pot as ladies are said to gaze on precious stones*]. Is that — but I suppose I'm dreaming again. [*Timidly.*] It isn't by any chance a pot on top of a fire, is it?

LADY MARY. Indeed, it is, dearest. It is our supper.

LORD LOAM. I have been dreaming of a pot on a fire for two days. [*Quivering.*] There's nothing in it, is there?

ERNEST. Sniff, uncle. [LORD LOAM *sniffs.*]

LORD LOAM [*reverently*]. It smells of onions!

[*There is a sudden diversion.*]

CATHERINE. Father, you have boots!

LADY MARY. So he has.

LORD LOAM. Of course I have.

ERNEST [*with greedy cunning*]. You are actually wearing boots, uncle. It's very unsafe, you know, in this climate.

LORD LOAM. Is it?

ERNEST. We have all abandoned them, you observe. The blood, the arteries, you know.

LORD LOAM. I hadn't a notion.

[*He holds out his feet, and* ERNEST *kneels.*]

ERNEST. O Lord, yes.

[*In another moment those boots will be his.*]

LADY MARY [*quickly*]. Father, he is trying to get your boots from you. There is nothing in the world we wouldn't give for boots.

ERNEST [*rising haughtily, a proud spirit misunderstood*]. I only wanted the loan of them.

AGATHA [*running her fingers along them lovingly*]. If you lend them to anyone, it will be to us, won't it, father?

LORD LOAM. Certainly, my child.

ERNEST. Oh, very well. [*He is leaving these selfish ones.*] I don't want your old boots. [*He gives his uncle a last chance.*] You don't think you could spare me *one* boot?

LORD LOAM [*tartly*]. I do not.

ERNEST. Quite so. Well, all I can say is I'm sorry for you.

[*He departs to recline elsewhere.*]

LADY MARY. Father, we thought we should never see you again.

LORD LOAM. I was washed ashore, my dear, clinging to a hen-coop. How awful that first night was.

LADY MARY. Poor father.

LORD LOAM. When I woke, I wept. Then I began to feel extremely hungry. There was a large turtle on the beach. I remembered from the *Swiss Family Robinson* that if you turn a turtle over he is helpless. My dears, I crawled towards him, I flung myself upon him — [*here he pauses to rub his leg*] — the nasty, spiteful brute.

LADY MARY. You didn't turn him over?

LORD LOAM [*vindictively, though he is a kindly man*]. Mary, the senseless thing wouldn't wait; I found that none of them would wait.

CATHERINE. We should have been as badly off if Crichton hadn't —

LADY MARY [*quickly*]. Don't praise Crichton.

LORD LOAM. And then those beastly monkeys. I always understood that if you flung stones at them they would retaliate by flinging cocoa-nuts at you. Would you believe it, I flung a hundred stones, and not one monkey had sufficient intelligence to grasp my meaning. How I longed for Crichton.

LADY MARY [*wincing*]. For us also, father?

LORD LOAM. For you also. I tried for hours to make a fire. The authors say that when wrecked on an island you can obtain a light by rubbing two pieces of stick together. [*With feeling.*] The liars!

LADY MARY. And all this time you thought there was no one on the island but yourself?

LORD LOAM. I thought so until this morning. I was searching the pools for little fishes, which I caught in my hat, when suddenly I saw before me — on the sand —

CATHERINE. What?

LORD LOAM. A hairpin.

LADY MARY. A hairpin! It must be one of ours. [*Greedily.*] Give it to me, father.

AGATHA. No, it's mine.

LORD LOAM. I didn't keep it.

LADY MARY [*speaking for all three*]. Didn't keep it? Found a hairpin on an island, and didn't keep it?

LORD LOAM [*humbly*]. My dears.

AGATHA [*scarcely to be placated*]. Oh, father, we have returned to Nature more than you bargained for.

LADY MARY. For shame, Agatha. [*She has something on her mind.*] Father, there is something I want you to do at once — I mean to assert your position as the chief person on the island.

[*They are all surprised.*]

LORD LOAM. But who would presume to question it?

CATHERINE. She must mean Ernest.

LADY MARY. Must I?

AGATHA. It is cruel to say anything against Ernest.

LORD LOAM [*firmly*]. If any one presumes to challenge my position, I shall make short work of him.

AGATHA. Here comes Ernest; now see if you can say these horrid things to his face.

LORD LOAM. I shall teach him his place at once.

LADY MARY [*anxiously*]. But how?

LORD LOAM [*chuckling*]. I have just thought of an extremely amusing way of doing it. [*As ERNEST approaches.*] Ernest.

ERNEST [*loftily*]. Excuse me, uncle, I'm thinking. I'm planning out the building of this hut.

LORD LOAM. I also have been thinking.

ERNEST. That don't matter.

LORD LOAM. Eh?

ERNEST. Please, please, this is important.

LORD LOAM. I have been thinking that I ought to give you my boots.

ERNEST. What!

LADY MARY. Father.

LORD LOAM [*genially*]. Take them, my boy. [*With a rapidity we had not thought him capable of, ERNEST becomes the wearer of the boots.*] And now I dare say you want to know why I give them to you, Ernest?

ERNEST [*moving up and down in them deliciously*]. Not at all.
The great thing is, 'I've got 'em, I've got 'em.'

LORD LOAM [*majestically, but with a knowing look at his daughter*]. My reason is that, as head of our little party, you, Ernest,
shall be our hunter, you shall clear the forests of these savage
beasts that make them so dangerous. [*Pleasantly.*] And now
you know, my dear nephew, why I have given you my boots.

ERNEST. This is my answer.

[*He kicks off the boots.*]

LADY MARY [*still anxious*]. Father, assert yourself.

LORD LOAM. I shall now assert myself. [*But how to do it? He
has a happy thought.*] Call Crichton.

LADY MARY. Oh father.

[CRICHTON *comes in answer to a summons, and is followed
by* TREHERNE.]

ERNEST [*wondering a little at* LADY MARY'S *grave face*].
Crichton, look here.

LORD LOAM [*sturdily*]. Silence! Crichton, I want your advice as
to what I ought to do with Mr. Ernest. He has defied me.

ERNEST. Pooh!

CRICHTON [*after considering*]. May I speak openly, my lord?

LADY MARY [*keeping her eyes fixed on him*]. That is what we
desire.

CRICHTON [*quite humbly*]. Then I may say, your lordship, that
I have been considering Mr. Ernest's case at odd moments ever
since we were wrecked.

ERNEST. My case?

LORD LOAM [*sternly*]. Hush.

CRICHTON. Since we landed on the island, my lord, it seems to
me that Mr. Ernest's epigrams have been particularly brilliant.

ERNEST [*gratified*]. Thank you, Crichton.

CRICHTON. But I find — I seem to find it growing wild, my lord,
in the woods, that sayings which would be justly admired in
England are not much use on an island. I would therefore most

respectfully propose that henceforth every time Mr. Ernest favours us with an epigram his head should be immersed in a bucket of cold spring water.

[*There is a terrible silence.*]

LORD LOAM [*uneasily*]. Serve him right.

ERNEST. I should like to see you try to do it, uncle.

CRICHTON [*ever ready to come to the succour of his lordship*]. My feeling, my lord, is that at the next offence I should convey him to a retired spot, where I shall carry out the undertaking in as respectful a manner as is consistent with a thorough immersion.

[*Though his manner is most respectful, he is resolute; he evidently means what he says.*]

LADY MARY [*a ramrod*]. Father, you must not permit this; Ernest is your nephew.

LORD LOAM [*with his hand to his brow*]. After all, he is my nephew, Crichton; and, as I am sure, he now sees that I am a strong man —

ERNEST [*foolishly in the circumstances*]. A strong man. You mean a stout man. You are one of mind to two of matter.

[*He looks round in the old way for approval. No one has smiled, and to his consternation he sees that* CRICHTON *is quietly turning up his sleeves.* ERNEST *makes an appealing gesture to his uncle; then he turns defiantly to* CRICHTON.]

CRICHTON. Is it to be before the ladies, Mr. Ernest, or in the privacy of the wood? [*He fixes* ERNEST *with his eye.* ERNEST *is cowed.*] Come.

ERNEST [*after a long time*]. Oh, all right.

CRICHTON [*succinctly*]. Bring the bucket.

[ERNEST *hesitates. He then lifts the bucket and follows* CRICHTON *to the nearest spring.*]

LORD LOAM [*rather white*]. I'm sorry for him, but I had to be firm.

LADY MARY. Oh father, it wasn't you who was firm. Crichton did it himself.

LORD LOAM. Bless me, so he did.

LADY MARY. Father, be strong.

LORD LOAM [*bewildered*]. You can't mean that my faithful Crichton —

LADY MARY. Yes, I do.

TREHERNE. Lady Mary, I stake my word that Crichton is incapable of acting dishonourably.

LADY MARY. I know that; I know it as well as you. Don't you see, that is what makes him so dangerous?

TREHERNE. By Jove, I — I believe I catch your meaning.

CATHERINE. He is coming back.

LORD LOAM [*who has always known himself to be a man of ideas*]. Let us all go into the hut, just to show him at once that it is *our* hut.

LADY MARY [*as they go*]. Father, I implore you, assert yourself now and for ever.

LORD LOAM. I will.

LADY MARY. And, please, don't ask him how you are to do it.

[CRICHTON *returns with sticks to mend the fire.*]

LORD LOAM [*loftily, from the door of the hut*]. Have you carried out my instructions, Crichton?

CRICHTON [*deferentially*]. Yes, my lord.

[ERNEST *appears, mopping his hair, which has become very wet since we last saw him. He is not bearing malice, he is too busy drying, but* AGATHA *is specially his champion.*]

AGATHA. It's infamous, infamous.

LORD LOAM [*strongly*]. *My* orders, Agatha.

LADY MARY. Now, father, please.

LORD LOAM [*striking an attitude*]. Before I give you any further orders, Crichton —

CRICHTON. Yes, my lord.

LORD LOAM [*delighted*]. Pooh! It's all right.

LADY MARY. No. Please go on.

LORD LOAM. Well, well. This question of the leadership; what do you think now, Crichton?

CRICHTON. My lord, I feel it is a matter with which *I* have nothing to do.

LORD LOAM. Excellent. Ha, Mary? That settles it, I think.

LADY MARY. It seems to, but — I'm not sure.

CRICHTON. It will settle itself naturally, my lord, without any interference from us.

[*The reference to Nature gives general dissatisfaction.*]

LADY MARY. Father.

LORD LOAM [*a little severely*]. It settled itself long ago, Crichton, when I was born a peer, and you, for instance, were born a servant.

CRICHTON [*acquiescing*]. Yes, my lord, that was how it all came about quite naturally in England. We had nothing to do with it there, and we shall have as little to do with it here.

TREHERNE [*relieved*]. That's all right.

LADY MARY [*determined to clinch the matter*]. One moment. In short, Crichton, his lordship will continue to be our natural head.

CRICHTON. I dare say, my lady, I dare say.

CATHERINE. But you must *know*.

CRICHTON. Asking your pardon, my lady, one can't be sure — on an island.

[*They look at each other uneasily.*]

LORD LOAM [*warningly*]. Crichton, I don't like this.

CRICHTON [*harassed*]. The more I think of it, your lordship, the more uneasy I become myself. When I heard, my lord, that you had left that hairpin behind —

[*He is pained.*]

LORD LOAM [*feebly*]. One hairpin among so many would only have caused dissension.

CRICHTON [*very sorry to have to contradict him*]. Not so, my lord. From that hairpin we could have made a needle; with that needle we could, out of skins, have sewn trousers — of which your lordship is in need; indeed, we are all in need of them.

LADY MARY [*suddenly self-conscious*]. All?

CRICHTON. On an island, my lady.

LADY MARY. Father.

CRICHTON [*really more distressed by the prospect than she*]. My lady, if Nature does not think them necessary, you may be sure she will not ask you to wear them. [*Shaking his head.*] But among all this undergrowth —

LADY MARY. Now you see this man in his true colours.

LORD LOAM [*violently*]. Crichton, you will either this moment say, 'Down with Nature,' or —

CRICHTON [*scandalised*]. My Lord!

LORD LOAM [*loftily*]. Then this is my last word to you; take a month's notice.

[*If the hut had a door he would now shut it to indicate that the interview is closed.*]

CRICHTON [*in great distress*]. Your lordship, the disgrace —

LORD LOAM [*swelling*]. Not another word: you may go.

LADY MARY [*adamant*]. And don't come to me, Crichton, for a character.

ERNEST [*whose immersion has cleared his brain*]. Aren't you all forgetting that this is an island?

[*This brings them to earth with a bump. LORD LOAM looks to his eldest daughter for the fitting response.*]

LADY MARY [*equal to the occasion*]. It makes only this difference — that you may go at once, Crichton, to some other part of the island.

[*The faithful servant has been true to his superiors ever since he was created, and never more true than at this moment; but his fidelity is founded on trust in Nature, and to be untrue to it would be to be untrue to them. He lets the wood he has been gathering slip to the ground, and bows his sorrowful head. He turns to obey. Then affection for these great ones wells up in him.*]

CRICHTON. My lady, let me work for you.

LADY MARY. Go.

CRICHTON. You need me so sorely; I can't desert you; I won't.

LADY MARY [*in alarm, lest the others may yield*]. Then, father, there is but one alternative, *we* must leave him.

[LORD LOAM *is looking yearningly at* CRICHTON.]

TREHERNE. It seems a pity.

CATHERINE [*forlornly*]. *You* will work for us?

TREHERNE. Most willingly. But I must warn you all that, so far, Crichton has done nine-tenths of the scoring.

LADY MARY. The question is, are we to leave this man?

LORD LOAM [*wrapping himself in his dignity*]. Come, my dears.

CRICHTON. My lord!

LORD LOAM. Treherne — Ernest — get our things.

ERNEST. We don't have any, uncle. They all belong to Crichton.

TREHERNE. Everything we have he brought from the wreck — he went back to it before it sank. He risked his life.

CRICHTON. My lord, anything you would care to take is yours.

LADY MARY [*quickly*]. Nothing.

ERNEST. Rot! If I could have your socks, Crichton —

LADY MARY. Come, father; we are ready.

[*Followed by the others, she and* LORD LOAM *pick their way up the rocks. In their indignation they scarcely notice that daylight is coming to a sudden end.*]

CRICHTON. My lord, I implore you — *I* am not desirous of being head. Do you have a try at it, my lord.

LORD LOAM [*outraged*]. A try at it!

CRICHTON [*eagerly*]. It may be that you will prove to be the best man.

LORD LOAM. *May* be! My children, come.

[*They disappear proudly but gingerly up those splintered rocks.*]

TREHERNE. Crichton, I'm sorry; but of course I must go with them.

CRICHTON. Certainly, sir.

[*He calls to* TWEENY, *and she comes from behind the hut, where she has been watching breathlessly.*]

Will you be so kind, sir, as to take her to the others?

TREHERNE. Assuredly.

TWEENY. But what do it all mean?

CRICHTON. Does, Tweeny, does. [*He passes her up the rocks to* TREHERNE.] We shall meet again soon, Tweeny. Good-night, sir.

TREHERNE. Good-night. I dare say they are not far away.

CRICHTON [*thoughtfully*]. They went westward, sir, and the wind is blowing in that direction. That may mean, sir, that Nature is already taking the matter into her own hands. They are all hungry, sir, and the pot has come a-boil. [*He takes off the lid.*] The smell will be borne westward. That pot is full of Nature, Mr. Treherne. Good-night, sir.

TREHERNE. Good-night.

[*He mounts the rocks with* TWEENY, *and they are heard for a little time after their figures are swallowed up in the fast growing darkness.* CRICHTON *stands motionless, the lid in his hand, though he has forgotten it, and his reason for taking it off the pot. He is deeply stirred, but presently is ashamed of his dejection, for it is as if he doubted his principles. Bravely true to his faith that Nature will decide now as ever before, he proceeds manfully with his preparations for the night. He lights a ship's lantern, one of several treasures he has brought ashore, and is filling his pipe with crumbs of tobacco from various pockets, when the stealthy movement of some animal in the grass startles him. With the lantern in one hand and his cutlass in the other, he searches the ground around the hut. He returns, lights his pipe, and sits down by the fire, which casts weird moving shadows. There is a red gleam on his face; in the darkness he is a strong and perhaps rather sinister figure. In the great stillness that has fallen over the land, the wash of the surf seems to have increased in volume. The sound is indescribably mournful. Except where the fire is, desolation has fallen on the island like a pall.*]

Once or twice, as Nature dictates, CRICHTON *leans forward to stir the pot, and the smell is borne westward. He then resumes his silent vigil.*

Shadows other than those cast by the fire begin to descend the rocks. They are the adventurers returning. One by one they steal nearer to the pot until they are squatted round it, with their hands out to the blaze. LADY MARY *only is absent. Presently she comes within sight of the others, then stands against a tree with her teeth clenched. One wonders, perhaps, what Nature is to make of her.*]

ACT THREE

THE HAPPY HOME

The scene is the hall of their island home two years later. This sturdy log-house is no mere extension of the hut we have seen in process of erection, but has been built a mile or less to the west of it, on higher ground and near a stream. When the master chose this site, the others thought that all he expected from the stream was a sufficiency of drinking water. They know better now every time they go down to the mill or turn on the electric light.

This hall is the living-room of the house, and walls and roof are of stout logs. Across the joists supporting the roof are laid many home-made implements, such as spades, saws, fishing-rods, and from hooks in the joists are suspended cured foods, of which hams are specially in evidence. Deep recesses half-way up the walls contain various provender in barrels and sacks. There are some skins, trophies of the chase, on the floor, which is otherwise bare. The chairs and tables are in some cases hewn out of the solid wood, and in others the result of rough but efficient carpentering. Various pieces of wreckage from the yacht have been turned to novel uses: thus the steering-wheel now hangs from the centre of the roof, with electric lights attached to it encased in bladders. A lifebuoy has become the back of a chair. Two barrels have been halved and turn coyly from each other as a settee.

The farther end of the room is more strictly the kitchen, and is a great recess, which can be shut off from the hall by folding-doors. There is a large open fire on it. The chimney is half of one of the boats of the yacht. On the walls of the kitchen proper are many plate-racks, containing shells; there are rows of these of one size and shape, which mark them off as dinner plates or bowls; others are as obviously tureens. They are arranged primly as in a well-conducted kitchen; indeed, neatness and cleanliness are the note struck everywhere, yet the effect of the whole is romantic and barbaric.

The outer door into this hall is a little peculiar on an island. It is covered with skins and is in four leaves, like the swing-doors of fashionable restaurants, which allow you to enter without allowing the hot air to escape. During the winter season our castaways have found this contrivance useful, but CRICHTON'S brain was perhaps a little lordly when he conceived it. Another door leads by a passage to the sleeping-rooms of the house, which are all on the ground-floor, and to CRICHTON'S work-room, where he is at this moment, and whither we should like to follow him, but in a play we may not, as it is out of sight. There is a large window space without a window, which, however, can be shuttered, and through this we have a view of cattle-sheds, fowl-pens, and a field of grain. It is a fine summer evening.

TWEENY is sitting there, very busy plucking the feathers off a bird and dropping them on a sheet placed for that purpose on the floor. She is trilling to herself in the lightness of her heart. We may remember that TWEENY, alone among the women, had dressed wisely for an island when they fled the yacht, and her going-away gown still adheres to her, though in fragments. A score of pieces have been added here and there as necessity compelled, and these have been patched and repatched in incongruous colours; but, when all is said and done, it can still be maintained that TWEENY wears a skirt. She is deservedly proud of her skirt, and sometimes lends it on important occasions when approached in the proper spirit.

Some one outside has been whistling to TWEENY; the guarded whistle which, on a less savage island, is sometimes assumed to be an indication to cook that the constable is willing, if the coast be clear. TWEENY, however, is engrossed, or perhaps she is not in the mood for a follower, so he climbs in at the window undaunted, to take her willy-nilly. He is a jolly-looking labouring man, who answers to the name of Daddy, and — But though that may be his island name, we recognise him at once. He is LORD LOAM, settled down to the new conditions, and enjoying life heartily as handy-man about the happy home. He is comfortably attired in skins. He is still stout, but all the flabbiness has dropped from him; gone too is his pomposity; his eye is clear, brown his skin; he could leap a gate.

In his hands he carries an island-made concertina, and such is the exuberance of his spirits that, as he alights on the floor, he bursts into music and song, something about his being a chickety chickety chick chick, and will TWEENY please to tell him whose chickety chick is she. Retribution follows sharp. We hear a whir, as if from insufficiently oiled machinery, and over the passage door appears a placard showing the one word 'Silence.' His lordship stops, and steals to TWEENY on his tiptoes.

LORD LOAM. I thought the Gov. was out.

TWEENY. Well, you see he ain't. And if he were to catch you here idling —

[LORD LOAM *pales. He lays aside his musical instrument and hurriedly dons an apron.* TWEENY *gives him the bird to pluck, and busies herself laying the table for dinner.*]

LORD LOAM [*softly*]. What is he doing now?

TWEENY. I think he's working out that plan for laying on hot and cold.

LORD LOAM [*proud of his master*]. And he'll manage it too. The man who could build a blacksmith's forge without tools —

TWEENY [*not less proud*]. He made the tools.

LORD LOAM. Out of half a dozen rusty nails. The sawmill, Tweeny; the speaking-tube; the electric lighting; and look at the use he has made of the bits of the yacht that were washed ashore. And all in two years. He is a master I'm proud to pluck for.

[*He chirps happily at his work, and she regards him curiously.*]

TWEENY. Daddy, you're of little use, but you're a bright, cheerful creature to have about the house. [*He beams at this commendation.*] Do you ever think of old times now? We was a bit different.

LORD LOAM [*pausing*]. Circumstances alter cases.

[*He resumes his plucking contentedly.*]

TWEENY. But, Daddy, if the chance was to come of getting back?

LORD LOAM. I have given up bothering about it.

TWEENY. You bothered that day long ago when we saw a ship passing the island. How we all ran like crazy folk into the water, Daddy, and screamed and held out our arms. [*They are both a little agitated.*] But it sailed away, and we've never seen another.

LORD LOAM. If the electrical contrivance had been made then that we have now we could have attracted that ship's notice. [*Their eyes rest on a mysterious apparatus that fills a corner of the hall.*] A touch on that lever, Tweeny, and in a few moments bonfires would be blazing all round the shore.

TWEENY [*backing from the lever as if it might spring at her*]. It's the most wonderful thing he has done.

LORD LOAM [*in a reverie*]. And then — England — home!

TWEENY [*also seeing visions*]. London of a Saturday night!

LORD LOAM. My lords, in rising once more to address this historic chamber —

TWEENY. There was a little ham and beef shop off the Edgware Road —

[*The visions fade; they return to the practical.*]

LORD LOAM. Tweeny, do you think I could have an egg to my tea?

[*At this moment a wiry, athletic figure in skins darkens the window. He is carrying two pails, which are suspended from a pole on his shoulder, and he is* ERNEST. *We should say that he is* ERNEST *completely changed if we were of those who hold that people change. As he enters by the window he has heard* LORD LOAM'S *appeal, and is perhaps justifiably indignant.*]

ERNEST. What is that about an egg? Why should you have an egg?

LORD LOAM [*with hauteur*]. That is my affair, sir. [*With a Parthian shot as he withdraws stiffly from the room.*] The Gov. has never put *my* head in a bucket.

ERNEST [*coming to rest on one of his buckets, and speaking with excusable pride*]. Nor mine for nearly three months. It was only last week, Tweeny, that he said to me, 'Ernest, the water cure has worked marvels in you, and I question whether I shall require to dip you any more.' [*Complacently.*] Of course that sort of thing encourages a fellow.

TWEENY [*who has now arranged the dinner-table to her satisfaction*]. I will say, Erny, I never seen a young chap more improved.

ERNEST [*gratified*]. Thank you, Tweeny; that's very precious to me.

[*She retires to the fire to work the great bellows with her foot, and* ERNEST *turns to* TREHERNE, *who has come in looking more like a cow-boy than a clergyman. He has a small box in his hand which he tries to conceal.*]

What have you got there, John?

TREHERNE. Don't tell anybody. It is a little present for the Gov.; a set of razors. One for each day in the week.

ERNEST [*opening the box and examining its contents*]. Shells! He'll like that. He likes sets of things.

TREHERNE [*in a guarded voice*]. Have you noticed that?

ERNEST. Rather.

TREHERNE. He is becoming a bit magnificent in his ideas.

ERNEST [*huskily*]. John, it sometimes gives me the creeps.

TREHERNE [*making sure that* TWEENY *is out of hearing*]. What do you think of that brilliant robe he got the girls to make for him?

ERNEST [*uncomfortably*]. I think he looks too regal in it.

TREHERNE. Regal! I sometimes fancy that is why he is so fond of wearing it. [*Practically.*] Well, I must take these down to the grindstone and put an edge on them.

ERNEST [*button-holing him*]. I say, John, I want a word with you.

TREHERNE. Well?

ERNEST [*become suddenly diffident*]. Dash it all, you know, you're a clergyman.

TREHERNE. One of the best things the Gov. has done is to insist that none of you forget it.

ERNEST [*taking his courage in his hands*]. Then — would you, John?

TREHERNE. What?

ERNEST [*wistfully*]. Officiate at a marriage ceremony, John?

TREHERNE [*slowly*]. Now, that is really odd.

ERNEST. Odd? Seems to me it's natural. And whatever is natural, John, is right.

TREHERNE. I mean that same question has been put to me to-day already.

ERNEST [*eagerly*]. By one of the women?

TREHERNE. Oh no; they all put it to me long ago. This was by the Gov. himself.

ERNEST. By Jove! [*Admiringly.*] I say, John, what an observant beggar he is.

TREHERNE. Ah! You fancy he was thinking of you?

ERNEST. I do not hesitate to affirm, John, that he has seen the love-light in my eyes. You answered —

TREHERNE. I said Yes, I thought it would be my duty to officiate if called upon.

ERNEST. You're a brick.

TREHERNE [*still pondering*]. But I wonder whether he *was* thinking of you?

ERNEST. Make your mind easy about that.

TREHERNE. Well, my best wishes. Agatha is a very fine girl.

ERNEST. Agatha? What made you think it was Agatha?

TREHERNE. Man alive, you told me all about it soon after we were wrecked.

ERNEST. Pooh! Agatha's all very well in her way, John, but I am flying at bigger game.

TREHERNE. Ernest, which is it?

ERNEST. Tweeny, of course.

TREHERNE. Tweeny? [*Reprovingly.*] Ernest, I hope her cooking has nothing to do with this.

ERNEST [*with dignity*]. Her cooking has very little to do with it.

TREHERNE. But does she return your affection?

ERNEST [*simply*]. Yes, John, I believe I may say so. I am unworthy of her, but I think I have touched her heart.

TREHERNE [*with a sigh*]. Some people seem to have all the luck. As you know, Catherine won't look at me.

ERNEST. I'm sorry, John.

TREHERNE. It's my desserts; I'm a second eleven sort of chap. Well, my heartiest good wishes, Ernest.

ERNEST. Thank you, John. How is the little black pig to-day?

TREHERNE [*departing*]. He has begun to eat again.

[*After a moment's reflection* ERNEST *calls to* TWEENY.]

ERNEST. Are you very busy, Tweeny?

TWEENY [*coming to him good-naturedly*]. There is always work to do; but if you want me, Ernest —

ERNEST. There is something I should like to say to you if you could spare me a moment.

TWEENY. Willingly. What is it?

ERNEST. What an ass I used to be, Tweeny.

TWEENY [*tolerantly*]. Oh, let bygones be bygones.

ERNEST [*sincerely, and at his very best*]. I'm no great shakes even now. But listen to this, Tweeny; I have known many women, but until I knew you I never knew any woman.

TWEENY [*to whose uneducated ear this sounds dangerously like an epigram*]. Take care — the bucket.

ERNEST [*hurriedly*]. I didn't mean it in that way. [*He goes chivalrously on his knees.*] Ah, Tweeny, I don't undervalue the bucket, but what I want to say now is that the sweet refinement of a dear girl has done more for me than any bucket could do.

TWEENY [*with large eyes*]. Are you offering to walk out with me, Erny?

ERNEST [*passionately*]. More than that. I want to build a little house for you — in the sunny glade down by Porcupine Creek. I want to make chairs for you and tables; and knives and forks, and a sideboard for you.

TWEENY [*who is fond of language*]. I like to hear you. [*Eyeing him.*] Would there be any one in the house except myself, Ernest?

ERNEST [*humbly*]. Not often; but just occasionally there would be your adoring husband.

TWEENY [*decisively*]. It won't do, Ernest.

ERNEST [*pleading*]. It isn't as if I should be much there.

TWEENY. I know, I know; but I don't love you, Ernest. I'm that sorry.

ERNEST [*putting his case cleverly*]. Twice a week I should be away altogether — at the dam. On the other days you would never see me from breakfast time to supper.

[*With the self-abnegation of the true lover.*]

If you like I'll even go fishing on Sundays.

TWEENY. It's no use, Erny.

ERNEST [*rising manfully*]. Thank you, Tweeny; it can't be helped. [*Then he remembers.*] Tweeny, we shall be disappointing the Gov.

TWEENY [*quaking*]. What's that?

ERNEST. He wanted us to marry.

TWEENY [*blankly*]. You and me? the Gov.! [*Her head droops woefully. From without is heard the whistling of a happier spirit, and* TWEENY *draws herself up fiercely.*] That's her; that's the thing what has stole his heart from me.

[*A stalwart youth appears at the window, so handsome and tingling with vitality that, glad to depose* CRICHTON, *we cry thankfully, 'The hero at last.' But it is not the hero; it is the heroine. This splendid boy, clad in skins, is what Nature has done for* LADY MARY. *She carries bow and arrows and a blow-pipe, and over her shoulder is a fat buck, which she drops with a cry of triumph. Forgetting to enter demurely, she leaps through the window.*]

[*Sourly.*] Drat you, Polly, why don't you wipe your feet?

LADY MARY [*good-naturedly*]. Come, Tweeny, be nice to me. It's a splendid buck.

[*But* TWEENY *shakes her off, and retires to the kitchen fire.*]

ERNEST. Where did you get it?

LADY MARY [*gaily*]. I sighted a herd near Penguin's Creek, but had to creep round Silver Lake to get to windward of them. However, they spotted me and then the fun began. There was nothing for it but to try and run them down, so I singled out a fat buck and away we went down the shore of the lake, up the valley of rolling stones; he doubled into Brawling River and took to the water, but I swam after him; the river is only half a mile broad there, but it runs strong. He went spinning down the rapids, down I went in pursuit; he clambered ashore, I clambered ashore; away we tore helter-skelter up the hill and down again. I lost him in the marshes, got on his track again near Bread Fruit Wood, and brought him down with an arrow in Firefly Grove.

TWEENY [*staring at her*]. Aren't you tired?

LADY MARY. Tired! It was gorgeous.

[*She runs up a ladder and deposits her weapons on the joists. She is whistling again.*]

TWEENY [*snapping*]. I can't abide a woman whistling.

LADY MARY [*indifferently*]. I like it.

TWEENY [*stamping her foot*]. Drop it, Polly, I tell you.

LADY MARY. I won't. I'm as good as you are.

[*They are facing each other defiantly.*]

ERNEST [*shocked*]. Is this necessary? Think how it would pain *him.*

[LADY MARY'S *eyes take a new expression. We see them soft for the first time.*]

LADY MARY [*contritely*]. Tweeny, I beg your pardon. If my whistling annoys you, I shall try to cure myself of it.

[*Instead of calming* TWEENY, *this floods her face in tears.*]

Why, how can that hurt you, Tweeny dear?

TWEENY. Because I can't make you lose your temper.

LADY MARY [*divinely*]. Indeed, I often do. Would that I were nicer to everybody.

TWEENY. There you are again. [*Large-eyed.*] What makes you want to be so nice, Polly?

LADY MARY [*with fervour*]. Only thankfulness, Tweeny. [*She exults.*] It is such fun to be alive.

[*So also seem to think* CATHERINE *and* AGATHA, *who bounce in with fishing-rods and creel. They, too, are in manly attire.*]

CATHERINE. We've got some ripping fish for the Gov.'s dinner. Are we in time? We ran all the way.

TWEENY [*tartly*]. You'll please to cook them yourself, Kitty, and look sharp about it.

[*She retires to her hearth, where* AGATHA *follows her.*]

AGATHA [*yearning*]. Has the Gov. decided who is to wait upon him to-day?

CATHERINE [*who is cleaning her fish*]. It's my turn.

AGATHA [*hotly*]. I don't see that.

TWEENY [*with bitterness*]. It's to be neither of you, Aggy; he wants Polly again.

[LADY MARY *is unable to resist a joyous whistle.*]

AGATHA [*jealously*]. Polly, you toad.

[*But they cannot make* LADY MARY *angry.*]

TWEENY [*storming*]. How dare you look so happy?

LADY MARY [*willing to embrace her*]. I wish, Tweeny, there was anything I could do to make you happy also.

TWEENY. Me! Oh, I'm happy. [*She remembers* ERNEST, *whom it is easy to forget on an island.*] I've just had a proposal, I tell you.

[LADY MARY *is shaken at last, and her sisters with her.*]

AGATHA. A proposal?

CATHERINE [*going white*]. Not — not —

[*She dare not say his name.*]

ERNEST [*with singular modesty*]. You needn't be alarmed; it was only me.

LADY MARY [*relieved*]. Oh, you!

AGATHA [*happy again*]. Ernest, you dear, I got such a shock.

CATHERINE. It was only Ernest [*showing him her fish in thankfulness*]. They are beautifully fresh; come and help me to cook them.

ERNEST [*with simple dignity*]. Do you mind if I don't cook fish to-night? [*She does not mind in the least. They have all forgotten him. A lark is singing in three hearts.*] I think you might all be a little sorry for a chap. [*But they are not even sorry, and he addresses* AGATHA *in these winged words.*] I'm particularly disappointed in you, Aggy; seeing that I was half engaged to you, I think you might have had the good feeling to be a little more hurt.

AGATHA. Oh, bother.

ERNEST [*summing up the situation in so far as it affects himself*]. I shall now go and lie down for a bit.

[*He retires coldly but unregretted.* LADY MARY *approaches* TWEENY *with her most insinuating smile.*]

LADY MARY. Tweeny, as the Gov. has chosen me to wait on him, please may I have the loan of *it* again?

[*The reference made with such charming delicacy is evidently to* TWEENY'S *skirt.*]

TWEENY [*doggedly*]. No, you mayn't.

AGATHA [*supporting* TWEENY]. Don't you give it to her.

LADY MARY [*still trying sweet persuasion*]. You know quite well that he prefers to be waited on in a skirt.

TWEENY. I don't care. Get one for yourself.

LADY MARY. It is the only one on the island.

TWEENY. And it's mine.

LADY MARY [*an aristocrat after all*]. Tweeny, give me that skirt directly.

CATHERINE. Don't.

TWEENY. I won't.

LADY MARY [*clearing for action*]. I shall make you.

TWEENY. I should like to see you try.

[*An unseemly fracas appears to be inevitable, but something happens. The whir is again heard, and the notice is displayed 'Dogs delight to bark and bite.' Its effect is instantaneous and cheering. The ladies look at each other guiltily and immediately proceed on tiptoe to their duties. These are all concerned with the master's dinner.* CATHERINE *attends to his fish.* AGATHA fills a quaint toast-rack and brings the menu, which is written on a shell.* LADY MARY *twists a wreath of green leaves around her head, and places a flower beside the master's plate.* TWEENY *signs that all is ready, and she and the younger sisters retire into the kitchen, closing the screen that separates it from the rest of the room.* LADY MARY *beats a tom-tom, which is the dinner-bell. She then gently works a punkah, which we have not hitherto observed, and stands at attention. No doubt she is in hopes that the Gov. will enter into conversation with her, but she is too good a parlour-maid to let her hopes appear in her face. We may watch her manner* *with complete approval. There is not one of us who would not give her £26 a year.*

The master comes in quietly, a book in his hand, still the only book on the island, for he has not thought it worth while to build a printing-press. His dress is not noticeably different from that of the others, the skins are similar, but perhaps these are a trifle more carefully cut or he carries them better. One sees somehow that he has changed for his evening meal. There is an odd suggestion of a dinner jacket about his doeskin coat. It is, perhaps, too grave a face for a man of thirty-two, as if he were overmuch immersed in affairs, yet there is a sunny smile left to lighten it at times and bring back its youth; perhaps too intellectual a face to pass as strictly handsome, not sufficiently suggestive of oats. His tall figure is very straight, slight rather than thick-set, but nobly muscular. His big hands, firm and hard with labour though they be, are finely shaped — note the fingers so much more tapered, the nails better tended than those of his domestics; they are one of many indications that he is of a superior breed. Such signs, as has often been pointed out, are infallible. A romantic figure, too. One can easily see why the women-folks of this strong man's house both adore and fear him.

He does not seem to notice who is waiting on him to-night, but inclines his head slightly to whoever it is, as she takes her place at the back of his chair. LADY MARY respectfully places the menu-shell before him, and he glances at it.]

CRICHTON. Clear, please.

[LADY MARY *knocks on the screen, and a serving hutch in it opens, through which* TWEENY *offers two soup plates.* LADY MARY *selects, the clear, and the aperture is closed. She works the punkah while the master partakes of the soup.*]

CRICHTON [*who always gives praise where it is due*]. An excellent soup, Polly, but still a trifle too rich.

LADY MARY. Thank *you.*

[*The next course is the fish, and while it is being passed through the hutch we have a glimpse of three jealous women.* LADY MARY'S *movements are so deft and noiseless that any observant spectator can see that she was born to wait at table.*]

CRICHTON [*unbending as he eats*]. Polly, you are a very smart girl.

LADY MARY [*bridling, but naturally gratified*]. La!

CRICHTON [*smiling*]. And I'm not the first you've heard it from, I'll swear.

LADY MARY [*wriggling*]. Oh Gov.!

CRICHTON. Got any followers on the island, Polly?

LADY MARY [*tossing her head*]. Certainly not.

CRICHTON. I thought that perhaps John or Ernest —

LADY MARY [*tilting her nose*]. I don't say that it's for want of asking.

CRICHTON [*emphatically*]. I'm sure it isn't.

[*Perhaps he thinks he has gone too far.*]

You may clear.

[*Flushed with pleasure, she puts before him a bird and vegetables, sees that his beaker is filled with wine, and returns to the punkah. She would love to continue their conversation, but it is for him to decide. For a time he seems to have forgotten her.*]

CRICHTON [*presently*]. Did you lose any arrows to-day?

LADY MARY. Only one in Firefly Grove.

CRICHTON. You were as far as that? How did you get across the Black Gorge?

LADY MARY. I went across on the rope.

CRICHTON. Hand over hand?

LADY MARY [*swelling at the implied praise*]. I wasn't in the least dizzy.

CRICHTON [*moved*]. You brave girl! [*He sits back in his chair a little agitated.*] But never do that again.

LADY MARY [*pouting*]. It is such fun, Gov.

CRICHTON [*decisively*]. I forbid it.

LADY MARY [*the little rebel*]. I shall.

CRICHTON [*surprised*]. Polly!

[*He signs to her sharply to step forward, but for a moment she holds back petulantly, and even when she does come it is less obediently than like a naughty, sulky child. Nevertheless, with the forbearance that is characteristic of the man, he addresses her with grave gentleness rather than severely.*]

You must do as I tell you, you know.

LADY MARY [*strangely passionate*]. I won't.

CRICHTON [*smiling at her fury*]. We shall see. Frown at me, Polly; there, you do it at once. Clench your little fists, stamp your feet, bite your ribbons —

[*A student of women, or at least of this woman, he knows that she is about to do those things, and thus she seems to do them to order. LADY MARY screws up her face like a baby and cries. He is immediately kind.*]

You child of Nature; was it cruel of me to wish to save you from harm?

LADY MARY [*drying her eyes*]. I'm an ungracious wretch. Oh Gov., I don't try half hard enough to please you. I'm even wearing — [*she looks down sadly*] — when I know you prefer *it*.

CRICHTON [*thoughtfully*]. I admit I do prefer *it*. Perhaps I am a little old-fashioned in these matters.

[*Her tears again threaten.*]

Ah, don't, Polly; that's nothing.

LADY MARY. If I could only please you, Gov.

CRICHTON [*slowly*]. You do please me, child, very much — [*he half rises*] — very much indeed. [*If he meant to say more he checks himself. He looks at his plate.*] No more, thank you.

[*The simple island meal is soon ended, save for the walnuts and the wine, and CRICHTON is too busy a man to linger long over them. But he is a stickler for etiquette, and the table is cleared charmingly, though with dispatch, before they are placed before him. LADY MARY is an artist with the crumb-brush, and there are few arts more delightful to watch. Dusk has come sharply, and she turns on the electric light. It awakens CRICHTON from a reverie in which he has been regarding her.*]

CRICHTON. Polly, there is only one thing about you that I don't quite like.

[*She looks up, making a* moue, *if that can be said of one who so well knows her place. He explains.*]

That action of the hands.

LADY MARY. What do I do?

CRICHTON. This — like one washing them. I have noticed that the others tend to do it also. It seems odd.

LADY MARY [*archly*]. Oh Gov., have you forgotten?

CRICHTON. What?

LADY MARY. That once upon a time a certain other person did that.

CRICHTON [*groping*]. You mean myself? [*She nods, and he shudders.*] Horrible!

LADY MARY [*afraid she has hurt him*]. You haven't for a very long time. Perhaps it is natural to servants.

CRICHTON. That must be it. [*He rises.*] Polly! [*She looks up expectantly, but he only sighs and turns away.*]

LADY MARY [*gently*]. You sighed, Gov.

CRICHTON. Did I? I was thinking. [*He paces the room and then turns to her agitatedly, yet with control over his agitation. There is some mournfulness in his voice.*] I have always tried to do the right thing on this island. Above all, Polly, I want to do the right thing by you.

LADY MARY [*with shining eyes*]. How we all trust you. That is your reward, Gov.

CRICHTON [*who is having a fight with himself*]. And now I want a greater reward. Is it fair to you? Am I playing the game? Bill Crichton would like always to play the game. If we were in England —

[*He pauses so long that she breaks in softly.*]

LADY MARY. We know now that we shall never see England again.

CRICHTON. I am thinking of two people whom neither of us has seen for a long time — Lady Mary Lasenby, and one Crichton, a butler.

[*He says the last word bravely, a word he once loved, though it is the most horrible of all words to him now.*]

LADY MARY. That cold, haughty, insolent girl. Gov., look around you and forget them both.

CRICHTON. I had nigh forgotten them. He has had a chance, Polly — that butler — in these two years of becoming a man, and he has tried to take it. There have been many failures, but there has been some success, and with it I have let the past drop off me, and turned my back on it. That butler seems a far-away figure to me now, and not myself. I hail him, but we scarce know each other..If I am to bring him back it can only be done by force, for in my soul he is now abhorrent to me. But if I thought it best for you I'd haul him back; I swear as an honest man, I would bring him back with all his obsequious ways and deferential airs, and let you see the man you call your Gov. melt for ever into him who was your servant.

LADY MARY [*shivering*]. You hurt me. You say these things, but you say them like a king. To me it is the past that was not real.

CRICHTON [*too grandly*]. A king! I sometimes feel —

[*For a moment the yellow light gleams in his green eyes. We remember suddenly what* TREHERNE *and* ERNEST *said about his regal look. He checks himself.*]

I say it harshly, it is so hard to say, and all the time there is another voice within me crying — [*He stops.*]

LADY MARY [*trembling but not afraid*]. If it is the voice of Nature —

CRICHTON [*strongly*]. I know it to be the voice of Nature.

LADY MARY [*in a whisper*]. Then, if you want to say it very much, Gov., please say it to Polly Lasenby.

CRICHTON [*again in the grip of an idea*]. A king! Polly, some people hold that the soul but leaves one human tenement for another, and so lives on through all the ages. I have occasionally thought of late that, in some past existence, I may have been a king. It has all come to me so naturally, not as if I had to work it out, but — as — if — I — remembered.

'Or ever the knightly years were gone,
With the old world to the grave,
I was a *king* in Babylon,
And you were a Christian slave.'

It may have been; you hear me, it may have been.

LADY MARY [*who is as one fascinated*]. It may have been.

CRICHTON. I am lord over all. They are but hewers of wood and drawers of water for me. These shores are mine. Why should I hesitate; I have no longer any doubt. I do believe I am doing the right thing. Dear Polly, I have grown to love you; are you afraid to mate with me? [*She rocks her arms; no words will come from her.*]

'I was a king in Babylon,
And you were a Christian slave.'

LADY MARY [*bewitched*]. You are the most wonderful man I have ever known, and I am not afraid.

[*He takes her to him with mastership. Presently he is seated, and she is at his feet looking up adoringly in his face. As the tension relaxes she speaks with a smile.*]

I want you to tell me — every woman likes to know — when was the first time you thought me nicer than the others?

CRICHTON [*stroking her hair*]. I think a year ago. We were chasing goats on the Big Slopes, and you out-distanced us all; you were the first of our party to run a goat down; I was proud of you that day.

LADY MARY [*blushing with pleasure*]. Oh Gov., I only did it to please you. Everything I have done has been out of the desire to please you. [*Suddenly anxious.*] If I thought that in taking a wife from among us you were imperilling your dignity —

CRICHTON [*decisively*]. Have no fear of that, dear. I have thought it all out. The wife, Polly, always takes the same position as the husband.

LADY MARY. But I am so unworthy. It was sufficient to me that I should be allowed to wait on you at that table.

CRICHTON. You shall wait on me no longer. At whatever table I sit, Polly, you shall soon sit there also. [*Boyishly.*] Come, let us try what it will be like.

LADY MARY. As your servant at your feet.

CRICHTON. No, as my consort by my side.

[*They are sitting thus when the hatch is again opened and coffee offered. But* LADY MARY *is no longer there to receive it.*

Her sisters peep through in consternation. In vain they rattle the cup and saucer. AGATHA *brings the coffee to* CRICHTON.]

CRICHTON [*forgetting for the moment that it is not a month hence*]. Help your mistress first, girl. [*Three women are bereft of speech, but he does not notice it. He addresses* CATHERINE *vaguely.*] Are you a good girl, Kitty?

CATHERINE [*when she finds her tongue*]. I try to be, Gov.

CRICHTON [*still more vaguely*]. That's right.

[*He takes command of himself again, and signs to them to sit down.* ERNEST *comes in cheerily, but finding* CRICHTON *here is suddenly weak. He subsides on a chair, wondering what has happened.*]

CRICHTON [*surveying him*]. Ernest. [ERNEST *rises.*] You are becoming a little slovenly in your dress, Ernest; I don't like it.

ERNEST [*respectfully*]. Thank you. [ERNEST *sits again.* DADDY *and* TREHERNE *arrive.*]

CRICHTON. Daddy, I want you.

LORD LOAM [*gloomily*]. Is it because I forgot to clean out the dam?

CRICHTON [*encouragingly*]. No, no. [*He pours some wine into a goblet.*] A glass of wine with you, Daddy.

LORD LOAM [*hastily*]. Your health, Gov.

[*He is about to drink, but the master checks him.*]

CRICHTON. And hers. Daddy, this lady has done me the honour to promise to be my wife.

LORD LOAM [*astounded*]. Polly!

CRICHTON [*a little perturbed*]. I ought first to have asked your consent. I deeply regret — but Nature; may I hope I have your approval?

LORD LOAM. May you, Gov.? [*Delighted.*] Rather! Polly!

[*He puts his proud arms round her.*]

TREHERNE. We all congratulate you, Gov., most heartily.

ERNEST. Long life to you both, sir.

[*There is much shaking of hands, all of which is sincere.*]

TREHERNE. When will it be, Gov.?

CRICHTON [*after turning to* LADY MARY, *who whispers to him*]. As soon as the bridal skirt can be prepared. [*His manner has been most indulgent, and without the slightest suggestion of patronage. But he knows it is best for all that he should keep his place, and that his presence hampers them.*] My friends, I thank you for your good wishes, I thank you all. And now, perhaps you would like me to leave you to yourselves. Be joyous. Let there be song and dance to-night. Polly, I shall take my coffee in the parlour — you understand.

[*He retires with pleasant dignity. Immediately there is a rush of two girls at* LADY MARY.]

LADY MARY. Oh, oh! Father, they are pinching me.

LORD LOAM [*taking her under his protection*]. Agatha, Catherine, never presume to pinch your sister again. On the other hand, she may pinch you henceforth as much as ever she chooses.

[*In the meantime* TWEENY *is weeping softly, and the two are not above using her as a weapon.*]

CATHERINE. Poor Tweeny, it's a shame.

AGATHA. After he had almost promised *you.*

TWEENY [*loyally turning on them*]. No, he never did. He was always honourable as could be. 'Twas me as was too vulgar. Don't you dare say a word agin that man.

ERNEST [*to* LORD LOAM]. You'll get a lot of tit-bits out of this, Daddy.

LORD LOAM. That's what I was thinking.

ERNEST [*plunged in thought*]. I dare say *I* shall have to clean out the dam now.

LORD LOAM [*heartlessly*]. I dare say.

[*His gay old heart makes him again proclaim that he is a chickety chick. He seizes the concertina.*]

TREHERNE [*eagerly*]. That's the proper spirit.

[*He puts his arm around* CATHERINE, *and in another mo-*

ment they are all dancing to Daddy's music. Never were people happier on an island. A moment's pause is presently created by the return of CRICHTON, *wearing the wonderful robe of which we have already had dark mention. Never has he looked more regal, never perhaps felt so regal. We need not grudge him the one foible of his rule, for it is all coming to an end.*]

CRICHTON [*graciously, seeing them hesitate*]. No, no; I am delighted to see you all so happy. Go on.

TREHERNE. We don't like to before you, Gov.

CRICHTON [*his last order*]. It is my wish.

[*The merrymaking is resumed, and soon* CRICHTON *himself joins in the dance. It is when the fun is at its fastest and most furious that all stop abruptly as if turned to stone. They have heard the boom of a gun. Presently they are alive again.* ERNEST *leaps to the window.*]

TREHERNE [*huskily*]. It was a ship's gun. [*They turn to* CRICHTON *for confirmation; even in that hour they turn to* CRICHTON.] Gov.?

CRICHTON. Yes.

[*In another moment* LADY MARY *and* LORD LOAM *are alone.*]

LADY MARY [*seeing that her father is unconcerned*]. Father, you heard.

LORD LOAM [*placidly*]. Yes, my child.

LADY MARY [*alarmed by his unnatural calmness*]. But it was a gun, father.

LORD LOAM [*looking an old man now, and shuddering a little*]. Yes — a gun — I have often heard it. It's only a dream, you know; why don't we go on dancing?

[*She takes his hands, which have gone cold.*]

LADY MARY. Father. Don't you see, they have all rushed down to the beach? Come.

LORD LOAM. Rushed down to the beach; yes, always that — I often dream it.

LADY MARY. Come, father, come.

LORD LOAM. Only a dream, my poor girl.

[CRICHTON *presently returns. He is pale but firm.*]

CRICHTON. We can see lights within a mile of the shore — a great ship.

LORD LOAM. A ship — always a ship.

LADY MARY. Father, this is no dream.

LORD LOAM [*looking timidly at* CRICHTON]. It's a dream, isn't it? There's no ship?

CRICHTON [*soothing him with a touch*]. You are awake, Daddy, and there is a ship.

LORD LOAM [*clutching him*]. You are not deceiving me?

CRICHTON. It is the truth.

LORD LOAM [*reeling*]. True? — a ship — at last!

[*He goes after the others pitifully.*]

CRICHTON [*quietly*]. There is a small boat between it and the island; they must have sent it ashore for water.

LADY MARY. Coming in?

CRICHTON. No. That gun must have been a signal to recall it. It is going back. They can't hear our cries.

LADY MARY [*pressing her temples*]. Going away. So near — so near. [*Almost to herself.*] I think I'm glad.

CRICHTON [*cheerily*]. Have no fear. I shall bring them back.

[*He goes towards the table on which is the electrical apparatus.*]

LADY MARY [*standing on guard as it were between him and the table*]. What are you going to do?

CRICHTON. To fire the beacons.

LADY MARY. Stop! [*She faces him.*] Don't you see what it means?

CRICHTON [*firmly*]. It means that our life on the island has come to a natural end.

LADY MARY [*huskily*]. Gov., let the ship go.

CRICHTON. The old man — you saw what it means to him.

LADY MARY. But I am afraid.

CRICHTON [*adoringly*]. Dear Polly.

LADY MARY. Gov., let the ship go. [*She clings to him, but though it is his death sentence he loosens her hold.*]

CRICHTON. Bill Crichton has got to play the game.

[*He pulls the levers. Soon through the window one of the beacons is seen flaring red. There is a long pause. Alarms and excursions outside.* ERNEST *is the first to reappear.*]

ERNEST. Polly, Gov., the boat has turned back. [*He is gone. There is more disturbance. He returns.*] They are English sailors; they have landed! We are rescued, I tell you, rescued!

LADY MARY [*wanly*]. Is it anything to make so great a to-do about?

ERNEST [*staring*]. Eh?

LADY MARY. Have we not been happy here?

ERNEST. Happy? lord, yes.

LADY MARY [*catching hold of his sleeve*]. Ernest, we must never forget all that the Gov. has done for us.

ERNEST [*stoutly*]. Forget it? The man who could forget it would be a selfish wretch and a — But I say, this makes a difference!

LADY MARY [*quickly*]. No, it doesn't.

ERNEST [*his mind tottering*]. A mighty difference!

[*The others come running in, some weeping with joy, others boisterous. For some time dementia rules. Soon we see blue-jackets gazing through the window at the curious scene.* LORD LOAM *comes accompanied by a naval officer, whom he is continually shaking by the hand.*]

LORD LOAM. And here, sir, is our little home. Let me thank you in the name of us all, again and again and again.

OFFICER. Very proud, my lord. It is indeed an honour to have been able to assist so distinguished a gentleman as Lord Loam.

LORD LOAM. A glorious, glorious day. I shall show you our other room. Come, my pets. Come, Crichton.

[*He has not meant to be cruel. He does not know he has said it.*

*It is the old life that has come back to him. They all go. All
leave* CRICHTON *except* LADY MARY.]

LADY MARY [*stretching out her arms to him*]. Dear Gov., I will
never give you up.

[*There is a salt smile on his face as he shakes his head to her.
He lets the cloak slip to the ground. She will not take this for
an answer; again her arms go out to him. Then comes the great
renunciation. By an effort of will he ceases to be an erect
figure; he has the humble bearing of a servant. His hands come
together as if he were washing them.*]

CRICHTON [*it is the speech of his life*]. My lady. [*She goes away.
There is none to salute him now, unless we do it.*]

ACT FOUR

THE OTHER ISLAND

Some months have elapsed, and we have again the honour of waiting upon LORD LOAM *in his London home. It is the room of the first act, but with a new scheme of decoration, for on the walls are exhibited many interesting trophies from the island, such as skins, stuffed birds, and weapons of the chase, labelled 'Shot by Lord Loam,' 'Hon. Ernest Woolley's Blow-pipe,' etc. There are also two large glass cases containing other odds and ends, including, curiously enough, the bucket in which* ERNEST *was first dipped, but there is no label calling attention to the incident.*

It is not yet time to dress for dinner, and his lordship is on a couch, hastily yet furtively cutting the pages of a new book. With him are his two younger daughters and his nephew, and they also are engaged in literary pursuits; that is to say, the ladies are eagerly but furtively reading the evening papers, on copies of which ERNEST *is sitting complacently but furtively, doling them out as called for. Note the frequent use of the word 'furtive.' It implies that they are very reluctant to be discovered by their butler, say, at their otherwise delightful task.*

AGATHA [*reading aloud, with emphasis on the wrong words*]. 'In conclusion, we most heartily congratulate the Hon. Ernest Woolley. This book of his, regarding the adventures of himself and his brave companions on a desert isle, stirs the heart like a trumpet.'

[*Evidently the book referred to is the one in* LORD LOAM'S *hands.*]

ERNEST. Here is another.

CATHERINE [*reading*]. 'From the first to the last of Mr. Woolley's engrossing pages it is evident that he was an ideal man to be wrecked with, and a true hero.' [*Half-admiringly.*] Ernest!

ERNEST [*calmly*]. That's how it strikes *them*, you know. Here's another one.

AGATHA [*reading*]. 'There are many kindly references to the two servants who were wrecked with the family, and Mr. Woolley pays the butler a glowing tribute in a footnote.'

[*Some one coughs uncomfortably.*]

317

LORD LOAM [*who has been searching the index for the letter L*]. Excellent, excellent. At the same time I must say, Ernest, that the whole book is about yourself.

ERNEST [*genially*]. As the author —

LORD LOAM. Certainly, certainly. Still, you know, as a peer of the realm — [*with dignity*] — I think, Ernest, you might have given me one of your adventures.

ERNEST. I say it was you who taught us how to obtain a fire by rubbing two pieces of stick together.

LORD LOAM [*beaming*]. Do you, do you? I call that very handsome. What page?

[*Here the door opens, and the well-bred* CRICHTON *enters with the evening papers as subscribed for by the house. Those we have already seen have perhaps been introduced by* ERNEST '*furtively.*' *Every one except the intruder is immediately self-conscious, and when he withdraws there is a general sigh of relief. They pounce on the new papers.* ERNEST *evidently gets a shock from one, which he casts contemptuously on the floor.*]

AGATHA [*more fortunate*]. Father, see page 81. 'It was a tiger-cat,' says Mr. Woolley, 'of the largest size. Death stared Lord Loam in the face, but he never flinched.'

LORD LOAM [*searching his book eagerly*]. Page 81.

AGATHA. 'With presence of mind only equalled by his courage, he fixed an arrow in his bow.'

LORD LOAM. Thank you, Ernest; thank you, my boy.

AGATHA. 'Unfortunately he missed.'

LORD LOAM. Eh?

AGATHA. 'But by great good luck I heard his cries' —

LORD LOAM. My cries?

AGATHA. — 'and rushing forward with drawn knife, I stabbed the monster to the heart.'

[LORD LOAM *shuts his book with a pettish slam. There might be a scene here were it not that* CRICHTON *reappears and goes to one of the glass cases. All are at once on the alert, and his lordship is particularly sly.*]

LORD LOAM. Anything in the papers, Catherine?

CATHERINE. No, father, nothing — nothing at all.

ERNEST [*it pops out as of yore*]. The papers! The papers are guides that tell us what we ought to do, and then we don't do it.

[CRICHTON *having opened the glass case has taken out the bucket, and* ERNEST, *looking round for applause, sees him carrying it off and is undone. For a moment of time he forgets that he is no longer on the island, and with a sigh he is about to follow* CRICHTON *and the bucket to a retired spot. The door closes, and* ERNEST *comes to himself.*]

LORD LOAM [*uncomfortably*]. I told him to take it away.

ERNEST. I thought — [*he wipes his brow*] — I shall go and dress.

[*He goes.*]

CATHERINE. Father, it's awful having Crichton here. It's like living on tiptoe.

LORD LOAM [*gloomily*]. While he is here we are sitting on a volcano.

AGATHA. How mean of you! I am sure he has only stayed on with us to — to help us through. It would have looked so suspicious if he had gone at once.

CATHERINE [*revelling in the worst*]. But suppose Lady Brocklehurst were to get at him and pump him. She's the most terrifying, suspicious old creature in England; and Crichton simply can't tell a lie.

LORD LOAM. My dear, that is the volcano to which I was referring. [*He has evidently something to communicate.*] It is all Mary's fault. She said to me yesterday that she would break her engagement with Brocklehurst unless I told him about — you know what.

[*All conjure up the vision of* CRICHTON.]

AGATHA. Is she mad?

LORD LOAM. She calls it common honesty.

CATHERINE. Father, have you told him?

LORD LOAM [*heavily*]. She thinks I have, but I couldn't. She is sure to find out to-night.

[*Unconsciously he leans on the island concertina, which he has perhaps been lately showing to an interviewer as something he made for* TWEENY. *It squeaks, and they all jump.*]

CATHERINE. It is like a bird of ill-omen.

LORD LOAM [*vindictively*]. I must have it taken away; it has done that twice.

[LADY MARY *comes in. She is in evening dress. Undoubtedly she meant to sail in, but she forgets, and despite her garments it is a manly entrance. She is properly ashamed of herself. She tries again, and has an encouraging success. She indicates to her sisters that she wishes to be alone with papa.*]

AGATHA. All right, but we know what it's about. Come along, Kit.

[*They go.* LADY MARY *thoughtlessly sits like a boy, and again corrects herself. She addresses her father, but he is in a brown study, and she seeks to draw his attention by whistling. This troubles them both.*]

LADY MARY. How horrid of me!

LORD LOAM [*depressed*]. If you would try to remember —

LADY MARY [*sighing*]. I do; but there are so many things to remember.

LORD LOAM [*sympathetically*]. There are — [*in a whisper*]. Do you know, Mary, I constantly find myself secreting hair-pins.

LADY MARY. I find it so difficult to go up steps one at a time.

LORD LOAM. I was dining with half a dozen members of our party last Thursday, Mary, and they were so eloquent that I couldn't help wondering all the time how many of their heads *he* would have put in the bucket.

LADY MARY. I use so many of his phrases. And my appetite is so scandalous. Father, I usually have a chop before we sit down to dinner.

LORD LOAM. As for my clothes — [*wriggling*]. My dear, you can't think how irksome collars are to me nowadays.

LADY MARY. They can't be half such an annoyance, father, as —

[*She looks dolefully at her skirt.*]

LORD LOAM [*hurriedly*]. Quite so — quite so. You have dressed early to-night, Mary.

LADY MARY. That reminds me; I had a note from Brocklehurst saying that he would come a few minutes before his mother as — as he wanted to have a talk with me. He didn't say what about, but of course we know.

[*His lordship fidgets.*]

[*With feeling.*] It was good of you to tell him, father. Oh, it is horrible to me — [*covering her face*]. It seemed so natural at the time.

LORD LOAM [*petulantly*]. Never again make use of that word in this house, Mary.

LADY MARY [*with an effort*]. Father, Brocklehurst has been so loyal to me for these two years that I should despise myself were I to keep my — my extraordinary lapse from him. Had Brocklehurst been a little less good, then you need not have told him my strange little secret.

LORD LOAM [*weakly*]. Polly — I mean Mary — it was all Crichton's fault, he —

LADY MARY [*with decision*]. No, father, no; not a word against him, though I haven't the pluck to go on with it; I can't even understand how it ever was. Father, do you not still hear the surf? Do you see the curve of the beach?

LORD LOAM. I have begun to forget — [*in a low voice*]. But they were happy days; there was something magical about them.

LADY MARY. It was glamour. Father, I have lived Arabian nights. I have sat out a dance with the evening star. But it was all in a past existence, in the days of Babylon, and I am myself again. But he has been chivalrous always. If the slothful, indolent creature I used to be has improved in any way, I owe it all to him. I am slipping back in many ways, but I am determined not to slip back altogether — in memory of him and his island. That is why I insisted on your telling Brocklehurst. He can break our engagement if he chooses. [*Proudly.*] Mary Lasenby is going to play the game.

LORD LOAM. But my dear —

[LORD BROCKLEHURST *is announced.*]

LADY MARY [*meaningly*]. Father, dear, oughtn't you to be dressing?

LORD LOAM [*very unhappy*]. The fact is — before I go — I want to say —

LORD BROCKLEHURST. Loam, if you don't mind, I wish very specially to have a word with Mary before dinner.

LORD LOAM. But —

LADY MARY. Yes, father.

[*She induces him to go, and thus courageously faces* LORD BROCKLEHURST *to hear her fate.*]

I am ready, George.

LORD BROCKLEHURST [*who is so agitated that she ought to see he is thinking not of her but of himself*]. It is a painful matter — I wish I could have spared you this, Mary.

LADY MARY. Please go on.

LORD BROCKLEHURST. In common fairness, of course, this should be remembered, that two years have elapsed. You and I had no reason to believe that we should ever meet again.

[*This is more considerate than she had expected.*]

LADY MARY [*softening*]. I was so lost to the world, George.

LORD BROCKLEHURST [*with a groan*]. At the same time, the thing is utterly and absolutely inexcusable —

LADY MARY [*recovering her hauteur*]. Oh!

LORD BROCKLEHURST. And so I have already said to mother.

LADY MARY [*disdaining him*]. You have told her?

LORD BROCKLEHURST. Certainly, Mary, certainly; I tell mother everything.

LADY MARY [*curling her lip*]. And what did she say?

LORD BROCKLEHURST. To tell the truth, mother rather pooh-poohed the whole affair.

LADY MARY [*incredulous*]. Lady Brocklehurst pooh-poohed the whole affair!

LORD BROCKLEHURST. She said, 'Mary and I will have a good laugh over this.'

LADY MARY [*outraged*]. George, your mother is a hateful, depraved old woman.

LORD BROCKLEHURST. Mary!

LADY MARY [*turning away*]. Laugh indeed, when it will always be such a pain to me.

LORD BROCKLEHURST [*with strange humility*]. If only you would let me bear all the pain, Mary.

LADY MARY [*who is taken aback*]. George, I think you are the noblest man —

[*She is touched, and gives him both her hands. Unfortunately he simpers.*]

LORD BROCKLEHURST. She was a pretty little thing.

[*She stares, but he marches to his doom.*]

Ah, not beautiful like you. I assure you it was the merest folly; there were a few letters, but we have got them back. It was all owing to the boat being so late at Calais. You see she had such large, helpless eyes.

LADY MARY [*fixing him*]. George, when you lunched with father to-day at the club —

LORD BROCKLEHURST. I didn't He wired me that he couldn't come.

LADY MARY [*with a tremor*]. But he wrote you?

LORD BROCKLEHURST. No.

LADY. MARY [*a bird singing in her breast*]. You haven't seen him since?

LORD BROCKLEHURST. No.

[*She is saved. Is he to be let off also? Not at all. She bears down on him like a ship of war.*]

LADY MARY. George, who and what is this woman?

LORD BROCKLEHURST [*cowering*]. She was — she is — the shame of it — a lady's-maid.

LADY MARY [*properly horrified*]. A what?

LORD BROCKLEHURST. A lady's-maid. A mere servant, Mary. [LADY MARY *whirls round so that he shall not see her face.*]

I first met her at this house when you were entertaining the servants; so you see it was largely your father's fault.

LADY MARY [*looking him up and down*]. A lady's-maid?

LORD BROCKLEHURST [*degraded*]. Her name was Fisher.

LADY MARY. My maid!

LORD BROCKLEHURST [*with open hands*]. Can you forgive me, Mary?

LADY MARY. Oh George, George!

LORD BROCKLEHURST. Mother urged me not to tell you anything about it; but —

LADY MARY [*from her heart*]. I am so glad you told me.

LORD BROCKLEHURST. You see there was nothing catastrophic in it.

LADY MARY [*thinking perhaps of another incident*]. No, indeed.

LORD BROCKLEHURST [*inclined to simper again*]. And she behaved awfully well. She quite saw that it was because the boat was late. I suppose the glamour to a girl in service of a man in high position —

LADY MARY. Glamour! — yes, yes, that was it.

LORD BROCKLEHURST. Mother says that a girl in such circumstances is to be excused if she loses her head.

LADY MARY [*impulsively*]. George, I am so sorry if I said anything against your mother. I am sure she is the dearest old thing.

LORD BROCKLEHURST [*in calm waters at last*]. Of course for women of our class she has a very different standard.

LADY MARY [*grown tiny*]. Of course.

LORD BROCKLEHURST. You see, knowing how good a woman she is herself, she was naturally anxious that I should marry some one like her. That is what has made her watch your conduct so jealously, Mary.

LADY MARY [*hurriedly thinking things out*]. I know. I — I think, George, that before your mother comes I should like to say a word to father.

LORD BROCKLEHURST [*nervously*]. About this?

LADY MARY. Oh no; I shan't tell him of this. About something else.

LORD BROCKLEHURST. And you do forgive me, Mary?

LADY MARY [*smiling on him*]. Yes, yes. I — I am sure the boat was *very* late, George.

LORD BROCKLEHURST [*earnestly*]. It really was.

LADY MARY. I am even relieved to know that you are not quite perfect, dear. [*She rests her hands on his shoulders. She has a moment of contrition.*] George, when we are married, we shall try to be not an entirely frivolous couple, won't we? We must endeavour to be of some little use, dear.

LORD BROCKLEHURST [*the ass*]. *Noblesse oblige.*

LADY MARY [*haunted by the phrases of a better man*]. Mary Lasenby is determined to play the game, George.

[*Perhaps she adds to herself, 'Except just this once.' A kiss closes this episode of the two lovers; and soon after the departure of* LADY MARY *the* COUNTESS OF BROCKLEHURST *is announced. She is a very formidable old lady.*]

LADY BROCKLEHURST. Alone, George?

LORD BROCKLEHURST. Mother, I told her all; she has behaved magnificently.

LADY BROCKLEHURST [*who has not shared his fears*]. Silly boy. [*She casts a supercilious eye on the island trophies.*] So these are the wonders they brought back with them. Gone away to dry her eyes, I suppose?

LORD BROCKLEHURST [*proud of his mate*]. She didn't cry, mother.

LADY BROCKLEHURST. No? [*She reflects.*] You're quite right. I wouldn't have cried. Cold, icy. Yes, that was it.

LORD BROCKLEHURST [*who has not often contradicted her*]. I assure you, mother, that wasn't it at all. She forgave me at once.

LADY BROCKLEHURST [*opening her eyes sharply to the full*]. Oh!

LORD BROCKLEHURST. She was awfully nice about the boat being late; she even said she was relieved to find that I wasn't quite perfect.

LADY BROCKLEHURST [*pouncing*]. She said that?

LORD BROCKLEHURST. She really did.

LADY BROCKLEHURST. I mean *I* wouldn't. Now if *I* had said that, what would have made me say it? [*Suspiciously.*] George, is Mary all we think her?

LORD BROCKLEHURST [*with unexpected spirit*]. If she wasn't, mother, you would know it.

LADY BROCKLEHURST. Hold your tongue, boy. We don't really know what happened on that island.

LORD BROCKLEHURST. You were reading the book all the morning.

LADY BROCKLEHURST. How can I be sure that the book is true?

LORD BROCKLEHURST. They all talk of it as true.

LADY BROCKLEHURST. How do I know that they are not lying?

LORD BROCKLEHURST. Why should they lie?

LADY BROCKLEHURST. Why shouldn't they? [*She reflects again.*] If I had been wrecked on an island, I think it highly probable that I should have lied when I came back. Weren't some servants with them?

LORD BROCKLEHURST. Crichton, the butler.

[*He is surprised to see her ring the bell.*]

Why, mother, you are not going to —

LADY BROCKLEHURST. Yes, I am. [*Pointedly.*] George, watch whether Crichton begins any of his answers to my questions with 'The fact is.'

LORD BROCKLEHURST. Why?

LADY BROCKLEHURST. Because that is usually the beginning of a lie.

LORD BROCKLEHURST [*as* CRICHTON *opens the door*].

Mother, you can't do these things in other people's houses.

LADY BROCKLEHURST [*cooly, to* CRICHTON]. It was I who rang. [*Surveying him through her eyeglass.*] So you were one of the castaways, Crichton?

CRICHTON. Yes, my lady.

LADY BROCKLEHURST. Delightful book Mr. Woolley has written about your adventures. [CRICHTON *bows.*] Don't you think so?

CRICHTON. I have not read it, my lady.

LADY BROCKLEHURST. Odd that they should not have presented you with a copy.

LORD BROCKLEHURST. Presumably Crichton is no reader.

LADY BROCKLEHURST. By the way, Crichton, were there any books on the island?

CRICHTON. I had one, my lady — Henley's poems.

LORD BROCKLEHURST. Never heard of him.

[CRICHTON *again bows.*]

LADY BROCKLEHURST [*who has not heard of him either*]. I think you were not the only servant wrecked?

CRICHTON. There was a young woman, my lady.

LADY BROCKLEHURST. I want to see her. [CRICHTON *bows, but remains.*] Fetch her up.

[*He goes.*]

LORD BROCKLEHURST [*almost standing up to his mother*]. This is scandalous.

LADY BROCKLEHURST [*defining her position*]. I am a mother.

[CATHERINE *and* AGATHA *enter in dazzling confections, and quake in secret to find themselves practically alone with* LADY BROCKLEHURST.]

[*Even as she greets them.*] How d' you do, Catherine — Agatha? You didn't dress like this on the island, I expect! By the way, how did you dress?

[*They have thought themselves prepared, but —*]

AGATHA. Not — not so well, of course, but quite the same idea.

[*They are relieved by the arrival of* TREHERNE, *who is in clerical dress.*]

LADY BROCKLEHURST. How do you do, Mr. Treherne? There is not so much of you in the book as I had hoped.

TREHERNE [*modestly*]. There wasn't very much of me on the island, Lady Brocklehurst.

LADY BROCKLEHURST. How d' ye mean?

[*He shrugs his honest shoulders.*]

LORD BROCKLEHURST. I hear you have got a living, Treherne. Congratulations.

TREHERNE. Thanks.

LORD BROCKLEHURST. Is it a good one?

TREHERNE. So-so. They are rather weak in bowling, but it's a good bit of turf.

[*Confidence is restored by the entrance of* ERNEST, *who takes in the situation promptly, and, of course, knows he is a match for any old lady.*]

ERNEST [*with ease*]. How do you do, Lady Brocklehurst.

LADY BROCKLEHURST. Our brilliant author!

ERNEST [*impervious to satire*]. Oh, I don't know.

LADY BROCKLEHURST. It is as engrossing, Mr. Woolley, as if it were a work of fiction.

ERNEST [*suddenly uncomfortable*]. Thanks, awfully. [*Recovering.*] The fact is —

[*He is puzzled by seeing the Brocklehurst family exchange meaning looks.*]

CATHERINE [*to the rescue*]. Lady Brocklehurst, Mr. Treherne and I — we are engaged.

AGATHA. And Ernest and I.

LADY BROCKLEHURST [*grimly*]. I see, my dears; thought it wise to keep the island in the family.

[*An awkward moment this for the entrance of* LORD LOAM

and LADY MARY, *who, after a private talk upstairs, are feeling happy and secure.*]

LORD LOAM [*with two hands for his distinguished guest*]. Aha! ha, ha! younger than any of them, Emily.

LADY BROCKLEHURST. Flatterer. [*To* LADY MARY.] You seem in high spirits, Mary.

LADY MARY [*gaily*]. I am.

LADY BROCKLEHURST [*with a significant glance at* LORD BROCKLEHURST]. After —

LADY MARY. I — I mean. The fact is —

[*Again that disconcerting glance between the Countess and her son.*]

LORD LOAM [*humorously*]. She hears wedding bells, Emily, ha, ha!

LADY BROCKLEHURST [*coldly*]. Do you, Mary? Can't say I do; but I'm hard of hearing.

LADY MARY [*instantly her match*]. If you don't, Lady Brocklehurst, I'm sure I don't.

LORD LOAM [*nervously*]. Tut, tut. Seen our curios from the island, Emily; I should like you to examine them.

LADY BROCKLEHURST. Thank you, Henry. I am glad you say that, for I have just taken the liberty of asking two of them to step upstairs.

[*There is an uncomfortable silence, which the entrance of* CRICHTON *with* TWEENY *does not seem to dissipate.* CRICHTON *is impenetrable, but* TWEENY *hangs back in fear.*]

LORD BROCKLEHURST [*stoutly*]. Loam, I have no hand in this.

LADY BROCKLEHURST [*undisturbed*]. Pooh, what have I done? You always begged me to speak to the servants, Henry, and I merely wanted to discover whether the views you used to hold about equality were adopted on the island; it seemed a splendid opportunity, but Mr. Woolley has not a word on the subject.

[*All eyes turn to* ERNEST.]

ERNEST [*with confidence*]. The fact is —

[*The fatal words again.*]

LORD LOAM [*not quite certain what he is to assure her of*]. I assure you, Emily —

LADY MARY [*as cold as steel*]. Father, nothing whatever happened on the island of which I for one, am ashamed, and I hope Crichton will be allowed to answer Lady Brocklehurst's questions.

LADY BROCKLEHURST. To be sure. There's nothing to make a fuss about, and we're a family party. [*To* GRICHTON.] Now, truthfully, my man.

CRICHTON [*calmly*]. I promise that, my lady.

[*Some hearts sink, the hearts that could never understand a* CRICHTON.]

LADY BROCKLEHURST [*sharply*]. Well, were you all equal on the island?

CRICHTON. No, my lady. I think I may say there was as little equality there as elsewhere.

LADY BROCKLEHURST. All the social distinctions were preserved?

CRICHTON. As at home, my lady.

LADY BROCKLEHURST. The servants?

CRICHTON. They had to keep their place.

LADY BROCKLEHURST. Wonderful. How was it managed? [*With an inspiration.*] You, girl, tell me that?

[*Can there be a more critical moment?*]

TWEENY [*in agony*]. If you please, my lady, it was all the Gov.'s doing.

[*They give themselves up for lost.* LORD LOAM *tries to sink out of sight.*]

CRICHTON. In the regrettable slang of the servant's hall, my lady, the master is usually referred to as the Gov.

LADY BROCKLEHURST. I see. [*She turns to* LORD LOAM.] You —

LORD LOAM [*reappearing*]. Yes, I understand that is what they called me.

LADY BROCKLEHURST [*to* CRICHTON]. You didn't even take your meals with the family?

CRICHTON. No, my lady, I dined apart.

[*Is all safe?*]

LADY BROCKLEHURST [*alas*]. You, girl, also? Did you dine with Crichton?

TWEENY [*scared*]. No, your ladyship.

LADY BROCKLEHURST [*fastening on her*]. With whom?

TWEENY. I took my bit of supper with — with Daddy and Polly and the rest.

[*Væ victis.*]

ERNEST [*leaping into the breach*]. Dear old Daddy — he was our monkey. You remember our monkey, Agatha?

AGATHA. Rather! What a funny old darling he was.

CATHERINE [*thus encouraged*]. And don't you think Polly was the sweetest little parrot, Mary?

LADY BROCKLEHURST. Ah! I understand; animals you had domesticated?

LORD LOAM [*heavily*]. Quite so — quite so.

LADY BROCKLEHURST. The servant's teas that used to take place here once a month —

CRICHTON. They did not seem natural on the island, my lady, and were discontinued by the Gov.'s orders.

LORD BROCKLEHURST. A clear proof, Loam, that they were a mistake here.

LORD LOAM [*seeing the opportunity for a diversion*]. I admit it frankly. I abandon them. Emily, as the result of our experiences on the island, I think of going over to the Tories.

LADY BROCKLEHURST. I am delighted to hear it.

LORD LOAM [*expanding*]. Thank you, Crichton, thank you; that is all.

[*He motions to them to go, but the time is not yet.*]

LADY BROCKLEHURST. One moment. [*There is a universal but stifled groan.*] Young people, Crichton, will be young people, even on an island; now, I suppose there was a certain amount of — shall we say sentimentalising, going on?

CRICHTON. Yes, my lady, there was.

LORD BROCKLEHURST [*ashamed*]. Mother!

LADY BROCKLEHURST [*disregarding him*]. Which gentleman? [*To* TWEENY] You, girl, tell me.

TWEENY [*confused*]. If you please, my lady —

ERNEST [*hurriedly*]. That fact is —

[*He is checked as before, and probably says 'D—n' to himself, but he has saved the situation.*]

TWEENY [*gasping*]. It was him — Mr. Ernest, your ladyship.

LADY BROCKLEHURST [*counsel for the prosecution*]. With which lady?

AGATHA. I have already told you, Lady Brocklehurst, that Ernest and I —

LADY BROCKLEHURST. Yes, *now;* but you were two years on the island. [*Looking at* LADY MARY.] Was it this lady?

TWEENY. No, your ladyship.

LADY BROCKLEHURST. Then I don't care which of the others it was. [TWEENY *gurgles.*] Well, I suppose that will do.

LORD BROCKLEHURST. Do! I hope you are ashamed of yourself, mother. [*To* CRICHTON, *who is going.*] You are an excellent fellow, Crichton; and if, after we are married, you ever wish to change your place, come to us.

LADY MARY [*losing her head for the only time*]. Oh no, impossible.

LADY BROCKLEHURST [*at once suspicious*]. Why impossible? [LADY MARY *cannot answer, or perhaps she is too proud.*] Do you see why it should be impossible, my man?

[*He can make or mar his unworthy* MARY *now. Have you any doubt of him?*]

CRICHTON. Yes, my lady. I had not told you, my lord, but as soon as your lordship is suited I wish to leave service.

[*They are all immensely relieved, except poor* TWEENY.]

TREHERNE [*the only curious one*]. What will you do, Crichton?

[CRICHTON *shrugs his shoulders.*]

CRICHTON. Shall I withdraw, my lord?

[*He withdraws with* TWEENY; *the thunderstorm is over.*]

LADY BROCKLEHURST [*thankful to have made herself unpleasant*]. Horrid of me, wasn't it? But if one wasn't disagreeable now and again, it would be horribly tedious to be an old woman. He will soon be yours, Mary, and then — think of the opportunities you will have of being disagreeable to me. On that understanding, my dear, don't you think we might —?

[*Their cold lips meet.*]

LORD LOAM [*vaguely*]. Quite so — quite so.

[CRICHTON *announces dinner, and they file out.* LADY MARY *stays behind a moment and impulsively holds out her hand.*]

LADY MARY. To wish you every dear happiness.

CRICHTON [*an enigma to the last*]. The same to you, my lady.

LADY MARY. Do you despise me, Crichton? [*The man who could never tell a lie makes no answer.*] I am ashamed of myself, but I am the sort of woman on whom shame sits lightly. [*He does not contradict her.*] You are the best man among us.

CRICHTON. On an island, my lady, perhaps; but in England, no.

LADY MARY [*not inexcusably*]. Then there is something wrong with England.

CRICHTON. My lady, not even from you can I listen to a word against England.

LADY MARY. Tell me one thing: you have not lost your courage?

CRICHTON. No, my lady.

[*She goes. He turns out the lights.*]

The Admirable Crichton

Springboard

1.   James M. Barrie wrote many plays, of which *Peter Pan* is most famous. Find out what you can about Barrie and his other plays. Is *The Admirable Crichton* representative (or typical) of Barrie's work? Why or why not?

2.   Despite abundant humor in *The Admirable Crichton,* the play makes some serious comments about the structure of social classes. What are some of these observations? How is Barrie's view of social order and change different from, say, Shaw's view in *Pygmalion?*

3.   Why does the title of this play describe Crichton as admirable? Precisely what qualities or actions earn Crichton this appellation? In light of the play's theme, do you find any irony in Barrie's title?

4.   In reading the stage directions for this play, we notice that Barrie often explains or describes much that will not be seen on stage; e.g., in Act One, Barrie gives an elaborate account of events that take place even before the curtain rises. What audience does Barrie have in mind for this information? Why does he provide such information?

5.   Consider the tone of voice Barrie uses in his stage directions. What seems to be his attitude toward his subject matter?

6.   Why do the stage directions at the opening of Act One focus on Ernest Woolley instead of on Crichton? Why is Crichton himself (including any close description of him) virtually ignored until Act Two?

7.   Acts One and Four are set at Loam House. Look up "loam" in an unabridged dictionary. What might Barrie be suggesting about Lord Loam's character — and indeed about his entire social class?

8.   Early in the play, Crichton asserts his belief that whatever is natural is right. But "natural" is a chameleon word that

334

means different things to different people. What does the word signify to Crichton? To the others at Loam House? To the others on the island? To Barrie? To us today?

(Act One)

9.   Ernest Woolley is excessively fond of epigrams. Find out what you can about the literary history of the epigram. What kinds of plays traditionally feature epigrams? What are the peculiar strengths and weaknesses of the epigram, as a comment about life? Discuss Ernest's epigram at the opening of Act One: "Life, Crichton, is like a cup of tea; the more heartily we drink, the sooner we reach the dregs."

10.   In this act, we witness the inhabitants of Loam House playing at role reversal. What is the point of such a game? What is the audience invited to conclude about the experiment?

11.   Some of the servants — specifically the ladies' maids — refuse to accompany the three ladies and Lord Loam on the yachting trip under the conditions that Lord Loam sets forth. What is ironic about the servants' attitude?

12.   Lady Mary tells Treherne that Crichton's inability to act dishonorably is precisely what makes him so dangerous. What does she mean by this remark? What is the danger she envisions?

(Act Two)

13.   In Act Two, how is leadership determined? What part does "nature" play in deciding who will lead and who will follow?

(Act Three)

14.   What do we see of "natural" behavior in Act Three? Do all the characters display this behavior? What do the changes in Lady Mary's behavior suggest?

15.   How are clothes (e.g., Crichton's uniform at Loam House and his colorful robe on the island) used to denote position and class in society? What effect does the outward show have on the inward reality?

16.   What significance does Crichton's habitual motion of washing his hands have for him? What biblical allusion is in-

tended by Barrie? What is Crichton's reaction, on the island, when he notices Lady Mary adopting his gesture?

17. Why do we feel sympathy for Lord Loam at the end of Act Three? Why is his first reaction at being rescued pain instead of joy?

18. How does Crichton's disciplined restraint serve to highlight the strength and power of emotions at the ends of Acts Three and Four?

(Act Four)

19. What behavior do we expect from Lady Mary, Ernest, and Crichton upon their return to Loam House? How much of a change do we expect their island experience to have had on them?

20. Is it as difficult for Crichton to resume the demeanor and habits of servitude as it is for Lady Mary to resume the role of privilege? Why or why not?

21. While the members of Loam House openly lie about their island experience, Crichton resorts to equivocation, which greatly discomforts him. What motivates each of the characters to avoid clear truth?

22. Does Mary understand what she has asked Crichton in the final lines of the play? What is the full meaning of his reply?

THE GLASS MENAGERIE

by Tennessee Williams

Nobody, not even the rain, has such small hands.

e. e. cummings

The Glass Menagerie

Introduction

The name Thomas Lanier Williams is not widely recognized, but almost everybody has heard of Tennessee Williams. Early obscurity ended abruptly and permanently with *The Glass Menagerie;* the play won the 1945 New York Drama Critics Circle award and established its thirty-one year-old creator as one of the most celebrated young writers of post-war America. Unlike so many plays that have their season and then fade away, *The Glass Menagerie* has stayed around to become a classic of the modern theatre. Much the same could be said of the play's author. A prolific writer, Williams remains active now that he is in his sixties, although in recent years he has concentrated on what he calls chamber music rather than full-scale symphonies.

For many people, *The Glass Menagerie* is not at all typical of Tennessee Williams. Such plays as *The Rose Tattoo, A Streetcar Named Desire* (1947 winner of the Drama Critics Circle award and a Pulitzer Prize), *Cat on a Hot Tin Roof* (yet another Pulitzer winner, 1955), *Sweet Bird of Youth,* and *Night of the Iguana* are stark and shocking studies in decadence, delusion, and despair. *The Glass Menagerie,* while it deals with the same themes, does so with a gentleness, a sweet poignancy, that does seem rare among Williams' works.

Williams himself argues that each of his plays is unique, and yet the special fragility or delicacy of mood of *The Glass Menagerie* demands an explanation. Perhaps the epigram to the play offers one answer; the line comes from poem LVII ("somewhere i have never travelled, gladly beyond") of *W (ViVa)* (1931) by E.E. Cummings (1894-1962). We also find an allusion to Cummings' later 1944 book of poems, *1x1 (One Times One),* in Scene VII when Jim O'Connor tells Laura, "The different people are not like other people, but being different is nothing to be ashamed of. Because other people are not such wonderful people. They're one hundred times one thousand. You're one times one!" Numerous other similarities in texture, tone, and mood are to be found between the introduction to Cummings' *New Poems* (1938) and the speeches Jim and Tom deliver to and about Laura. Although Cummings has many moods and voices in his poetry, he is in particular a modern master of sweet melancholy and tender lyricism. A fine artist in his own right, one of Cummings' triumphs may well be the mellowing influence he seems to have had on the Williams of *The Glass Menagerie.*

CHARACTERS

AMANDA WINGFIELD, *the mother*

A little woman of great but confused vitality clinging frantically to another time and place. Her characterization must be carefully created, not copied from type. She is not paranoiac, but her life is paranoia. There is much to admire in AMANDA, and as much to love and pity as there is to laugh at. Certainly she has endurance and a kind of heroism, and though her foolishness makes her unwittingly cruel at times, there is tenderness in her slight person.

LAURA WINGFIELD, *her daughter*

AMANDA, having failed to establish contact with reality, continues to live vitally in her illusions, but LAURA'S situation is even graver. A childhood illness has left her crippled, one leg slightly shorter than the other, and held in a brace. This defect need not be more than suggested on the stage. Stemming from this, LAURA'S separation increases till she is like a piece of her own glass collection, too exquisitely fragile to move from the shelf.

TOM WINGFIELD, *her son*

And the narrator of the play. A poet with a job in a warehouse. His nature is not remorseless, but to escape from a trap he has to act without pity.

JIM O'CONNOR, *the gentleman caller*

A nice, ordinary, young man.

SCENE: AN ALLEY IN ST. LOUIS

PART I. Preparation for a Gentleman Caller.

PART II. The Gentleman calls.

TIME: Now and the Past.

TONE: How Author feels

mood: Atmosphere of play as seen by characters

339

Scene I

[*The Wingfield apartment is in the rear of the building, one of those vast hive-like conglomerations of cellular living-units that flower as warty growths in overcrowded urban centers of lower middle-class population and are symptomatic of the impulse of this largest and fundamentally enslaved section of American society to avoid fluidity and differentiation and to exist and function as one interfused mass of automatism.* ᴀᴜᴛᴏᴍᴀᴛɪᴄ

The apartment faces an alley and is entered by a fire-escape, a structure whose name is a touch of accidental poetic truth, for all of these huge buildings are always burning with the slow and implacable fires of human desperation. The fire-escape is included in the set — that is, the landing of it and steps descending from it. ✳ CONSTANT

The scene is memory and is therefore nonrealistic. Memory takes a lot of poetic license. It omits some details; others are exaggerated, according to the emotional value of the articles it touches, for memory is seated predominantly in the heart. The interior is therefore rather dim and poetic.

At the rise of the curtain, the audience is faced with the dark, grim rear wall of the Wingfield tenement. This building, which runs parallel to the footlights, is flanked on both sides by dark, narrow alleys which run into murky canyons of tangled clotheslines, garbage cans and the sinister latticework of neighboring fire-escapes. It is up and down these side alleys that exterior entrances and exits are made, during the play. At the end of TOM'S opening commentary, the dark tenement wall slowly reveals (by means of a transparency) the interior of the ground floor Wingfield apartment.

Downstage is the living room, which also serves as a sleeping room for LAURA, the sofa unfolding to make her bed. Upstage, center, and divided by a wide arch or second proscenium with transparent faded portieres (or second curtain), is the dining room. In an old-fashioned what-not in the living room are seen scores of transparent glass animals. A blown-up photograph of the father hangs on the wall of the living room, facing the audience, to the left of the archway. It is the face of a very handsome young man in a doughboy's First World War cap. He is gallantly smiling, ineluctably smiling, as if to say, "I will be smiling forever."

The audience hears and sees the opening scene in the dining room through both the transparent fourth wall of the building and the transparent gauze portieres of the dining-room arch. It

is during this revealing scene that the fourth wall slowly ascends, out of sight. This transparent exterior wall is not brought down again until the very end of the play, during TOM'S final speech.

The narrator is an undisguised convention of the play. He takes whatever license with dramatic convention as is convenient to his purposes.

TOM enters dressed as a merchant sailor from alley, stage left, and strolls across the front of the stage to the fire-escape. There he stops and lights a cigarette. He addresses the audience.]

TOM. Yes, I have tricks in my pocket, I have things up my sleeve. But I am the opposite of a stage magician. He gives you illusion that has the appearance of truth. I give you truth in the pleasant disguise of illusion. To begin with, I turn back time. I reverse it to that quaint period, the thirties, when the huge middle class of America was matriculating in a school for the blind. Their eyes had failed them, or they had failed their eyes, and so they were having their fingers pressed forcibly down on the fiery Braille alphabet of a dissolving economy. In Spain there was revolution. Here there was only shouting and confusion. In Spain there was Guernica. Here there were disturbances of labor, sometimes pretty violent, in otherwise peaceful cities such as Chicago, Cleveland, Saint Louis . . . This is the social background of the play.

[MUSIC.]

The play is memory. Being a memory play, it is dimly lighted, it is sentimental, it is not realistic. In memory everything seems to happen to music. That explains the fiddle in the wings. I am the narrator of the play, and also a character in it. The other characters are my mother, Amanda, my sister, Laura, and a gentleman caller who appears in the final scenes. He is the most realistic character in the play, being an emissary from a world of reality that we were somehow set apart from. But since I have a poet's weakness for symbols, I am using this character also as a symbol; he is the long delayed but always expected something that we live for. There is a fifth character in the play who doesn't appear except in this larger-than-life photograph over the mantel. This is our father who left us a long time ago. He was a telephone man who fell in love with long distances; he gave up his job with the telephone company and skipped the light fantastic out of town . . . The last we heard of him was a picture post-card from Mazatlan, on the Pacific coast of Mexico, containing a message of two words — "Hello — Good-bye!" and no address. I think the rest of the play will explain itself . . . .

[AMANDA'S *voice becomes audible through the portieres.*]

[LEGEND ON SCREEN: "OU SONT LES NEIGES."]

[*He divides the portieres and enters the upstage area.*]

[AMANDA *and* LAURA *are seated at a drop-leaf table. Eating is indicated by gestures without food or utensils.* AMANDA *faces the audience.* TOM *and* LAURA *are seated in profile.*]

[*The interior has lit up softly and through the scrim we see* AMANDA *and* LAURA *seated at the table in the upstage area.*]

AMANDA [*calling*]. Tom?

TOM. Yes, Mother.

AMANDA. We can't say grace until you come to the table!

TOM. Coming, Mother. [*He bows slightly and withdraws, reappearing a few moments later in his place at the table.*]

AMANDA [*to her son*]. Honey, don't *push* with your *fingers*. If you have to push with something, the thing to push with is a crust of bread. And chew — chew! Animals have sections in their stomachs which enable them to digest food without mastication, but human beings are supposed to chew their food before they swallow it down. Eat food leisurely, son, and really enjoy it. A well-cooked meal has lots of delicate flavors that have to be held in the mouth for appreciation. So chew your food and give your salivary glands a chance to function!

[TOM *deliberately lays his imaginary fork down and pushes his chair back from the table.*]

TOM. I haven't enjoyed one bite of this dinner because of your constant directions on how to eat it. It's you that make me rush through meals with your hawk-like attention to every bite I take. Sickening — spoils my appetite — all this discussion of animals' secretion — salivary glands — mastication!

AMANDA [*lightly*]. Temperament like a Metropolitan star! [*He rises and crosses downstage.*] You're not excused from the table.

TOM. I'm getting a cigarette.

AMANDA. You smoke too much.

[LAURA *rises*.]

LAURA. I'll bring in the blanc mange.

[*He remains standing with his cigarette by the portieres during the following.*]

AMANDA [*rising*]. No, sister, no, sister — you be the lady this time and I'll be the darky.

LAURA. I'm already up.

AMANDA. Resume your seat, little sister — I want you to stay fresh and pretty — for gentlemen callers!

LAURA. I'm not expecting any gentlemen callers.

AMANDA [*crossing out to kitchenette. Airily*]. Sometimes they come when they are least expected! Why, I remember one Sunday afternoon in Blue Mountain — [*Enters kitchenette.*]

TOM. I know what's coming!

LAURA. Yes. But let her tell it.

TOM. Again?

LAURA. She loves to tell it.

[AMANDA *returns with bowl of dessert.*]

AMANDA. One Sunday afternoon in Blue Mountain — your mother received — *seventeen!* — gentlemen callers! Why, sometimes there weren't chairs enough to accommodate them all. We had to send the nigger over to bring in folding chairs from the parish house.

TOM [*remaining at portieres*]. How did you entertain those gentlemen callers?

AMANDA. I understood the art of conversation!

TOM. I bet you could talk.

AMANDA. Girls in those days *knew* how to talk, I can tell you.

TOM. Yes?

[IMAGE: AMANDA AS A GIRL ON A PORCH, GREETING CALLERS.]

AMANDA. They knew how to entertain their gentlemen callers. It wasn't enough for a girl to be possessed of a pretty face and a graceful figure — although I wasn't slighted in either respect. She also needed to have a nimble wit and a tongue to meet all occasions.

TOM. What did you talk about?

AMANDA. Things of importance going on in the world! Never anything coarse or common or vulgar. [*She addresses* TOM *as though he were seated in the vacant chair at the table though he remains by portieres. He plays this scene as though he held the book.*] My callers were gentlemen — all! Among my callers were some of the most prominent young planters of the Mississippi Delta — planters and sons of planters!

[TOM *motions for music and a spot of light on* AMANDA.]

[Her eyes lift, her face glows, her voice becomes rich and elegiac.]

[SCREEN LEGEND: "OU SONT LES NEIGES."]

There was young Champ Laughlin who later became vice-president of the Delta Planters Bank. Hadley Stevenson who was drowned in Moon Lake and left his widow one hundred and fifty thousand in Government bonds. There were the Cutrere brothers, Wesley and Bates. Bates was one of my bright particular beaux! He got in a quarrel with that wild Wainwright boy. They shot it out on the floor of Moon Lake Casino. Bates was shot through the stomach. Died in the ambulance on his way to Memphis. His widow was also well-provided for, came into eight or ten thousand acres, that's all. She married him on the rebound — never loved her — carried my picture on him the night he died! And there was that boy that every girl in the Delta had set her cap for! That beautiful, brilliant young Fitzhugh boy from Greene County!

TOM. What did he leave his widow?

AMANDA. He never married! Gracious, you talk as though all of my old admirers had turned up their toes to the daisies!

TOM. Isn't this the first you've mentioned that still survives?

AMANDA. That Fitzhugh boy went North and made a fortune — came to be known as the Wolf of Wall Street! He had the Midas touch, whatever he touched turned to gold! And I could have been

Mrs. Duncan J. Fitzhugh, mind you! But — I picked your *father!*

LAURA [*rising*]. Mother, let me clear the table.

AMANDA. No, dear, you go in front and study your typewriter chart. Or practice your shorthand a little. Stay fresh and pretty! — It's almost time for our gentlemen callers to start arriving. [*She flounces girlishly toward the kitchenette.*] How many do you suppose we're going to entertain this afternoon?

[TOM *throws down the paper and jumps up with a groan.*]

LAURA [*alone in the dining room*]. I don't believe we're going to receive any, Mother.

AMANDA [*reappearing, airily*]. What? No one — not one? You must be joking! [LAURA *nervously echoes her laugh. She slips in a fugitive manner through the half-open portieres and draws them gently behind her. A shaft of very clear light is thrown on her face against the faded tapestry of the curtains.* MUSIC: "THE GLASS MENAGERIE" UNDER FAINTLY. *Lightly:*] Not one gentleman caller? It can't be true! There must be a flood, there must have been a tornado!

LAURA. It isn't a flood, it's not a tornado, Mother. I'm just not popular like you were in Blue Mountain . . . . [TOM *utters another groan.* LAURA *glances at him with a faint, apologetic smile. Her voice catching a little.*] Mother's afraid I'm going to be an old maid.

(The Scene Dims Out With "GLASS MENAGERIE" *Music.)*

Scene II

[*"Laura, Haven't You Ever Liked Some Boy?"*
    On the dark stage the screen is lighted with the image of blue roses.
    Gradually LAURA'S *figure becomes apparent and the screen goes out.*
    The music subsides.
    LAURA *is seated in the delicate ivory chair at the small claw-foot table.*
    She wears a dress of soft violet material for a kimono — her hair tied back from her forehead with a ribbon.
    She is washing and polishing her collection of glass.

[AMANDA *appears on the fire-escape steps. At the sound of her ascent,* LAURA *catches her breath, thrusts the bowl of ornaments away and seats herself stiffly before the diagram of the typewriter keyboard as though it held her spellbound. Something has happened to* AMANDA. *It is written in her face as she climbs to the landing: a look that is grim and hopeless and a little absurd.*

NERVOUS

She has on one of those cheap or imitation velvety-looking cloth coats with imitation fur collar. Her hat is five or six years old, one of those dreadful cloche hats that were worn in the late twenties and she is clasping an enormous black patent-leather pocketbook with nickel clasps and initials. This is her full-dress outfit, the one she usually wears to the D.A.R.

Before entering she looks through the door.

She purses her lips, opens her eyes wide, rolls them upward and shakes her head.

Then she slowly lets herself in the door. Seeing her mother's expression LAURA *touches her lips with a nervous gesture.*]

LAURA. Hello, Mother, I was — [*She makes a nervous gesture toward the chart on the wall.* AMANDA *leans against the shut door and stares at* LAURA *with a martyred look.*]

AMANDA. Deception? Deception? [*She slowly removes her hat and gloves, continuing the sweet suffering stare. She lets the hat and gloves fall on the floor — a bit of acting.*]

LAURA [*shakily*]. How was the D.A.R. meeting? [AMANDA *slowly opens her purse and removes a dainty white handkerchief which she shakes out delicately and delicately touches to her lips and nostrils.*] Didn't you go to the D.A.R. meeting, Mother?

AMANDA [*faintly, almost inaudibly*]. — No. — No. [*Then more forcibly:*] I did not have the strength — to go to the D.A.R. In fact, I did not have the courage! I wanted to find a hole in the ground and hide myself in it forever! [*She crosses slowly to the wall and removes the diagram of the typewriter keyboard. She holds it in front of her for a second, staring at it sweetly and sorrowfully — then bites her lips and tears it in two pieces.*]

LAURA [*faintly*]. Why did you do that, Mother? [AMANDA *repeats the same procedure with the chart of the Gregg Alphabet.*] Why are you —

AMANDA. Why? Why? How old are you, Laura?

LAURA. Mother, you know my age.

AMANDA. I thought that you were an adult; it seems that I was mistaken. [*She crosses slowly to the sofa and sinks down and stares at* LAURA.]

LAURA. Please don't stare at me, Mother.

[AMANDA *closes her eyes and lowers her head. Count ten.*]

AMANDA. What are we going to do, what is going to become of us, what is the future?

[*Count ten.*]

LAURA. Has something happened, Mother? [AMANDA *draws a long breath and takes out the handkerchief again. Dabbing process.*] Mother, has — something happened?

AMANDA. I'll be all right in a minute. I'm just bewildered — [*Count five*] — by life . . . .

LAURA. Mother, I wish that you would tell me what's happened!

AMANDA. As you know, I was supposed to be inducted into my office at the D.A.R. this afternoon. [IMAGE: A SWARM OF TYPEWRITERS.] But I stopped off at Rubicam's business college to speak to your teachers about your having a cold and ask them what progress they thought you were making down there.

LAURA. Oh . . . .

AMANDA. I went to the typing instructor and introduced myself as your mother. She didn't know who you were. Wingfield, she said. We don't have any such student enrolled at the school! I assured her she did, that you had been going to classes since early in January. "I wonder," she said, "if you could be talking about that terribly shy little girl who dropped out of school after only a few days' attendance?" "No," I said, "Laura, my daughter, has been going to school every day for the past six weeks!" "Excuse me," she said. She took the attendance book out and there was your name, unmistakably printed, and all the dates you were absent until they decided that you had dropped out of school. I still said, "No, there must have been some mistake! There must have been some mix-up in the records!" And she said, "No — I remember her perfectly now. Her hands shook so that she couldn't hit the right keys! The first time we gave a speed-test, she broke down completely — was sick at the stomach and almost had to be carried into the wash-room! After that morning she never showed up any more. We phoned the house but never got any answer" — while I was working at Famous and Barr, I suppose, demonstrating those — Oh! I felt so weak I could barely keep on my feet! I had to sit down while they got me a glass of water! Fifty dollars' tuition, all of our plans — my hopes and ambitions for you — just gone up the spout, just gone up the spout like that. [LAURA *draws a long breath and gets awkwardly to her feet. She crosses to the victrola and winds it up.*] What are you doing?

LAURA. Oh! [*She releases the handle and returns to her seat.*]

AMANDA. Laura, where have you been going when you've gone out pretending that you were going to business college?

LAURA. I've just been going out walking.

AMANDA. That's not true.

LAURA. It is. I just went walking.

AMANDA. Walking? Walking? In winter? Deliberately courting pneumonia in that light coat? Where did you walk to, Laura?

LAURA. All sorts of places — mostly in the park.

AMANDA. Even after you'd started catching that cold?

LAURA. It was the lesser of two evils, Mother. [IMAGE: WINTER SCENE IN PARK.] I couldn't go back up. I — threw up — on the floor!

AMANDA. From half past seven till after five every day you mean to tell me you walked around in the park, because you wanted to make me think that you were still going to Rubicam's Business College?

LAURA. It wasn't as bad as it sounds. I went inside places to get warmed up.

AMANDA. Inside where?

LAURA. I went in the art museum and the bird-houses at the Zoo. I visited the penguins every day! Sometimes I did without lunch and went to the movies. Lately I've been spending most of my afternoons in the Jewel-box, that big glass house where they raise the tropical flowers.

AMANDA. You did all this to deceive me, just for deception? [LAURA *looks down.*] Why?

LAURA. Mother, when you're disappointed, you get that awful suffering look on your face, like the picture of Jesus' mother in the museum!

AMANDA. Hush!

LAURA. I couldn't face it.

[*Pause. A whisper of strings.*]

[LEGEND: "THE CRUST OF HUMILITY."]

AMANDA [*hopelessly fingering the huge pocketbook*]. So what are we going to do the rest of our lives? Stay home and watch the parades go by? Amuse ourselves with the glass menagerie, darling? Eternally play those worn-out phonograph records your father left as a painful reminder of him? We won't have a business career — we've given that up because it gave us nervous indigestion! [*Laughs wearily.*] What is there left but dependency all our lives? I know so well what becomes of unmarried women who aren't prepared to occupy a position. I've seen such pitiful cases in the South — barely tolerated spinsters living upon the grudging patronage of sister's husband or brother's wife! — stuck away in some little mouse-trap of a room — encouraged by one in-law to visit another — little birdlike women without any nest — eating the crust of humility all their life! Is that the future that we've mapped out for ourselves? I swear it's the only alternative I can think of! It isn't a very pleasant alternative, is it? Of course — some girls *do marry*. [LAURA *twists her hands nervously.*] Haven't you ever liked some boy?

LAURA. Yes. I liked one once. [*Rises.*] I came across his picture a while ago.

AMANDA [with some interest]. He gave you his picture?

LAURA. No, it's in the year-book.

AMANDA [*disappointed*]. Oh — a high-school boy.

[SCREEN IMAGE: JIM AS HIGH-SCHOOL HERO BEARING A SILVER CUP.]

LAURA. Yes. His name was Jim. [LAURA *lifts the heavy annual from the claw-foot table.*] Here he is in *The Pirates of Penzance*.

LAURA. The operetta the senior class put on. He had a wonderful voice and we sat across the aisle from each other Mondays, Wednesdays and Fridays in the Aud. Here he is with the silver cup for debating! See his grin?

AMANDA [*absently*]. He must have had a jolly disposition.

LAURA. He used to call me — Blue Roses.

[IMAGE: BLUE ROSES.]

AMANDA. Why did he call you such a name as that?

LAURA. When I had that attack of pleurosis — he asked me what was the matter when I came back. I said pleurosis — he thought that I said Blue Roses! So that's what he always called me after that. Whenever he saw me, he'd holler, "Hello, Blue Roses!" I didn't care for the girl that he went out with. Emily Meisenbach. Emily was the best-dressed girl at Soldan. She never struck me, though, as being sincere . . . It says in the Personal Section — they're engaged. That's — six years ago! They must be married by now.

AMANDA. Girls that aren't cut out for business careers usually wind up married to some nice man. [*Gets up with a spark of revival.*] Sister, that's what you'll do!

[LAURA *utters a startled, doubtful laugh. She reaches quickly for a piece of glass.*]

LAURA. But, Mother —

AMANDA. Yes? [*Crossing to photograph.*]

LAURA [*in a tone of frightened apology*]. I'm — crippled!

[IMAGE: SCREEN.]

AMANDA. Nonsense! Laura, I've told you never, never to use that word. Why, you're not crippled, you just have a little defect — hardly noticeable, even! When people have some slight disadvantage like that, they cultivate other things to make up for it — develop charm — and vivacity — and — *charm!* That's all you have to do! [*She turns again to the photograph.*] One thing your father had *plenty of* — was *charm!*

[TOM *motions to the fiddle in the wings.*]

(*The Scene Fades Out With Music.*)

Scene III

LEGEND ON SCREEN: "AFTER THE FIASCO —"

[TOM *speaks from the fire-escape landing.*]

TOM. After the fiasco at Rubicam's Business College, the idea of getting a gentleman caller for Laura began to play a more important part in Mother's calculations. It became an obsession. Like some archetype of the universal unconscious, the image of the gentleman caller haunted our small apartment. . . . [IMAGE: YOUNG MAN AT DOOR WITH FLOWERS.] An evening at home rarely passed without some allusion to this image, this spectre, this hope. . . . Even when he wasn't mentioned, his presence hung in Mother's preoccupied look and in my sister's frightened, apologetic manner — hung like a sentence passed upon the Wingfields! Mother was a woman of action as well as words. She began to take logical steps in the planned direction. Late that winter and in the early spring — realizing that extra money would be needed to properly feather the nest and plume the bird — she conducted a vigorous campaign on the telephone, roping in subscribers to one of those magazines for matrons called *The Home-maker's Companion,* the type of journal that features the serialized sublimations of ladies of letters who think in terms of delicate cup-like breasts, slim, tapering waists, rich, creamy thighs, eyes like woodsmoke in autumn, fingers that soothe and caress like strains of music, bodies as powerful as Etruscan sculpture.

[SCREEN IMAGES: GLAMOR MAGAZINE COVER.]

[AMANDA *enters with phone on long extension cord. She is spotted in the dim stage.*]

AMANDA. Ida Scott? This is Amanda Wingfield! We *missed* you at the D.A.R. last Monday! I said to myself: She's probably suffering with that sinus condition! How is that sinus condition? Horrors! Heaven have mercy! — You're a Christian martyr, yes, that's what you are, a Christian martyr! Well, I just now happened to notice that your subscription to the *Companion's* about to expire! Yes, it expires with the next issue, honey! — just when that wonderful new serial by Bessie Mae Hopper is getting off to such an exciting start. Oh, honey, it's something that you can't miss! You remember how *Gone With the Wind* took everybody by storm? You simply couldn't go out if you hadn't read it. All everybody *talked* was Scarlett

351

O'Hara. Well, this is a book that critics already compare to *Gone With the Wind*. It's the *Gone With the Wind* of the post-World War generation! — What? — Burning? — Oh, honey, don't let them burn, go take a look in the oven and I'll hold the wire! Heavens — I think she's hung up!

DIM OUT

[LEGEND ON SCREEN: "YOU THINK I'M IN LOVE WITH CONTINENTAL SHOEMAKERS?"]

[*Before the stage is lighted, the violent voices of* TOM *and* AMANDA *are heard.*]

[*They are quarreling behind the portieres. In front of them stands* LAURA *with clenched hands and panicky expression.*]

[*A clear pool of light on her figure throughout this scene.*]

TOM. What in Christ's name am I —

AMANDA [*shrilly*]. Don't you use that —

TOM. Supposed to do!

AMANDA. Expression! Not in my —

TOM. Ohhh!

AMANDA. Presence! Have you gone out of your senses?

TOM. I have, that's true, *driven* out!

AMANDA. What is the matter with you, you — big — big — IDIOT!

TOM. Look — I've got *no thing,* no single thing —

AMANDA. Lower your voice!

TOM. In my life here that I can call my OWN! Everything is —

AMANDA. Stop that shouting!

TOM. Yesterday you confiscated my books! You had the nerve to —

AMANDA. I took that horrible novel back to the library — yes! That hideous book by that insane Mr. Lawrence. [TOM *laughs wildly.*] I cannot control the output of diseased minds or people who cater to them — [TOM *laughs still more wildly.*] BUT I WON'T ALLOW SUCH FILTH BROUGHT INTO MY HOUSE! No, no, no, no, no!

TOM. House, house! Who pays rent on it, who makes a slave of himself to —

AMANDA [*fairly screeching*]. Don't you DARE to —

TOM. No, no, *I* mustn't say things! *I've* got to just —

AMANDA. Let me tell you —

TOM. I don't want to hear any more! [*He tears the portieres open. The upstage area is lit with a turgid smoky red glow.*]

[*AMANDA'S hair is in metal curlers and she wears a very old bathrobe, much too large for her slight figure, a relic of the faithless Mr. Wingfield.*]

[*An upright typewriter and a wild disarray of manuscripts is on the drop-leaf table. The quarrel was probably precipitated by AMANDA'S interruption of his creative labor. A chair lying overthrown on the floor.*]

[*Their gesticulating shadows are cast on the ceiling by the fiery glow.*]

AMANDA. You *will* hear more, you —

TOM. No, I won't hear more, I'm going out!

AMANDA. You come right back in —

TOM. Out, out, out! Because I'm —

AMANDA. Come back here, Tom Wingfield! I'm not through talking to you!

TOM. Oh, go —

LAURA [*desperately*]. — Tom!

AMANDA. You're going to listen, and no more insolence from you! I'm at the end of my patience! [*He comes back toward her.*]

TOM. What do you think I'm at? Aren't I supposed to have any patience to reach the end of, Mother? I know, I know. It seems unimportant to you, what I'm *doing* — what I *want* to do — having a little *difference* between them! You don't think that —

AMANDA. I think you've been doing things that you're ashamed of. That's why you act like this. I don't believe that you go every night to the movies. Nobody goes to the movies night after night. Nobody in their right mind goes to the movies as often as you pretend to. People don't go to the movies at nearly midnight, and movies don't let out at two A.M. Come in stumbling. Muttering to yourself like a maniac! You get three hours' sleep and then go to work. Oh, I can picture the way you're doing down there. Moping, doping, because you're in no condition.

TOM [*wildly*]. No, I'm in no condition!

AMANDA. What right have you got to jeopardize your job? Jeopardize the security of us all? How do you think we'd manage if you were —

TOM. Listen! You think I'm crazy *about* the *warehouse?* [*He bends fiercely toward her slight figure.*] You think I'm in love with the Continental Shoemakers? You think I want to spend fifty-five *years* down there in that — *celotex interior!* with — *fluorescent* — *tubes!* Look! I'd rather somebody picked up a crowbar and battered out my brains — than go back mornings! I *go!* Every time you come in yelling that God damn *"Rise and Shine!" "Rise and Shine!"* I say to myself, "How *lucky dead* people are!" But I get up. I *go!* For sixty-five dollars a month I give up all that I dream of doing and being *ever!* And you say self — *self's* all I ever think of. Why, listen, if self is what I thought of, Mother, I'd be where he is — GONE! [*Pointing to father's picture.*] As far as the system of transportation reaches! [*He starts past her. She grabs his arm.*] Don't grab at me, Mother!

AMANDA. Where are you going?

TOM. I'm going to the *movies!*

AMANDA. I don't believe that lie!

TOM [*crouching toward her, overtowering her tiny figure. She backs away, gasping*]. I'm going to opium dens! Yes, opium dens, dens of vice and criminals' hang-outs, Mother. I've joined the Hogan gang, I'm a hired assassin, I carry a tommy-gun in a violin case! I run a string of cat-houses in the Valley! They call me Killer, Killer Wingfield, I'm leading a double-life, a simple, honest warehouse worker by day, by night, a dynamic *czar* of the *underworld, Mother.* I go to gambling casinos, I spin away fortunes on the roulette table! I wear a patch over one eye and a false mustache, sometimes I put on green whiskers. On those occasions they call me — *El Diablo!* Oh, I could tell you things to make you sleepless! My enemies plan to dynamite this place.

They're going to blow us all sky-high some night! I'll be glad, very happy, and so will you! You'll go up, up on a broomstick, over Blue Mountain with seventeen gentlemen callers! You ugly — babbling old — witch. . . . [*He goes through a series of violent, clumsy movements, seizing his overcoat, lunging to the door, pulling it fiercely open. The women watch him, aghast. His arm catches in the sleeve of the coat as he struggles to pull it on. For a moment he is pinioned by the bulky garment. With an outraged groan he tears the coat off again, splitting the shoulder of it, and hurls it across the room. It strikes against the shelf of* LAURA'S *glass collection, there is a tinkle of shattering glass.* LAURA *cries out as if wounded.*]

[MUSIC LEGEND: "THE GLASS MENAGERIE."]

LAURA [*shrilly*]. *My glass!* — menagerie. . . . [*She covers her face and turns away.*]

[*But* AMANDA *is still stunned and stupefied by the "ugly witch" so that she barely notices this occurrence. Now she recovers her speech.*]

AMANDA [*in an awful voice*]. I won't speak to you — until you apologize! [*She crosses through portieres and draws them together behind her.* TOM *is left with* LAURA. LAURA *clings weakly to the mantel with her face averted.* TOM *stares at her stupidly for a moment. Then he crosses to shelf. Drops awkwardly on his knees to collect the fallen glass, glancing at* LAURA *as if he would speak but couldn't.*]

"The Glass Menagerie" steals in as

(The Scene Dims Out.)

Scene IV

[*The interior is dark. Faint light in the alley.*

A deep-voice bell in a church is tolling the hour of five as the scene commences.

TOM *appears at the top of the alley. After each solemn boom of the bell in the tower, he shakes a little noise-maker or rattle as if to express the tiny spasm of man in contrast to the sustained power and dignity of the Almighty. This and the unsteadiness of his advance make it evident that he has been drinking.*

MAN INSIGNIF.

MOTIF: TOM'S ESCAPE

As he climbs the few steps to the fire-escape landing light steals up inside. LAURA appears in night-dress, observing TOM'S empty bed in the front room.

TOM fishes in his pockets for door-key, removing a motley assortment of articles in the search, including a perfect shower of movie-ticket stubs and an empty bottle. At last he finds the key, but just as he is about to insert it, it slips from his fingers. He strikes a match and crouches below the door.]

STORY ✽TOM [*bitterly*]. One crack — and it falls through!

OF TOM'S   [LAURA *opens the door.*]

LIFE   LAURA. Tom! Tom, what are you doing?

TOM. Looking for a door-key.

LAURA. Where have you been all this time?

TOM. I have been to the movies.

LAURA. All this time at the movies?

TOM. There was a very long program. There was a Garbo picture and a Mickey Mouse and a travelogue and a newsreel and a preview of coming attractions. And there was an organ solo and a collection for the milk-fund — simultaneously — which ended up in a terrible fight between a fat lady and an usher!

LAURA [*innocently*]. Did you have to stay through everything?

TOM. Of course! And, oh, I forgot! There was a big stage show! The headliner on this stage show was Malvolio the Magician. He performed wonderful tricks, many of them, such as pouring water back and forth between pitchers. First it turned to wine and then it turned to beer and then it turned to whiskey. I know it was whiskey it finally turned into because he needed somebody to come up out of the audience to help him, and I came up — both shows! It was Kentucky Straight Bourbon. A very generous fellow, he gave souvenirs. [*He pulls from his back pocket a shimmering rainbow-colored scarf.*] He gave me this. This is his magic scarf. You can have it, Laura. You wave it over a canary cage and you get a bowl of gold-fish. You wave it over the gold-fish bowl and they fly away canaries. . . . But the wonderfullest trick of all was the coffin trick. We nailed him into a coffin and he got out of the coffin without removing one nail. [*He has come inside.*] There is a trick that would come in handy for me — get me out of this 2 by 4 situation! [*Flops onto bed and starts removing shoes.*]

LAURA. Tom — Shhh!

TOM. What're you shushing me for?

LAURA. You'll wake up Mother.

TOM. Goody, goody! Pay 'er back for all those "Rise an' Shines." [*Lies down, groaning.*] You know it don't take much intelligence to get yourself into a nailed-up coffin, Laura. But who in hell ever got himself out of one without removing one nail?

[*As if in answer, the father's grinning photograph lights up.*]

SCENE DIMS OUT

[*Immediately following: The church bell is heard striking six. At the sixth stroke the alarm clock goes off in* AMANDA'S *room, and after a few moments we hear her calling: "Rise and Shine! Rise and Shine! Laura, go tell your brother to rise and shine!"*]

TOM [*Sitting up slowly*]. I'll rise — but I won't shine.

[*The light increases.*]

AMANDA. Laura, tell your brother his coffee is ready.

[LAURA *slips into front room.*]

LAURA. Tom, it's nearly seven. Don't make Mother nervous. [*He stares at her stupidly. Beseechingly.*] Tom, speak to Mother this morning. Make up with her, apologize, speak to her!

TOM. She won't to me. It's her that started not speaking.

LAURA. If you just say you're sorry she'll start speaking.

TOM. Her not speaking — is that such a tragedy?

LAURA. Please — please!

AMANDA [*calling from kitchenette*]. Laura, are you going to do what I asked you to do, or do I have to get dressed and go out myself?

LAURA. Going, going — soon as I get on my coat! [*She pulls on a shapeless felt hat with nervous, jerky movement, pleadingly glancing at* TOM. *Rushes awkwardly for coat. The coat is one of* AMANDA'S, *inaccurately made-over, the sleeves too short for* LAURA.] Butter and what else?

AMANDA [*entering upstage*]. Just butter. Tell them to charge it.

LAURA. Mother, they make such faces when I do that.

AMANDA. Sticks and stones can break our bones, but the expression on Mr. Garfinkel's face won't harm us! Tell your brother his coffee is getting cold.

LAURA [*at door*]. Do what I asked you, will you, will you, Tom?

[*He looks sullenly away.*]

AMANDA. Laura, go now or just don't go at all!

LAURA [*rushing out*]. Going — going! [*A second later she cries out.* TOM *springs up and crosses to door.* AMANDA *rushes anxiously in.* TOM *opens the door.*]

TOM. Laura?

LAURA. I'm all right. I slipped, but I'm all right.

AMANDA [*peering anxiously after her*]. If anyone breaks a leg on those fire-escape steps, the landlord ought to be sued for every cent he possesses! [*She shuts door. Remembers she isn't speaking and returns to other room.*]

[*As* TOM *enters listlessly for his coffee, she turns her back to him and stands rigidly facing the window on the gloomy gray vault of the areaway. Its light on her face with its aged but childish features is cruelly sharp, satirical as a Daumier print.*]

[MUSIC UNDER: "AVE MARIA."]

[TOM *glances sheepishly but sullenly at her averted figure and slumps at the table. The coffee is scalding hot; he sips it and gasps and spits it back in the cup. At his gasp,* AMANDA *catches her breath and half turns. Then catches herself and turns back to window.*]

[TOM *blows on his coffee, glancing sideways at his mother. She clears her throat.* TOM *clears his. He starts to rise. Sinks back down again, scratches his head, clears his throat again.* AMANDA *coughs.* TOM *raises his cup in both hands to blow on it, his eyes staring over the rim of it at his mother for several moments. Then he slowly sets the cup down and awkwardly and hesitantly rises from the chair.*]

TOM [*hoarsely*]. Mother. I — I apologize. Mother. [AMANDA *draws a quick, shuddering breath. Her face works grotesquely.*

She breaks into childlike tears.] I'm sorry for what I said, for everything that I said, I didn't mean it.

AMANDA [*sobbingly*]. My devotion has made me a witch and so I make myself hateful to my children!

TOM. *No,* you *don't.*

AMANDA. I worry so much, don't sleep, it makes me nervous!

TOM [*gently*]. I understand that.

AMANDA. I've had to put up a solitary battle all these years. But you're my right-hand bower! Don't fall down, don't fail!

TOM [*gently*]. I try, Mother.

AMANDA [*with great enthusiasm*]. Try and you will SUCCEED! [*The notion makes her breathless.*] Why, you — you're just *full* of natural endowments! Both of my children — they're *unusual* children! Don't you think I know it? I'm so — *proud!* Happy and — feel I've — so much to be thankful for but — Promise me one thing, son!

TOM. What, Mother?

AMANDA. Promise, son, you'll — never be a drunkard!

TOM [*turns to her grinning*]. I will never be a drunkard, Mother.

AMANDA. That's what frightened me so, that you'd be drinking! Eat a bowl of Purina!

TOM. Just coffee, Mother.

AMANDA. Shredded wheat biscuit?

TOM. No. No, Mother, just coffee.

AMANDA. You can't put in a day's work on an empty stomach. You've got ten minutes — don't gulp! Drinking too-hot liquids makes cancer of the stomach. . . . Put cream in.

TOM. No, thank you.

AMANDA. To cool it.

TOM. No! No, thank you, I want it black.

AMANDA. I know, but it's not good for you. We have to do all that we can to build ourselves up. In these trying times we live in, all that we have to cling to is — each other. . . . That's why it's so important to — Tom, I — I sent out your sister so I could discuss something with you. If you hadn't spoken I would have spoken to you. [*Sits down.*]

TOM [*gently*]. What is it, Mother, that you want to discuss?

AMANDA. *Laura!*

[TOM *puts his cup down slowly.*]

[LEGEND ON SCREEN: "LAURA."]

[MUSIC: "THE GLASS MENAGERIE."]

TOM. — Oh. — Laura . . .

AMANDA [*touching his sleeve*]. You know how Laura is. So quiet but — still water runs deep! She notices things and I think she — broods about them. [TOM *looks up*]. A few days ago I came in and she was crying.

TOM. What about?

AMANDA. You.

TOM. Me?

AMANDA. She has an idea that you're not happy here.

TOM. What gave her that idea?

AMANDA. What gives her any idea? However, you do act strangely. I — I'm not criticizing, understand *that!* I know your ambitions do not lie in the warehouse, that like everybody in the whole wide world — you've had to — make sacrifices, but — Tom — Tom — life's not easy, it calls for — Spartan endurance! There's so many things in my heart that I cannot describe to you! I've never told you but I — *loved* your father. . . .

TOM [*gently*]. I know that, Mother.

AMANDA. And you — when I see you taking after his ways! Staying out late — and — well, you *had* been drinking the night you were in that — terrifying condition! Laura says that you hate the apartment and that you go out nights to get away from it! Is that true, Tom?

TOM. No. You say there's so much in your heart that you can't describe to me. That's true of me, too. There's so much in my heart that I can't describe to *you!* So let's respect each other's —

AMANDA. But, why — *why,* Tom — are you always so *restless?* Where do you *go* to, nights?

TOM. I — go to the movies.

AMANDA. Why do you go to the movies so much, Tom?

TOM. I go to the movies because — I like adventure. Adventure is something I don't have much of at work, so I go to the movies.

AMANDA. But, Tom, you go to the movies *entirely* too *much!*

TOM. I like a lot of adventure.

[AMANDA *looks baffled, then hurt. As the familiar inquisition resumes he becomes hard and impatient again.* AMANDA *slips back into her querulous attitude toward him.*]

[IMAGE ON SCREEN: SAILING VESSEL WITH JOLLY ROGER.]

AMANDA. Most young men find adventure in their careers.

TOM. Then most young men are not employed in a warehouse.

AMANDA. The world is full of young men employed in warehouses and offices and factories.

TOM. Do all of them find adventure in their careers?

AMANDA. They do or they do without it! Not everybody has a craze for adventure.

TOM. Man is by instinct a lover, a hunter, a fighter, and none of those instincts are given much play at the warehouse!

AMANDA. Man is by instinct! Don't quote instinct to me! Instinct is something that people have got away from! It belongs to animals! Christian adults don't want it!

TOM. What do Christian adults want, then, Mother?

AMANDA. Superior things! Things of the mind and the spirit! Only animals have to satisfy instincts! Surely your aims are somewhat higher than theirs! Than monkeys — pigs —

TOM. I reckon they're not.

AMANDA. You're joking. However, that isn't what I wanted to discuss.

TOM [*rising*]. I haven't much time.

AMANDA [*pushing his shoulders*]. Sit down.

TOM. You want me to punch in red at the warehouse, Mother?

AMANDA. You have five minutes. I want to talk about Laura.

[LEGEND: "PLANS AND PROVISIONS."]

TOM. All right! What about Laura?

AMANDA. We have to be making plans and provisions for her. She's older than you, two years, and nothing has happened. She just drifts along doing nothing. It frightens me terribly how she just drifts along.

TOM. I guess she's the type that people call home girls.

AMANDA. There's no such type, and if there is, it's a pity! That is unless the home is hers, with a husband!

TOM. What?

AMANDA. Oh, I can see the handwriting on the wall as plain as I see the nose in front of my face! It's terrifying! More and more you remind me of your father! He was out all hours without explanation — Then *left! Good-bye!* And me with the bag to hold. I saw that letter you got from the Merchant Marine. I know what you're dreaming of. I'm not standing here blindfolded. Very well, then. Then *do* it! But not till there's somebody to take your place.

TOM. What do you mean?

AMANDA. I mean that as soon as Laura has got somebody to take care of her, married, a home of her own, independent — why, then you'll be free to go wherever you please, on land, on sea, whichever way the wind blows you! But until that time you've got to look out for your sister. I don't say me because I'm old and don't matter! I say for your sister because she's young and dependent. I put her in business college — a dismal failure! Frightened her so it made her sick to her stomach. I took her over to the Young People's League at the church. Another fiasco. She spoke to nobody, nobody spoke to her. Now all she does is fool with those pieces of glass and play those worn-out records. What kind of a life is that for a girl to lead?

TOM. What can I do about it?

AMANDA. Overcome selfishness! Self, self, self is all that you ever think of! [TOM *springs up and crosses to get his coat. It is ugly and bulky. He pulls on a cap with earmuffs.*] Where is your muffler? Put your wool muffler on! [*He snatches it angrily from the closet and tosses it around his neck and pulls both ends tight.*] Tom! I haven't said what I had in mind to ask you.

TOM. I'm too late to —

AMANDA. [*catching his arm — very importunately. Then shyly*]. Down at the warehouse, aren't there some — nice young men?

TOM. No!

AMANDA. There *must* be — *some* . . .

TOM. Mother —

[*Gesture.*]

AMANDA. Find out one that's clean-living — doesn't drink and — ask him out for sister!

TOM. What?

AMANDA. For *sister!* To *meet!* Get *acquainted!*

TOM [*stamping to door*]. Oh, my *go-osh!*

AMANDA. Will you? [*He opens door. Imploringly.*] Will you? [*He starts down.*] Will you? *Will* you, dear?

TOM [*calling back*]. YES!

[AMANDA *closes the door hesitantly and with a troubled but faintly hopeful expression.*]

[SCREEN IMAGE: GLAMOR MAGAZINE COVER.]

[*Spot* AMANDA *at phone.*]

AMANDA. Ella Cartwright? This is Amanda Wingfield! How are you, honey? How is that kidney condition? [*Count five.*] *Horrors!* [*Count five.*] You're a Christian martyr, yes, honey, that's what you are, a Christian martyr! Well, I just happened to notice in my little red book that your subscription to the *Companion* has just run out! I knew that you wouldn't want to miss out on the wonderful serial starting in this new issue. It's by Bessie Mae Hopper, the first thing she's written since *Honeymoon for Three.* Wasn't that a strange and interesting story? Well, this one is even lovelier, I believe. It has a sophisticated, society background. It's all about the horsey set on Long Island!

(Fade Out.)

Scene V

[*It is early dusk of a spring evening. Supper has just been finished in the Wingfield apartment. AMANDA and LAURA in light colored dresses are removing dishes from the table, in the upstage area, which is shadowy, their movements formalized almost as a dance or ritual, their moving forms as pale and silent as moths.*

TOM, in white shirt and trousers, rises from the table and crosses toward the fire-escape.]

AMANDA [*as he passes her*]. Son, will you do me a favor?

TOM. What?

AMANDA. Comb your hair! You look so pretty when your hair is combed! [TOM *slouches on sofa with evening paper. Enormous caption "Franco Triumphs."*] There is only one respect in which I would like you to emulate your father.

TOM. What respect is that?

AMANDA. The care he always took of his appearance. He never allowed himself to look untidy. [*He throws down the paper and crosses to fire-escape.*] Where are you going?

TOM. I'm going out to smoke.

AMANDA. You smoke too much. A pack a day at fifteen cents a pack. How much would that amount to in a month? Thirty times fifteen is how much, Tom? Figure it out and you will be astounded at what you could save. Enough to give you a night-school course in accounting at Washington U! Just think what a wonderful thing that would be for you, son!

[TOM *is unmoved by the thought.*]

TOM. I'd rather smoke. [*He steps out on landing, letting the screen door slam.*]

AMANDA [*sharply*]. I know! That's the tragedy of it. . . . [*Alone, she turns to look at her husband's picture.*]

[DANCE MUSIC: "ALL THE WORLD IS WAITING FOR THE SUNRISE!"]

TOM [*to the audience*]. Across the alley from us was the Paradise

Dance Hall. On evenings in spring the windows and doors were open and the music came outdoors. Sometimes the lights were turned out except for a large glass sphere that hung from the ceiling. It would turn slowly about and filter the dusk with delicate rainbow colors. Then the orchestra played a waltz or a tango, something that had a slow and sensuous rhythm. Couples would come outside, to the relative privacy of the alley. You could see them kissing behind ash-pits and telephone poles. This was the compensation for lives that passed like mine, without any change or adventure. Adventure and change were imminent in this year. They were waiting around the corner for all these kids. Suspended in the mist over Berchtesgaden, caught in the folds of Chamberlain's umbrella — In Spain there was Guernica! But here there was only hot swing music and liquor, dance halls, bars, and movies, and sex that hung in the gloom like a chandelier and flooded the world with brief, deceptive rainbows. . . . All the world was waiting for bombardments!

[AMANDA *turns from the picture and comes outside.*]

AMANDA [*Sighing*]. A fire-escape landing's a poor excuse for a porch. [*She spreads a newspaper on a step and sits down, gracefully and demurely as if she were settling into a swing on a Mississippi veranda.*] What are you looking at?

TOM. The moon.

AMANDA. Is there a moon this evening?

TOM. It's rising over Garfinkel's Delicatessen.

AMANDA. So it is! A little silver slipper of a moon. Have you made a wish on it yet?

TOM. Um-hum.

AMANDA. What did you wish for?

TOM. That's a secret.

AMANDA. A secret, huh? Well, I won't tell mine either. I will be just as mysterious as you.

TOM. I bet I can guess what yours is.

AMANDA. Is my head so transparent?

TOM. You're not a sphinx.

AMANDA. No, I don't have secrets. I'll tell you what I wished for on the moon. Success and happiness for my precious children! I wish for that whenever there's a moon, and when there isn't a moon, I wish for it, too.

TOM. I thought perhaps you wished for a gentleman caller.

AMANDA. Why do you say that?

TOM. Don't you remember asking me to fetch one?

AMANDA. I remember suggesting that it would be nice for your sister if you brought home some nice young man from the warehouse. I think that I've made that suggestion more than once.

TOM. Yes, you have made it repeatedly.

AMANDA. Well?

TOM. We are going to have one.

AMANDA. *What?*

TOM. A gentleman caller!

[THE ANNUNCIATION IS CELEBRATED WITH MUSIC.]

[AMANDA *rises.*]

[IMAGE ON SCREEN: CALLER WITH BOUQUET.]

AMANDA. You mean you have asked some nice young man to come over?

TOM. Yep. I've asked him to dinner.

AMANDA. You really did?

TOM. I did!

AMANDA. You did, and did he — *accept?*

TOM. He did!

AMANDA. Well, well — well, well! That's — lovely!

TOM. I thought that you would be pleased.

AMANDA. It's definite, then?

TOM. Very definite.

AMANDA. Soon?

TOM. Very soon.

AMANDA. For heaven's sake, stop putting on and tell me some things, will you?

TOM. What things do you want me to tell you?

AMANDA. *Naturally* I would like to know when he's *coming!*

TOM. He's coming tomorrow.

AMANDA. *Tomorrow?*

TOM. Yep. Tomorrow.

AMANDA. But, Tom!

TOM. Yes, Mother?

AMANDA. Tomorrow gives me no time!

TOM. Time for what?

AMANDA. Preparations! Why didn't you phone me at once, as soon as you asked him, the minute that he accepted? Then, don't you see, I could have been getting ready!

TOM. You don't have to make any fuss.

AMANDA. Oh, Tom, Tom, Tom, of course I have to make a fuss! I want things nice, not sloppy! Not thrown together. I'll certainly have to do some fast thinking, won't I?

TOM. I don't see why you have to think at all.

AMANDA. You just don't know. We can't have a gentleman caller in a pig-sty! All my wedding silver has to be polished, the monogrammed table linen ought to be laundered! The windows have to be washed and fresh curtains put up. And how about clothes? We have to *wear* something, don't we?

TOM. Mother, this boy is no one to make a fuss over!

AMANDA. Do you realize he's the first young man we've introduced to your sister? It's terrible, dreadful, disgraceful that poor little sister has never received a single gentleman caller! Tom, come inside! [*She opens the screen door.*]

TOM. What for?

AMANDA. I want to ask you some things.

TOM. If you're going to make such a fuss, I'll call it off, I'll tell him not to come!

AMANDA. You certainly won't do anything of the kind. Nothing offends people worse than broken engagements. It simply means I'll have to work like a Turk! We won't be brilliant, but we will pass inspection. Come on inside. [TOM *follows, groaning.*] Sit down.

TOM. Any particular place you would like me to sit?

AMANDA. Thank heavens I've got that new sofa! I'm also making payments on a floor lamp I'll have sent out! And put the chintz covers on, they'll brighten things up! Of course I'd hoped to have these walls re-papered. . . . What is the young man's name?

TOM. His name is O'Connor.

AMANDA. That, of course, means fish — tomorrow is Friday! I'll have that salmon loaf — with Durkee's dressing! What does he do? He works at the warehouse?

TOM. Of course! How else would I —

AMANDA. Tom, he — doesn't drink?

TOM. Why do you ask me that?

AMANDA. Your father *did!*

TOM. Don't get started on that!

AMANDA. He *does* drink, then?

TOM. Not that I know of!

AMANDA. Make sure, be certain! The last thing I want for my daughter's a boy who drinks!

TOM. Aren't you being a little bit premature? Mr. O'Connor has not yet appeared on the scene!

AMANDA. But will tomorrow. To meet your sister, and what do I know about his character? Nothing! Old maids are better off than wives of drunkards!

TOM. Oh, my God!

AMANDA. Be still!

TOM [*leaning forward to whisper*]. Lots of fellows meet girls whom they don't marry!

AMANDA. Oh, talk sensibly, Tom — and don't be sarcastic! [*She has gotten a hairbrush.*]

TOM. What are you doing?

AMANDA. I'm brushing that cow-lick down! What is this young man's position at the warehouse?

TOM [*submitting grimly to the brush and the interrogation*]. This young man's position is that of a shipping clerk, Mother.

AMANDA. Sounds to me like a fairly responsible job, the sort of a job *you* would be in if you just had more *get-up*. What is his salary? Have you any idea?

TOM. I would judge it to be approximately eighty-five dollars a month.

AMANDA. Well — not princely, but —

TOM. Twenty more than I make.

AMANDA. Yes, how well I know! But for a family man, eighty-five dollars a month is not much more than you can just get by on. . . .

TOM. Yes, but Mr. O'Connor is not a family man.

AMANDA. He might be, mightn't he? Some time in the future?

TOM. I see. Plans and provisions.

AMANDA. You are the only young man that I know of who ignores the fact that the future becomes the present, the present the past, and the past turns into everlasting regret if you don't plan for it!

TOM. I will think that over and see what I can make of it.

AMANDA. Don't be supercilious with your mother! Tell me some more about this — what do you call him?

TOM. James D. O'Connor. The D. is for Delaney.

AMANDA. Irish on *both* sides! *Gracious!* And doesn't drink?

TOM. Shall I call him up and ask him right this minute?

AMANDA. The only way to find out about those things is to make discreet inquiries at the proper moment. When I was a girl in Blue Mountain and it was suspected that a young man drank, the girl whose attentions he had been receiving, if any girl *was,* would sometimes speak to the minister of his church, or rather her father would if her father was living, and sort of feel him out on the young man's character. That is the way such things are discreetly handled to keep a young woman from making a tragic mistake!

TOM. Then how did you happen to make a tragic mistake?

AMANDA. That innocent look of your father's had everyone fooled! He *smiled* — the world was *enchanted!* No girl can do worse than put herself at the mercy of a handsome appearance! I hope that Mr. O'Connor is not too good-looking.

TOM. No, he's not too good-looking. He's covered with freckles and hasn't too much of a nose.

AMANDA. He's not right-down homely, though?

TOM. Not right-down homely. Just medium homely, I'd say.

AMANDA. Character's what to look for in a man.

TOM. That's what I've always said, Mother.

AMANDA. You've never said anything of the kind and I suspect you would never give it a thought.

TOM. Don't be so suspicious of me.

AMANDA. At least I hope he's the type that's up and coming.

TOM. I think he really goes in for self-improvement.

AMANDA. What reason have you to think so?

TOM. He goes to night school.

AMANDA [*beaming*]. Splendid! What does he do, I mean study?

TOM. Radio engineering and public speaking!

AMANDA. Then he has visions of being advanced in the world! Any young man who studies public speaking is aiming to have an executive job some day! And radio engineering? A thing for the future! Both of these facts are very illuminating. Those are the sort of things that a mother should know concerning any young man who comes to call on her daughter. Seriously or — not.

TOM. One little warning! He doesn't know about Laura. I didn't let on that we had dark ulterior motives. I just said, why don't you come and have dinner with us? He said okay and that was the whole conversation.

AMANDA. I bet it was! You're eloquent as an oyster. However, he'll know about Laura when he gets here. When he sees how lovely and sweet and pretty she is, he'll thank his lucky stars he was asked to dinner.

TOM. Mother, you mustn't expect too much of Laura.

AMANDA. What do you mean?

TOM. Laura seems all those things to you and me because she's ours and we love her. We don't even notice she's crippled any more.

AMANDA. Don't say crippled! You know that I never allow that word to be used!

TOM. But face facts, Mother. She is and — that's not all —

AMANDA. What do you mean "not all"?

TOM. Laura is very different from other girls.

AMANDA. I think the difference is all to her advantage.

TOM. Not quite all — in the eyes of others — strangers — she's terribly shy and lives in a world of her own and those things make her seem a little peculiar to people outside the house.

AMANDA. Don't say peculiar.

TOM. Face the facts. She is.

[THE DANCE-HALL MUSIC CHANGES TO A TANGO THAT HAS A MINOR AND SOMEWHAT OMINOUS TONE.]

AMANDA. In what way is she peculiar — may I ask?

TOM [*gently*]. She lives in a world of her own — a world of — little glass ornaments, Mother. . . . [*Gets up.* AMANDA *remains holding brush, looking at him, troubled.*] She plays old phonograph records and — that's about all — [*He glances at himself in the mirror and crosses to door.*]

AMANDA [*sharply*]. Where are you going?

TOM. I'm going to the movies. [*Out screen door.*]

AMANDA. Not to the movies, every night to the movies! [*Follows quickly to screen door.*] I don't believe you always go to the movies! [*He is gone.* AMANDA *looks worriedly after him for a moment. Then vitality and optimism return and she turns from the door. Crossing to portieres.*] Laura! Laura! [LAURA *answers from kitchenette.*]

LAURA. Yes, Mother.

AMANDA. Let those dishes go and come in front! [LAURA *appears with dish towel. Gaily.*] Laura, come here and make a wish on the moon!

LAURA [*entering*]. Moon — moon?

AMANDA. A little silver slipper of a moon. Look over your left shoulder, Laura, and make a wish! [LAURA *looks faintly puzzled as if called out of sleep.* AMANDA *seizes her shoulders and turns her at an angle by the door.*] No! Now, darling, *wish!*

LAURA. What shall I wish for, Mother?

AMANDA [*her voice trembling and her eyes suddenly filling with tears*]. Happiness! Good Fortune!

[*The violin rises and the stage dims out.*]

Scene VI

[IMAGE: HIGH SCHOOL HERO.]

TOM. And so the following evening I brought Jim home to dinner. I had known Jim slightly in high school. In high school Jim was a hero. He had tremendous Irish good nature and vitality with the scrubbed and polished look of white chinaware. He seemed to move in a continual spotlight. He was a star in basketball, captain of the debating club, president of the senior class and the glee club and he sang the male lead in the annual light operas. He was always running or bounding, never just walking. He seemed always at the point of defeating the law of gravity. He was shooting with such velocity through his adolescence that you would logically expect him to arrive at nothing short of the White House by the time he was thirty. But Jim apparently ran into more interference after his graduation from Soldan. His speed had definitely slowed. Six years after he left high school he was holding a job that wasn't much better than mine.

[IMAGE: CLERK.]

He was the only one at the warehouse with whom I was on friendly terms. I was valuable to him as someone who could remember his former glory, who had seen him win basketball games and the silver cup in debating. He knew of my secret practice of retiring to a cabinet of the washroom to work on poems when business was slack in the warehouse. He called me Shakespeare. And while the other boys in the warehouse regarded me with suspicious hostility, Jim took a humorous attitude toward me. Gradually his attitude affected the others, their hostility wore off and they also began to smile at me as people smile at an oddly fashioned dog who trots across their path at some distance.

I knew that Jim and Laura had known each other at Soldan, and I had heard Laura speak admiringly of his voice. I didn't know if Jim remembered her or not. In high school Laura had been as unobtrusive as Jim had been astonishing. If he did remember Laura, it was not as my sister, for when I asked him to dinner, he grinned and said, "You know, Shakespeare, I never thought of you as having folks!"

He was about to discover that I did. . . .

[LIGHT UP STAGE.]

[LEGEND ON SCREEN: "THE ACCENT OF A COMING FOOT."]

[*Friday evening. It is about five o'clock of a late spring evening which comes "scattering poems in the sky."*]

[*A delicate lemony light is in the Wingfield apartment.*]

[AMANDA *has worked like a Turk in preparation for the gentleman caller. The results are astonishing. The new floor lamp with its rose-silk shade is in place, a colored paper lantern conceals the broken light fixture in the ceiling, new billowing white curtains are at the windows, chintz covers are on chairs and sofa, a pair of new sofa pillows make their initial appearance.*]

[*Open boxes and tissue paper are scattered on the floor.*]

[LAURA *stands in the middle with lifted arms while* AMANDA *crouches before her, adjusting the hem of the new dress, devout and ritualistic. The dress is colored and designed by memory. The arrangement of* LAURA'S *hair is changed; it is softer and more becoming. A fragile, unearthly prettiness has come out in* LAURA: *she is like a piece of translucent glass touched by light, given a momentary radiance, not actual, not lasting.*]

AMANDA [*impatiently*]. Why are you trembling?

LAURA. Mother, you've made me so nervous!

AMANDA. How have I made you nervous?

LAURA. By all this fuss! You make it seem so important!

AMANDA. I don't understand you, Laura. You couldn't be satisfied with just sitting home, and yet whenever I try to arrange something for you, you seem to resist it. [*She gets up.*] Now take a look at yourself. No, wait! Wait just a moment — I have an idea!

LAURA. What is it now?

[AMANDA *produces two powder puffs which she wraps in handkerchiefs and stuffs in* LAURA'S *bosom.*]

LAURA. Mother, what are you doing?

AMANDA. They call them "Gay Deceivers"!

LAURA. I won't wear them!

AMANDA. You will!

LAURA. Why should I?

AMANDA. Because, to be painfully honest, your chest is flat.

LAURA. You make it seem like we were setting a trap.

AMANDA. All pretty girls are a trap, a pretty trap, and men expect them to be. [LEGEND: "A PRETTY TRAP."] Now look at yourself, young lady. This is the prettiest you will ever be! I've got to fix myself now! You're going to be surprised by your mother's appearance! [*She crosses through portieres, humming gaily.*]

[LAURA *moves slowly to the long mirror and stares solemnly at herself.*]

[*A wind blows the white curtains inward in a slow, graceful motion and with a faint, sorrowful sighing.*]

AMANDA [*off stage*]. It isn't dark enough yet. [*She turns slowly before the mirror with a troubled look.*]

[LEGEND ON THE SCREEN: "THIS IS MY SISTER: CELEBRATE HER WITH STRINGS!" MUSIC.]

AMANDA [*laughing, off*]. I'm going to show you something. I'm going to make a spectacular appearance!

LAURA. What is it, Mother?

AMANDA. Possess your soul in patience — you will see! Something I've resurrected from that old trunk! Styles haven't changed so terribly much after all. . . . [*She parts the portieres.*] Now just look at your mother! [*She wears a girlish frock of yellowed voile with a blue silk sash. She carries a bunch of jonquils — the legend of her youth is nearly revived. Feverishly*] This is the dress in which I led the cotillion. Won the cakewalk twice at Sunset Hill, wore one spring to the Governor's ball in Jackson! See how I sashayed around the ballroom, Laura? [*She raises her skirt and does a mincing step around the room.*] I wore it on Sundays for my gentlemen callers! I had it on the day I met your father — I had malaria fever all that spring. The change of climate from East Tennessee to the Delta — weakened resistance — I had a little temperature all the time — not enough to be serious — just enough to make me restless and giddy! Invitations poured in — parties all over the Delta! — "Stay in bed," said Mother, "you have fever!" — but I just wouldn't. — I took quinine but kept on going, going! — Evenings, dances! — Afternoons, long, long rides! Picnics — lovely! — So lovely, that country in May. — All lacy with dogwood, literally flooded with jonquils! — That was the spring I had the craze for jonquils. Jonquils became an absolute obsession. Mother said, "Honey, there's no more room for jonquils." And still I kept on bringing in more jonquils. Whenever, wherever I saw them, I'd say, "Stop! Stop! I see jonquils!" I made the young men help me gather the jonquils! It was a joke, Amanda and her jonquils! Finally there were no more vases to hold them, every available space was filled with jonquils. No vases to hold them? All right, I'll hold them myself! And then I — [*She stops in front of the picture. MUSIC.*] met your father! Malaria fever and jonquils and then — this — boy. . . . [*She switches on the rose-colored lamp.*] I hope they get here before it starts to rain. [*She crosses upstage and places the jonquils in bowl on table.*] I gave your brother a little extra change so he and Mr. O'Connor could take the service car home.

LAURA [*with altered look*]. What did you say his name was?

AMANDA. O'Connor.

LAURA. What is his first name?

AMANDA. I don't remember. Oh, yes, I do. It was — Jim!

[LAURA *sways slightly and catches hold of a chair.*]

[LEGEND ON SCREEN: "NOT JIM!"]

LAURA [*faintly*]. Not — Jim!

AMANDA. Yes, that was it, it was Jim! I've never known a Jim that wasn't nice!

[MUSIC: OMINOUS.]

LAURA. Are you sure his name is Jim O'Connor?

AMANDA. Yes. Why?

LAURA. Is he the one that Tom used to know in high school?

AMANDA. He didn't say so. I think he just got to know him at the warehouse.

LAURA. There was a Jim O'Connor we both knew in high school — [*Then, with effort.*] If that is the one that Tom is bringing to dinner — you'll have to excuse me, I won't come to the table.

AMANDA. What sort of nonsense is this?

LAURA. You asked me once if I'd ever liked a boy. Don't you remember I showed you this boy's picture?

AMANDA. You mean the boy you showed me in the year book?

LAURA. Yes, that boy.

AMANDA. Laura, Laura, were you in love with that boy?

LAURA. I don't know, Mother. All I know is I couldn't sit at the table if it was him!

AMANDA. It won't be him! It isn't the least bit likely. But whether it is or not, you will come to the table. You will not be excused.

LAURA. I'll have to be, Mother.

AMANDA. I don't intend to humor your silliness, Laura. I've had too much from you and your brother, both! So just sit down and compose yourself till they come. Tom has forgotten his key so you'll have to let them in, when they arrive.

LAURA [*panicky*]. Oh, Mother — *you* answer the door!

AMANDA [*lightly*]. I'll be in the kitchen — busy!

LAURA. Oh, Mother, please answer the door, don't make me do it!

AMANDA [*crossing into kitchenette*]. I've got to fix the dressing for the salmon. Fuss, fuss — silliness! — over a gentleman caller!

[*Door swings shut.* LAURA *is left alone.*]

[LEGEND: "TERROR!"]

[*She utters a low moan and turns off the lamp — sits stiffly on the edge of the sofa, knotting her fingers together.*]

[LEGEND ON SCREEN: "THE OPENING OF A DOOR!"]

[TOM *and* JIM *appear on the fire-escape steps and climb to landing. Hearing their approach,* LAURA *rises with a panicky gesture. She retreats to the portieres.*]

[*The doorbell.* LAURA *catches her breath and touches her throat. Low drums.*]

AMANDA [*calling*]. Laura, sweetheart! The door!

[LAURA *stares at it without moving.*]

JIM. I think we just beat the rain.

TOM. Uh-huh. [*He rings again, nervously.* JIM *whistles and fishes for a cigarette.*]

AMANDA [*very, very gaily*]. Laura, that is your brother and Mr. O'Connor! Will you let them in, darling?

[LAURA *crosses toward kitchenette door.*]

LAURA [*breathlessly*]. Mother — you go to the door!

[AMANDA *steps out of kitchenette and stares furiously at* LAURA. *She points imperiously at the door.*]

LAURA. Please, please!

AMANDA [*in a fierce whisper*]. What is the matter with you, you silly thing?

LAURA [*desperately*]. Please, you answer it, *please!*

AMANDA. I told you I wasn't going to humor you, Laura. Why have you chosen this moment to lose your mind?

LAURA. Please, please, please, you go!

AMANDA. You'll have to go to the door because I can't!

LAURA [*despairingly*]. I can't either!

AMANDA. *Why?*

LAURA. I'm *sick!*

AMANDA. I'm sick, too — of your nonsense! Why can't you and your brother be normal people? Fantastic whims and behavior! [TOM *gives a long ring.*] Preposterous goings on! Can you give me one reason — [*Calls out lyrically:*] COMING! JUST ONE SECOND! — why you should be afraid to open a door? Now you answer it, Laura!

LAURA. Oh, oh, oh . . . [*She returns through the portieres. Darts to the victrola and winds it frantically and turns it on.*]

AMANDA. Laura Wingfield, you march right to that door!

LAURA. Yes — yes, Mother!

[*A faraway, scratchy rendition of "Dardanella" softens the air and gives her strength to move through it. She slips to the door and draws it cautiously open.*]

[TOM *enters with the caller,* JIM O'CONNOR.]

TOM. Laura, this is Jim. Jim, this is my sister, Laura.

JIM [*stepping inside*]. I didn't know that Shakespeare had a sister!

LAURA [*retreating stiff and trembling from the door*]. How — how do you do?

JIM [*heartily extending his hand*]. Okay!

[LAURA *touches it hesitantly with hers.*]

JIM. Your hand's *cold,* Laura!

LAURA. Yes, well — I've been playing the victrola. . . .

JIM. Must have been playing classical music on it! You ought to play a little hot swing music to warm you up!

LAURA. Excuse me — I haven't finished playing the victrola. . . .

[*She turns awkwardly and hurries into the front room. She pauses a second by the victrola. Then catches her breath and darts through the portieres like a frightened deer.*]

JIM [*grinning*]. What was the matter?

TOM. Oh — with Laura? Laura is — terribly shy.

JIM. Shy, huh? It's unusual to meet a shy girl nowadays. I don't believe you ever mentioned you had a sister.

TOM. Well, now you know. I have one. Here is the *Post Dispatch*. You want a piece of it?

JIM. Uh-huh.

TOM. What piece? The comics?

JIM. Sports! [*Glances at it.*] Ole Dizzy Dean is on his bad behavior.

TOM [*disinterest*]. Yeah? [*Lights cigarette and crosses back to fire-escape door.*]

JIM. Where are *you* going?

TOM. I'm going out on the terrace.

JIM [*goes after him*]. You know, Shakespeare — I'm going to sell you a bill of goods!

TOM. What goods?

JIM. A course I'm taking.

TOM. Huh?

JIM. In public speaking! You and me, we're not the warehouse type.

TOM. Thanks — that's good news. But what has public speaking got to do with it?

JIM. It fits you for — executive positions!

TOM. Awww.

JIM. I tell you it's done a helluva lot for me.

   [IMAGE: EXECUTIVE AT DESK.]

TOM. In what respect?

JIM. In every! Ask yourself what is the difference between you an' me and men in the office down front? Brains? — No! — Ability? — No! Then what? Just one little thing —

TOM. What is that one little thing?

JIM. Primarily it amounts to — social poise! Being able to square up to people and hold your own on any social level!

AMANDA [*off stage*]. Tom?

TOM. Yes, Mother?

AMANDA. Is that you and Mr. O'Connor?

TOM. Yes, Mother.

AMANDA. Well, you just make yourselves comfortable in there.

TOM. Yes, Mother.

AMANDA. Ask Mr. O'Connor if he would like to wash his hands.

JIM. Aw, no — no — thank you — I took care of that at the warehouse. Tom —

TOM. Yes?

JIM. Mr. Mendoza was speaking to me about you.

TOM. Favorably?

JIM. What do you think?

TOM. Well —

JIM. You're going to be out of a job if you don't wake up.

TOM. I am waking up —

JIM. You show no signs.

TOM. The signs are interior.

[IMAGE ON SCREEN: THE SAILING VESSEL WITH JOLLY ROGER AGAIN.]

TOM. I'm planning to change. [*He leans over the rail speaking with quiet exhilaration. The incandescent marquees and signs of the first-run movie houses light his face from across the alley. He looks like a voyager.*] I'm right at the point of committing myself to a future that doesn't include the warehouse and Mr. Mendoza or even a night-school course in public speaking.

JIM. What are you gassing about?

TOM. I'm tired of the movies.

JIM. Movies!

TOM. Yes, movies! Look at them — [*A wave toward the marvels of Grand Avenue.*] All of those glamorous people — having adventures — hogging it all, gobbling the whole thing up! You know what happens? People go to the *movies* instead of *moving!* Hollywood characters are supposed to have all the adventures for everybody in America, while everybody in America sits in a dark room and watches them have them! Yes, until there's a war. That's when adventure becomes available to the masses! *Everyone's* dish, not only Gable's! Then the people in the dark room come out of the dark room to have some adventures themselves — Goody, goody! — It's our turn now, to go to the South Sea Island — to make a safari — to be exotic, far-off! — But I'm not patient. I don't want to wait till then. I'm tired of the *movies* and I am *about* to *move!*

JIM [*incredulously*]. Move?

TOM. Yes.

JIM. When?

TOM. Soon!

JIM. Where? Where?

[THEME THREE MUSIC SEEMS TO ANSWER THE QUESTION, WHILE TOM THINKS IT OVER. HE SEARCHES AMONG HIS POCKETS.]

TOM. I'm starting to boil inside. I know I seem dreamy, but inside — well, I'm boiling! Whenever I pick up a shoe, I shudder a little thinking how short life is and what I am doing! — Whatever that means, I know it doesn't mean shoes — except as something to wear on a traveler's feet! [*Finds paper.*] Look —

JIM. What?

TOM. I'm a member.

JIM [*reading*]. The Union of Merchant Seamen.

TOM. I paid my dues this month, instead of the light bill.

JIM. You will regret it when they turn the lights off.

TOM. I won't be here.

JIM. How about your mother?

TOM. I'm like my father. The bastard son of a bastard! See how he grins? And he's been absent going on sixteen years!

JIM. You're just talking, you drip. How does your mother feel about it?

TOM. Shhh! — Here comes Mother! Mother is not acquainted with my plans!

AMANDA [*enters portieres*]. Where are you all?

TOM. On the terrace, Mother.

[*They start inside. She advances to them.* TOM *is distinctly shocked at her appearance. Even* JIM *blinks a little. He is making his first contact with girlish Southern vivacity and in spite of the night-school course in public speaking is somewhat thrown off the beam by the unexpected outlay of social charm.*]

[*Certain responses are attempted by* JIM *but are swept aside by* AMANDA'S *gay laughter and chatter.* TOM *is embarrassed but after the first shock* JIM *reacts very warmly. Grins and chuckles, is altogether won over.*]

[IMAGE: AMANDA AS A GIRL.]

AMANDA [*coyly smiling, shaking her girlish ringlets*]. Well, well, well, so this is Mr. O'Connor. Introductions entirely unnecessary. I've heard so much about you from my boy. I finally said to him, Tom — good gracious! — why don't you bring this paragon to supper? I'd like to meet this nice young man at the warehouse! — Instead of just hearing him sing your praises so much! I don't know why my son is so standoffish — that's not Southern behavior! Let's sit down and — I think we could stand a little more air in here! Tom, leave the door open. I felt a nice fresh breeze a moment ago. Where has it gone to? Mmm, so warm already! And not quite summer, even. We're going to burn up when summer really gets started. However, we're having — we're having a very light supper. I think light things are better fo' this time of year. The same as light clothes are. Light clothes an' light food are what warm weather calls fo'. You know our blood gets so thick during th' winter — it takes a while fo' us to *adjust* ou'selves! — when the season changes . . . It's come so quick this year. I wasn't prepared. All of a sudden — heavens! Already summer! — I ran to the trunk an' pulled out this light dress — Terribly old! Historical almost! But feels so good — so good an' co-ol, y'know. . . .

TOM. Mother —

AMANDA. Yes, honey?

TOM. How about — supper?

AMANDA. Honey, you go ask Sister if supper is ready! You know that Sister is in full charge of supper! Tell her you hungry boys are waiting for it. [*To* JIM.] Have you met Laura?

JIM. She —

AMANDA. Let you in? Oh, good, you've met already! It's rare
for a girl as sweet an' pretty as Laura to be domestic! But Laura
is, thank heavens, not only pretty but also very domestic. I'm
not at all. I never was a bit. I never could make a thing but
angel-food cake. Well, in the South we had so many servants.
Gone, gone, gone. All vestige of gracious living! Gone completely! I wasn't prepared for what the future brought me. All
of my gentlemen callers were sons of planters and so of course I
assumed that I would be married to one and raise my family on
a large piece of land with plenty of servants. But man proposes
— and woman accepts the proposal! — To vary that old, old
saying a little bit — I married no planter! I married a man who
worked for the telephone company! — That gallantly smiling
gentleman over there! [*Points to the picture.*] A telephone man
who — fell in love with long-distance! — Now he travels and I
don't even know where! — But what am I going on for about
my — tribulations? Tell me yours — I hope you don't have any!
Tom?

TOM [*returning*]. Yes, Mother?

AMANDA. Is supper nearly ready?

TOM. It looks to me like supper is on the table.

AMANDA. Let me look — [*She rises prettily and looks through
portieres.*] Oh, lovely! — But where is Sister?

TOM. Laura is not feeling well and she says that she thinks she'd
better not come to the table.

AMANDA. What? — Nonsense! — Laura? Oh, Laura!

LAURA [*off stage, faintly*]. Yes, Mother.

AMANDA. You really must come to the table. We won't be seated
until you come to the table! Come in, Mr. O'Connor. You sit
over there, and I'll — Laura? Laura Wingfield! You're keeping
us waiting, honey! We can't say grace until you come to the
table!

[*The back door is pushed weakly open and* LAURA *comes in.
She is obviously quite faint, her lips trembling, her eyes wide
and staring. She moves unsteadily toward the table.*]

[LEGEND: "TERROR!"]

[*Outside a summer storm is coming abruptly. The white curtains billow inward at the windows and there is a sorrowful murmur and deep blue dusk.*]

[LAURA *suddenly stumbles — she catches at a chair with a faint moan.*]

TOM. Laura!

AMANDA. Laura! [*There is a clap of thunder.*] [LEGEND: "AH!"] [*Despairingly.*] Why, Laura, you *are* sick, darling! Tom, help your sister into the living room, dear! Sit in the living room, Laura — rest on the sofa. Well! [*To the gentleman caller.*] Standing over the hot stove made her ill! — I told her that it was just too warm this evening, but — [TOM *comes back in.* LAURA *is on the sofa.*] Is Laura all right now?

TOM. Yes.

AMANDA. What *is* that? Rain? A nice cool rain has come up! [*She gives the gentleman caller a frightened look.*] I think we may — have grace — now . . . [TOM *looks at her stupidly.*] Tom, honey — you say grace!

TOM. Oh . . . "For these and all thy mercies —" [*They bow their heads,* AMANDA *stealing a nervous glance at* JIM. *In the living room* LAURA, *stretched on the sofa, clenches her hand to her lips, to hold back a shuddering sob.*] God's Holy Name be praised —

(The Scene Dims Out.)

Scene VII

[A Souvenir.]

[*Half an hour later. Dinner is just being finished in the upstage area which is concealed by the drawn portieres.*

As the curtain rises LAURA *is still huddled upon the sofa, her feet drawn under her, her head resting on a pale blue pillow, her eyes wide and mysteriously watchful. The new floor lamp with its shade of rose-colored silk gives a soft, becoming light to her face, bringing out the fragile, unearthly prettiness which usually escapes attention. There is a steady murmur of rain, but it is slackening and stops soon after the scene begins; the air out-*

side becomes pale and luminous as the moon breaks out.
A moment after the curtain rises, the lights in both rooms
flicker and go out.]

JIM. Hey, there, Mr. Light Bulb!

[AMANDA *laughs nervously.*]

[LEGEND: "SUSPENSION OF A PUBLIC SERVICE."]

AMANDA. Where was Moses when the lights went out? Ha-ha.
Do you know the answer to that one, Mr. O'Connor?

JIM. No, Ma'am, what's the answer?

AMANDA. In the dark! [JIM *laughs appreciably.*] Everybody sit
still. I'll light the candles. Isn't it lucky we have them on the
table? Where's a match? Which of you gentlemen can provide
a match?

JIM. Here.

AMANDA. Thank you, sir.

JIM. Not at all, Ma'am!

AMANDA. I guess the fuse has burnt out. Mr. O'Connor, can you
tell a burnt-out fuse? I know I can't and Tom is a total loss
when it comes to mechanics. [SOUND: GETTING UP:
VOICES RECEDE A LITTLE TO KITCHENETTE.] Oh, be
careful you don't bump into something. We don't want our
gentleman caller to break his neck. Now wouldn't that be a fine
howdy-do?

JIM. Ha-ha! Where is the fuse-box?

AMANDA. Right here next to the stove. Can you see anything?

JIM. Just a minute.

AMANDA. Isn't electricity a mysterious thing? Wasn't it Benjamin
Franklin who tied a key to a kite? We live in such a mysterious
universe, don't we? Some people say that science clears up all
the mysteries for us. In my opinion it only creates more! Have
you found it yet?

JIM. No, Ma'am. All these fuses look okay to me.

AMANDA. Tom!

TOM. Yes, Mother?

AMANDA. That light bill I gave you several days ago. The one I told you we got the notices about?

TOM. Oh. — Yeah.

[LEGEND: "HA!"]

AMANDA. You didn't neglect to pay it by any chance?

TOM. Why, I —

AMANDA. Didn't! I might have known it!

JIM. Shakespeare probably wrote a poem on that light bill, Mrs. Wingfield.

AMANDA. I might have known better than to trust him with it! There's such a high price for negligence in this world!

JIM. Maybe the poem will win a ten-dollar prize.

AMANDA. We'll just have to spend the remainder of the evening in the nineteenth century, before Mr. Edison made the Mazda lamp!

JIM. Candlelight is my favorite kind of light.

AMANDA. That shows you're romantic! But that's no excuse for Tom. Well, we got through dinner. Very considerate of them to let us get through dinner before they plunged us into everlasting darkness, wasn't it, Mr. O'Connor?

JIM. Ha-ha!

AMANDA. Tom, as a penalty for your carelessness you can help me with the dishes.

JIM. Let me give you a hand.

AMANDA. Indeed you will not!

JIM. I ought to be good for something.

AMANDA. Good for something? [*Her tone is rhapsodic.*] *You?* Why, Mr. O'Connor, nobody, *nobody's* given me this much entertainment in years — as you have!

JIM. Aw, now, Mrs. Wingfield!

AMANDA. I'm not exaggerating, not one bit! But Sister is all by her lonesome. You go keep her company in the parlor! I'll give you this lovely old candelabrum that used to be on the altar at the church of the Heavenly Rest. It was melted a little out of shape when the church burnt down. Lightning struck it one spring. Gypsy Jones was holding a revival at the time and he intimated that the church was destroyed because the Episcopalians gave card parties.

JIM. Ha-ha.

AMANDA. And how about you coaxing Sister to drink a little wine? I think it would be good for her! Can you carry both at once?

JIM. Sure. I'm Superman!

AMANDA. Now, Thomas, get into this apron!

[*The door of kitchenette swings closed on* AMANDA'S *gay laughter; the flickering light approaches the portieres.*]

[LAURA *sits up nervously as he enters. Her speech at first is low and breathless from the almost intolerable strain of being alone with a stranger.*]

[THE LEGEND: "I DON'T SUPPOSE YOU REMEMBER ME AT ALL!"]

[*In her first speeches in this scene, before* JIM'S *warmth overcomes her paralyzing shyness,* LAURA'S *voice is thin and breathless as though she has just run up a steep flight of stairs.*]

[JIM'S *attitude is gently humorous. In playing this scene it should be stressed that while the incident is apparently unimportant, it is to* LAURA *the climax of her secret life.*]

JIM. Hello, there, Laura.

LAURA [*faintly*]. Hello. [*She clears her throat.*]

JIM. How are you feeling now? Better?

LAURA. Yes. Yes, thank you.

JIM. This is for you. A little dandelion wine. [*He extends it toward her with extravagant gallantry.*]

LAURA. Thank you.

JIM. Drink it — but don't get drunk! [*He laughs heartily.* LAURA *takes the glass uncertainly; laughs shyly.*] Where shall I set the candles?

LAURA. Oh — oh, anywhere . . .

JIM. How about here on the floor? Any objections?

LAURA. No.

JIM. I'll spread a newspaper under to catch the drippings. I like to sit on the floor. Mind if I do?

LAURA. Oh, no.

JIM. Give me a pillow?

LAURA. What?

JIM. A pillow!

LAURA. Oh . . . [*Hands him one quickly.*]

JIM. How about you? Don't you like to sit on the floor?

LAURA. Oh — yes.

JIM. Why don't you, then?

LAURA. I — will.

JIM. Take a pillow! [LAURA *does. Sits on the other side of the candelabrum.* JIM *crosses his legs and smiles engagingly at her.*] I can't hardly see you sitting way over there.

LAURA. I can — see you.

JIM. I know, but that's not fair, I'm in the limelight. [LAURA *moves her pillow closer.*] Good! Now I can see you! Comfortable?

LAURA. Yes.

JIM. So am I. Comfortable as a cow. Will you have some gum?

LAURA. No, thank you.

JIM. I think that I will indulge, with your permission. [*Musingly unwraps it and holds it up.*] Think of the fortune made by the guy that invented the first piece of chewing gum. Amazing, huh? The Wrigley Building is one of the sights of Chicago. — I saw it summer before last when I went up to the Century of Progress. Did you take in the Century of Progress?

LAURA. No, I didn't.

JIM. Well, it was quite a wonderful exposition. What impressed me most was the Hall of Science. Gives you an idea of what the future will be in America, even more wonderful than the present time is! [*Pause. Smiling at her.*] Your brother tells me you're shy. Is that right, Laura?

LAURA. I — don't know.

JIM. I judge you to be an old-fashioned type of girl. Well, I think that's a pretty good type to be. Hope you don't think I'm being too personal — do you?

LAURA [*hastily, out of embarrassment*]. I believe I *will* take a piece of gum, if you — don't mind. [*Clearing her throat.*] Mr. O'Connor, have you — kept up with your singing?

JIM. Singing? Me?

LAURA. Yes. I remember what a beautiful voice you had.

JIM. When did you hear me sing?

[VOICE OFF STAGE IN THE PAUSE.]

VOICE [*off stage*].
      O blow, ye winds, heigh-ho,
      A-roving I will go!
        I'm off to my love
        With a boxing glove —
      Ten thousand miles away!

JIM. You say you've heard me sing?

LAURA. Oh, yes! Yes, very often . . . I — don't suppose you remember me — at all?

JIM [*smiling doubtfully*]. You know I have an idea I've seen you before. I had that idea soon as you opened the door. It seemed almost like I was about to remember your name. But the name that I started to call you — wasn't a name! And so I stopped myself before I said it.

LAURA. Wasn't it — Blue Roses?

JIM [*springs up. Grinning*]. Blue Roses! My gosh, yes — Blue Roses! That's what I had on my tongue when you opened the door! Isn't it funny what tricks your memory plays? I didn't connect you with high school somehow or other. But that's where it was; it was high school. I didn't even know you were Shakespeare's sister! Gosh, I'm sorry.

LAURA. I didn't expect you to. You — barely knew me!

JIM. But we did have a speaking acquaintance, huh?

LAURA. Yes, we — spoke to each other.

JIM. When did you recognize me?

LAURA. Oh, right away!

JIM. Soon as I came in the door?

LAURA. When I heard your name I thought it was probably you. I knew that Tom used to know you a little in high school. So when you came in the door — Well, then I was — sure.

JIM. Why didn't you *say* something, then?

LAURA [*breathlessly*]. I didn't know what to say, I was — too surprised!

JIM. For goodness' sakes! You know, this sure is funny!

LAURA. Yes! Yes, isn't it, though . . .

JIM. Didn't we have a class in something together?

LAURA. Yes, we did.

JIM. What class was that?

LAURA. It was — singing — Chorus!

JIM. Aw!

LAURA. I sat across the aisle from you in the Aud.

JIM. Aw.

LAURA. Mondays, Wednesdays and Fridays.

JIM. Now I remember — you always came in late.

LAURA. Yes, it was so hard for me, getting upstairs. I had that brace on my leg — it clumped so loud!

JIM. I never heard any clumping.

LAURA [*wincing at the recollection*]. To me it sounded like — thunder!

JIM. Well, well, well, I never even noticed.

LAURA. And everybody was seated before I came in. I had to walk in front of all those people. My seat was in the back row. I had to go clumping all the way up the aisle with everyone watching!

JIM. You shouldn't have been self-conscious.

LAURA. I know, but I was. It was always such a relief when the singing started.

JIM. Aw, yes, I've placed you now! I used to call you Blue Roses. How was it that I got started calling you that?

LAURA. I was out of school a little while with pleurosis. When I came back you asked me what was the matter. I said I had pleurosis — you thought I said Blue Roses. That's what you always called me after that!

JIM. I hope you didn't mind.

LAURA. Oh, no — I liked it. You see, I wasn't acquainted with many — people. . . .

JIM. As I remember you sort of stuck by yourself.

LAURA. I — I — never have had much luck at — making friends.

JIM. I don't see why you wouldn't.

LAURA. Well, I — started out badly.

JIM. You mean being —

LAURA. Yes, it sort of — stood between me —

JIM. You shouldn't have let it!

LAURA. I know, but it did, and —

JIM. You were shy with people!

LAURA. I tried not to be but never could —

JIM. Overcome it?

LAURA. No, I — I never could!

JIM. I guess being shy is something you have to work out of kind of gradually.

LAURA [*sorrowfully*]. Yes — I guess it —

JIM. Takes time!

LAURA. Yes —

JIM. People are not so dreadful when you know them. That's what you have to remember! And everybody has problems, not just you, but practically everybody has got some problems. You think of yourself as having the only problems, as being the only one who is disappointed. But just look around you and you will see lots of people as disappointed as you are. For instance, I hoped when I was going to high school that I would be further along at this time, six years later, than I am now — You remember that wonderful write-up I had in *The Torch?*

LAURA. Yes! [*She rises and crosses to table.*]

JIM. It said I was bound to succeed in anything I went into! [LAURA *returns with the annual.*] Holy Jeez! *The Torch!* [*He accepts it reverently. They smile across it with mutual wonder. LAURA crouches beside him and they begin to turn through it. LAURA'S shyness is dissolving in his warmth.*]

LAURA. Here you are in *Pirates of Penzance!*

JIM [*wistfully*]. I sang the baritone lead in that operetta.

LAURA [*rapidly*]. So — *beautifully!*

JIM [*protesting*]. Aw —

LAURA. Yes, yes — beautifully — beautifully!

JIM. You heard me?

LAURA. All three times!

JIM. No!

LAURA. Yes!

JIM. All three performances?

LAURA [*looking down*]. Yes.

JIM. Why?

LAURA. I — wanted to ask you to — autograph my program.

JIM. Why didn't you ask me to?

LAURA. You were always surrounded by your own friends so much that I never had a chance to.

JIM. You should have just —

LAURA. Well, I — thought you might think I was —

JIM. Thought I might think you was — what?

LAURA. Oh —

JIM [*with reflective relish*]. I was beleaguered by females in those days.

LAURA. You were terribly popular!

JIM. Yeah —

LAURA. You had such a — friendly way —

JIM. I was spoiled in high school.

LAURA. Everybody — liked you!

JIM. Including you?

LAURA. I — yes, I — I did, too — [*She gently closes the book in her lap.*]

JIM. Well, well, well! — Give me that program, Laura. [*She hands it to him. He signs it with a flourish.*] There you are — better late than never!

LAURA. Oh, I — what a — surprise!

JIM. My signature isn't worth very much right now. But some day — maybe — it will increase in value! Being disappointed is one thing and being discouraged is something else. I am disappointed but I am not discouraged. I'm twenty-three years old. How old are you?

LAURA. I'll be twenty-four in June.

JIM. That's not old age!

LAURA. No, but —

JIM. You finished high school?

LAURA [*with difficulty*]. I didn't go back.

JIM. You mean you dropped out?

LAURA. I made bad grades in my final examinations. [*She rises and replaces the book and the program. Her voice strained.*] How is — Emily Meisenbach getting along?

JIM. Oh, that kraut-head!

LAURA. Why do you call her that?

JIM. That's what she was.

LAURA. You're not still — going with her?

JIM. I never see her.

LAURA. It said in the Personal Section that you were — engaged!

JIM. I know, but I wasn't impressed by that — propaganda!

LAURA. It wasn't — the truth?

JIM. Only in Emily's optimistic opinion!

LAURA. Oh —

[LEGEND: "WHAT HAVE YOU DONE SINCE HIGH SCHOOL?"]

[JIM *lights a cigarette and leans indolently back on his elbows smiling at LAURA with a warmth and charm which lights her inwardly with altar candles. She remains by the table and turns in her hands a piece of glass to cover her tumult.*]

JIM [*after several reflective puffs on a cigarette*]. What have you done since high school? [*She seems not to hear him.*] Huh? [LAURA *looks up.*] I said what have you done since high school, Laura?

LAURA. Nothing much.

JIM. You must have been doing something these six long years.

LAURA. Yes.

JIM. Well, then, such as what?

LAURA. I took a business course at business college —

JIM. How did that work out?

LAURA. Well, not very — well — I had to drop out, it gave me — indigestion —

[JIM *laughs gently.*]

JIM. What are you doing now?

LAURA. I don't do anything — much. Oh, please don't think I sit around doing nothing! My glass collection takes up a good deal of time. Glass is something you have to take good care of.

JIM. What did you say — about glass?

LAURA. Collection I said — I have one — [*She clears her throat and turns away again, acutely shy.*]

JIM [*abruptly*]. You know what I judge to be the trouble with you? Inferiority complex! Know what that is? That's what they call it when someone low-rates himself! I understand it because I had it, too. Although my case was not so aggravated as yours seems to be. I had it until I took up public speaking, developed my voice, and learned that I had an aptitude for science. Before that time I never thought of myself as being outstanding in any way whatsoever! Now I've never made a regular study of it, but I have a friend who says I can analyze people better than doctors that make a profession of it. I don't claim that to be necessarily true, but I can sure guess a person's psychology, Laura! [*Takes out his gum.*] Excuse me, Laura. I always take it out when the flavor is gone. I'll use this scrap of paper to wrap it in. I know how it is to get it stuck on a shoe. Yep — that's what I judge to be your principal trouble. A lack of confidence in yourself as a person. You don't have the proper amount of faith in yourself. I'm basing that fact on a number of your remarks and also on certain observations I've made. For instance that clumping you thought was so awful in high school. You say that you even dreaded to walk into class. You see what you did? You dropped out of school, you gave up an education because of a clump, which as far as I know was practically non-existent! A little physical defect is what you have. Hardly noticeable even! Magnified thousands of times by imagination! You know what my strong advice to you is? Think of yourself as *superior* in some way!

LAURA. In what way would I think?

JIM. Why, man alive, Laura! Just look about you a little. What do you see? A world full of common people! All of 'em born and all of 'em going to die! Which of them has one-tenth of your good points! Or mine! Or anyone else's, as far as that goes — Gosh! Everybody excels in some one thing. Some in many! [*Unconsciously glances at himself in the mirror.*] All you've got to do is discover in *what!* Take me, for instance. [*He adjusts his tie at the mirror.*] My interest happens to lie in electrodynamics. I'm taking a course in radio engineering at night school, Laura, on top of a fairly responsible job at the warehouse. I'm taking that course and studying public speaking.

LAURA. Ohhhh.

JIM. Because I believe in the future of television! [*Turning back to her.*] I wish to be ready to go up right along with it. Therefore I'm planning to get in on the ground floor. In fact I've already made the right connections and all that remains is for the industry itself to get under way! Full steam — [*His eyes are starry.*] Knowledge — Zzzzzp! Money — Zzzzzzp! — Power!

That's the cycle democracy is built on! [*His attitude is convincingly dynamic.* LAURA *stares at him, even her shyness eclipsed in her absolute wonder. He suddenly grins.*] I guess you think I think a lot of myself!

LAURA. No — o-o-o, I —

JIM. Now how about you? Isn't there something you take more interest in than anything else?

LAURA. Well, I do — as I said — have my — glass collection —

[*A peal of girlish laughter from the kitchen.*]

JIM. I'm not right sure I know what you're talking about. What kind of glass is it?

LAURA. Little articles of it, they're ornaments mostly! Most of them are little animals made out of glass, the tiniest little animals in the world. Mother calls them a glass menagerie! Here's an example of one, if you'd like to see it! This one is one of the oldest. It's nearly thirteen. [MUSIC: "THE GLASS MENAGERIE."] [*He stretches out his hand.*] Oh, be careful — if you breathe, it breaks!

JIM. I'd better not take it. I'm pretty clumsy with things.

LAURA. Go on, I trust you with him! [*Places it in his palm.*] There now — you're holding him gently! Hold him over the light, he loves the light! You see how the light shines through him?

JIM. It sure does shine!

LAURA. I shouldn't be partial, but he is my favorite one.

JIM. What kind of a thing is this one supposed to be?

LAURA. Haven't you noticed the single horn on his forehead?

JIM. A unicorn, huh?

LAURA. Mmm-hmmm!

JIM. Unicorns, aren't they extinct in the modern world?

LAURA. I know!

JIM. Poor little fellow, he must feel sort of lonesome.

LAURA [*smiling*]. Well, if he does he doesn't complain about it. He stays on a shelf with some horses that don't have horns and all of them seem to get along nicely together.

JIM. How do you know?

LAURA [*lightly*]. I haven't heard any arguments among them!

JIM [*grinning*]. No arguments, huh? Well, that's a pretty good sign! Where shall I set him?

LAURA. Put him on the table. They all like a change of scenery once in a while!

JIM [*stretching*]. Well, well, well, well — Look how big my shadow is when I stretch!

LAURA. Oh, oh, yes — it stretches across the ceiling!

JIM [*crossing to door*]. I think it's stopped raining. [*Opens fire-escape door.*] Where does the music come from?

LAURA. From the Paradise Dance Hall across the alley.

JIM. How about cutting the rug a little, Miss Wingfield?

LAURA. Oh, I —

JIM. Or is your program filled up? Let me have a look at it. [Grasps imaginary card.] Why, every dance is taken! I'll just have to scratch some out. [WALTZ MUSIC: "LA GOLONDRINA"] Ahhh, a waltz! [*He executes some sweeping turns by himself then holds his arms toward* LAURA.]

LAURA [*breathlessly*]. I — can't dance!

JIM. There you go, that inferiority stuff!

LAURA. I've never danced in my life!

JIM. Come on, try!

LAURA. Oh, but I'd step on you!

JIM. I'm not made out of glass.

LAURA. How — how — how do we start?

JIM. Just leave it to me. You hold your arms out a little.

LAURA. Like this?

JIM. A little bit higher. Right. Now don't tighten up, that's the main thing about it — relax.

LAURA [*laughing breathlessly*]. It's hard not to.

JIM. Okay.

LAURA. I'm afraid you can't budge me.

JIM. What do you bet I can't? [*He swings her into motion.*]

LAURA. Goodness, yes, you can!

JIM. Let yourself go, now, Laura, just let yourself go.

LAURA. I'm —

JIM. Come on!

LAURA. Trying!

JIM. Not so stiff — Easy does it!

LAURA. I know but I'm —

JIM. Loosen th' backbone! There now, that's a lot better.

LAURA. Am I?

JIM. Lots, lots better! [*He moves her about the room in a clumsy waltz.*]

LAURA. Oh, my!

JIM. Ha-ha!

LAURA. Oh, my goodness!

JIM. Ha-ha-ha! [*They suddenly bump into the table.* JIM *stops.*] What did we hit on?

LAURA. Table.

JIM. Did something fall off it? I think —

LAURA. Yes.

JIM. I hope that it wasn't the little glass horse with the horn!

LAURA. Yes.

JIM. Aw, aw, aw. Is it broken?

LAURA. Now it is just like all the other horses.

JIM. It's lost its —

LAURA. Horn! It doesn't matter. Maybe it's a blessing in disguise.

JIM. You'll never forgive me. I bet that was your favorite piece of glass.

LAURA. I don't have favorites much. It's no tragedy, Freckles.

Glass breaks so easily. No matter how careful you are. The traffic jars the shelves and things fall off them.

JIM. Still I'm awfully sorry that I was the cause.

LAURA [*smiling*]. I'll just imagine he had an operation. The horn was removed to make him feel less — freakish! [*They both laugh.*] Now he will feel more at home with the other horses, the ones that don't have horns . . .

JIM. Ha-ha, that's very funny! [*Suddenly serious.*] I'm glad to see that you have a sense of humor. You know — you're — well — very different! Surprisingly different from anyone else I know! [*His voice becomes soft and hesitant with a genuine feeling.*] Do you mind me telling you that? [LAURA *is abashed beyond speech.*] I mean it in a nice way . . . [LAURA *nods shyly, looking away.*] You make me feel sort of — I don't know how to put it! I'm usually pretty good at expressing things, but — This is something that I don't know how to say! [LAURA *touches her throat and clears it — turns the broken unicorn in her hands.*] [*Even softer.*] Has anyone ever told you that you were pretty? [PAUSE: MUSIC.] [LAURA *looks up slowly, with wonder, and shakes her head.*] Well, you are! In a very different way from anyone else. And all the nicer because of the difference, too. [*His voice becomes low and husky.* LAURA *turns away, nearly faint with the novelty of her emotions.*] I wish that you were my sister. I'd teach you to have some confidence in yourself. The different people are not like other people, but being different is nothing to be ashamed of. Because other people are not such wonderful people. They're one hundred times one thousand. You're one times one! They walk all over the earth. You just stay here. They're common as — weeds, but — you — well, you're — *Blue Roses!*

[IMAGE ON SCREEN: BLUE ROSES.]

[MUSIC CHANGES.]

LAURA. But blue is wrong for — roses . . .

JIM. It's right for you — You're — pretty!

LAURA. In what respect am I pretty?

JIM. In all respects — believe me! Your eyes — your hair — are pretty! Your hands are pretty! [*He catches hold of her hand.*] You think I'm making this up because I'm invited to dinner and have to be nice. Oh, I could do that! I could put on an act for you, Laura, and say lots of things without being very sincere. But this time I am. I'm talking to you sincerely. I happened to notice you had this inferiority complex that keeps you from feeling comfortable with people. Somebody needs to build your confidence up and make you proud instead of shy and turning away and — blushing — Somebody ought to — Ought to — *kiss* you, Laura! [*His hand slips slowly up her arm to her shoulder.*] [MUSIC SWELLS TUMULTUOUSLY.] [*He suddenly turns her about and kisses her on the lips.*] [*When he releases her* LAURA *sinks on the sofa with a bright, dazed look.*] [JIM *backs away and fishes in his pocket for a cigarette.*] [LEGEND ON SCREEN: "SOUVENIR."] Stumble-john! [*He lights the cigarette, avoiding her look.*] [*There is a peal of girlish laughter from* AMANDA *in the kitchen.*] [LAURA *slowly raises and opens her hand. It still contains the little broken glass animal. She looks at it with a tender, bewildered expression.*] Stumble-john! I shouldn't have done that — That was way off the beam. You don't smoke, do you? [*She looks up, smiling, not hearing the question.*] [*He sits beside her a little gingerly. She looks at him speechlessly — waiting.*] [*He coughs decorously and moves a little farther aside as he considers the situation and senses her feelings, dimly, with perturbation.*] [*Gently.*] Would you — care for a — mint? [*She doesn't seem to hear him but her look grows brighter even.*] Peppermint — Life Saver? My pocket's a regular drug store — wherever I go . . . [*He pops a mint in his mouth. Then gulps and decides to make a clean breast of it. He speaks slowly and gingerly.*] Laura, you know, if I had a sister like you, I'd do the same thing as Tom. I'd bring out fellows and — introduce her to them. The right type of boys of a type to — appreciate her. Only — well — he made a mistake about me. Maybe I've got no call to be saying this. That may not have been the idea in having me over. But what if it was? There's nothing wrong about that. The only trouble is that in my case — I'm not in a situation to — do the right thing. I can't take down your number and say I'll phone. I can't call up next week and — ask for a date. I thought I had better explain the situation in case you misunderstood it and — hurt your feelings. . . . [*Pause.*] [*Slowly, very slowly,* LAURA'S *look changes, her eyes returning slowly from his to the ornament in her palm.*]

[AMANDA *utters another gay laugh in the kitchen.*]

LAURA [*faintly*]. You — won't — call again?

JIM. No, Laura, I can't. [*He rises from the sofa.*] As I was just explaining, I've — got strings on me, Laura, I've — been going steady! I go out all the time with a girl named Betty. She's a home-girl like you, and Catholic, and Irish, and in a great many ways we — get along fine. I met her last summer on a moonlight boat trip up the river to Alton, on the *Majestic.* Well — right away from the start it was — love! [LEGEND: LOVE!] [LAURA *sways slightly forward and grips the arm of the sofa. He fails to notice, now enrapt in his own comfortable being.*] Being in love has made a new man of me! [*Leaning stiffly forward, clutching the arm of the sofa,* LAURA *struggles visibly with her storm. But* JIM *is oblivious, she is a long way off.*] The power of love is really pretty tremendous! Love is something that — changes the whole world, Laura! [*The storm abates a little and* LAURA *leans back. He notices her again.*] It happened that Betty's aunt took sick, she got a wire and had to go to Centralia. So Tom — when he asked me to dinner — I naturally just accepted the invitation, not knowing that you — that he — that I — [*He stops awkwardly.*] Huh — I'm a stumble-john! [*He flops back on the sofa.*] [*The holy candles in the altar of* LAURA'S *face have been snuffed out. There is a look of almost infinite desolation.*] [JIM *glances at her uneasily.*] I wish that you would — say something. [*She bites her lip which was trembling and then bravely smiles. She opens her hand again on the broken glass ornament. Then she gently takes his hand and raises it level with her own. She carefully places the unicorn in the palm of his hand, then pushes his fingers closed upon it.*] What are you — doing that for? You want me to have him? — Laura? [*She nods.*] What for?

LAURA. A — souvenir . . .

[*She rises unsteadily and crouches beside the victrola to wind it up.*]

[LEGEND ON SCREEN: "THINGS HAVE A WAY OF TURNING OUT SO BADLY!"]

[OR IMAGE: "GENTLEMAN CALLER WAVING GOOD-BYE! — GAILY."]

[*At this moment* AMANDA *rushes brightly back in the front room. She bears a pitcher of fruit punch in an old-fashioned cut-glass pitcher and a plate of macaroons. The plate has a gold border and poppies painted on it.*]

AMANDA. Well, well, well! Isn't the air delightful after the shower? I've made you children a little liquid refreshment. [*Turns gaily to the gentleman caller.*] Jim, do you know that song about lemonade?

> "Lemonade, lemonade
>> Made in the shade and stirred with a spade —
> Good enough for any old maid!"

JIM [*uneasily*]. Ha-ha! No — I never heard it.

AMANDA. Why, Laura! You look so serious!

JIM. We were having a serious conversation.

AMANDA. Good! Now you're better acquainted!

JIM [*uncertainly*]. Ha-ha! Yes.

AMANDA. You modern young people are much more serious-minded than my generation. I was so gay as a girl!

JIM. You haven't changed, Mrs. Wingfield.

AMANDA. Tonight I'm rejuvenated! The gaiety of the occasion, Mr. O'Connor! [*She tosses her head with a peal of laughter. Spills lemonade.*] Oooo! I'm baptizing myself!

JIM. Here — let me —

AMANDA [*setting the pitcher down*]. There now. I discovered we had some maraschino cherries. I dumped them in, juice and all!

JIM. You shouldn't have gone to that trouble, Mrs. Wingfield.

AMANDA. Trouble, trouble? Why it was loads of fun! Didn't you hear me cutting up in the kitchen? I bet your ears were burning! I told Tom how outdone with him I was for keeping you to himself so long a time! He should have brought you over much, much sooner! Well, now that you've found your way, I want you to be a very frequent caller! Not just occasional but all the time. Oh, we're going to have a lot of gay times together! I see them coming! Mmm, just breathe that air! So fresh, and the moon's so pretty! I'll skip back out — I know where my place is when young folks are having a — serious conversation!

JIM. Oh, don't go out, Mrs. Wingfield. The fact of the matter is I've got to be going.

AMANDA. Going, now? You're joking! Why, it's only the shank of the evening, Mr. O'Connor!

JIM. Well, you know how it is.

AMANDA. You mean you're a young workingman and have to keep workingmen's hours. We'll let you off early tonight. But only on the condition that next time you stay later. What's the best night for you? Isn't Saturday night the best night for you workingmen?

JIM. I have a couple of time-clocks to punch, Mrs. Wingfield. One at morning, another one at night!

AMANDA. My, but you *are* ambitious! You work at night, too?

JIM. No, Ma'am, not work but — Betty! [*He crosses deliberately to pick up his hat. The band at the Paradise Dance Hall goes into a tender waltz.*]

AMANDA. Betty? Betty? Who's — Betty! [*There is an ominous cracking sound in the sky.*]

JIM. Oh, just a girl. The girl I go steady with! [*He smiles charmingly. The sky falls.*]

[LEGEND: "THE SKY FALLS."]

AMANDA [*a long-drawn exhalation*]. Ohhhh . . . Is it a serious romance, Mr. O'Connor?

JIM. We're going to be married the second Sunday in June.

AMANDA. Ohhhh — how nice! Tom didn't mention that you were engaged to be married.

JIM. The cat's not out of the bag at the warehouse yet. You know how they are. They call you Romeo and stuff like that. [*He stops at the oval mirror to put on his hat. He carefully shapes the brim and the crown to give a discreetly dashing effect.*] It's been a wonderful evening, Mrs. Wingfield. I guess this is what they mean by Southern hospitality.

AMANDA. It really wasn't anything at all.

JIM. I hope it don't seem like I'm rushing off. But I promised Betty I'd pick her up at the Wabash depot, an' by the time I get my jalopy down there her train'll be in. Some women are pretty upset if you keep 'em waiting.

AMANDA. Yes, I know — The tyranny of women! [*Extends her hand.*] Good-bye, Mr. O'Connor. I wish you luck — and happiness — and success! All three of them, and so does Laura! — Don't you, Laura?

LAURA. Yes!

JIM [*taking her hand*]. Good-bye, Laura. I'm certainly going to treasure that souvenir. And don't you forget the good advice I gave you. [*Raises his voice to a cheery shout.*] So long, Shakespeare! Thanks again, ladies — Good night!

[*He grins and ducks jauntily out.*]

[*Still bravely grimacing,* AMANDA *closes the door on the gentleman caller. Then she turns back to the room with a puzzled expression. She and* LAURA *don't dare to face each other.* LAURA *crouches beside the victrola to wind it.*]

AMANDA [*faintly*]. Things have a way of turning out so badly. I don't believe that I would play the victrola. Well, well — well — Our gentleman caller was engaged to be married! Tom!

TOM [*from back*]. Yes, Mother?

AMANDA. Come in here a minute. I want to tell you something awfully funny.

TOM [*enters with macaroon and a glass of the lemonade*]. Has the gentleman caller gotten away already?

AMANDA. The gentleman caller has made an early departure. What a wonderful joke you played on us!

TOM. How do you mean?

AMANDA. You didn't mention that he was engaged to be married.

TOM. Jim? Engaged?

AMANDA. That's what he just informed us.

TOM. I'll be jiggered! I didn't know about that.

AMANDA. That seems very peculiar.

TOM. What's peculiar about it?

AMANDA. Didn't you call him your best friend down at the warehouse?

TOM. He is, but how did I know?

AMANDA. It seems extremely peculiar that you wouldn't know your best friend was going to be married!

TOM. The warehouse is where I work, not where I know things about people!

AMANDA. You don't know things anywhere! You live in a dream; you manufacture illusions! [*He crosses to door.*] Where are you going?

TOM. I'm going to the movies.

AMANDA. That's right, now that you've had us make such fools of ourselves. The effort, the preparations, all the expense! The new floor lamp, the rug, the clothes for Laura! All for what? To entertain some other girl's fiance! Go to the movies, go! Don't think about us, a mother deserted, an unmarried sister who's crippled and has no job! Don't let anything interfere with your selfish pleasure! Just go, go, go — to the movies!

TOM. All right, I will! The more you shout about my selfishness to me the quicker I'll go, and I won't go to the movies!

AMANDA. Go, then! Then go to the moon — you selfish dreamer!

[TOM *smashes his glass on the floor. He plunges out on the fire-escape, slamming the door.* LAURA *screams — cut by door.*]

[*Dance-hall music up.* TOM *goes to the rail and grips it desperately, lifting his face in the chill white moonlight penetrating the narrow abyss of the alley.*]

[LEGEND ON SCREEN: "AND SO GOOD-BYE . . ."]

[TOM'S *closing speech is timed with the interior pantomime. The interior scene is played as though viewed through sound-proof glass.* AMANDA *appears to be making a comforting speech to* LAURA *who is huddled upon the sofa. Now that we cannot hear the mother's speech, her silliness is gone and she has dignity and tragic beauty.* LAURA'S *dark hair hides her face until at the end of the speech she lifts it to smile at her mother.* AMANDA'S *gestures are slow and graceful, almost dancelike, as she comforts the daughter. At the end of her speech she glances a moment at the father's picture — then withdraws through the portieres. At close of* TOM'S *speech,* LAURA *blows out the candles, ending the play.*]

TOM. I didn't go to the moon, I went much further — for time is the longest distance between two places — Not long after that I was fired for writing a poem on the lid of a shoe-box. I left Saint Louis. I descended the steps of this fire-escape for a last time and followed, from then on, in my father's footsteps, attempting to find in motion what was lost in space — I traveled around a great deal. The cities swept about me like dead leaves, leaves that were brightly colored but torn away from the branches. I would have stopped, but I was pursued by something. It always came upon me unawares, taking me altogether by surprise. Perhaps it was a familiar bit of music. Perhaps it was only a piece of transparent glass — Perhaps I am walking along a street at night, in some strange city, before I have found companions. I pass the lighted window of a shop where perfume is sold. The window is filled with pieces of colored glass, tiny transparent bottles in delicate colors, like bits of a shattered rainbow. Then all at once my sister touches my shoulder. I turn around and look into her eyes . . . Oh, Laura, Laura, I tried to leave you behind me, but I am more faithful than I intended to be! I reach for a cigarette, I cross the street, I run into the movies or a bar, I buy a drink, I speak to the nearest stranger — anything that can blow your candles out! [LAURA *bends over the candles.*] — for nowadays the world is lit by lightning! Blow out your candles, Laura — and so good-bye. . . .

[*She blows the candles out.*]

(*The Scene Dissolves.*)

PRODUCTION NOTES

Being a "memory play," *The Glass Menagerie* can be presented with unusual freedom of convention. Because of its considerably delicate or tenuous material, atmospheric touches and subtleties of direction play a particularly important part. Expressionism and all other unconventional techniques in drama have only one valid aim, and that is a closer approach to truth. When a play employs unconventional techniques, it is not, or certainly shouldn't be, trying to escape its responsibility of dealing with reality, or interpreting experience, but is actually or should be attempting to find a closer approach, a more penetrating and vivid expression of things as they are. The straight realistic play with its genuine Frigidaire and authentic ice-cubes, its characters that speak exactly as its audience speaks, corresponds to the academic landscape and has the same virtue of a photographic likeness. Everyone should know nowadays the unimportance of the photographic in art: that truth, life, or reality is an organic thing which the poetic imagination can represent or suggest, in essence, only through transformation, through changing into other forms than those which were merely present in appearance.

These remarks are not meant as comments only on this particular play. They have to do with a conception of a new, plastic theatre which must take the place of the exhausted theatre of realistic conventions if the theatre is to resume vitality as a part of our culture.

THE SCREEN DEVICE

There is *only one important difference between the original and acting version of the play* and that is the *omission* in the latter of the device which I tentatively included in my *original* script. This device was the use of a screen on which were projected magic-lantern slides bearing images or titles. I do not regret the omission of this device from the present Broadway production. The extraordinary power of Miss Taylor's performance made it suitable to have the utmost simplicity in the physical production. But I think it may be interesting to some readers to see how this device was conceived. So I am putting it into the published manuscript. These images and legends, projected from behind, were cast on a section of wall between the front-room and dining-room areas, which should be indistinguishable from the rest when not in use.

The purpose of this will probably be apparent. It is to give accent to certain values in each scene. Each scene contains a particular point (or several) which is structurally the most important. In an episodic play, such as this, the basic structure or narrative line may be obscured from the audience; the effect may seem fragmentary rather than architectural. This may not be the fault of the play so much as a lack of attention in the audience. The legend or image upon the screen will strengthen the effect of what is merely allusion in the writing and allow the primary point to be made more simply and lightly than if the entire responsibility were on the spoken lines. Aside from this structural value, I think the screen will have a definite emotional appeal, less definable but just as important. An imaginative producer or director may invent many other uses for this device than those indicated in the present script. In fact the possibilities of the device seem much larger to me than the instance of this play can possibly utilize.

THE MUSIC

Another extra-literary accent in this play is provided by the use of music. A single recurring tune, "The Glass Menagerie," is used to give emotional emphasis to suitable passages. This tune is like circus music, not when you are on the grounds or in the immediate vicinity of the parade, but when you are at some distance and very likely thinking of something else. It seems under those circumstances to continue almost interminably and it weaves in and out of your preoccupied consciousness; then it is the lightest, most delicate music in the world and perhaps the saddest. It expresses the surface vivacity of life with the underlying strain of immutable and inexpressible sorrow. When you look at a piece of delicately spun glass you think of two things: how beautiful it is and how easily it can be broken. Both of those ideas should be woven into the recurring tune, which dips in and out of the play as if it were carried on a wind that changes. It serves as a thread of connection and allusion between the narrator with his separate point in time and space and the subject of his story. Between each episode it returns as a reference to the emotion, nostalgia, which is the first condition of the play. It is primarily Laura's music and therefore comes out most clearly when the play focuses upon her and the lovely fragility of glass which is her image.

THE LIGHTING

The lighting in the play is not realistic. In keeping with the atmosphere of memory, the stage is dim. Shafts of light are focused on selected areas or actors, sometimes in contra-distinction to what is the apparent center. For instance, in the quarrel scene between Tom and Amanda, in which Laura has no active part, the clearest pool of light is on her figure. This is also true of the supper scene, when her silent figure on the sofa should remain the visual center. The light upon Laura should be distinct from the others, having a peculiar pristine clarity such as light used in early religious portraits of female saints or madonnas. A certain correspondence to light in religious paintings, such as El Greco's, where the figures are radiant in atmosphere that is relatively dusky, could be effectively used throughout the play. (It will also permit a more effective use of the screen.) A free, imaginative use of light can be of enormous value in giving a mobile, plastic quality to plays of a more or less static nature.

The Glass Menagerie

Springboard

1.   If *The Glass Menagerie* is Tom's memory of the past, why doesn't he tell us things exactly as they happened? What characteristics of memory does this "memory play" make use of? (For example, why is the play written in seven scenes, instead of the traditional three acts or five acts?)

2.   In what ways does the title *The Glass Menagerie* refer to Laura, Amanda, Tom, Jim?

3.   Laura and Amanda obviously have difficulty facing reality. However, Tom also struggles with the same problem. Cite instances.

4.   The play associates Laura with blue roses and Amanda with yellow jonquils. What do the characteristics of these flowers explain about the women?

5.   Tom's closing speech is coordinated with an interior pantomime involving Laura and Amanda. Read the stage directions for the pantomime, and then read Tom's closing speech. What meaning does Williams intend us to understand through the juxtaposition?

6.   In Scene I, once Tom leaves the apron of the stage and enters the apartment area upstage, Williams moves quickly to delineate character through dialogue. Immediately we witness bickering between Amanda and Tom. We hear a recitation of the past as Amanda remembers it, and we observe Laura's view of her own present. Using what you hear and see in this scene, describe each of the three Wingfields: what kind of people are they, in this first impression?

7.   Why does Amanda use the pronoun "we" in her long speech to Laura in Scene II, and again in Scene VII? Is Amanda aware of any other meaning in her use of the pronoun?

8.   Study Scene III, considering the dialogue, action, placement of actors, and lighting. Pay particular attention to the pantomime at the end of the scene — Tom trapped in his coat, Tom on his knees unable to speak — and to the sound of shattering glass. How does this short scene present in miniature everything the play as a whole is about?

9.   In Scene IV, Tom tells Laura of a magician's wonderful coffin trick. Explain how Tom's reference to this bit of "magic" reflects Tom's own situation and is connected to Mr. Wingfield's desertion of his family. What is Williams telling the audience when a spotlight suddenly illuminates the father's grinning photograph displayed so prominently over the mantle?

10.   In Scene V, Tom steps out onto the fire escape landing and talks to the audience about the Paradise Dance Hall. In what ways is Tom like those who patronize the dance hall?

11.   In Scene VI, when Tom and Jim arrive at the Wingfield apartment, Laura does not want to be the one to let them in. What are the implications in Amanda's question to Laura, "Can you give me one reason . . . why you should be afraid to open a door?" Look at the stage directions for this part of the scene. What does "opening a door" mean to Laura here?

12.   In Scene VII, when the glass unicorn falls from the table, breaking off its horn, Laura says that now the unicorn is just like all the other horses. Later, she gives Jim the unicorn as a souvenir. Study what happens between these two events. How do you interpret the unicorn and Laura's action?

13.   In Scene VII, assess Jim's character, paying close attention to the stage directions which describe the gestures and actions accompanying his dialogue. For example, Jim looks in the mirror often; does he notice that he does this? What is his impression of himself? Does he see himself clearly?

14.   When Williams calls *The Glass Menagerie* a memory play, he asks us to consider not only the nature of memory itself but also the personal memories of Amanda, Laura, and Jim. The entire play is presented as Tom's memory. What can we judge about the way each character sees his past? How does each see his present? His future?

15.   Amanda's first words to Laura in Scene II are "Deception? Deception?" Read again the opening stage directions for this scene, which describe Amanda's entry into the apartment. In what way does the word *deception* apply to Amanda, too?

16.   In Scene V, Amanda tells Tom, "You are the only young man that I know of who ignores the fact that the future becomes the present, the present the past, and the past turns

into everlasting regret if you don't plan for it!" Is Amanda's accusation true about Tom? Is it true about herself?

17. Scene III shows us an angry, fiery argument between Amanda and Tom. Such arguments, we notice from the set and lighting clues, tear the whole family apart. Scene V, however, shows us another facet of the relationship between mother and son. Discuss these new insights into Tom and Amanda's feelings for one another. Would the tenderness between them make it harder for Tom to leave home?

18. In Scene VI, Tom and Jim talk on the fire escape. In what respect are Jim's remarks an echo of Amanda's advice to Tom? Does Tom react to Jim the same way he had to Amanda?

19. In Tom's speech to the audience at the opening of the play, he calls himself a magician. He makes a distinction, however, between what he does as a weaver of magic and what the stage magician does: "He gives you truth in the pleasant disguise of illusion." In what way can Tom's description also apply to the playwright?

20. In the opening stage directions Williams tells us that "the narrator is an undisguised convention of the play." The setting is described as "now and the past." On stage, Tom speaks directly to the audience, sometimes blurring the distinction between what is the play and what is not the play. How can Williams' use of the narrator as orchestrator and interpreter of the action help articulate the play's theme? In what way can we see the play as a kind of "confession" that helps Tom unburden himself of the guilt he has been carrying?

GLOSSARY

Act — The major division of a play, breaking the larger action into unified, logical segments. An act may present important advances in the plot, for example, or changes in time or location.

Apron — The area of the stage in front of the main curtain, often containing the footlights.

Aside — A dramatic convention which enables a character to speak to the audience or to someone else on stage, but without everybody on stage hearing. It is a necessary convention, since a realistically quiet speech (or even whisper) would not carry far in the theatre.

Catharsis — Aristotle's term for the experience a tragedy conveys. Witnessing the play purges members of the audience, draining them of pity and fear, and teaches them to avoid such evil as the hero has succumbed to.

Character — A person in a play; also, the word for the personality, moral qualities, and motivation that define that person.

Climax — The point at which the conflict in the plot is most intense; the pivot or fulcrum or turning point in the action.

Comedy — That which is amusing. In drama, a generic name for any play that is intended to amuse, that pokes fun at manners, social behavior and customs, people or institutions, and that ends happily.

Conflict — The struggle, either internal or external, between opposing characters or forces or ideas; the conflict highlights the main issue or issues of a play.

Denouement — The *untying* of the complications of plot. The point following the climax, at which time disclosure or discovery of some sort allows a resolution.

Deus ex Machina — A term which literally means "god from the machine." In Greek drama, it referred to the arrival of an actor who was lowered onto the stage by a mechanical crane and who brought about a solution. The term has now come to mean the resolution of the plot by any sort of artificial or unexpected means (e.g., the ship in *The Admirable Crichton*).

413

Dialogue — Speeches that the actors deliver in a play, either in exchange with each other or directed toward the audience.

Director — The person who imposes his interpretation of a work on the actors, scenery, script, etc. He is responsible for the staging and ultimate form of the performance the audience sees.

Drama — In Greek the word means "to do"; a form of story meant to be acted out by performers in front of an audience.

Dramatic Convention — A tacit agreement between artists (playwright, director, actors, et al.) and audience to regard patent lies as if they were truths. What Coleridge called "that willing suspension of disbelief for the moment which constitutes poetic faith" is essential for theatre to succeed. As Aristotle observed, the drama is an "imitation" of life; the staged life is a fake, a forgery, and yet it must be regarded by the audience as if it were the real thing, or something like the real thing. The link between staged life and real life, the link that constitutes this "as if," is made of conventions. There are too many to be enumerated, but they include the aside, the soliloquy, the stage whisper, spotlighting, rhymed discourse, and the stage as the actual geographical location of action. One reason experimental plays seldom succeed at first is simply because the conventions employed are new, or at least are not the ones the audience consciously or unconsciously anticipates.

Dramatic Irony — An ancient figure of speech indicating a discrepancy between what is expected and what occurs, between what is said and what is meant, or between what is said and what is actually understood. Irony can be quite complex, and scholars distinguish many different forms (e.g., irony of fate, verbal irony, Romantic irony, Sophoclean irony, Socratic irony, irony of situation); hyperbole, understatement, and sarcasm are all varieties of verbal irony. While these types of irony can all prove applicable to the theatre, dramatic irony is especially important. Dramatic irony, which can range in its effect from tragedy to comedy, occurs when the audience knows more than a character on stage does.

Episode — A brief unit of action and dialogue, distinct in itself but part of a larger sequence. In Greek tragedy, an episode was the part between two choric songs; the term is less precise now.

Expressionism — A style of drama that attempts to project inner emotional or psychological experience, rather than any kind of traditional, external reality. Expressionism employs such techniques as dreamlike lighting, distorted sets, stretched or compressed time, and fragmented dialogue. In the theatre, expressionism flourished after World War I, especially in Europe, as if to say that that cataclysmic war had demonstrated that "reality" could no longer be dealt with "realistically."

Falling Action — The opposite of rising action (when the tempo quickens and excitement builds), falling action allows the audience a time to relax after intense dramatic action.

Foreshadowing — A hint or clue in the plot that prepares the audience for some future event, often of a tragic nature.

Form — An exceedingly difficult term because it can mean so many different things, all of them abstract. Two general meanings may be distinguished: first, "form" refers to those characteristics of a play which enable us to associate it with other plays and thus recognize it as a comedy or tragedy or farce or melodrama; second, "form" refers to the organic form of the individual play, its own inherent structure or design or arrangement of particulars that gives it unity. Form, then, always has to do with unity, either unity between the given play and other plays, or unity arising from related elements within the play itself.

Image, Imagery — Although these terms would seem to relate to sight, by extension they cover anything that appeals to any of the five senses.

Monologue — A lengthy speech delivered by one speaker, heard but not interrupted by other characters on stage.

Mood — The atmosphere or feeling established by the setting and by the actors. Not to be confused with *tone*.

Motif — A pattern of recurring words, ideas, objects, or actions, suggesting significance and unity.

Narrator — A storyteller who controls the information the listener receives, thus affecting the listener's understanding and evaluation of events.

Naturalism — See Realism.

Pantomime — Communication entirely through gestures, not words.

Picture Frame Stage — A stage framed by a proscenium arch that separates the actors (and action) from the audience. The audience views the play with a sense of distance, as if looking at a picture in a frame.

Plot — The arrangement given by the playwright to the events or episodes of the play's action, moving from the introduction of the conflict to climax and resolution.

Proscenium — From the Greek *proskenion,* meaning the space before the scene. The term denotes the walls that frame the stage as well as the opening in the wall through which the audience sees the play.

Proscenium Arch — The arch that forms the frame of the proscenium wall and its opening facing the audience.

Realism — A style of writing and presenting a play that attempts to show people and life as they actually are or as they appear to be in real life. Realism has been a major influence in the theatre since the late nineteenth century. It should not be confused with *naturalism,* which implies a deterministic view of man.

Reversal — Aristotle's *peripeteia,* referring to a sudden and drastic change in the fortunes or expectations of the protagonist (main character). Such a reversal of circumstances is often seen in the context of some irony, either tragic or comic.

Rising Action — The sequence of plot complications leading up to a climax or turning point.

Scene — The setting of a play (locale, props, etc.), or a separate portion of an act containing its own unifying situation and development.

Scrim — Netting or gauze-like material upon which scenery can be painted and which appears transparent or opaque with changes in the direction of the lighting.

Set — The arrangement of scenery and props for a play or for any scene within the play.

Setting — The designation of time and place in which the action of the play occurs.

Soliloquy — A dramatic convention whereby a character "thinks aloud" to himself, so that the audience overhears him revealing emotions, inner conflicts, or motivations. The most famous instances of soliloquy are in *Hamlet.*

Stage Directions — Instructions in the script, usually parenthetical or italicized, explaining how and where the action of the play should be staged; at their most useful, these instructions can reveal the playwright's ideas about how the substance and theme of the play should be interpreted. Some stage directions are intended for the actors alone, others for the reading audience. Common technical terms include *downstage* (the area of the stage nearest the audience), *upstage* (the back part of the stage, farthest from the audience), and *stage right, stage left* (the actor's right and left as he faces the audience.)

Structure — See *form.*

Symbol — A word, gesture, object or situation that suggests meaning beyond itself. In literature, symbols unify and enlarge the work.

Theme — The dominating idea (e.g., a particular view of life and of human nature) conveyed through a play.

Tone — The playwright's attitude toward his subject, inevitably reflected throughout the play. Tone is not to be confused with *mood,* which pertains to the characters' world rather than the playwright's.

Tragedy — A serious dramatic representation of action in which a character of moral worth struggles, suffers, and undergoes a catastrophic reversal of fortune. In the working out of the character's fate or "punishment," there must appear to be the necessary loss of some good in order for the evil to be fully expiated; hence, the audience is uplifted at finding justice triumphant, but saddened over the accompanying sacrifice of good.